THE EUROPEAN UNION SERIES

General Editors: Neill Nugent, William E. Paterson, Vincent Wright

The Eur... ... ...
Europ... ...sme
of key in...ation and ...is, ...es and policy processes, and the role of mem
states.

Books in the series are written by leading scholars in their fields and reflect the mc
up-to-date research and debate. Particular attention is paid to accessibility and cle
presentation for a wide audience of students, practitioners and interested general
readers.

The series consists of four major strands:

- general textbooks
- the major institutions and actors
- the main areas of policy
- the member states and the Union

Published titles

Michelle Cini and Lee McGowan
Competition Policy in the European Union

Renaud Dehousse
The European Court of Justice

Desmond Dinan
Ever Closer Union: An Introduction to European Integration (2nd edn)

Wyn Grant
The Common Agricultural Policy

Justin Greenwood
Representing Interests in the European Union

Alain Guyomarch, Howard Machin and Ella Ritchie
France in the European Union

Fiona Hayes-Renshaw and Helen Wallace
The Council of Ministers

Simon Hix
The Political System of the European Union

Simon Hix and Christopher Lord
Political Parties in the European Union

Brigid Laffan
The Finances of the European Union

Janne Haaland Matláry
Energy Policy in the European Union

John McCormick
Understanding the European Union: A Concise Introduction

Neill Nugent
The Government and Politics of the European Union (4th edn)

John Peterson and Elizabeth Bomberg
Decision-Making in the European Union

John Peterson and Margaret Sharp
Technology Policy in the European Union

European Union Series
Series Standing Order
ISBN 0-333-71695-7 hardcover
ISBN 0-333-69352-3 paperback
(outside North America only)

You can receive future titles in this series as they are published by placing a standing order.
Please contact your bookseller or, in the case of difficulty, write to us at the address below
with your name and address, the title of the series and one of the ISBNs quoted above.

Customer Services Department, Macmillan Distribution Ltd
Houndmills, Basingstoke, Hampshire RG21 6XS, England

Forthcoming

Simon Bulmer and Drew Scott
European Union: Economics, Policy and Politics

Ben Rosamond
Theories of European Integration

Richard Sinnott
Understanding European Integration

•   •   •   •

Simon Bulmer and Wolfgang Wessels
The European Council

David Earnshaw and David Judge
The European Parliament

Neill Nugent
The European Commission

Anne Stevens
The Administration of the European Union

•   •   •   •

David Allen and Geoffrey Edwards
The External Economic Relations of the European Union

Laura Cram
Social Policy in the European Union

Wyn Grant, Duncan Matthews and Peter Newell
The Greening of the European Union?

Martin Holland
The European Union and the Third World

Malcolm Levitt and Christopher Lord
The Political Economy of Monetary Union

Anand Menon
Defence Policy and the European Union

James Mitchell and Paul McAleavey
Regionalism and Regional Policy in the European Union

Jörg Monar
Justice and Home Affairs in the European Union

John Redmond and Lee Miles
Enlarging the European Union

Hazel Smith
The Foreign Policy of the European Union

Mark Thatcher
The Politics of European High Technology

Rüdiger Wurzel
Environmental Policy in the European Union

•   •   •   •

Simon Bulmer and William E. Paterson
Germany and the European Union

Carlos Closa and Paul Heywood
Spain and the European Union

Phil Daniels and Ella Ritchie
Britain and the European Union

Other titles planned include

The History of the European Union
The European Union Source Book
The European Union Reader
The Political Economy of the European Union

•   •   •   •

Political Union
The USA and the European Union

•   •   •   •

The European Union and its Member States
Reshaping the States of the Union
Italy and the European Union

Decision-Making in the European Union

John Peterson

and

Elizabeth Bomberg

First published 1999 by
MACMILLAN PRESS LTD
Houndmills, Basingstoke, Hampshire RG21 2XS
and London
Companies and representatives
throughout the world

ISBN 0–333–60491–1 hardcover
ISBN 0–333–60492–X paperback

A catalogue record for this book is available
from the British Library.

10   9   8   7   6   5   4   3   2   1
08 07 06 05 04 03 02 01 00 99

Copy-edited and typeset by Povey–Edmondson
Tavistock and Rochdale, England

Printed in Great Britain by
Antony Rowe Ltd
Chippenham, Wiltshire   1003098152

Published in the United States of America by
ST. MARTIN'S PRESS, INC.,
Scholarly and Reference Division
175 Fifth Avenue, New York, N.Y. 10010

ISBN 0–312–22529–6 clothbound
ISBN 0–312–22521–0 paperback

To Margaret Bomberg, for her courage and spirit

Contents

List of Exhibits and Tables

Exhibits

Tables

Preface

Writing this book has been a labour of love in more ways than one. It has been delayed by the joyous distractions of the two children – Miles and Calum – born during its writing. It has been brought to closure primarily because our publisher Steven Kennedy has encouraged and harassed (in equal measure) so diligently. It has been supported by generous grants from the UK Economic and Social Research Council (grant R000235829), the Joseph Rowntree Foundation, the Carnegie Foundation and the European Commission. We have also received crucial institutional support from the Institute of Governmental Studies (University of California, Berkeley) and the Centre for European Policy Studies (Brussels), as well as our own Universities of York, Stirling and Glasgow. Perhaps above all, we must thank our interviewees, nearly all of whom showed patience, kindness and a genuine desire to help.

If the book achieves its purpose, it is largely because so many trusted colleagues have generously commented on earlier drafts of our manuscripts. For their time, expertise and constructive criticism, we owe a huge debt to David Allen, Iain Begg, Simon Bulmer, Youri Devuyst, Neil Fligstein, Jonathon Golub, Wyn Grant, Francis Jacobs, David Judge, Paul MacAleavey, Kathleen McNamara, Gary Marks, David Martin MEP, Andrew Moravcsik, Neill Nugent, Mark Pollack, Nelson Polsby, Rod Rhodes, Eric Schickler, Michael Shackleton, Alan Swinbank, Helen Wallace, William Wallace, Martin Westlake, J. Nicholas Ziegler and Anthony Zito. Antje Brown, Richard Doherty, Monica Frassoni, Franz Heimel, Clare McManus and Catherine Tulloch gave generously of themselves to the project. The contribution of Ricardo Gomez was critical, essential and well beyond the call of duty.

Finally, we inevitably must thank each other. If nothing else, this book represents a huge achievement: we have managed to push each other to achieve better things, while still remaining great pals.

JOHN PETERSON AND ELIZABETH BOMBERG

List of Abbreviations

ACEA	Association of European Automobile Manufacturers
ACP	African, Caribbean and Pacific Countries
AEA	Association of European Airlines
APEC	Asia–Pacific Economic Cooperation Forum
APME	Association of Plastics Manufacturers in Europe
ASEAN	Association of South East Asian Nations
ASEM	Asia–Europe Meeting
AV	audio-visual
BAP	Biotechnology Action Programme
BEUC	Bureau Européen des Unions de Consommateurs
BRITE	Basic Research in Industrial Technologies for Europe
BSE	bovine spongiform encephalopathy
BST	bovine somatotropin
BT	British Telecom
BTR	banana trade regime
CAP	Common Agricultural Policy
CCMC	Comité des Constructeurs du Marché Commun
CCP	Common Commercial Policy
CEECs	Central and Eastern Europe Countries
CEEP	European Centre of Public Enterprises
CFCs	chlorofluorocarbons
CFSP	Common Foreign and Security Policy
CIs	Community Initiatives
CJTF	Combined Joint Task Forces
CLT	Luxembourg Television Company
CO2	carbon dioxide
CODEST	European Science and Technology Development Committee
COMITEXTIL	Committee for the European Textile and Clothing Industry
COPA	Committee of Professional Agricultural Organisations
CoR	Committee of the Regions and Local Authorities
COREPER	Committee of Permanent Representatives
CREST	Comité de la Recherche Scientifique et Technique
DBV	Deutsche Bauernverband
DG	Directorate-General (European Commission)
DT	Deutsche Telekom
DTI	Department of Trade and Industry (UK)

EAGGF	European Agricultural Guidance and Guarantee Fund
EAPs	Environmental Action Programmes
EC	European Community
ECB	European Central Bank
ECHO	European Community Humanitarian Office
ECJ	European Court of Justice
ECOFIN	(Council of) Economic and Finance Ministers
ECSC	European Coal and Steel Community
ECU	European Currency Unit
EDF	European Development Fund
EEA	European Environmental Agency
EEC	European Economic Community
EFPIA	European Federation of Pharmaceutical Industry Associations
EFTA	European Free Trade Association
EMU	Economic and Monetary Union
EP	European Parliament
EPC	European Political Co-operation
ERDF	European Regional Development Fund
ERRA	European Recovery and Recycling Association
ERT	European Round Table of Industrialists
ESCB	European System of Central Banks
ESDI	European Security and Defence Identity
ESF	European Social Fund
ESNBA	European Secretariat of National Biotechnology Associations
ESPRIT	European Strategic Programme for Information Technologies
ESTA	European Science and Technology Assembly
ETUC	European Trades Union Congress
EU	European Union
EURAM	European Research in Advanced Materials
EUREKA	European Research Co-ordinating Agency
EUROPEN	European Organisation for Packaging and the Environment
FDA	Food and Drug Administration
FEM	Federation of European Motorcyclists
FERA	European Federation of Audiovisual Producers
FIFG	Financial Instrument for Fisheries Guidance
FTA	free trade area or agreement
G7	Group of seven industrialised nations
GAC	General Affairs Council
GATS	General Agreement on Trade in Services

GATT	General Agreement on Tariffs and Trade
GDP	gross domestic product
GMOs	genetically modified organisms
GNP	Gross National Product
GSP	Generalised System of Preferences
HDTV	high-definition television
ICL	International Computers Limited
IGC	intergovernmental conference
IMF	International Monetary Fund
INCPEN	Industry Council for Packaging and the Environment
IO	international organisation
IR	international relations
IRDAC	Industrial Research and Development Advisory Committee
IRI	Institute for Industrial Reconstruction
IT	information technology
ITTF	Information Technologies Task Force
JESSI	Joint European Silicon Structures Initiative
LI	liberal intergovernmentalism
MAC	multiplexed analogue components
MCAs	Monetary Compensatory Amounts
MCR	Merger Control Regulation
MEP	member of the European Parliament
MFA	Multifibre Arrangement
MLG	multi-level governance
MNCs	multinational corporations
MPC	Monetary Policy Committee (UK)
NAFTA	North American Free Trade Association
NATO	North Atlantic Treaty Organisation
NGO	non-governmental organisation
NI	new institutionalism
NPT	Non-proliferation Treaty
NTA	New Transatlantic Agenda
OECD	Organisation for Economic Co-operation and Development
OSCE	Organisation for Security and Co-operation in Europe (formerly CSCE)
PCF	Packaging Chain Forum
PermReps	Permanent Representations (of EU Member States)
PESC	Politique étrangère et de sécurité commune
PHARE	Poland and Hungary: Aid for the Restructuring of Economies
QMV	qualified majority voting

RACE	Research in Advanced Communications for Europe
RAM	random access memory
R&D	research and development
RTD	research and technological development
SAGB	Senior Advisory Group on Biotechnology
SCA	Special Committee on Agriculture
SCF	Scientific Committee for Food
SEA	Single European Act
SLIM	Simplification of Legislation in the Internal Market
SNAs	sub-national authorities
SPAN	Sustainable Packaging Action Network
TABD	Transatlantic Business Dialogue
TWF	Television Without Frontiers
UK	United Kingdom
UN	United Nations
UNICE	Union of Industrial and Employers' Confederations of Europe
USA	United States
WEU	Western European Union
WTO	World Trade Organisation

Introduction

This book has two fundamental purposes. First, it represents our attempt to make an original scholarly contribution to the literature on EU politics and policy-making. It is the product of a four-year research project on EU decision-making, which has focused primarily on specific cases of decision-making in the period 1994–8. We have done the legwork: tracking policy proposals as they have evolved from the 'twinkle in the eye' of a policy entrepreneur to the 'setting' of an EU policy. We have conducted nearly 500 interviews in Brussels and eight national capitals, collected archive material from EU and national holdings, and trawled the fast-expanding EU literature. Our research has been systematic but we are unashamed to describe our methodology, following Fenno (1996), as 'soaking and poking': soaking up archive and interview material (particularly concerning our selected case studies) and then poking around to answer questions that arose from the 'soaking', or finding explanations for things that just did not quite add up.

Our second, and equally important, task is to bring the EU alive for a wide and general audience. Politics and policy in the EU are dense, complex and often incomprehensible to all but specialists. We have tried to write a clear, enticing, user-friendly text that is useful to students and non-specialists. In particular, we offer a large dose of 'oral wisdom' about how the EU makes decisions. Thus our book is peppered liberally with direct quotations from EU decision-makers, particularly from our interviews. It is far too easy, as scholars, to become seduced by the jargon and arcana of the EU, and to forget that decisions are taken by 'flesh and blood individuals, real *people*' (Fenno 1996: 8). The view we offer is of a lively, often humorous and always fascinating operation of a unique experiment in modern governance.

We have faced three basic problems in writing this book. First, the European Union has refused to stand still for us. During our period of research, new, transformative, 'history-making' decisions have been taken, as manifest above all in the move to Economic and Monetary Union (EMU) and agreement on the Amsterdam Treaty. The EU is very difficult to 'photograph' because it is almost always moving and changing (see Pierson 1996).[1]

Second, the EU has taken steps towards eastern enlargement which make the process irreversible. The EU may be on the verge of evolving into a fundamentally different type of institution, and thus we sometimes wonder how durable the patterns we have studied are likely to be.

1

However, we have tried to identify themes that will continue to dominate EU decision-making into the early 21st century. We think we have uncovered certain patterns that are now established so firmly that they will persist even after the EU expands to include a far larger and more heterogeneous collection of Member States.

Third, we have had to be selective, concentrating on policy sectors where the Union's competence is established and relatively clear patterns of governance are visible. The EU is most involved in sectors where demand has arisen for supranational rules, regulation or support as a consequence of the Union's ambitions to have a single, 'internal' market (see Sandholtz and Stone Sweet 1998). However, the Union's policy role is now firmly established in sectors (such as foreign policy) where the link to economic integration is indirect. Moreover, the EU's policy role is constantly changing. The transition to EMU has already had a considerable impact on the EU, which is central to our analysis. But considerable uncertainty surrounds monetary union and we can offer only glimpses of what effects it will have on the Union's future (see Chapter 10).

Our first two chapters introduce theories of EU decision-making (Chapter 1) and the Union's institutions, decision rules and informal norms (Chapter 2). Subsequent chapters all follow a single pattern. First, they examine the broad context – historical, political and economic – in which the EU makes decisions in specific sectors. Second, they focus on 'history-making' decisions that are taken at a level which transcends the day-to-day operation of the Union as a political system, or what we call the 'super-systemic' level of decision-making. Third, we examine how the EU makes decisions which 'set' policy, usually after interinstitutional bargaining at what could be termed the 'systemic' level. Fourth, and perhaps most importantly, we look at the way decisions are taken which do not 'make' but rather 'shape' policy at the sub-systemic level of EU decision-making, where mainly officials and private or non-governmental actors bargain with each other over policy details. We argue that this level is both neglected and crucial.

Our approach is to 'work down', from top to bottom, through the Union's multiple levels of governance in a way that may appear non-chronological (examining policy-setting before agenda-setting) and non-traditional. We have chosen this approach for two reasons: first, the EU's broad agenda is often set from the 'top-down' (that is, on the initiative of its Member States); and second, it is usually impossible to make sense of decision-making at the sub-systemic level unless the analyst has a clear grasp of the *system*, or the EU's degree of competence, institutional balance and decision rules, in specific policy sectors.

One of the most vexing problems of studying the EU is moving from the general (a raft of treaty reforms) to the specific (an anti-dumping decision on cotton imports) and back again. We solve this problem by offering abundant exhibits of particular policy episodes or key touchstones in the study of EU decision-making.[2] They are used to illustrate more general points of argument or analysis. The reader in a hurry, or one who finds one of our chapters less than central to their own interests, may skip over the exhibits without losing the 'narrative' in our story. But the exhibits are intended to enrich and deepen the reader's understanding of the EU.

We have thought carefully about the likely place of our book in the existing literature. Recent EU scholarship features as much (maybe more) theory-*building* than theory-testing. The result is new and 'original' theories before older ones have been validated or debunked. The over-abundance of theory may be a simple consequence of modern academic pressures to publish and the reality that it is easier to 'construct' theory than to go out and conduct rigorous, detailed empirical research.[3] But another, wholly compatible explanation is that we are witnessing the residual effect of the disillusion of scholars with early attempts at theorising about the pace and direction of European integration. Controversy still surrounds the question of precisely what one of the fathers of modern integration theory, Ernst Haas (1975: 1), meant when he appeared to declare that theorising about European integration was 'obsolete' and 'probably not worth our while'. In any case, the practical effect was that an entire academic sub-discipline was shut down: few scholars or students wanted to conduct research on a topic that was, apparently, 'obsolete'. There seemed little pay-off in developing new models to describe, explain or predict how the (then) European Community made decisions, particularly because it did not *make* many important ones (this point is controversial, but the perception was widespread; see Caporaso and Keeler 1995).

Then, of course, the EU was 'relaunched' in the mid-1980s, and set on a trajectory that – while not straight or untroubled – culminated in EMU by the late 1990s. In the decade or so in between, the understandable response to leaving the dry, desert-like period of 'theoretical obsolescence' was a good deal of scurrying around to develop theory which could shed light on terribly interesting and apparently extraordinary events in Western Europe.

This book is *not* another exercise in theory-building. It is certainly theoretically 'pregnant', in that it uses theory to shed light on the way the EU works as a system for making decisions. However, our primary aim is to shed light on the EU in a way that makes it understandable and interesting to a broad readership.[4]

Chapter 1

Making Sense of EU Decision-Making

Decision-making and EU Politics
Three types of decision
Conclusion

Why study decision-making in the European Union (EU)? A deceptively simple answer is: because a large share of public policy affecting 370 million European citizens (and many beyond the EU's borders) is now decided at this level of governance. The accuracy of Jacques Delors' famous prediction that 80 per cent of all economic and social legislation would be decided at the EU level by the late 1990s remains disputed.[1] What *is* clear is that trying to measure how much legislation is decided at different levels of government in Europe is both pointless and beside the point. What makes the EU novel, interesting and worthy of close study is 'its unique *combination* of national and supranational rules and institutions'[2](Begg 1996: 527).

This book is about how national and supranational (and sometimes subnational) institutions and actors combine in the making of *decisions*: that is, choices or solutions that end some uncertainty or reduce contention. A decision is not the same as a *policy*: action (or inaction) by public authorities facing choices between alternative courses of public action (see Colebatch 1998). When *any* choice is made, the result is a decision. All policies are a product of decisions about what to do, how to do it, and how to decide what to do. Decisions are the building blocks of policies.

Yet some decisions are 'bigger' than policies. Decisions to embrace quasi-constitutional change, such as reform of the EU's Treaties, transcend 'ordinary' choices about what action (or inaction) should be taken by the EU within its defined areas of competence. 'Big' decisions may redefine the EU's competence or alter its institutions in ways that lead to changes in EU policy.

Our strategy for understanding the EU, and all that it does, is to study the lowest common unit of every move it makes: the individual decision. This research strategy particularly befits the European Union because it is a unique system of 'multi-level governance' (see Marks *et al.* 1996a;

Hooghe and Marks 1997). The term *governance* is everywhere in the recent EU literature (see Armstrong and Bulmer 1998; Bulmer 1998; Hix 1998; Sandholtz and Stone Sweet 1998), but it is rarely defined very clearly. We define governance as the imposition of overall direction or control on the allocation of valued resources. Governance is synthetic: it results from a mix of factors, including political leadership, state–society relations, institutional competition, electoral politics, and so on. The EU's existence as an extra level or layer of governance that has been 'fused' onto the nation-state (Wessels 1997a) makes the mix unusually eclectic in Europe compared to other parts of the world.[3]

Quite a lot of work on the EU – in fact, much of the best work – is concerned with decision-making. Our own contribution is to supply the 'two things' that Caporaso (1998) finds missing from existing work. First, we specify a clear continuum of different types of decision in EU governance (see Table 1.1). Second, we offer 'representative cases of major decisions and minor and intermediate decisions' (Caporaso 1998: 11).

This chapter introduces our framework for analysis, which specifies three analytical categories or types of EU decision. We begin by introducing decision-making as a general approach to understanding politics, and consider how theory can help us make sense of EU decision-making.

Table 1.1   *Multi-level EU decision-making*

LEVEL	Decision type	Dominant actors*	Example
Super-systemic	history-making	European Council; governments in IGCs; European Court of Justice	endorse white paper on internal market
Systemic	policy-setting	Council; COREPER; European Parliament (under 'co-decision')	agree directives to create an internal market for motorbikes
Sub-systemic	policy-shaping	Commission; Council working groups; EP committees	propose that all motorbikes licensed in the EU must observe specified power limits.

*See Exhibit 2.1 for a basic introduction to the EU's institutions.

Source: adapted from Peterson (1995a).

Decision-Making and EU Politics

Some of the best-known, classic works of political science have focused on decision-making. A prime example is Graham Allison's (1971) *Essence of Decision*, which 'mines' competing models of decision-making to explain American policy during the Cuban missile crisis. Allison's is one of the shrewdest works ever in the study of decision-making, yet he admits there are stark limits to our ability to explain what happens in the real political world:

> In attempting to explain a particular event, the analyst cannot simply describe the full state of the world leading up to that event. The logic of explanation requires that he [*sic*] single out the relevant, important determinants of the occurrence. (Allison 1971: 4)

There have been few systematic studies of the key determinants of EU decision-making.[4] Rosenthal's (1975) study of decision-making in the early years of the European Economic Community (EEC) is an exception. Following Allison, it tests three competing models of decision-making: intergovernmentalism (with Member States controlling decision-making), pressure politics (with decisions determined by 'grass-roots, interest group and parliamentary pressures') and what Rosenthal (1975: 4–5) calls 'elite networks'. During a period (1968–71) when intergovernmentalism appeared to dominate, Rosenthal nonetheless found that 'elite networks' offered the most compelling explanations for the outcomes of EEC decision-making. Within elite networks, decision-making was a product of 'subtle, behind-the-scenes lobbying and elaborate committee work' (Rosenthal 1975: 6). Investigating this type of informal, backroom decision-making is not easy, yet Rosenthal's evidence suggests it cannot be ignored.

This type of decision-making *has* been ignored, or dismissed as unimportant, by most international relations (IR) scholars. IR scholars can be relied upon to raise important, basic questions about *power*, including questions about who or what determines which issues are subjected to EU decisions. Most students of IR concede that the European Union's mere existence poses a challenge to 'neo-realism', which remains a dominant paradigm in the study of IR. Neo-realism assumes that 'states are the key actors in world politics; they are substantively and instrumentally rational; and their preferences and choices are largely shaped by the absence of a centralized international authority, i.e. inter-state anarchy' (Grieco 1995: 27). For neo-realists, EU decision-making is 'the practice of ordinary diplomacy' although 'under conditions creating unusual opportunities for providing collective goods through highly institutionalized exchange' (Pierson 1996: 124). Thus the European Union is *only* as powerful as its Member States wish it to be.

Inspired but not abducted by neo-realism, Milward (1992) and Moravcsik (1994) both argue that the EU strengthens the nation-state, as opposed to weakening it. EU decision-making, according to them, is primarily *intergovernmental. It* is dominated by national interests and allows governments to 'escape' from pesky domestic pressures that limit their room for manoeuvre at the national level.

For instance, given its neo-liberal policy agenda, the EU may empower national governments by 'limiting decision-making to relatively noncontroversial matters' (Bachrach and Baratz 1970: 8–9). The difficulty of securing agreements at the EU level may 'prevent certain grievances from developing into fully-fledged issues which call for decisions' (Bachrach and Baratz 1963: 642): EU commitments (such as the EMU convergence criteria) may effectively preclude measures (such as higher taxes to fund redistribution) that benefit the poor or powerless. The result is a 'mobilisation of bias', as 'some issues are organized into politics while other are organized out' (Schattschneider 1960: 71). Put another way, the Union may guarantee the sanctity of 'non decisions' that lead it to ignore or neglect certain problems: *not* to choose is, in a way, to make a choice.

The problem, of course, is how to organise a research agenda to investigate 'non decisions' (see Polsby 1980). Moreover, EU decision-making is clearly *not* always limited to non-controversial matters, or issues that all its Member States can agree should be on the Union's agenda, as we would expect under conditions of 'ordinary diplomacy'. Explaining why means engaging in *policy analysis*, or dissecting a choice to act (or not to act) and examining which actors or interests determine the outcome, and why. Policy analysis suggests, contrary to intergovernmentalist assumptions, that the EU may be as much like New Haven, Connecticut as like the United Nations, in that it sometimes features pluralistic competition in 'subject matter domains encompassing both routine and nonroutine decisions, conflict and innovation, with a rather heavy emphasis on innovation' (Polsby 1980: 192).

Intergovernmentalists have a counterattack: when the EU becomes a source of innovative public policy it is because one or more Member States has managed to 'seize' the policy agenda in pursuit of its national interest (Héritier 1996). Yet because Member States are the source of most policy ideas does not mean that they exert tight control over EU decision-making. The Union's institutions, particularly the European Commission, often welcome the initial 'push' of a certain Member State (or group of them) to put an issue on the agenda. They then may grab control of the decision-making process in a way that is unwelcome to the national initiator (see Weale 1996; Cram 1997).

More generally, the EU has become a polity in its own right, in which decision-making is not a simple matter of intergovernmental bargaining. Important decisions arise from bargaining which is inter*institutional* (see Exhibit 2.1), involving the Commission, the Council of Ministers, European Parliament (EP) and (sometimes) the European Court of Justice (ECJ). Power is shared at the supranational level, and not *only* between states.

The EU is a powerful level of governance, and in fact is the main regulator of the most highly regulated societies in the word. It must craft policy solutions that surmount conflicts of national interest in a system that features abundant and widely distributed vetoes. Yet it often seems that 'the policy-making capacities of the Union have not been strengthened nearly as much as capabilities at the level of Member States have declined' (Scharpf 1994a: 220). The EU itself is resource-poor, spending less than 2 per cent of all public money in the Union. It must aggregate an enormous number of interests, in a polity of 370 million EU citizens, without the benefit of strong, Europe-wide political parties, pressure groups or trades unions. The EU has an almost impossible job with few means to do it. Often the only plausible strategy is to encourage the formation of something like Rosenthal's elite networks, or 'policy networks', which can 'prepare' decisions and build consensus through informal exchange and backroom bargaining.

Policy networks are conceptual tools of public policy analysis. They help describe and explain decision-making which 'shapes' policy away from the limelight (see Peterson 1995a; Richardson 1996c). The term 'policy network' is a metaphor for a cluster of actors, each of which has an interest, or 'stake', in a given EU policy sector and the capacity to help determine policy success or failure. EU policy networks usually bring together a diverse variety of institutional actors (see Table 1.1) and other 'stakeholders': private and public, national and supranational, political and administrative.

Actors in policy networks are dependent on each other for scarce resources, such as information, expertise or legitimacy. They thus have incentives to share resources, bargain and agree on how to try to 'shape' policy in the interests of their sector. Much of what the EU does is highly technical. Policy structures are highly fragmented – between, say, agriculture or environmental or cohesion policy. Thus EU policy networks tend to be technocratic, consensual and policy-specific. Policy networks play an important functional role in EU governance: they aggregate the interests of a variety of different actors in a highly 'differentiated polity' marked by 'the fragmentation of policies and politics' (Rhodes 1997: 7).

Policy network analysis seeks to determine how decisions are negotiated within such networks. It seems apt for a system of governance that is weakly institutionalised, resource-poor and has no 'government', yet which often takes a strong lead in governing Europe. In this system, 'the capacity of individuals and small groups to influence decisions' remains striking (Rosenthal 1975: 134).

However, the 'big' decisions that determine the pace and direction of European integration preoccupy the highest political levels where power is concentrated, regardless of how 'fragmented' or technocratic the EU is. At this level of decision-making, the Union has a firm, intergovernmental backbone. The student of EU decision-making thus must be concerned with explaining a range of different decisions taken at different levels in a multi-level system of governance. Our approach is to draw on a range of theories that are 'pitched' at different levels of decision-making (see Table 1.2 below), on the assumption that 'different kinds of theories are appropriate for different parts of the EU puzzle' (Sandholtz 1996: 427). Otherwise, we run headlong into the classic 'level of analysis' problem which has preoccupied international relations scholars (see Singer 1961).[5] Put simply, a theory which seeks to explain or predict 'big decisions', such as the launch of EMU, should not be judged by how well it explains or predicts a decision to change the way that pig carcasses are measured.

Of course, advocates of particular theories often claim (implicitly, at least) that 'their' theory can tell us everything we really need to know about EU decision-making. Espousers of a single, 'meta-theory' of EU politics may accuse us of being magpies or engaging in 'intellectual ad-hocery'.[6] Yet, echoing Hix (1998: 46), we know of 'no general theory of American or German government', and thus question the wisdom of searching for a general theory of the EU (see also Moravcsik and Nicolaïdis 1999). Moreover, we know of no other international organisation (IO) which approaches the EU's decision-making power. European integration has produced a distinctive model of 'deep regionalism' (Laffan 1998) that resists simple characterisations. EU decision-making is heavily nuanced, constantly changing and even kaleidoscopic.

Table 1.2 *Putting theory in its place*

Level	Type of decision	Bargaining mode	Rationality	'Best' theory
Super-systemic	history-making	intergovernmental	political	liberal intergovernmetalism; neofunctionalism
Systemic	policy-setting	interinstitutional	political; technocratic	new institutionalism
Sub-systemic	policy-shaping	resource exchange	technocratic; consensual	policy network analysis

Three Types of Decision

Our framework for analysis of EU decision-making (see Table 1.2) acknowledges the multi-level character of the Union. It specifies the different actors (see Table 1.1), modes of bargaining, and rationalities – or criteria for determining what are 'good' decisions – which 'drive' decision-making at different levels. It categorises different types of decision by outcome, and specifies which actors tend to dominate choices which produce a specific kind of outcome, and why.

The framework is a heuristic one: that is, one which aids learning, discovery or problem-solving. It is *not* intended to imply that only one type of decision is ever taken at each level of governance, or that these levels are demarcated by neat, dividing lines (like boundaries on a map). Issues often 'jump' up and down between levels of decision-making before they are resolved. Our framework's three levels do not always correspond to organisational aggregation (that is national cabinets at the top, the Council in the middle and the Commission at the bottom) or political jurisdiction (as in supranational, national and sub-national). The framework offers analytical categories of different kinds of decision, not explanatory variables which specify which factors will determine outcomes. In that sense, it is theoretically neutral: it does not seek to 'referee' debates between competing models so much as it tries to combine the insights of different theories by specifying precisely where they are 'pitched'. It applies them were they have the most analytical leverage: to the most appropriate 'piece of the EU puzzle'. In short, our framework is a template for making sense of EU policy episodes, which result from an accumulation of different kinds of decision.[7]

High Politics and 'History-Making' Decisions

History-making decisions do precisely what the term implies: they 'make history' by changing the EU – altering its procedures, rebalancing the relative powers of its institutions, or adjusting the Union's remit. They are taken at a 'super-systemic' level, or one that transcends the EU's policy process. Because they are quasi-constitutional in character, they preoccupy decision-makers at the highest political levels.

Generally, history-making decisions emerge in one of three ways. First, they are taken as a consequence of intergovernmental conferences (IGCs) called to revise the EU's founding treaties. Second, they are taken by the European Council and determine the EU's agenda, priorities or finances. Increasingly, in an enlarged Union, they may determine the sub-group of EU Member States that undertakes specific, integrative projects. Third, more rarely, they come in the form of legal decisions taken by the ECJ, which set out the limits of the EU's powers or define principles of governance.

History-making decisions usually come at 'high-political junctures, moments when new high-level deals make it possible for specific linkages and interdependencies to become important' (Ross 1995: 12). For example, a decision was taken in spring 1985 to convene a European Council in Milan to discuss the Dooge Report, a paper on reform of the Community's institutions. Only later did the Commission, sensing that the time was right for a more general relaunch of the EU, decide to table its *White Paper on Completing the Internal Market* at the June 1985 summit. The market liberalisation programme it promised became linked to institutional reform in a way that, for example, overcame the objections of the United Kingdom (UK) to making more decisions by qualified majority voting (QMV) as opposed to unanimous voting.

Budgetary decisions which 'make history' now occur in regular cycles when the European Council adopts multi-annual 'financial perspectives' (Laffan 1997a: 9–13). The first, agreed in 1988, was truly historic in that it reduced the need for more budgetary wrangling over the next five years and set the precedent for the successor 'Delors II' package covering 1993–9 (see Shackleton 1991). Subsequent financial agreements were adopted as complex package deals that set clear parameters for EU spending. They did not change EU governance in abrupt or dramatic terms, but went far towards determining, in practical terms, the EU's policy remit for years at a time.

Decisions about how much money the EU will spend on what are often the end results of very hard-nosed intergovernmental negotiations about policy details. However, the role of ideas is perhaps more important in the EU than in any other system of governance, given the Union's ambitions to transform and modernise European political economies. Simply put, ideas are 'shared causal beliefs' (McNamara 1998: 4): accepted knowledge about which policy measures will cause desirable outcomes to occur. In particular, neo-liberal ideas – inflation and wage control, monetarism, stable interest rates – inspired the decisions to launch the so-called 1992 project to 'complete' the internal market. Similarly, the creation of the Euro was underpinned by the emergence of 'a new consensus opposed to demand management and wedded to the concept of sound money as the single most important goal of economic policy' (Ludlow 1997: 27).

More broadly, as Helen Wallace (1993) has argued, European integration as a process has always been driven by *ideals*: in equal measure, by shadows of the past and shadows of the future. The process stagnates when principal decision-makers forget how European integration rescued Europe from the chaos of the 1940s and made possible its post-war political stability and economic prosperity (see Exhibit 1.1).

Exhibit 1.1   The Franco-German alliance

Alongside the prosperity that European integration has engendered, its most important achievement has been to make the border between France and Germany – transgression of which sparked three wars between 1870 and 1940 – superfluous, and almost non-existent. Arguably, the relationship between France and Germany is the most extraordinary relationship between any two sovereign states in the world. The Franco-German alliance has been the driving force for nearly all 'history-making' decisions, from the formation of the European Coal and Steel Community in the early post-war period to the creation of the Euro. Without the ties that link France and Germany, the EU would be a rather unremarkable international organisation (IO); with the Franco-German axis, the Union is a system of governance in its own right and an international superpower (of sorts).

Franco-German co-operation in EU decision-making is now habitual. The 1964 Elysée Treaty requires regular exchanges between national cabinets and sometimes leads to closer relationships between, say, French and German environment ministers than between these ministers and their national colleagues (see Bulmer and Paterson 1987). Yet bilateral co-operation is rarely automatic. French and German EU policy preferences are fundamentally at odds in a range of sectors, particularly the internal market and trade policy. Common positions often must be imposed from the highest political levels, and the strength of the axis has been fundamentally determined by the personal affinity of successive German Chancellors and French Presidents (see Dinan 1994).

At first, German unification seemed to threaten the Franco-German alliance. Before 1990, the two had been rough political equals. Afterwards, Germany's population became more than 30 per cent larger, and its economy 40 per cent bigger (Messerlin 1996). Even when the impetus behind 'early' German unification began to appear unstoppable, the French government, especially President François Mitterrand, cast profoundly negative aspersions on the prospect. Eventually, however, a Franco-German bargain was struck: in crude terms, Germany could have early unification if France was 'given' the Deutschmark, or a commitment to EMU. A joint letter from Mitterrand and the German Chancellor Helmut Kohl urged moves 'to accelerate the political construction' of Europe and 'transform relations as a whole among member states into a European Union' (quoted in Dinan 1994: 165). The eventual result was the Maastricht Treaty. Other than insisting on an increase in the number of German Members of the European Parliament (MEPs),

→

→

Germany did not seek a 'reweighting' of its formal representation in EU decision-making.

The new challenge to the Franco-German alliance became EU enlargement. All EU enlargements have diluted the combined power of France and Germany: their joint share of the EU's economy shrank from 70 per cent in 1960 to less than half by 1990. But eastern enlargement threatens to drive a wedge between Germany, which remains on the front-line of the EU's eastern border, and France, for whom agricultural reforms needed to facilitate enlargement are an anathema.

The Franco-German motor continued to power the post-Maastricht European project largely because Helmut Kohl (German Chancellor from 1982 to 1998) was so personally committed to both the motor and the project. In the words of a senior German official, Kohl continued to 'believe very strongly in the idea that the bigger that Europe gets, the more important it is that the big states – and the original, old, founding members – should send impulses to the whole project. Kohl is very convinced that the Franco-German motor is essential, and that it is still valid'.[8] Yet even Kohl showed great reluctance to accept more integrated EU decision-making in the Amsterdam Treaty (see Exhibit 1.2). Subsequently, Germany's unprecedented protests about its net budgetary contribution to the EU led one seasoned observer to foresee increasingly 'glacial' Franco-German relations posing 'the greatest threat to the EU in its 40 years' existence'.[9] The onset of the post-Kohl era, following the 1998 election of a Social Democratic-led government under Gerhard Schröder, raised new questions about Germany's continued commitment to European integration, despite Schröder's immediate plans to seek joint Franco-German positions on preparations for EMU, EU institutional reform and enlargement.

Regardless of who heads Germany's government, Bulmer (1997) detects a strikingly close fit between EU and German interests (especially in free trade), institutions (multi-level and even 'federal') and identity (strongly European). The 'fit' between France and the EU will never be so comfortable, but German influence on French perceptions, and the essential French interest in co-operation with Germany, has proved remarkably durable. Asked in 1996 to explain a sudden German policy U-turn (on the reform of post offices) to support the French position, the (German) Commissioner for Industry, Martin Bangemann, called the Franco-German story 'a love story, and matters of love cannot be explained'.[10]

Equally, European integration stalls when political leaders begin to doubt that closer European unity can bring about a future that is better than the present.

Most theoretical work on the EU is concerned with 'history-making' decisions that determine the general pace and direction of European integration. The longest established theory of integration, neo-functionalism, is concerned with how one quasi-constitutional decision to integrate might 'spill over' and provoke further, related acts of integration (Haas 1964, 1968; Lindberg and Scheingold 1970, 1971). Neo-functionalism assumes that integration feeds upon itself through two linked processes. The first is societal: social actors demand integration, and the demand is satisfied by using – or, more likely, adjusting – existing rules, institutions and structures in ways that further integration. The second is a technocratic process: leadership is provided by the 'power of the expert, the ability of supranational technocrats to structure the agenda, and the variable ability of the Commission to broker deals' (Caporaso 1998: 8). The essence of political integration is the gradual emergence of a 'collective decision-making system' (Lindberg 1970: 650).

The unidirectional logic of neo-functionalism was heavily criticised when European integration appeared to stagnate and even reverse in the late 1960s and 1970s. The theory appeared to make a comeback in the 1980s as the pace of European integration accelerated again (Taylor 1989; Tranholm-Mikkelsen 1991; Burley and Mattli 1993), yet dissatisfaction with neo-functionalism, especially amongst IR scholars, led to the development of alternative theoretical models, especially 'liberal intergovernmentalism' (see Moravcsik 1998).

Liberal intergovernmentalism (LI) focuses firmly on 'major decisions in the history of the E[U]' (Moravcsik 1993: 517). The core assumptions of LI are that 'states are rational self-interested actors, that they "read" the demands of society, that these demands are somehow aggregated . . . and that [states] negotiate over their differences in the international arena' (Caporaso 1998: 9). LI is compatible with the insight that the EU may *strengthen* the state, instead of weakening it, by giving European leaders strategic opportunities to make decisions in forums insulated from domestic pressures. The EU also gives them policy tools for managing the complex interdependence that makes Europe's destiny a more or less collective one (see Putnam 1988; Evans *et al.* 1993; Moravcsik 1994). Yet, in line with the demands of IR scholarship, LI purports to be a general theory of international co-operation that is not specific to Europe.

LI assumes that 'governments first define a set of interests, then bargain amongst themselves to realize those interests' (Moravcsik 1993: 481). Governments act with more or less autonomy depending on how effectively and with what intensity domestic groups make demands on them.

Yet Sandholtz (1993: 3) argues that 'the national interests of EC states do not have independent existence; they are not formed in a vacuum and then brought to Brussels. Those interests are defined and redefined in an international and institutional context that includes the EC' itself. There is little theoretical room within LI for the shaping of national interests *within* the context of EU bargaining.

In particular, intergovernmentalists who approach the EU from an international relations paradigm have almost naturally tended to miss the importance of the ECJ because 'An international organization, almost by definition, does not have a court that exercises judicial review in the sphere of constitutional law as opposed to international law' (Sbragia 1993: 34). More generally, the role of the Court in pushing integration forward through history-making legal decisions boosts neo-functionalism. Its advocates 'argue that in the march toward European Union, as community building gathered speed, the issues before the court have become more politically salient' (Mattli and Slaughter 1995: 189; see also Burley and Mattli 1993; Mattli and Slaughter 1998). The ECJ has taken numerous, highly political decisions, based on ostensibly *legal* rationale, to extend or deepen integration.

Neo-functionalism's most glaring weakness is its implicit assumption that the EU is a uniquely efficient solution to a set of functional problems (Hooghe and Marks 1999). In many respects, the Union is highly *inefficient*; it is simply the most readily available means for organising co-operation. Moreover, neo-functionalism tends to ignore the fundamentally political (as opposed to technocratic) rationality of history-making decisions.

Nevertheless, LI and neo-functionalism are complementary more than they are competitive. Intergovernmentalism is primarily a theory that explains the *process* of bargaining between Member States. Neo-functionalism is a theory of how the *context* of EU decision-making evolves (see Sbragia 1993). This view is echoed by Pierson (1996: 125), who qualifies LI's image of near-total Member State control yet concedes the 'strong institutional position' of national actors. Central to Pierson's (1996: 126) account are 'the lags between decisions and long-term consequences'. History-making decisions are often 'leaps in the dark' with consequences that cannot be foreseen with clarity (Lindberg 1965: 58). The result is 'control gaps': national governments lose control over a process created originally to strengthen them, and the EU evolves according to its own integrative logic. An important source of this logic is the ECJ, which is more autonomous than most national courts and all other EU institutions. Another source is the 'dense networks of experts' (Pierson 1996: 133) which limit the range of future institutional or policy choices by controlling access to the EU's agenda in specific sectors. The result, paradoxically, is 'a highly fragmented but increasingly integrated polity' (Pierson 1996: 158).[11]

Intergovernmentalists argue that what is most important about the super-systemic level is that it *exists*: Member States can always revise the treaties if they are unhappy with the 'increasingly integrated policy' they have created (see Exhibit 1.2). The ECJ cannot stop them. Yet neo-functionalist logic is visible in many history-making decisions. It may be true to claim that states retain the 'ultimate right to decide' in EU governance (Caporaso 1998: 12), but the range of choice open to EU Member States is constrained, in important ways, by the logic of the project they themselves have created.

Setting Policy: the Systemic Level

Most EU decisions – certainly all important ones – are preceded by bargaining. The character of much of the bargaining is intergovernmental, with Member States mobilising their ministers, officials and even their nationals in EU institutions to press forward their national preferences. Yet 'the fact that many (or most) EU decisions look like interstate bargains . . . tells us nothing about how the institutional context shapes preferences and EU decision-making' (Sandholtz 1996: 404). Even theorists who use 'rational choice' models insist that 'One can understand the legislative process in Europe only through detailed institutional analysis of the interactions among the Council, the Commission and the EP, and in particular the sequencing of decisions' (Garrett and Tsebelis 1996: 269–70; see also Tsebelis 1994; Pollack 1997a).

'Policy-setting' decisions are taken at the end of the EU's legislative process, or when the EU arrives at a 'policy *decision* point' (Richardson 1996b: 282). When the EU legislates, it operates as a political system in which powers are shared between institutions (as opposed to an international organisation in which power is monopolised by states). Most EU policies are 'set' when the terms of a directive are agreed according to the 'Community method' of decision-making (Devuyst 1999): the Commission proposes, the Council disposes, the EP amends, and so on. Yet policy is 'set' in a variety of ways and it occurs whenever the Union chooses between alternative courses of action in policy sectors where it has legal competence or the will to act. Few policies are set without a good measure of interinstitutional sparring.

A valuable approach for understanding the policy effects of such institutional politics is the so-called 'new institutionalism' (NI). Its basic lesson is that institutions *matter*: they are the source of much political behaviour and not impartial 'black boxes' which simply transform preferences into policies. Like the EU itself, the NI crosses the boundary between international relations and comparative politics: informing the analysis of IR scholars concerned with interdependence and institutionalised cooperation (see Keohane 1998), while also occupying a 'central place in comparative political science' (Peters 1998a: 122; see also March and Olsen 1989).

The NI offers powerful diagnostic tools for understanding systemic level EU decision-making (Bulmer 1994, 1998; Armstrong and Bulmer 1998). Not only does it shed light on bitterly fought battles for institutional advantage between the Council, EP and Commission. It also reminds us that EU institutions do *not* give equal access to all that wish to influence the policy process. Above all, a new institutionalist analysis of the EU reveals that the Union's common institutions are often more than mere arbiters in the decision-making process, and have become key players in their own right.

What makes the new institutionalism new? Primarily, it is its concern with factors *beyond* the formal roles or legal powers of executives, parliaments, and so on, and its focus on values, norms and informal conventions that govern exchanges between actors. The NI differentiates between 'institutions' and 'organisations': institutions are 'rules' of the game and organisations are 'the players' (North 1990: 3–4).[16] The NI thus highlights how 'players' become socialised to the rules of the game in EU decision-making, and its ethos of bargaining towards consensus. For example, Member States fight pitched battles to place their own nationals in key posts in the Commission and EP, but Bellier's (1995, 1997) fascinating anthropological research suggests that most of the EU's officials 'go native' and adopt a truly supranational European identity.

When the NI has been applied to national politics, it has shed most light on federal systems (see Scharpf 1988; Campbell *et al.* 1991; Weaver and Rockman 1993; Pierson 1995). As in federal systems, the EU is the scene of dilemmas associated with shared decision-making. It is thus prone to 'least common denominator' solutions, which offend few policy stakeholders, or actors with an interest in EU decisions but may not solve policy problems very effectively. In the EU, as in the United States (USA) or Germany, it remains difficult to form minimum winning coalitions for most policy proposals because decisions are easily blocked and veto points are so plentiful. Regardless of whether QMV applies, informal institutional norms in the Council often dictate that unanimity – or something close to it – is needed for the setting of any important policy. Even when QMV is strictly applied, a relatively small group of states can block decisions. Scharpf (1988) argues that the EU combines *de facto* unanimous decision rules, diffused power and a 'bargaining' style of decision-making which seeks, above all, a 'deal' as opposed to the solution to a problem. The result is a 'joint decision trap' which renders the EU a relatively ineffective

Exhibit 1.2   The Amsterdam Treaty[12]

The 1996–7 IGC took place because of a political decision taken in late 1991 when the Maastricht Treaty was agreed: German dissatisfaction with Maastricht's depth of commitment to political union and (particularly) French unhappiness with its provisions for creating a 'common' foreign defence and policy were appeased by an agreement to do it all again and hold *another* IGC in 5 years' time. The subsequent IGC was probably the most carefully prepared and considered of any of the three convened after 1985 (see Edwards and Pijpers 1997; Moravcsik and Nicolaïdis 1998, 1999). Its result – the Amsterdam Treaty – embodied far fewer history-making decisions than either the Single European Act or the Maastricht Treaty (despite Amsterdam's tacit endorsement of a deal to reform the EU's institutions to prepare for enlargement; see Chapter 2). The Treaty *did* decree landmark changes to decision-making on justice and home affairs policies, and potentially important reforms of the Common Foreign and Security Policy (CFSP; see Exhibit 9.1). Yet four outcomes of the IGC were even more striking.

First, the negotiations produced a series of 'non-decisions' on the extension of qualified majority voting (QMV). Member States reacted coyly to the Commission's (1996c: 21) proposal to enshrine QMV as 'the general rule' in EU decision-making. Proposals for a significant extension of QMV, tabled by the 1997 Dutch Council Presidency, were whittled away as the negotiations proceeded. Yet, at the 1997 Amsterdam summit, delegates were still astounded to find Germany's Helmut Kohl blocking the extension of QMV to all but the EU's Framework R&D programme and an obscure Treaty article on national subsidies for imports of raw materials. Even the new British Labour government under Tony Blair was willing to agree a broader extension of majority voting. Kohl's reticence was mainly a consequence of his weakened domestic position in Germany, and particularly the need for any deal to be ratified by the German states (Länder), which were dominated by Kohl's political opponents and/or Eurosceptics. Kohl's legendary skills in the playing of 'two level games' (see Putnam 1988) – using real or imagined constraints at one level of negotiations (such as the domestic level) to secure concessions at another (the EU) – failed him this time.

⟶

system of governance. According to this view, the Union is usually incapable of true policy innovation.

Perhaps above all, the NI helps explain why the setting of precedents is so fiercely contested in the EU. At the heart of most NI analyses is the concept of '*path dependency*', or the notion that 'Once an historical choice is made, it both precludes and facilitates others. Political change follows a branching model. Once a particular fork is chosen, it is very difficult to get

⟶

Second, the Amsterdam Treaty gave legal sanction to a future EU of multiple speeds. It added new provisions on 'flexibility' – or 'reinforced co-operation' in specific policy areas between a sub-set of EU Member States (see de La Serre and Wallace 1997; Edwards and Phillipart 1999). Flexibility as a concept had been championed primarily by France and Germany, and opposed most staunchly by the UK, with support from Greece, Denmark, Sweden and Ireland. The Blair government insisted that any Member State should be able to veto any proposed flexible arrangement. This idea was rejected by France and Germany, which settled for the compromise that a qualified majority could elect to move forward, with reluctant states allowed to stop them only by citing 'important and stated reasons of national policy' (see Exhibit 2.5). It was not clear that the new flexibility provisions would be used very often, but the Amsterdam Treaty moved the EU closer to a system of differentiated, 'multi-speed' integration, as opposed to an institution in which all Member States sailed at one speed.

Third, the Amsterdam Treaty significantly extended the so-called 'co-decision procedure', the EU decision rule which gives veto power to the EP (see Exhibit 1.3). After Amsterdam, the Parliament was measurably closer to being 'on equal footing with the Council' (Moravcsik and Nicolaïdis 1998: 21). The extension of co-decision certainly did not make the European Union a parliamentary democracy, but it pushed the EU in that direction.

Fourth and finally, the Amsterdam Treaty fuelled the conviction shared by many scholars (see Weiler 1997; Dinan 1998) that IGCs are a poor way of 'constitution-building' (if it is accepted that the EU's treaties have the character of a 'constitution').[13] The Amsterdam summit broke up in the middle of the night in a state of some chaos, with many delegations unsure about precisely what had been decided. One senior Nordic official complained that 'different members of the Dutch presidency were telling us different things about what had been agreed'.[14] One British official, described the negotiations as 'sad. Old men sitting around arguing at 3 o'clock in the morning'[15] (although the advantage enjoyed by the relatively young and energetic Blair must have been some consolation). A strange way to build Europe, indeed.

back on the rejected path' (Krasner 1984: 225). Path dependency may be viewed as a product of the joint decision trap: the need for agreement between so many different decision-makers – including many beyond Brussels – does not only mean that it is achingly difficult to 'set' policy in the first place. It becomes even harder to *change* policy, even when it outlives its usefulness. The 'sunk costs' of agreeing a policy in the first place are often considerable, leading to situations where EU policies become analogous to the QWERTY system of organising letters on a computer keyboard:[17] one solution may prevail over others even though it proves to be far less efficient than discarded alternatives would have been.

Unanimity is almost always required at the super-systemic level for any major institutional change, yet the EU continues to trundle along, even when it appears in danger of falling apart, because unanimity is also needed for decisions which *roll back* integration (Marks *et al.* 1996a: 354; Pierson 1996: 143). More generally, political institutions are 'sticky' and tend to change more slowly than governments or the preferences of policy-makers. Thus institutions become a force for continuity more than change.

In particular, institutionalised arrangements differ markedly between EU policy sectors. Reforms designed to rationalise decision-making or make it simpler and more transparent are difficult to agree unanimously. Path dependency leads to an 'organic accretion' of decision-making procedures: new ones are fastened onto old ones in the same way that lichens attach themselves first to a tree, then to other lichens, adding layer upon layer, overlapping but never shedding.[18] In the EU, the result is enormous procedural differentiation, with the number of different, formal decision-making procedures increasing steadily (the Amsterdam Treaty offered a modest 'shedding'). After the Maastricht Treaty, the EU had more than 23 distinct procedures for making binding decisions (Westlake 1995: 77; Wessels 1997b: 24–7).

In a system marked less by competition between different political philosophies than by competition between institutions, the new institutionalism highlights how apparently consensual policy-making does not preclude clandestine attempts to shift boundary and decision rules: 'the triangular relationship between the Commission, Council and Parliament is a dynamic . . . or unstable one in which the institutions frequently use all political and legal means available to increase their impact on the decision-making process or defend their prerogatives' (Monar 1994: 695). Attempts to 'shift' decision rules are abetted by the proliferation of so many different decision rules.

In particular, the EU's abundance of decision-making procedures acts to empower the Court of Justice. They ECJ must frequently adjudicate in interinstitutional disputes about which procedure should apply to a particular legislative initiative. Most ECJ decisions are relatively undramatic, concerning the application of competition policy or the implementation of directives at the national level. Yet the Court is still a powerful institutional actor at the systemic level, particularly because it must rule on disputes about procedure and act as a 'court of appeal' for interests which cannot get a hearing from other institutions.

At the same time, the discretion of national governments and courts in applying Community law is wide. Rates of compliance with EU rules are patchy and uneven between Member States (see Jordan 1997; Haas 1998). Governments have shown great creative imagination in resisting or subverting the Court's rulings. The ECJ lacks any police force or army to enforce its will and must earn its authority by reputation. Thus new institutionalism stresses both the capacity of the Court to influence Union policy and its inability to enforce its decisions directly. One important reason why nearly everything is negotiable in EU decision-making is that the 'EU legal system is not based on a solid institutional foundation' (Garrett 1992: 556).

The new institutionalism is more a set of assumptions, a 'method for deriving analytical insights' (Armstrong and Bulmer 1998: 61), than a proper theory, which can describe, explain and predict the outcomes of systemic decision-making. The NI's virtues are clear, yet even its staunchest advocates concede that 'the EU is not yet a state with a stable institutional system, so the development of a convincing grand-theoretical explanation of its governance seems to be highly unlikely' (Armstrong and Bulmer 1998: 61). The EU remains a relatively young and experimental system of governance. As such, 'informal political processes have to bear rather more weight than in a long-established polity, with entrenched rules and engrained practices' (Wallace 1997: 11). Yet, if we treat informal processes (particularly at the sub-systemic level) as 'institutions', surely we are stretching the concept of institutions to its breaking point.[19]

Shaping Policy: the Sub-Systemic Level

Policy-shaping decisions do not 'decide' EU policy. Rather, they determine policy details or what policy options will be considered 'by ruling some policy alternatives as permissible or impermissible' (Pollack 1997a: 100). Article 211[20] of the treaties explicitly mandates that the Commission should 'participate in the *shaping* of measures taken by the Council and the European Parliament'. Most 'policy-shaping' decisions are taken early in the policy process when policies are being formulated and, in fact, before the EU's formal legislative process even begins. These early stages are when most lobbying activity occurs. Once political agreement begins to emerge at the systemic level even an informal deal 'often tends to be rather inflexible. Modifying it in any way may mean starting the bargaining process all over again, as once part of it has been unstitched, the whole garment starts to unravel' (Grant 1993: 31–2).

In particular, the margins for changing the content of EU legislation seem to shrink quite quickly after the Commission has tabled a proposal. After that point, according to a senior Commission official, 'scope for changing the proposal exists only at the margins, involving about 20 per cent of the total proposal' (Hull 1993: 83). This allegation may seem to overstate the powers of the Commission, but it is indicative more of *when* crucial decisions are taken in the EU's policy process than who controls decision-making.

When policies are formulated, important decisions may emerge from consultations between the Commission and policy stakeholders in formal, purpose-built forums created to facilitate exchanges of ideas and agendas. 'However, at least as pertinent' – usually more so – 'are the informally constituted and flexible networks that are so much present' (Wallace 1997: 10). The EU is a 'hothouse' for relatively informal policy networks for four basic reasons. First, despite recent attempts to formalise consultation between the Commission and policy stakeholders (see Peterson 1995c), the EU continues to lack formal institutions which can adequately 'manag[e] the policy dialogue' (Wallace 1997: 10). The EU depends fundamentally on its ability to forge consensus between a wide variety of decision-makers before policies may be 'set'. It thus requires extensive, informal, 'pre-legislative' bargaining over the shape of most proposals before they have any chance of being accepted.

Second, rules of access to EU decision-making are usually unclear. For Wallace (1996b: 27), this ambiguity explains why policy networks, 'currently amongst the most attractive and rewarding areas of study, have become so important' (see also Kohler-Koch 1994, 1996). Informal networking allows the participation of a far larger number and wider range of different stakeholders than could ever be accommodated in formal consultative mechanisms.

Third, both the EU's multi-level character and policy remit encourage a sort of governing by co-ordination. Much EU legislation is decided in the form of directives, which set out a general set of objectives while leaving most details as to how they might be achieved to Member States themselves. To a considerable extent, the precise content of directives is determined later at a non-political level by various types of official, together with interested interest groups and lobbyists, in response to broad policy injunctions. Governments thus have incentives to engage with private actors, who 'have to be drawn into the policy networks because they provide necessary expertise and because effective implementation depends on their support' (Kohler-Koch 1997: 49).[21]

Fourth, and finally, the EU attracts actors interested in policy change, but it is a consensual system in which opposition is appeased or minimised (Kohler-Koch 1996: 373). Policy networks (in environmental policy) may promote change by facilitating bargaining over the terms and extent of new EU measures. Alternatively, some (in agriculture or external trade policy) consolidate the veto power of vested interests. Above all, policy networks facilitate the detailed bargaining which must precede attempts to satisfy different needs in different Member States with the same policy.

Most policy networks provide stability, and often outlast political changes such as the election of new governments. In this context, most interest groups in Europe continue to focus the bulk of their lobbying at the national level, where most of the resources are held that groups want or need. Relationships between interest groups and national administrations are usually more long-standing and routinised than is the case at the EU level. The result is that the national level is more likely to breed stable, tightly integrated networks, or '*policy communities*', which strictly control access to the policy agenda (Rhodes 1990).

Compared to most national systems of government, the Union seems a relatively open market for influence and access. Such 'open competition for scarce resources leads to shifting coalitions . . .[and] few "frozen" cleavages that lead to permanent coalitions' (Wessels 1997b: 36). It is plausible to suggest that most EU policy networks remain relatively unstable '*issue networks*', or the polar opposites of 'policy communities'. The memberships of issue networks are not drawn from a stable 'community' but rather are fluid and defined by specific issues that arise on the EU's agenda (Heclo 1978). Compared to their national equivalents, EU policy networks appear to be more complex, crowded and unstable.

Yet actors at the EU level are often dependent on each other and on the functional success of the EU as a successful manager of interdependence. The EU is more a technocracy than a democracy, in that 'political hegemony cannot be established by fighting ideological battles in the political market-place' and power is usually a function of resources which help solve problems: 'expert knowledge, political insight, and bargaining experience' (Kohler-Koch 1997: 48). Thus policy networks spring up around specific EU policy sectors, marshalling technocratic expertise and seeking to shape policy options which are likely to be endorsed by political decision-makers at the systemic level. The Commission usually plays the role of facilitator and 'ring-leader': 'There are always ministries, groups, and factions in each country which share to some degree the policy goals of the Commission and whose positions are strengthened by virtue of an alliance with it' (Lindberg 1965: 63). However, the bargaining mode within policy networks is resource exchange between mutually dependent actors (see Table 1.2) and thus the Commission must *negotiate* a policy agenda with its 'clients'.

Given the highly technical nature of EU governance, we can expect policy networks to be dominated by 'epistemic communities', or 'network[s] of professionals with recognized expertise and competence in a particular domain' who define problems, identify compromises and supply 'expert' arguments to justify political choices (Haas 1992: 3). Nonetheless, the EU also offers opportunities for political agency, or purposive action in pursuit of political goals. Policy networks may provide access to politically-minded 'advocacy coalitions' of elected and bureaucratic officials, interest group leaders, journalists and other actors which wish to 'steer' the EU's policy agenda (Sabatier and Jenkins-Smith 1993; Sabatier 1998). Advocacy coalitions are groups of actors with 'core policy beliefs', who are likely to be capable of effective political action when their members interact repeatedly, exchange information easily and unite in support of policies which will treat them fairly, if not all equally (Sabatier 1998: 116). Successful advocacy coalitions may shift the EU's policy agenda from the 'bottom-up', as appeared to occur when Member States accepted (first) the need for the Social Charter and then the Maastricht Treaty's social protocol to 'flank' the 1992 project with EU social policies (see Exhibit 3.5). Advocacy coalitions are not the same as epistemic communities: the former have political objectives while the latter tend to be motivated more by technocratic considerations. But both types of coalition compete for control of the EU's agenda, and thus seek to 'penetrate' policy networks that act as the sentinels of the agenda in specific sectors.

Institutional reforms often provide new openings for advocacy coalitions. The co-operation procedure – introduced by the Single European Act – not only induced considerable internal reform of the Commission (the creation of a new unit in its Secretariat-General for relations with the EP), it also offered MEPs 'membership cards' to selected policy networks. After the Maastricht Treaty went a step further and mandated 'co-decision' (see Exhibit 1.3), the Commission was forced to engage the EP's relevant committees early in the policy process in order to get its legislation accepted, sometimes even helping MEPs to draft mutually acceptable amendments to proposed legislation (Westlake 1994a: 17).

The EP became a far more powerful player in some sectors than in others, in part because co-decision applied to some (the internal market) but not all (agricultural policy). As such, policy network analysis helps us come to grips with how 'sectorised' EU decision-making is: there are quite separate and different types of policy networks for, say, environmental and cohesion policy despite overlaps between their memberships.

Because rival sectoral networks compete to control the EU's policy agenda, networks need an effective 'sherpa': an agent who can ensure that the sectoral actors have a guardian when an initiative reaches the systemic level of decision-making. The Commissioner with responsibility for a given portfolio is the most obvious candidate. Policy networks are empowered if 'their' Commissioner commands the trust of his/her colleagues on the college, as well as national ambassadors and ministers who ultimately set policy. When policy networks lack an effective sherpa, the interests of their members can be trounced by those of competing networks: for example, when a proposed consumer policy measure has implications for agricultural producers (see Exhibits 4.6 and 5.2).

Exhibit 1.3 Co-decision: the art of conciliation[22]

If EU policy networks became more accessible to a broader range of interests in the post-Maastricht period, it was largely because of co-decision. Article 251 of the Treaty[23] is generally (but not always) combined with QMV in the Council. Under co-decision, the Council shares legal responsibility for legislation jointly with the European Parliament (EP), with the EP and Council entering into direct negotiations if they cannot agree on a proposal. Negotiations take place in formal 'conciliation committees', in which the Council and EP are equally represented. If a joint text is *not* approved by a Conciliation Committee, the act falls. Put simply, co-decision gives the EP the power to veto any proposal that falls under its auspices.

The EP is strongest under co-decision when its members exercise collective judgement about how far they can push the Council to accept its proposed amendments. There is dispute about whether the EP or Commission is more dependent on the support of the Council under co-decision. However, the Commission cannot withdraw a proposal once it has become subject to conciliation, and it is possible for the EP and Council effectively to decide against the wishes of the Commission. One important effect is that the Commission and policy networks which shape proposals early in the decision-making process tend to be more open to MEPs (especially chairs of relevant EP Committees or '*rapporteurs*' who evaluate specific proposals) than they were before co-decision existed.

Under co-decision, deals struck when EU policies are 'set' are often interinstitutional as much as they are intergovernmental in nature. In particular, the procedure tends to produce one of two patterns of bargaining. Sometimes, particularly under a strong presidency, the Council acts with considerable unity and discipline but negotiates with a (crucial) degree of flexibility. Deals struck between Member States at the relatively early stages of decision-making – when the Council reaches a 'common position' on a proposal – are honoured, but a way is found to accommodate (or at least appease) the EP.

More rarely, co-decision fosters competition between alliances of Members States linked to EP factions. A group of MEPs may seek allies on the Council who agreed with reluctance to the terms of the Council's common position. Attempts are then made to 'peel them off' from the rest of the Council by agreeing a mutually acceptable 'raft' of amendments. This strategy is still uncommon, but when it works policy choices tend to reflect compromise between broad political tendencies (Socialist v. Christian Democratic), competing sectoral interests (industrial v. consumer interests) or visions of the EU's proper role in European governance. Potentially, at least, the co-decision procedure enhances 'the development and significance of socio-political cleavages at the European level' (Rhodes and Mazey 1995: 20). Above all, the need for broad 'winning' coalitions means that goalposts are often shifted so that all can claim that they are winners when policies are set through co-decision.

In this climate, policy networks that show solidarity and can bargain their way to internal consensus enjoy powerful advantages. The Commission thus 'goes to extraordinary lengths to establish constituencies of Euro-groups around each Directorate-General – practically "sponsoring" their formation' (McLaughlin and Jordan 1993: 157). The number of 'Euro-groups' featuring direct memberships (as opposed to being federations of national groups) that are officially recognised by the Commission has grown significantly. Relatively integrated Euro-groups in pharmaceuticals, information technology and automobiles have emerged as a result of the co-existence of three factors: the strong international orientation of the industries, the clear remit of the EU in these sectors and the domination of the industries by a relatively small number of firms (Grant 1994; Greenwood 1995b). Relatively tightly knit policy communities exist in all of these sectors.

It is worth recalling that the early neo-functionalists assigned to such interest groups a powerful role as an 'engine' of integration. However, the representatives of Euro-groups in Brussels rarely seem to act with much autonomy. In fact, 'Real power has shifted away from the representative bodies in Brussels to . . . national member organizations' (Wessels 1997b: 29) and many Euro-groups are not much more than the sum of their parts. The broad aggregation of interests in EU decision-making is difficult and rare.

Aspinwall (1998: 197) even sees an 'advocacy void' arising from lack of strong transnational pressure groups (or EU-wide political parties). The number of interest groups represented in Brussels increased exponentially from around 200 in 1960 to something like 2200 by the mid-1990s (Wessels 1997b: 17). Yet the clear majority remained national or sub-national (as opposed to transnational) in orientation. By the late 1990s, there were about 700 truly transnational groups in Brussels, but - for the sake of comparison – around 1900 organised groups in Denmark. There were something like 23 000 organisations organised nationally in the USA in the non-profit sector alone (Aspinwall 1998: 206).

Certainly, Brussels was crawling with more than 10 000 lobbyists by 1990, but most represented single companies or were their organisation's *only* representative (besides secretarial personnel) in Brussels. The estimate that the Commission brought together roughly 30 000 participants annually in its organised meetings (Wessels 1997b: 17) seemed slightly less like Euro-pluralism given that more than 80 per cent were national civil servants (Wessels and Rometsch 1996: 331). In fact, recent literature on EU interest representation often concludes that, contrary to what might be expected, multi-level decision-making appears to advantage state actors over private actors compared to centralised, hierarchical decision-making (see Grande 1996; Kohler-Koch 1996). The effective separation of powers between levels of EU governance has the Madisonian effect of curbing the power of private 'factions', which face enormous difficulties in 'capturing' all levels at once. Influence in EU decision-making tends to be wielded quite narrowly by private actors, in certain sectors and at certain levels of decision-making only. Meanwhile, the EU's Member States are powerful at all levels and in all sectors. One upshot is that the EU may 'strengthen the state' even at the deepest reaches of the sub-systemic level.

Consistent with this thesis is the notion that the EU is a 'mobiliser of bias' not only in favour of states, but also in favour of private interests that are most powerful at the state level: producers are advantaged more than consumers by the EU's existence and neo-liberal ethos. Narrow interests are privileged more than diffuse 'promotional' or 'cause' groups such as women's rights or environmental groups (see Kohler-Koch 1994; Pierson 1995: 460). Traditionally, the EU has tended to validate Olson's (1965) theory 'that successful collective action is more likely in settings where small groups will be strongly motivated to act' (Caporaso 1998: 10). In contrast, 'broadly-based interest organizations find it difficult to cope with the EU, because they cannot be as closely linked to issue-specific networks as sectoral interest groups' (Kohler-Koch 1997: 48).

Yet, the EU is a system in flux. Recent research suggests that the EU does not always empower the already powerful, particularly as it begins to legislate on broader, 'non-economic' questions (social policy, environmental protection, and so on). If 'policy determines politics' (Lowi 1972) then it makes sense that more and more diffuse interests have managed to shape decision-making over time (see McGowan and Wallace 1996; Peterson 1997; Pollack 1997b; Wallace and Young 1997; Greenwood and Aspinwall 1998; Mazey 1998). Usually, they have formed alliances with the Commission (environmental groups) and EP (consumer groups), or learned to use the ECJ (women's rights groups). Because the EU's institutions instinctively aim for pan-European solutions to policy problems, broadly based groups learn quickly that they enjoy more influence if they can present themselves as transnational in scope and 'pro-European' in ideology.

On balance, however, Euro-representation remains underdeveloped. The Brussels lobbying environment has become far more 'crowded', but relative to the Union's enormous scale, a remarkably small number of actors may 'capture' the EU's policy agenda. Remarkably few actors can sometimes shape (if not 'make') policies for the many in a polity of 370 million EU citizens, which is set to become significantly larger in the early 21st century (see Exhibit 1.4).

Given these contingencies, policy network analysis may be an 'inefficient research strategy' for making sense of EU decision-making.[24] It is often more 'efficient', sometimes even plausible, to link policy outcomes to a real or imagined set of national preferences, and then a process of intergovern-

---

Exhibit 1.4   Enlargement

In a different time and place, with the decidedly intergovernmental Council of Europe in his sights, the father of post-war European integration, Jean Monnet (1978: 271), insisted that 'the idea that *sixteen* nations can cooperate effectively is an illusion'. By 1995, the EU was one short of this number. In some respects it was surprising how little EU decision-making changed as a consequence of northern enlargement from 12 to 15 (see Peterson and Bomberg 1998). However, the post-Maastricht period was in important respects an unusually quiet period in EU decision-making, primarily because the European Commission under the presidency of Jacques Santer pledged to 'do less, but do it better'. There were far fewer policies to 'set', as the number of formal legislative proposals tabled by the Commission fell from 61 in 1990 to only 21 by 1996.

Yet the 1995 enlargement marked the final time that the EU could expand its membership without facing a choice between quite radical reform of its policies and institutions, or total stalemate in its decision-making (see Preston 1995; 1997). In policy terms, the EU's agenda became more crowded after the Commission tabled an ambitious range of proposals (31 in 1998), many in anticipation of eastern enlargement and arising from *Agenda 2000* (Commission 1997c), a 'package' of linked policy reforms. In institutional terms, it was accepted that decision-making would need to be reformed to cope with further enlargement (see Chapter 2). The Amsterdam Treaty required the EU to undertake a 'comprehensive review' of its decision-making procedures at least one year before its membership exceeded 20, thus creating

→

---

mental bargaining. Yet we recall Heclo's (1978: 102) warning when he first introduced the notion of 'issue networks': 'Looking for the few who are powerful, we tend to overlook the many whose webs of influence provoke and guide the exercise of power.' These 'webs of influence' may be opaque and difficult to study, but they clearly exist and shape EU policy in crucial ways.

Conclusion

We have ranged broadly across the existing literature in search of concepts and theory that can help us make sense of EU decision-making. It is clear that, whenever the EU decides, it is after a process of bargaining. As a consequence, we must be sensitive to the bargaining mode that characterises decision-making at different levels of analysis (see Table 1.2). Bargaining on the terms of most 'history-making' decisions seems

→

a psychological barrier to admitting more than five new Member States (with 12 lined up to join).[25]

From the Union's point of view, the creation of new 'accession partnerships', which mobilised all forms of EU assistance to applicant states, demonstrated its political commitment to enlargement (Council 1997: 6). From the perspective of applicant states, the EU moved at a snail's pace. In 1998, the six states closest to membership boldly committed themselves to accession by 2002, yet the Czech Republic's legendary President, Vaclav Havel, complained that the 'historical importance' of unifying East and West was being upstaged by 'battles about apples, fish or potatoes'.[26] Hungary's outspoken Prime Minister, Viktor Orban, implied that the Union was treating applicants 'like children'.[27] It was clear that the EU's next enlargement would occur only after a process of adjustment that would be wrenching for both sides.

Looking ahead, the difficulty of reaching agreements at the political level in an enlarged Union made it likely that more would be decided at the sub-systemic level within policy networks, many of which could not be expected to welcome actors from new Member States (see Peterson and Jones 1999). More generally, eastern enlargement seemed certain to foster intense new battles between policy networks for turf and resources. As Wessels (1997b: 39) suggested, a plausible future scenario was that 'the competition for access and influence among these networks would continue, with intensifying fights over scarce economic resources as the EU enlarged further'.

primarily intergovernmental. Yet, neo-functionalism helps explain why and how the context of European interigation evolved to the point where such bargaining resulted in the relaunch of European integration in the 1980s (Taylor 1989: 23–4) or was constrained by the ECJ and the process of legal integration (Burley and Mattli 1993).

When the EU sets policy, bargaining is often as much between institutions – the Commission, Council and EP – as between governments. Despite the EU's intergovernmental backbone, institutional objectives are far more important in the Union's policy process than in most other systems of government. The EU's institutions are often less concerned with substantive policy objectives than with gaining institutional ground (Wallace 1996a).

Finally, most EU policy outcomes are the ultimate products of overtly political choices taken by ministers or MEPs, but choices are shaped in crucial ways by decisions taken in sub-systemic policy networks. Actors who want to penetrate policy networks must have valued resources that they are willing to exchange in pursuit of their goals. Bargaining within EU policy networks is mostly informal, but 'sectoral networks, like states, operate within institutionalised rules that both enable and constrain action' (Jordan 1999: 30). Put another way, 'Networks will only function if they are embedded in overarching institutions, in a common understanding of the game they are in' (Kohler-Koch 1996: 374). Even if nearly everything is negotiable in EU decision-making, formal institutions, decision rules and accepted norms are crucial in determining how the game is played. It is these factors to which we turn in chapter 2.

Chapter 2

Institutions, Rules, Norms

Institutions
Decision rules
Norms
Conclusion

As we have seen, there is plenty of theory to help us understand EU decision-making.[1] Any theory of political action must confront basic questions, such as:

> Are the effects we wish to explain the products of actors displaying their agency, making unconstrained choices; [or] are these effects the products of an unfolding logic of a structure (or set of structures) over which agents (individual or collective) have no control?' (Hay 1995: 189; see also Wendt 1987)[2]

Applied to the EU, the question invites two possible answers. First, the EU's *structure* may determine decision-making. Structurally, the Union is enormously complex and potentially involves an extraordinary number, range and diversity of decision-makers. It is frequently difficult, sometimes impossible, to shift the EU in any one (especially new) policy direction, thus reinforcing the status quo. Vetoes are abundant and distributed widely, particularly on the Council and its offshoots, thus inviting lowest-common denominator decisions. Powers are separated between the EU's institutions, which are fundamentally weak and resource-poor. In any event, nearly any major decision requires the unanimous agreement of all Member States. In short, there are too many structural constraints in the EU for political agency to matter much or often.

A second possible answer is that *agency* often matters more than structure in EU decision-making. The Union is a young system of governance in which structures are fluid, experimental and changeable. The EU's treaties are astoundingly vague. Links between societal interests and EU decision-makers ('agents') are weak in the absence of traditional structures – such as strong political parties – for aggregating interests. EU policy networks may be 'captured' by agents who shape major decisions in ways that effectively predetermine them before Member States can 'make' them. Agency trumps structure: 'it is the men [*sic*] who govern the processes, and not the processes that govern the men' (Rosenthal 1975: 14).

Of course, these two views present a false dichotomy. Yet, the question of whether EU decisions are primarily determined by agency or structure is

---

Exhibit 2.1   The basics of EU decision-making

In a nutshell, the EU's main institutions and their decision-making procedures are as follows:

- The *European Council* consists of all national heads of government, the French and Finnish Presidents (since they are elected) and the President of the European Commission. It meets at least twice a year (but usually three times) at European summits and issues general political guidelines for the EU as a whole: that is for 'pillar I' (the European Community as traditionally defined) plus pillars II (for the Common Foreign and Security Policy) and III (Justice and Home Affairs policies), both of which were created by the Maastricht Treaty. In all but very rare cases, the European Council works on the basis of consensus and votes are not taken.
- The *Council of Ministers* is the EU's main legislative body. It brings together ministers from each Member State in specific policy sectors, such as the internal market, agriculture, the environment and so on. The Council usually decides on the basis of qualified majority voting (QMV), although procedural questions are decided by simple majority votes and some policy areas (such as taxation and most questions concerning pillars II and III) generally require unanimous agreement. The work of the Council is 'prepared' by the Committee of Permanent Representatives (COREPER), which groups together national ambassadors to the EU, as well as a plethora of working groups of national civil servants, including the Political Committee of senior national Foreign Ministry officials in the case of pillar II.

$\longrightarrow$

---

crucial, and engaging. In this chapter we arm the reader with a basic overview (beginning with Exhibit 2.1) of the institutions,[3] rules and norms which structure EU decision-making. This overview is essential background for understanding the rest of our analysis, and for equipping the reader to derive their own answer to the question of whether agency matters more than structure, or vice versa.

Institutions

The most fundamental insight of new institutionalist treatments of the EU is that the Union has a considerable measure of institutional autonomy and is not merely an instrument of nation-states (Armstrong and Bulmer 1996; Sandholtz and Stone Sweet 1998). The argument is *not* that individual EU institutions operate with much autonomy: powers are not so much separated as shared between them. Usually, important decisions may be made only if broad interinstitutional agreement exists. Yet the Union's

⟶

- The European Commission is the EU's civil service but it enjoys significant executive powers, many of which are delegated to it by the Council. It is given political direction by its President and the 'college' of 20 Commissioners, appointed by Member States for five-year terms, who decide (if necessary) by simple majority. Its functional tasks are carried out by 24 Directorates-General (DGs or 'services') which work on specific EU policies. The Commission's main power in EU decision-making is its monopoly on the right to initiate legislative proposals (within pillar I).
- The *European Parliament* (EP) consists of 626 elected members (MEPs), with each Member State electing (every five years) a number of members very roughly proportionate to its national population. The EP has gained powers – mostly to amend legislation – each time the treaties have been revised. The Parliament is most powerful when it vets appointees to the Commission and European Central Bank, and under the 'co-decision' (see Exhibit 1.3) and 'assent' procedures, both of which give the EP the power to veto measures by majority votes.
- The *European Court of Justice* (ECJ) consists of one judge per Member State, appointed for six-year terms. The ECJ mostly decides how Community law should be applied to specific cases or whether it is being applied uniformly across the Union. Because the EU's Treaties are so vague, the ECJ has considerable powers to fill 'gaps' in them, particularly by developing general principles of Community law.

institutions are endowed with powers that are, in important respects, placed beyond the control of any government or even coalitions of them. The EU is a polity, or system of governance, in its own right. It has its own will, agenda and institutional prerogatives (see Marks *et al.* 1996a).

The European Council

Any profile of the EU's institutions must begin with the European Council (see Bulmer and Wessels 1987; Werts 1992; Johnston 1994; Bulmer 1996). More than any other EU institution, its role has changed since the creation of the European Economic Community (EEC): it did not even become a formal Community institution until the SEA. Not only is the European Council the primary source of history-making decisions. Its 'Presidency conclusions', agreed at the end of European summits, have become 'bibles' which drive EU decision-making more generally.[4] In particular, the European Council has become far more involved in foreign policy: from mostly rubber-stamping decisions taken in the European Political

Co-operation framework in the late 1980s to becoming – at least formally – the primary decision-maker on the Common Foreign and Security Policy (CFSP; see Exhibit 9.4).

The European Council has enormous power but little time. Held over two days, summits usually offer only three formal sessions (of about three hours each) plus three official meals, during which business may be done. Scope for actual debate is strictly limited, particularly if all delegations wish to speak to a particular issue or (as is increasingly the case) summits include sessions with non-EU Member States, such as heads of government of Central and East European states. At times, European leaders discuss quite technical or detailed issues: the European Council chose maroon as the colour for EU passports after years of deadlock on the issue. Devices such as parallel Council meetings (farm ministers sorted out a row over sheep meat at the Luxembourg summit in 1980) or 'false B' points – items not for discussion but formally allowing ministerial input – help keep summits focused on 'big' decisions (Hayes-Renshaw and Wallace 1997: 80).

Crucially, the European Council is one of the only EU institutions whose sum *and* parts (individual Prime Ministers and Presidents) are not 'sectorised'. Summits can – and do – consider initiatives in any EU policy sector, and packages that tie disparate decisions together. The European Council is the EU's Board of Directors, and a source of 'high political' direction.

The Council of Ministers

In contrast to the European Council, the Council of Ministers[5] is highly sectorised despite its treaty status as a single institution (see Westlake 1995; Hayes-Renshaw and Wallace 1997). Alongside the European Council, it is the ultimate guardian of the territorial dimension in EU decision-making. The Council retains legal powers to legislate – increasingly alongside the EP – which the European Council 'takes over' only in special circumstances. The Council can (and often does) legislate across EU policy sectors via 'A points', which are decided by officials and then nodded through by ministers – *any* ministers – without discussion. The Council of Agricultural Ministers officially took decisions related to the European Coal and Steel Community, anti-dumping duties on video cassettes from Hong Kong, and the EC–Japan Centre for Industrial Co-operation in 1992 at the same time as it thrashed out a comprehensive farm reform package (see Swinbank 1996a).

Generally, however, the Council is highly fragmented between policy sectors. It thus reinforces the disaggregated, 'sectorised' nature of EU decision-making. The proliferation of new, specialised Councils, such as the Audio-Visual, Tourism and Culture Councils, gives ministers who are marginalised in their national capitals an opportunity to be active and assert the interests of 'their' sector. The General Affairs Council of Foreign Ministers meets more frequently (around 15 times a year) than any other Council and is meant to act as an overall co-ordinator of the Council's business. Yet, increasingly, the European Council has become the arbiter of difficult questions. As the Union's remit has expanded, particularly to include the CFSP and Economic and Monetary Union (EMU), the General Council has become both overloaded by absurdly crowded agendas and overshadowed by the Council of Economic and Finance Ministers (known by its French acronym, ECOFIN). By the late 1990s, the General Council had little or no time for discussions of anything besides external affairs (see Exhibit 9.5).

Political leadership of the Council falls to the rotating *Council Presidency*, which is held in turn by Member States for a period of six months. Representatives of the presidency chair all meetings of the Council at all levels. The Council presidency has become a more central player in EU politics as the Union has enlarged, used QMV more frequently, and assigned more executive functions to the Council. Even when the Community only consisted of 10 Member States, the British Ambassador, Michael Butler (1986: 26) found it 'almost impossible to get a conclusion out of a Council against the wishes of its President'. At the same time, each presidency is judged by how 'productive' it is, thus often inducing the state holding the chair to compromise its own national preferences to get deals agreed.

The Council Presidency has been empowered considerably by the co-decision procedure. Much of the real bargaining under co-decision takes place in informal 'trialogues' between representatives of the Council, Commission and EP, or 'informal conciliations' that precede formal meetings of conciliation committees. The difficulty of negotiating in formal conciliation committees puts a premium on such forums which facilitate informal bargaining, and which feature the Council Presidency speaking for (sometimes negotiating for) the Council as a whole.

In reality, ministerial meetings of the Council are just the tip of an iceberg. All Council meetings are prepared by *COREPER*, the spine of the 'single institutional framework' which is meant to tie together pillars I, II (for the CFSP) and III (for justice and home affairs). COREPER itself is split into two: COREPER I groups together national Deputy Ambassadors to the EU and is responsible for the internal market and other more technical sectors (such as research and trade). COREPER II, consisting of senior Ambassadors, prepares all meetings of the European Council, General Affairs, Development, ECOFIN and Budget Councils. Thus it confronts more divisive, politicised questions – although the rise of co-decision, which assigns Deputy Ambassadors a crucial role in negotiations with the EP, has boosted the relative power of COREPER I.

COREPER is a fascinating institution. Formally, at least, it 'has no autonomous decision-making power, and is in no way a substitute body for the Council' (Hayes-Renshaw and Wallace 1997: 81). Yet its members tend to serve in Brussels for long periods of time and develop a strong sense of complicity. Items decided by COREPER are forwarded to the Council as 'A points', which usually are not discussed by Ministers but formally agreed. In short, COREPER is a powerful engine in the decision-making process: its members frequently must 'manufacture' a national position in Council negotiations when instructions from national capitals are vague or reflect divisions between ministries. Lewis (1998: 499) argues that its role has been 'undervalued and overlooked' for two essential reasons:

> First is the combination of COREPER's *de facto* decision-making role *and* their causal influence and voice in the articulation of national preferences. And second is the collective, *communitarian* dimension of this authority, expressed through the routinization and diffuse exchange of viewpoints and a collective rationality which transcends individual, instrumental rationality.

COREPER works closely with the *Council General Secretariat*, the Council's own multinational, Brussels-based administration. Although not mentioned in any treaty before Maastricht, the Secretariat has always been a powerful player in EU decision-making. It continues to occupy 'an important and sometimes crucial role at all levels of the Council hierarchy in helping member state representatives to reach decisions efficiently and effectively' (Hayes-Renshaw and Wallace 1997: 102). Its officials (like those of COREPER) tend to serve for long periods of time. The Secretariat is relatively small, employing only about 300 'A' grade, or policy-making officials. They tend to be skilled at crafting compromises, particularly in drafting texts (including, crucially, Presidency Conclusions after European summits) which translate to all Community languages and on which all parties can agree.

The Secretary-General of the Council is an unsung heavyweight in EU decision-making. There is no set tenure for the post and only four individuals have held it since 1952 (Hayes-Renshaw and Wallace 1997: 107). All have been from small Member States (Luxembourg and Denmark) apart from the German, Jurgen Trumpf, who was appointed in 1994. The Amsterdam Treaty is certain to transform the role of the Secretary-General by making him or her the new 'High Representative' of the CFSP, and designating the Deputy Secretary-General 'responsible for the running of the General Secretariat'.

Much of the running in terms of actual Council decision-making falls to its approximately 150 *working groups*. Council groups bring together national officials and experts to scrutinise Commission proposals or undertake the technical groundwork needed before the Council can decide. Every working day, an average of around 1000 officials or experts attend 20 different Council group meetings in Brussels. About 70 per cent of the EU's legislative output is actually 'decided' at this level (Hayes-Renshaw and Wallace 1997: 15). An even higher percentage of all Council 'decisions' are taken in working groups (Rometsch and Wessels 1994: 213; van Schendelen 1996: 535).

Hayes-Renshaw and Wallace (1997: 98) go as far as to call working groups 'the backbone of the European system of integration'. Their political effect is to expand enormously the number of actors involved in EU decision-making, particularly by pulling in officials from national capitals. One seasoned Commission official argues that 'it is precisely at this level that most European legislation is made, where most lobbying takes place and where most of the "national interest" is defined and decided' (Spence 1993: 50). The expanding policy remit of the EU has been reflected in an upsurge in the activities of the Council at all levels, but the increase has been most dramatic at the working group level (see Table 2.1).

The central role of Council working groups reveals that EU decision-making is not only, or even mostly, a process that takes place in Brussels or Strasbourg. Many participants in working groups are based in Brussels in 'permanent representations' headed by national ambassadors to the EU, but a majority is based in national capitals. Moreover, the different ways in which Member States' national positions are determined and co-ordinated between domestic ministries *before* Council bargaining begins are a complicated, yet crucial variable in EU governance (see Romestch and Wessels 1996; Wright 1996). France (Lequesne 1993) and the UK (Armstrong and Bulmer 1996) have relatively centralised, decisive systems which often allow them to steal a march on Germany, with its traditionally decentralised, occasionally chaotic system[6] (Romestch 1996), despite the fact that all three have equal numbers of votes under QMV.

Table 2.1   *Days spent in session by the council and its sub-groups*

Year	Council	COREPER I & II	Working groups
1978	76.5	104.5	2090
1988	117.5	104	2000.5
1994	125	117	2580

Source: Hayes-Renshaw and Wallace (1997: 98).

A final issue that arises from the central role of national capitals in EU decision-making is whether the current system of Council presidencies is sustainable in the context of eastern enlargement. Could Estonia really handle the presidency? Could Cyprus or Malta? Any proposal to alter the system must be weighed against the fact that the presidency remains 'one of the very few ways in which large cohorts of home-based civil servants and ministers acquire an understanding of how the system works at the centre' (Ludlow 1997: 25).

The European Commission

At the centre in Brussels, of course, is the Commission. Its three principal parts are the college of Commissioners chosen by Member States (see Exhibit 2.2), the personal advisers or *cabinets* of the Commissioners, and the 'services' or Directorates-General, the Commission's equivalents of ministries. The Commission has formal agenda-setting powers: no important legislative decision may be taken unless the college of Commissioners decides to table a proposal.

As is so often the case, the Treaty is not entirely clear-cut on the Commission's right of initiative. Article 192[9] allows the Parliament – through a majority vote – to request the Commission to draw up a proposal on any matter covered in the Treaty. The 'ownership' of most new policy ideas is usually unclear in the EU and the Commission itself claims to generate few legislative proposals purely on its own initiative (see Table 2.2). Still, the Commission's control of the policy agenda is formidable. The EU lacks a 'government', but it is misleading to claim that the EU has 'no central agenda-setting and co-ordinating actor' (Hix 1998: 39).

Before the Commission sends a proposal to the Council and EP, the college of Commissioners must agree to it, if necessary by a simple majority vote. Once a vote is taken, all Commissioners must publicly support the decision. Collective responsibility is a source of strain in the

Table 2.2   *The Origins of Commission Proposals*

International obligations	35%
Amendment to or codification of existing law	25–30%
Response to requests from other EU institutions, Member States or interest groups	20%
Required by Treaty	10%
Pure 'spontaneous' Commission initiatives	5–10%

Source: European Commission (data collected in 1998), cited in Peterson 1999: 59.

college, which is united by no political party or ideology. However, the college seems to have become a more decisive (if not *united*) body since the early 1980s, with more actual voting taking place over time. According to David Williamson, the Commission's Secretary-General from 1987 to 1997 (see Exhibit 2.3), the post-1995 college under the Santer presidency did 'see themselves as part of a single college and they like to arrive at an agreement. There are more things thrown out and also more things adopted than in the past'.[10] The entire college under Santer was provoked into collective resignation in 1999 (to avoid being thrown out by the EP) amid charges of nepotism and mismanagement.

The college may be unelected, but it is the most 'political' level of the Commission. Since the mid-1980s, more than two-thirds of its members have had previous ministerial experience. Commissioners are required by the Treaty to act independently of 'their' governments and even take an oath of independence. In practice, most Commissioners may be relied upon to defend the interests of their Member States in the college.

One of the most enduring myths surrounding EU decision-making is that the Commission is a purposive, single-minded institution. In reality, it is highly fragmented, even if it often unites in defence of its institutional prerogatives, as it did in 1999 when the college resigned *en masse*. In the view of Ross (1995: 3), the Commission is 'divided into all sorts of interest groups, clans and cliques'. In particular, it is divided by policy sector, with ferocious rivalries existing between some DGs, such as III (Industry) and XI (Environment) or DGs I (External Economic Relations) and VI (Agriculture).

Moreover, the Commission's independence from national controls is undermined by the power of *cabinets* (Donnelly and Ritchie 1994). Each Commissioner has six to eight personal advisers serving in their *cabinet*, of whom one must be of a different nationality than the Commissioner. It may be wrong to claim, along with an official in the Secretariat-General, that 'intergovernmentalism starts when proposals hit the *cabinets*. They are mini-Councils within the Commission'.[12] Yet, *cabinets* became a target of plans for 'root and branch' reform of the Commission after 1999. McDonald (1997: 51) views them as a 'structural contradiction':

> They readily recruit people directly from national contexts, bypassing the services, and they have regular contacts with national administrations, national lobbyists and the permanent representations. They also notoriously 'parachute' their chosen national recruits directly into key service jobs, over the heads of well-qualified and experienced officials in the services.

The power of *cabinets* reflects, in part, the reluctance of Member States to ensure that the Commission is truly independent and well resourced. The Commission's full-time staff numbers around 16 000, but fewer than 10 000 are involved in actual policy-making (as opposed to translation or

Exhibit 2.2 How does the EU choose the Commission?

Over time, the appointment of the college of Commissioners has become one of the messiest, often nastiest, episodes of EU decision-making. The treaties tell us little, stating only that the Commission should be appointed by 'common accord'. In practice,

> The formal proceedings are private, and the important decisions are taken informally over lengthy periods within and between the various Member States. The final decision is reached at a meeting of national government representatives, normally at Foreign Minister level, but this is simply the formal conclusion of a series of intergovernmental consultations. (Macmullen 1997: 31)

Certain informal norms govern the appointment of the Commission. The treaties say that the Commission 'must include at least one national of each of the Member States, but may not include more than two Members having the same nationality'. In practice, the biggest five Member States – France, Germany, Italy, Spain and the UK – all appoint two Commissioners, with the remaining 10 Member States getting one each. Concerns that the Commission will become unwieldy as the EU enlarges have led smaller states to state clearly that they are prepared (in diplomatic parlance) to 'bleed for' their right to appoint a Commissioner. In the words of a State Secretary from a small, northern Member State, 'you simply can't ask any country to give up their Commissioner as long as the Commission retains the right of initiative and remains the "guardian of the Treaty"'.[7]

National governments, by convention, do not challenge each other's nominations to the Commission. Other conventions also narrow the range of choices: for example, the Commissioner for Agriculture is always from a small state (see Grant 1997c). However, there is no easy way around the political necessity for all Member States to choose a President by consensus. The point was first illustrated in 1965: in the midst of the crisis which culminated in the Luxembourg compromise (see Exhibit 2.5 below), the proposed renomination of Walter Hallstein, the first President of the

→

administration). Despite its vast responsibilities and reputation as a bloated, power-mad bureaucracy, the Commission is about the size of the UK's agricultural ministry. It is extraordinarily resource-poor, given its responsibilities, and traditionally has done a better job of generating new policy ideas than in managing existing EU policies (Metcalf 1992; Laffan 1997b).

Still, the Commission enjoys a position of considerable power, particularly when the Council is too split to decide what it wants, and circumstances dictate that the EU *must* make a decision (see Pollack 1997a). Above all, the Commission is empowered by its guardianship of

→

Commission and a devout (German) federalist, was opposed so fiercely by France that Germany withdrew it. Nearly 30 years later, a Conservative British government, under siege from Eurosceptic members of its own party, vetoed the favoured Franco-German candidate, the Belgian Prime Minister Jean-Luc Dehaene. Eventually, the job was offered to Jacques Santer, the Prime Minister of Luxembourg, whose political weight was on the light side (and who eventually resigned in disgrace). The EP approved Santer's nomination by the slimmest of margins, even if many MEPs were voting more against the shambolic procedure by which Santer was chosen than against the man himself. In any case, the days of an activist Commission under a forceful President, such as Hallstein or Jacques Delors (who served from 1985 to 1995), seemed over.

Yet Santer won a small but potentially important victory in the 1996–7 IGC: the Amsterdam Treaty promised that, in future, the Commission would be chosen 'in common accord' with the nominee for President, and not just (as previously) 'in consultation' with this individual. Amsterdam also mandated, for the first time, that the Commission would 'work under the political guidance of its President'.

Nonetheless, there was never much interest in reappointing Santer, even before he resigned in 1999. In 1998, Delors stepped forward to argue that 'the time has come to put a face on European democracy' and proposed that political groups in the EP should choose candidates to head the Commission. Their nominees would then join MEPs in fighting EP electoral campaigns, selling their vision of Europe to voters before governments actually chose a Commission President. The idea was to stimulate interest in EP elections and introduce 'personality politics' into the EU.[8] The proposal required no changes to the EU's treaties. It was always hard to imagine national governments signing up to it, even before the former Italian Prime Minister, Romano Prodi, was quickly chosen to replace Santer. Still, there were few that really were prepared to defend the old system for choosing the Commission as very adequate (see Ludlow 1992).

sectoral policy networks. Depending on the sector (such as the Common Agricultural Policy (CAP) v. CFSP), the Commission may or may not enjoy 'unparalleled access to information', but it certainly does enjoy a privileged place at the 'hub of numerous highly specialized policy networks of technical experts designing detailed regulations' (Marks *et al.* 1996a: 355).

Even if the Commission is at the 'hub' of most EU policy networks, the so-called 'comitology' system gives the Council three types of committee – all staffed by national 'experts' – to keep tabs on how the Commission uses its executive powers. Each type of committee gives national experts different powers to stall or overturn Commission decisions: advisory

Exhibit 2.3 The Commission's Secretary-General

The Secretariat-General is responsible for managing the Commission. Along with the legal service, the 'Sec-Gen', as it is commonly known, is the most important of the Commission's 'horizontal' services. Before the college can consider any proposal, it must be formally cleared by the Sec-Gen, which chairs meetings between different services (or DGs) with interests in any given proposal. These meetings are often caustic affairs featuring intense firefights between the services. The Sec-Gen plays an important role as an honest broker.

Its head, the Secretary-General, is the Commission's top *fonctionnaire*, or 'permanent' official. It is another key post in the Brussels machinery that does not change hands very often. The first Secretary-General of the Commission, the Frenchman Emile Nöel, retained the post for 30 years, from the origins of the EU in 1957 to 1987. Nöel was legendary both for his personal modesty – he diffidently observed that he mainly 'followed a lot of famous people into meeting rooms' – *and* his personal dominance of the Commission's bureaucracy. Several Commission Presidents clearly did not measure up to him in terms of influence within the Commission.

Nöel was finally replaced in 1987 by David Williamson, former deputy head of the British Cabinet office. A crafty behind-the-scenes operator, Williamson became a trusted member of Jacques Delors' personal and highly imperious network of allies (see Grant 1994; Ross 1995), even playing an important role in two intergovernmental conferences in 1987 and 1991. Yet Delors' own lack of interest in the internal management of the Commission left it overloaded and chaotic by the time that Jacques Santer replaced him as

$\longrightarrow$

committees simply give advice, management committees can suspend Commission decisions and refer them to the Council, and regulatory committees can vote to overturn them (see Nugent 1994: 109–12). But, in true EU style, there are many different variants: some regulatory committees can overrule the Commission by QMV, others only need a simple majority vote. A group of experts at a single sitting may be considered an advisory committee on one question and a regulatory committee on another. There are something like 1400 individual committees, which are 'highly complex and differentiated' (Wessels 1997b: 24).

The Commission's insistence that comitology does not limit its autonomy very much (see also Marks *et al*. 1996a: 367–8) is difficult to reconcile with the EP's fixation on comitology (Socialist Group 1989; Bradley 1992) or the Council's frequent, late night battles about what comitology procedure will apply to new legislation. Comitology is almost preposterously arcane but it is important for two reasons. First, it allows national interests, even in specialised groups of experts, to be wielded even in the

→

Commission President in 1995 (see Metcalf 1992; Peterson 1995c). Despite Santer's demise amid allegations of mismanagement in 1999, the Commission under his Presidency actually made tangible strides towards becoming better-administered (Laffan 1997b; Peterson 1999). Williamson could claim much of the credit. Yet, clashes between Williamson and Santer's brusque, forceful and experienced *chef du cabinet*, Jim Cloos, meant that Williamson played little role in the 1996–7 IGC, where the Commission was represented less effectively by the Commissioner for Institutional Affairs, Marcelino Oreja.

Williamson retired in 1997 and was replaced by his former deputy, Carlo Trojan. Of Dutch and Italian parentage, Trojan was a skilled linguist with enormous vigour and energy. Even before his promotion, he had helped broker deals on the EU aspects of German unification in 1990, the Structural Funds round in 1993 and the extension of the Commission President's powers in the 1996–7 IGC (where he 'backed up' Oreja). Yet, as a senior Commission official put it, 'Carlo is by no means a classic civil servant. He likes to "get around" rules and now he is at the top of a system to enforce them.[11] Trojan was damaged by the report on mismanagement which provoked Santer's resignation (EP 1999). Earlier, his strained relations with many top Commission officials had hardly been assets when controversial staff reforms were tabled. One result was an embarrassing walkout by Commission staff immediately prior to the historic Brussels summit on EMU in May 1998. Williamson was recalled from his retirement to head a high-level panel to re-examine the proposed staff reforms, in a classic illustration of the EU's frequent response when disputes boil over: call in a 'wise man', launch a study and delay decisions until later.

'deepest' recesses of the sub-systemic level. Second, comitology has the political effect of widening the number of actors involved in EU decision-making to include national officials, sub-national authorities and private actors (in fact, a majority of 'national' representatives on committees are interest group representatives and not officials;[13] see Buitendijk and van Schendelen 1995). The ubiquity of committees is a prime rationale for deploying a model of policy networks to make sense of sub-systemic decision-making.

The European Parliament

If comitology represents EU decision-making at its most arcane, the European Parliament (EP) is the Union's most open, public, democratic institution (see Westlake 1994b; Corbett *et al.* 1995). The EP suffers from its hapless image as a powerless, money-wasting 'talking shop' as well as from its impossible domestic arrangements. A member of the EP (MEP) must travel constantly between their constituency, Strasbourg (where plenary sessions are held), Brussels (for committees and occasional plenaries) and sometimes Luxembourg (where much of EP's administration is still based). An inexorable increase in the EP's powers since the mid-1980s has not prevented the rate of turnover of its members increasing with each successive election (held every five years).

Even the EP's staunchest supporters concede that the Parliament attracts incompetents and party hacks deemed unsuitable for national office, as well as committed and talented parliamentarians. Its members also include high-profile politicians whose political careers have peaked (Valéry Giscard-d'Estaing, Michel Rocard, Pol Schluter, Wilfred Martens) but who do not wish to leave politics altogether, as well as politicians 'on the rise' (such as Gijs De Vries, a long-time MEP who became a Dutch minister in 1998, and, most notably, Jacques Delors). Generally, however, the EP gives the Union an important measure of democratic credibility. It is not noticeably less effective than most national parliaments in Europe.

The EP has gained considerably in terms of interinstitutional respect in recent years. The Council Presidency informs and consults closely with the EP, although ministers sometimes have difficulty showing respect for MEPs who ask them silly questions or who clearly do not know their brief very well.[14] On balance, the Commission is more sympathetic to the views of the EP (see Sutherland 1988). Under the co-operation procedure, introduced by the Single European Act (SEA), the Commission accepted well over half of all amendments tabled by the Parliament, while the Council accepted less than 40 per cent.[15]

The introduction of co-decision (see Exhibit 1.3) significantly upgraded the EP's power in the legislative process. In particular, the procedure enhanced the importance of the EP's sectoral committees, in which most of its work has always been done, and particularly the political skills of committee chairs and MEPs (known as *rapporteurs*) who conduct evaluations of specific proposals. The most powerful MEPs are those, such as Ken Collins, the long-time chair of the Environment and Consumer Affairs Committee, who dominate their committees, penetrate the relevant sectoral policy networks and are consulted regularly by the Commission when policies are first formulated.

However, co-decision has also exposed the Parliament's weakness in dealing with highly technical matters. The EP lacks the resources in terms of expertise that the US Congress enjoys (such as the Congressional Research Service or Office of Technology Assessment). The peripatetic life of MEPs makes it difficult for them to co-ordinate their positions with each other or to consult experts in the EP's own administrative services (which employ about 3500 officials). The application of co-decision has been patchy to sectors where there is 'more room for political argument,

such as the environment, the social dimension, culture and education'
(Andersen and Eliassen 1996: 47), thus leaving MEPs with more interest
than power in these sectors.

Besides its powers to amend, the Parliament enjoys two further,
important prerogatives. One is the right to vet appointments to the
Commission and European Central Bank (ECB). After Member States
have nominated the Commission, it becomes subject to a vote of approval
by the EP. In 1994, the EP took it upon itself to organise US Senate-style
'confirmation hearings', followed by a Parliamentary debate and then a
roll-call vote on the Santer Commission. The Maastricht Treaty did not
say what the consequences of a negative vote might be, but the Amsterdam
Treaty makes it clear that the EP must vote to approve the Commission
before it may take office. The Parliament and Commission's five-year
mandates were synchronised by Maastricht, with the Parliament being
elected six months prior to the new Commission's nomination. Thus the
EP was allowed time to develop political priorities which it could then
insist the Commission take on board. The EP's right to question and 'vet'
prospective Commissioners also applies (in slightly different form) to the
process of nominating the board of the ECB (see Exhibit 10.2).

Another major EP power is that of 'assent': any association agreement
with a foreign country or the accession of new Member States must be
approved by an EP majority vote. The Maastricht Treaty extended the
assent procedure to some 'internal' policies such as the approval of the
general objectives of the structural funds (see Westlake 1994a: 41–2).
Assent is in some respects a 'cruder form of co-decision' (Corbett *et al.*
1995: 212): the EP is not allowed to propose amendments, but it can veto
anything that comes under the procedure. A negative EP vote is a 'nuclear
weapon' which the Parliament instinctively hesitates to drop, but assent
has still expanded the EP's powers in external relations well beyond what
the SEA's framers intended.

The European Court of Justice

Similarly, the evolution of the Community's legal system was not foreseen
by the EEC's founders, nor was the central role of the ECJ in EU decision-
making (Alter 1998). Community law has been expanded and strengthened
largely through the co-opting of national courts and legal administrations
(see Armstrong and Shaw 1998; Dehousse 1998). In fact, most ECJ
decisions are about the way national authorities should apply
Community law.

One view holds that the Court has kept Member States from challenging
the accretion of the EU's legal authority by hiding behind the treaties and

couching its behaviour in technical and apolitical terms (Weiler 1993). For holders of this view, the Court's role has been surreptitious: it has acted as a 'mask' that has hidden the political effects of legal integration and a 'shield' that has kept Member States from tampering with the EU's legal system (Burley and Mattli 1993). Often the Court has *not* acted in an impartial, legalistic way, sometimes using the Commission as a 'political bellwether': taking its view as an indicator of the political acceptability of any particular decision or line of reasoning in national capitals (Burley and Mattli 1993: 71).

Has the ECJ overridden national preferences in the construction of a 'new legal order'? The answer is 'yes' for advocates of a legal theory of integration with strong neo-functionalist overtones (Mattli and Slaughter 1995). For intergovernmentalists, the answer is 'no': the Court is fundamentally dependent on the willingness of national courts to respect its authority. Intergovernmentalists claim that 'the principles governing decisions of the European court and hence governing those of domestic

---

Exhibit 2.4   Cassis de Dijon and mutual recognition

Even students of politics who normally cringe at the mere mention of courts and 'legal studies' often find the ECJ a fascinating institution. A good case in point is the ECJ's *Cassis de Dijon* decision of 1979. Probably the most studied case in the EU's history, *Cassis* struck down Germany's ban on a French blackcurrant liqueur which did not meet German standards because its alcohol content was too low and thus threatened to confuse consumers. In the Court's view, the German policy objective was valid but the ban on the sale of *Cassis* in Germany was not, since Article 28[16] prohibits measures having the 'equivalent effect' of 'quantitative restrictions on imports' from another Member State. The solution was to require product label information on the liqueur's alcohol content. More broadly, the Court ruled that, since the liqueur met French standards, it could be marketed across the Union (see Alter and Meunier-Aitsahalia 1994). The *Cassis* decision thus gave the Commission an opening to build a case for the principle of 'mutual recognition' of national standards in its 1985 White Paper on the internal market.

The full impact of the *Cassis* decision became clear only in the mid-1980s, thus demonstrating that some decisions only 'make history' long after they have been taken. The case also illustrates how the EU may take up new policy ideas in roundabout ways. The Commission was still drafting its White Paper on the internal market in 1985 when the Council adopted a 'new approach' to setting standards. The Council's decision decreed that Article 94[17] (and unanimous voting) should apply to the establishment of essential health and

→

courts following its rulings are consistent with the preferences of France and Germany' (Garrett 1992: 558; see also Garrett 1995). However, more than any other EU institution, the ECJ 'minimizes the territorial dimension in its decision-making process' since it operates by secret, majority voting and Member States do not know how any judge has voted in any case unless a judge states so publicly (Sbragia 1993: 35).

It is above all the ECJ and Community law that make the EU unique amongst international organisations. The Court is an important source of the EU's supranational power and an important 'strategic actor' that is 'manifestly neither master nor servant' of the Union's Member States (Garrett *et al.* 1998: 174–5). However the ECJ is characterised, it is clearly *not* a wholly legalistic, apolitical arbiter in EU decision-making. Nor does it hand down only one kind of decision: 'Its weight has been felt at all levels of the decision-making process' (Dehousse 1998: 177). Yet the Court is most important as a source of history-making decisions (see Exhibit 2.4). ECJ judgements have 'utterly transformed the nature of the European

---

$\longrightarrow$

safety standards but otherwise that national variations in standards could exist as long as trade was not impeded (Dinan 1994: 338–9). Mutual recognition thus became established as a principle only after decisions by three separate EU institutions. However, it was above all the Court's 1979 case decision that established it as an essential cornerstone of the internal market.[18]

The principle of mutual recognition was never written into Community law: it is nothing more or less than the Commission's interpretation of how the ECJ is likely to rule on cases brought under Article 28. Member States can still ban imports from one another (providing they can justify it under a vague list of exemptions, see Chapter 3). They can even choose to defend essentially indefensible import bans in the Court, perhaps imposing so much expense and delay on a potential importer that the latter might just give up trying to sell their goods where governments are determined to ban them. Mutual recognition, like virtually everything else in EU politics, is subject to negotiation.

Nevertheless, mutual recognition played a major role in relaunching the EU in the 1980s. It had a powerful impact on EU decision-making on a range of questions concerning national standards and free trade. Crucially, the ECJ lurks in the background on all matters concerning mutual recognition: it provides a clear and powerful means for dispute settlement by judicial means, without which the removal of technical barriers to trade is almost always impossible (see Pelkmans 1995).

[Union] and its relations with national legal systems, conferring upon Community law an authority akin to that enjoyed by federal law in federal systems' (Dehousse 1998: 177).

Decision Rules

Even if a large 'slice' of EU decision-making is informal, the Union does produce formal legislation. The most important outcomes of the EU's legislative process are usually issued in the form of *directives*, which are binding in the result to be achieved, but leave to national authorities the choice of form and method to achieve the result. In contrast, *regulations* are binding in their entireties and directly applicable in all Member States without any further need for national implementing measures. Most regulations are technical and specific, issued by the Commission and apply to the CAP. *Decisions* are also binding in their entirety but are addressed to a specific party or Member State, resulting from competition policy rulings, the granting of exemptions to EU rules, trade policy measures taken against non-EU states, and so on. *Opinions* or *recommendations* issued by the Commission, Council or EP have no binding force, but the ECJ sometimes refers to them in its decisions, thus making their legal impact ambiguous.

For most of the EU's existence, unanimity was the accepted rule for virtually all important Council decisions (see Exhibit 2.5). The need for unanimity meant that only 270 directives were adopted between 1969 and 1985 (Schreiber 1991: 98). A breakthrough came in 1987, when the ratification of the Single European Act made QMV the most common formal decision rule. Just as important, if far less dramatic, was the Council's 1987 amendment of its own rules of procedure to make it far easier for a vote by QMV to be called. Previously, only the Council President could call a vote. Afterwards, any participant in the Council (including the Commission) could initiate a vote if supported by a simple majority of Member States.

It is often forgotten that the Council increasingly resorted to QMV in the early 1980s, long before the SEA was even mooted. Its more frequent use acted to 'reassure doubting governments . . . [Thus] the SEA built on already existing foundations and consolidated rather than invented a new policy method' (Wallace 1996a: 52–3). Yet the SEA made history in two respects. First, it substantively amended the founding treaties for the first time and thus established the principle that EU institutions could be revamped as needed. Second, it changed the nature of consensus building on the Council from 'a wooden insistence on unanimity to . . . a process of

Exhibit 2.5   The Luxembourg compromise

In 1965, the French President, Charles de Gaulle, pulled France out of all meetings of the Council in protest at Commission plans to extend the Community's powers generally, and particularly to expand the number of issues subject to QMV. The French 'empty chair policy' was far more consequential than the British 'non-co-operation' policy during the beef crisis of 1997 (see Exhibit 5.2) because it was clear that nothing very important could be discussed, let alone decided, without France in a Community of Six. De Gaulle was appeased by the Luxembourg compromise (so called because it was brokered under the 1966 Luxembourg Council presidency), an informal agreement which was communicated to the outside world in the form of a press release. It mandated that, wherever a decision was subject to QMV, the Council would postpone a decision if any Member State claimed that their 'vital national interests' (left entirely undefined) were threatened. Once invoked, the Luxembourg compromise meant that no decision could be taken until a unanimous agreement was reached. After 1966, a 'veto culture' emerged and most important decisions of the Council (except in the Budget Council) were taken by consensus, regardless of the Treaty's language about QMV.

After the 1973 enlargement, two new supporters of the Luxembourg compromise joined the French: the UK and Denmark. As Table 2.3 shows, the political equation on the Council was transformed. Even when QMV was observed, the UK and France by themselves could form a blocking minority. Consequently, the ethos that *all* decisions should be taken unanimously permeated the Council. Even if the Luxembourg compromise was formally invoked only about 10 times between 1966 and 1981 (Marks *et al.* 1996a: 362), its 'shadow' hung over the Council and gummed up decision-making considerably.

After agreement on the SEA, it was possible to argue that the Luxembourg compromise 'did in fact disappear . . . and no longer has any significant bearing on the way the Community functions' (Teasdale 1995: 104). Yet, its shadow occasionally became visible during particularly divisive negotiations, such as during the Uruguay Round of world trade talks (see Exhibit 4.3). The Amsterdam Treaty's provisions for 'flexibility', in both pillars I and II, allowed Member States to invoke 'important and stated reasons of national policy' to veto the plans of an *avant-garde* of states to move ahead with reinforced co-operation (see Exhibit 1.2). Reports of the death of the Luxembourg compromise seemed premature.

persuading the reluctant to shift position or to abandon opposition'
(Wallace 1996a: 54).

In the post-SEA period, formal EU decision rules continued to differ
markedly between policy sectors. Yet, the ubiquity of QMV became
established over time, making it the most important and contested EU
decision rule. QMV 'generally transformed the climate of decision-making'
(Weiler 1997: 107).

Table 2.3 shows the evolution of QMV over time. It gives a sense of
different minimum coalitions needed for qualified majorities and blocking
minorities. It also reveals significant inequities between Member States,
with post-unification Germany wielding only one vote per 8 million
citizens and each of Luxembourg's two votes representing just over
200 000 citizens. The EU, along with all quasi-federal systems, must

Table 2.3   *Qualified majority voting*

Member State	Number of votes with EC/EU consisting of					Population million (1999)
	6 (1958)	9 (1973)	10 (1981)	12 (1986)	15 (1995)	
Germany	4	10	10	10	10	82.425
France	4	10	10	10	10	59.148
Italy	4	10	10	10	10	57.714
Netherlands	2	5	5	5	5	15.761
Belgium	2	5	5	5	5	10.233
Luxembourg	1	2	2	2	2	0.432
UK	–	10	10	10	10	59.367
Denmark	–	3	3	3	3	5.316
Ireland	–	3	3	3	3	3.730
Greece	–	–	5	5	5	10.623
Spain	–	–	–	8	8	39.371
Portugal	–	–	–	5	5	9.896
Sweden	–	–	–	–	4	8.954
Austria	–	–	–	–	4	8.132
Finland	–	–	–	–	3	5.170
Qualified majority	12	41	45	54	62	
Blocking minority	6	18	19	23	26	

Source: Commission (1998c: annex 8).

provide for territorial representation, thus 'overweighting' the power of its constituent political units: in the EU's case, its Member States.

After the 1995 enlargement, a qualified majority required positive votes from states representing 62 out of a total of 87 votes. The 'big four' Member States – Germany, France, Italy and the UK – enjoyed a combined vote total of 40, only 46 per cent of the total. As Laffan (1996: 223) argued, this weighting 'amount[ed] to a serious under-representation of their 252 million citizens in contrast to the 115 million of the other eleven'. The problem was set to get worse, as some calculations suggested that a qualified majority could be assembled from governments representing only 48 per cent of the EU's population in a Union of 26 Member States (Moravcsik and Nicolaïdis 1998: 18).

One obvious solution was a 'dual majority' system of voting, in which positive decisions would require a percentage of weighted votes *as well as* votes from states representing a minimum percentage of the Union's total population (usually assumed to be 60 per cent). This type of system was favoured by most small states but was rejected by France in the 1996–7 IGC because it would have required accepting, for the first time, that Germany should have more votes than France. In the end, negotiators at the 1997 Amsterdam summit were left with a proposal for simple reweighting of votes, giving more to larger states in return for an acceptance that all Member States would appoint one Commissioner in future. The deal seemed done until very late in the summit, when Spanish negotiators insisted that they would only agree to give up 'their' second Commissioner if they were given as many votes as the 'big four' states in a new system of QMV. The deal collapsed, leaving the status quo in place. Yet the outlines of a deal were left so clear as to leave little doubt that the EU of the future give more weight to large states and feature a smaller Commission (Ludlow 1997; Moravcsik and Nicolaïdis 1998).[19]

Naturally, changes in formal decision rules are highly contested in the EU, and frequently so: the Union has undergone a sort of 'permanent revolution', with three treaty reforms and two enlargements (with more to come) since the mid-1980s. However, we can only assess the true significance of formal decision rules by considering, first, how pivotal individual Member States are likely to be in Council coalition-building, and, second, national preferences.

Various mathematical 'power indexes' exist to measure the actual negotiating power of states under QMV. They begin by assessing the extent to which a country is pivotal to the success or failure of various possible coalitions on the Council of Ministers (see Friedman 1990: 266–73). In mathematical terms, the more often a country is vital to the success of a possible majority, the more power it has in the Council. To illustrate the point, assume a measure is opposed by Britain, Italy and Ireland, which together wield 23 votes. Since a blocking minority consists of 26 votes, the power of Denmark or Finland (each with three votes) to determine the Council's decision on the measure becomes infinitely greater than Luxembourg's (with only two votes). A small country can exert enormous leverage on its larger colleagues when it can use its votes to transform an existing coalition into a qualified majority or blocking minority.

However, formal rules only matter as much as national preferences let them. States that are not instinctive supporters of one coalition or another in EU politics – such as 'spenders' v. budgetary sceptics – can become powerful swing voters that each opposing coalition seeks to attract. For example, France became a pivotal state in discussions about spending on EU research policy in the early 1990s when it wavered between being a supporter and an opponent of bigger budgets (see Peterson 1995b). When national preferences are factored in, it turns out that the power of small states is *not* disproportionately large, and indeed 'voting power . . . is close to actual relative population figures' (Kirman and Widgrén 1995: 434). This paradoxical result occurs because the number of votes assigned to particular countries matters far less than whether and when a state can hold the pivotal position at the margin of any particular decision (see Exhibit 5.4).

Arguably, power indexes give a better indication of what is at stake in enlargement than any simple comparison of population and voting shares. The clear message is that *all* existing EU Member States stand to lose negotiating power through eastern enlargement (Hosli 1993),[20] especially the larger states (Raunio and Wiberg 1998). To illustrate the point, in 1958 the 'big three' Member States – Germany, Italy and France – each had 20 per cent of the voting power under QMV (see Table 2.3), but their respective shares had fallen to just over 10 per cent by the time of the 1995 enlargement.

This diminution of national power helps explain British insistence on the 'Ioannina compromise', so called because it was agreed under the 1994 Greek Council presidency. The compromise appeased the UK after it lost a bid to keep the same blocking minority (23 votes, see Table 2.3) under QMV even after northern enlargement. Under the compromise, the adoption of any proposal opposed by Member States holding between 23 and 26 votes would be delayed until 'a satisfactory solution' was found (see Edwards 1996).

Concern for the details of formal voting rules obscures the hard, cold reality that weighting of states under QMV increasingly does not matter. In fact, the difference in coalition membership between a qualified majority and a *simple* majority of Member States (such as eight of 15 after 1995) gradually lessens with each enlargement. One analysis of voting power under QMV insists that the Council in future 'could move to adopt one decision method only – the simple majority rule – except when special matters are at stake, for which unanimity may still be required' (Lane *et al.* 1996: 184).

It is difficult to imagine such a move any time soon. What will matter most as the EU enlarges is how widely QMV will be extended, and how many measures will remain subject to unanimity. After the Amsterdam Treaty, around 65 Treaty articles (under pillar I) continued to require unanimity, although nearly half concerned monetary or financial issues and became redundant with the move to EMU. About a dozen others concerned basic institutional and financial matters (such as reforming the structural funds or appointing the Commission), while twice that number still required unanimity on measures linked to the internal market, such as social security, taxation, culture, industrial policy, and so on (Moravcsik and Nicolaïdis 1998: 23).

Regardless of how much further QMV is extended, the EU is likely to remain dependent on the 'Community method' of decision-making (Devuyst 1999) which itself depends 'on a kind of collusion behind the scenes' (Wallace 1996a: 43). Long discussions about formally reweighting votes under QMV in the 1996–7 IGC seemed pointless given evidence (bandied about by the Commission) suggesting that no Council vote in the previous three years would have changed if any of the new formulas being considered had been in place (Moravcsik and Nicolaïdis 1998: 19). However, formal decision rules are politically charged and highly contested symbols of power and influence in EU decision-making (see Exhibit 2.6), and they always will be.

Norms

Norms are principles of 'right action' serving to guide, control or regulate proper and acceptable behaviour in a group. Norms govern exchanges within and between EU institutions, and define the acceptable parameters for political action by agents in decision-making. Here we flag some particularly crucial norms in EU decision-making.

Soft Law

Alongside formally binding Community law, the EU also produces a considerable amount of 'soft law'. Sources include Commission action programmes, declarations by the European Council, interinstitutional agreements, and decisions taken in pillars II and III. It is accepted that 'Soft law is not subject to the control of the European Court of Justice (ECJ),

Exhibit 2.6   Consensus up to a point: 'losing' under QMV

The hypothetical example cited earlier in which the UK and Italy opposed a measure (with Ireland) under QMV, and thus had to court Denmark or Finland to form a blocking minority, is *entirely* hypothetical: it is a widely accepted norm that no measure should pass under QMV against the wishes of two large Member States. In a sense, this norm compensates for the over representation of smaller states under QMV. It is increasingly threatened each time the EU enlarges.

Yet, as a leading German negotiator insisted, 'Everyone wants to be part of the solution [under QMV]. Of course, it is also a question of domestic pressures at home. Bananas are a good example: we insisted on everything and lost everything in the end' (see Exhibit 4.5).[21] In fact, it became common knowledge that Germany was outvoted in the Council more often than any other Member State under QMV after the Single European Act (see below):

Member State	'No' votes*	Abstentions*	Total
Germany	40	12	52
UK	27	14	41
Italy	22	8	30
Sweden	20	2	22
Netherlands	16	3	19
Denmark	15	3	18
Spain	9	7	16
Portugal	8	7	15
France	6	6	12
Greece	9	1	10
Austria	8	2	10
Belgium	7	4	11
Ireland	7	2	9
Finland	7	0	7
Luxembourg	2	5	7

*In cases when EU legislation was adopted via positive votes.

Source: reproduced with permission from *European Voice*, 15–21 October 1998 (data from January 1995–July 1998)

but has nevertheless a kind of binding character and an impact' (Wessels 1997b: 21). Perhaps it is natural that different shades of law exist in a system where virtually everything is negotiable.

Negotiated Enforcement

A related norm is that decisions about the enforcement of EU rules are sensitive to the political context where they are applied. The result is that compliance is far less assured than in some (especially northern) national European contexts. The Commission, and by most accounts the ECJ, will almost always seek to avoid imposing an outcome on a Member State if it threatens to cause domestic problems for its government, and especially if it risks provoking an anti-EU backlash in public opinion. When the strict application of EU rules threatens either of these results, enforcement is almost always negotiated, not imposed (see Exhibits 3.2 and 4.6).

Waiting for a Policy Window

Another accepted norm of EU decision-making is that issues may remain on the Union's agenda for long periods of time, even though they remain far from resolution. A good example is the European Company Statute, a legal instrument allowing firms to incorporate themselves as 'European' (instead of French, German and so on). It was proposed originally in the 1970s and was still being discussed nearly 30 years later. Usually, initiatives that lie dormant for long periods, and then reappear in the form of fresh proposals, are kept on the agenda by the Commission (and/or the EP). The EU represents a 'multilateral inter-bureaucratic negotiation marathon' (Kohler-Koch 1996: 367), which allows policy entrepreneurs to bide their time waiting for political changes in key Member States, such as the replacement of a Gaullist government with a Socialist one in France. The Commission's longevity of tenure, as well as that of ECJ judges (Alter 1998), EP officials and certain MEPs, allows them to outlast national political cycles (of three to five years between elections). Longevity is an important source of advantage in waiting for 'policy windows' (Kingdon 1984), which may be fleeting but offer favourable opportunities for political agreement (see Exhibits 3.5 and 7.2). The Council does not (and legally cannot) tell the Commission: 'You've tried this one already and failed, so that's the end of the story.'

Punctuated Equilibriums

After the mid-1980s, the notion that dramatic, history-making decisions to change EU governance would often be needed to break stalemate and change EU *policy* became established as a norm. Instead of slow, steady change, the EU sometimes transforms itself by embracing sweeping changes to jettison a powerfully entrenched status quo (see Corbey 1995). When radical new initiatives are first tabled, they often provoke so much opposition that it initially appears they will never be agreed. Member States frequently attack them to placate threatened domestic interests, as well as to enhance their leverage in later negotiations, before they begin real bargaining. To illustrate the point, all 15 Member States in one way or another denounced the Commission's (1997b) proposals for quite radical changes to the CAP. Yet 'what is unthinkable one year may become the root of a crisis the next, and an ingredient in a "package deal" the third' (Lindberg 1965: 63). While parroting the line that the CAP as constituted was incompatible with eastern enlargement, the Commission also played down the battle ahead by noting that criticisms from farm ministers were actually less savage than those of a previous package of CAP reforms (agreed in 1992) when it was first tabled (see Exhibit 5.3).

Inertia is a powerful force in EU decision-making, and changing the status quo usually only happens after very intense and trenchant bargaining. However, classic examples of history-making decisions, such as agreement on the 1992 project or the creation of the CFSP, suggest that 'the EU model is to agree to it, bash on with it, and deal with problems later'.[22] One consequence of this pattern of 'punctuated equlibriums' (Baumgartner and Jones 1993) is that ambitious new initiatives – such as EMU or agricultural reform – may be agreed with relatively little deliberation about problems of implementation or execution.

Package Dealing

'Big decisions' which punctuate periods of equilibrium often result from package deals, or linked decisions – often across different policy sectors – which offer broad scope for trade-offs between different interests. 'Package dealing' is a long-established norm in EU decision-making. It produces decisions that are notoriously difficult to reverse without risking the unravelling of carefully balanced compromises.

Each subsequent enlargement of the EU has enhanced the importance of package dealing. Perhaps paradoxically, given the difficulties of striking carefully balanced deals between actors in different policy networks (see Hayes-Renshaw and Wallace 1997: 64–5), it is often easier to get linked decisions adopted than it is to strike bargains on a range of decisions between actors in only one sector. This pattern of 'bundling' decisions tends either to reproduce the status quo (when package dealing does not work) or to initiate quite abrupt, structural changes (see Kirman and Widgrén 1995).

Subsidiarity

The stubbornness of intergovernmental impulses in EU decision-making is guaranteed, in important respects, by the power of *subsidiarity* as a norm. Subsidiarity can be defined in a variety of ways, and indeed was given several different meanings in the Maastricht Treaty (see Scott *et al.* 1994). Like all constitutional principles, subsidiarity requires legal interpretation and political dialogue for its meaning to be revealed, but it is usually taken to mean that EU action is only justified when policy problems arise which cannot be better solved through national actions.

Subsidiarity became the *leitmotif* of EU decision-making after the political crisis over the Maastricht Treaty in the early 1990s. By the end of the decade, it was firmly established as a norm that all EU decisions had to respect. In particular, German, British and French preferences had converged, as never before in the Union's history, around a model in which as many decisions as possible were taken at the national or sub-national levels. Still, subsidiarity left the way open to increased 'policy transfer', or the process by which governments learn from each other by sharing notes on policy performance, mimicking each other's successes, and gradually achieving policy convergence. EMU, employment policy, taxation and compliance with internal market rules all went from 'no-go' areas to ones featuring institutionalised exchanges between EU Member States, thus producing considerable policy convergence (and even a single currency).

Informal Decision-Making

A particularly pervasive norm arises from the frequent failure of the EU's formal institutions to facilitate meaningful bargaining. *Informal* decision-making is considered natural and is usually welcomed. Nugent (1994: 298) observes that most 'set piece' occasions in EU decision-making (including meetings of the Council, the EP's plenary sessions, meetings of the college of Commissioners and conciliation committees)

> tend to be formal and structured. Partly because of this they are often, in themselves, not very well equipped to produce the training, the concessions, and the compromises that are so often necessary to build majorities, create agreements, and further progress. As a result they have come to be supported by a vast network of informal and unstructured channels between EU actors. (Nugent 1994: 298)

In particular, 'informal and social exchanges are an important though often-ignored aspect of inter-institutional relations, true at the level of both politicians and officials' (Westlake 1994a: 23). The Commission has often and explicitly acknowledged the importance of informal bargaining with the EP. In particular, the budgetary procedure has led to very intimate links between MEPs and DG XIX (Budget) and the assent procedure has produced similar links between the EP and DG I, the Commission service responsible for external relations.

Decision-making *within* EU institutions often reveals that informal 'rules of the game' matter more than formal prerogatives. For example, DG IV is meant to work as if it were an independent committee of inquiry when it investigates possible violations of competition rules. It, together with the Commissioner for Competition Policy, develops its own view on such cases. Yet, other Commissioners (and particularly their *cabinets*) often act as the agents of networks that seek to obstruct DG IV or shape its opinions. Even where the Commission is most powerful, politics should not matter and hierarchies are clear, there are plenty of opportunities for advocacy coalitions to mobilise to shape policy.

Consensus at (Almost) Any Cost

A final norm – perhaps the most powerful of any in EU decision-making – is that all steps should be taken to preserve at least the *appearance* of consensus. The 'Brussels style' of lobbying is thus informal, low-key and designed to identify compromises for political decision-makers (van Schendelen 1993; Middlemas 1995; Peterson and Cowles 1998). In a political system built on the assumption that European integration is, after all, a positive-sum process, it becomes imperative to ensure that outcomes produce as few visible losers as possible.

Conclusion

We have painted a general picture of the EU's structural landscape. When we examine this picture closely, what is perhaps most striking is the multiple sources of *unpredictability* in EU decision-making. A first and fundamental source of unpredictability is simply the lack of any 'government', let alone an opposition. The Commission sets out its work programme in the autumn for the year to come and the EP scrutinises it, and the timetable for this exercise has become more regularised in the interest of 'transparency' (Peterson 1995c: 488). Yet, despite its formal agenda-setting powers, the Commission is far from being a 'European government' and its work programme is a far cry from a party platform, election manifesto, or Queen's speech, which give far clearer pictures of future legislative agendas and likely policy outcomes.

Unpredictability is also an outgrowth of the EU's peculiar problems of collective action: its internally divided institutions, lack of mechanisms for meaningful interinstitutional bargaining and its representation void. At one time, when unanimity was the basic decision rule, the problem was simply one of inability to reach the 'policy decision point'. The more modern problem is an inability to ensure that the decision-making process will not be blown off course by factors that are difficult to control. An issue that seems to be the domain of experts, such as veterinary standards for cattle, can suddenly become a dramatic headline-grabber, as BSE ('mad cow disease') became in the late 1990s. Informal bargaining, away from the political limelight, becomes a means for controlling decision-making amidst considerable uncertainty. Yet interests that may be important to policy outcomes are often poorly represented in Brussels. There remain many 'principals' – constituencies from whom EU decision-makers derive authority and to whom they are accountable – which have only tenuous links to EU decision-making but which can intervene to affect outcomes.

Third, and finally, EU decision-making is unpredictable simply because it is such a young and experimental system of government and one currently pursuing two of the boldest experiments in its history: EMU and enlargement. While the birth of the Euro promises to create a more integrated, 'hard core' of Member States, eastern enlargement means the EU is set to become a considerably more heterogeneous collection of states in the early 21st century. Each past enlargement has expanded the diversity of national preferences and probably, on balance, reinforced the status quo owing to stalemate.

In short, if the EU seems structured in a way that ensures stalemate, it is constantly being reinvented. This process often unblocks stalemate while building on the means the Union has established for resolving conflicts. Territorial conflicts are resolved by the Council. Ideological battles may be fought within the Parliament. Functional disputes get sorted out within the Commission (Aspinwall 1998: 212). Without the benefit of any grand design, the EU has developed a flexible, and often surprisingly effective, set of mechanisms for the resolution of very complex conflicts. Still, it is difficult to see how this all could have happened without the Union's greatest strength: its capacity for improvisation.[23]

Chapter 3

The Internal Market

The 'core' of the EU
The 'super-systemic' level: launch, lapse, relaunch
The systemic level: institutions and 'path dependency'
The sub-systemic level: policy networks galore
Conclusion

It is impossible to imagine the European Union without the internal market. The quest for a 'common market' was the prime rationale for the creation of the European Economic Community (EEC) in the first place. Thirty years later, the launch of the '1992 project' marked a crucial turning point in EU decision-making. In subsequent years, the internal market – guaranteeing, in principle, the free movement of all goods, services, investment and people within the EU – accounted for as much as 70 per cent of all EU legislation. New policies for the environment, research, regional development and social policy were constructed to 'flank' the internal market, or to enhance or soften its impact.

The politics of the internal market have been something of an orphan in the EU literature. Part of the problem is that it is difficult to generalise about what, arguably, is not a distinct 'sector' of policy. For example, public subsidies to the air transport industry are policed by the Commission's DG VII (Transport), not DG IV (Competition). Decisions concerning taxation are made by Economic and Finance Ministers (ECOFIN), not the Internal Market Council.

Yet the internal market does have its own 'dedicated' institutions: a Council, a Commissioner and a Directorate-General (XV).[1] A variety of treaty articles can be used to legislate in the name of the internal market, but co-decision provides what is, for most intents and purposes, a single decision rule (see Table 3.1). The internal market may be viewed as a distinct sector for decision-making, but one that stretches to include to an extremely diverse variety of initiatives, actors and procedures. The quest for a truly single market – analogous to those of the USA, Japan or China – necessitates a considerable measure of political and legal solidarity, without which the EU would be just another international organisation.

60

Table 3.1   *Decision-making procedures for the internal market and related policies*

Policy	Treaty article*	Council vote	Parliament's role
Free movement of persons, services, capital	40: free movement of workers	QMV	co-decision
	44: freedom of establishment	QMV	co-decision
	46: co-ordination of provisions for foreign nationals	QMV	co-decision
	47: mutual recognition of qualifications	QMV	co-decision
	47: free movement of self-employed persons	unanimity	co-decision
	52: liberalisation of specific services	QMV	consultation
Approximation of laws	93: harmonisation of indirect taxation	unanimity	consultation
	94: common market[2]	unanimity	consultation
	95: internal market	**QMV**	**co-decision**
Social policy	137: workplace health & safety, working conditions, information and consultation of workers, labour markets, sexual equality	QMV	co-decision
Consumer protection	153: consumer protection	QMV	co-decision

*All post-Amsterdam Treaty.

The 'Core' Of the EU

The internal market is the heart of the Union: the vast majority of all EU decisions are taken to try to create or maintain a barrier-free market, or compensate for its economic, social or environmental costs. In principle, if not practice,[3] the internal market is underpinned by the single most powerful idea in the history of the study of economics: the law of comparative advantage (Ricardo 1911). Put simply, it holds that the more states trade with each another, the more they may specialise and the richer all become. The important political implication is that the internal market (like free trade more generally) promises benefits to all in the form of increased wealth.

The 1992 project was propelled by estimates (highly speculative ones) that its medium-term effects would include a 4.5 per cent rise in gross domestic product (GDP) and the creation of 1.8 million new jobs (Cecchini *et al.* 1988; Emerson *et al.* 1988). The drive to free the internal market fit with an emerging neo-liberal consensus on the desirability of policy ideas such as liberalisation, deregulation and privatisation. For a time, western Europe rallied behind these ideas at the policy level, but also behind the more symbolic notion of a 'Europe without Frontiers' at a political level. It is not wrong, just misleading, to see the 1992 project as the result of the 'depoliticization of the Common Market' (Majone 1997; Caporaso 1998) because the project, for a while anyway, was given a shove from the highest political levels by leaders who thought it would bring them political dividends.

Why was there a need for the 1992 project? After all, the EEC was created as a customs union which would guarantee the 'four freedoms', and aimed to harmonise national rules which restricted trade. The Treaty of Rome foresaw a gradual transition to qualified majority voting by the Council on most related measures. One problem, of course, was that the retention of the national veto slowed decision-making to the pace favoured by the most reluctant Member State (see Exhibit 2.5). Political commitment to the common market weakened perceptibly during the recessions of the 1970s, when many new barriers to internal trade emerged. The EU did not really have a 'common' market.

In key respects, all changed in 1985. At the Milan summit, the European Council endorsed the Commission's (1985b) White Paper on the internal market. It specified over 300 legislative acts needed to 'complete' the internal market and presented them as a single package with no picking and choosing allowed. A deadline of 31 December 1992 was set (hence the '1992 project') for agreeing all related decisions. After a brief intergovernmental conference, EU governments endorsed the Single European Act (SEA, ratified in 1987) which amended the Treaty of Rome for the first time and significantly extended qualified majority voting (QMV). No longer was the most notable feature of the EU its *inability* to take decisions.

The Four Freedoms

The 1985 White Paper refocused political attention on the four freedoms. The Union moved measurably closer to the free movement of *goods* by eliminating all border controls, which sharply reduced costs and delivery times. It proved far more difficult to liberalise the *service* sector (Oliver 1996). As the 1992 project's (essentially voluntary) deadline neared, the Commission discreetly downgraded several proposals, such as the Investment Services Directive, to 'non-priority status'. Services are generally less 'tradable' than goods, and language and geographical distance usually are more important barriers: it is easier to sell Danish bacon than Danish insurance in Portugal. However, services account for about two-thirds of the EU's economy. The scope for increased trade in services represents a large, unexploited opportunity for wealth creation.

The Union has moved far closer to free movement of *capital* than seemed possible in the early 1980s. The decisions of France and Italy in 1984–5 to lift domestic exchange controls (placing limits on how much money could be shifted abroad) were inevitable in the long run, but significant at the time: they helped secure the support of Helmut Kohl for the idea of endorsing the eventual goal of Economic and Monetary Union (EMU) in the preamble to the Single European Act (Taylor 1989: 10). By the time of the 1989 Madrid summit, at which EMU was given a crucial political push, a timetable had been agreed for the lifting of all restrictions on capital movements in the EU.

The lifting of exchange controls does not guarantee a 'single' market for capital. For example, attempts to agree common rules on the taxation of savings have been resisted particularly by the UK, on grounds of fiscal sovereignty, and Luxembourg, whose zero tax rate on savings and guarantees of banking secrecy are magnets for foreign capital. In any event, all Council decisions on taxation require unanimity. After limited harmonisation of VAT was agreed in 1992, taxation became a 'no go' area for the EU, with one ambassador (from a high-tax country) insisting, 'I have news for you: tax harmonization is not going to take place. So there will be no internal market in reality. Again, it all comes down to QMV versus unanimity. It is all that matters.'[4]

Free movement of *labour* has been the most difficult of the four freedoms to guarantee (Handoll 1995). A bitter dispute flared in the mid-1990s over 'posted workers' as richer Member States, especially Germany, refused to tolerate foreign guest workers (often from southern EU states) who priced their own nationals out of jobs at a time of high unemployment. The directive eventually agreed was thoroughly resented by southern states and had effects which were contrary to 'free movement'. Meanwhile, few Member States seemed bothered when several Italian universities decided to cope with revenue shortfalls after 1995 by dismissing 'foreign' (non-Italian) lecturers, even though many were EU citizens. The plea of one lecturers' rights activist – 'this is now a political question and requires political clout. We want this discussed by European government ministers'[5] – was indicative of how little the EU's common institutions often could do about violations of internal market rules without intervention from the Council.

The four freedoms often touch on acute national sensitivities. Sometimes the EU has needed anomalous institutions and decision rules to skirt them. For example, the elimination of passport checks was undertaken within the so-called 'Schengen Group'. Named after the small town in Luxembourg where it was created in 1985, the Group was born as an intergovernmental arrangement (cutting out the European Parliament: EP) which took decisions by consensus, did not include all EU Member States and had no binding rules.[6] Thus France reimposed border controls in 1995 on the grounds that Dutch laws on illegal drugs were too lax. Still, Schengen did much to promote free movement.

On the one hand, neo-functionalists could take comfort in the decision at the 1997 Amsterdam summit, in a clear case of 'spill-over' from the internal market, to give Schengen a proper treaty base, thus making it a part of the EU proper. On the other, Schengen shows how far the EU has to go even before it achieves the 'core' goals of the internal market. The four freedoms in some respects appear to validate Waltz's (1993) neo-realist insistence that the EU always will take the easiest decisions first, leaving the hardest ones subject to long-lasting, if not perpetual, wrangling.

Harmonisation and Approximation

The elimination of tariffs or quantitative restrictions on trade does not guarantee an internal market: national laws may have the 'equivalent effect' of such barriers (see Exhibit 2.4). For many years the Community tried to agree common rules where national laws diverged, going as far as trying to agree standards for the size and type of screws used in public buildings. With such ambitions, the only option was to try to *harmonise* national laws under what became Article 94,[7] which required unanimous Council decisions.

A huge backlog of cases built up by the mid-1980s. By this time, the Treaty's ban on technical barriers to trade was clearly impotent. Member States frequently hid behind treaty provisions which allowed divergent national product standards or other trade barriers for a variety of reasons, including health and safety.[8] Domestic producers were often sheltered from any meaningful competition.

The mid-1980s brought a 'new approach': Community directives sought to *approximate* national laws – that is, to eliminate differences between them which blocked trade, instead of trying to harmonise every detail. Employing the principle of 'mutual recognition' (see Exhibit 2.4), the Community's job became specifying only essential requirements to ensure health and safety. Member States were encouraged to develop common standards through the appropriate (non-EU) European and international standards organisations, thus potentially adding new, additional layers to 'multi-level governance'. When the system worked as intended, firms could offer lower prices because they no longer had to change their production methods to suit different national specifications.

A similar strategy was developed for public procurement, or purchases of goods or services by all levels of government. The Commission convinced Member States to harmonise procedures for advertising and awarding public contracts, which accounted for well over 10 per cent of total EU GDP. The hope was that more competition for public contracts would create large savings in public budgets.

Different decision rules continued to apply to different types of harmonisation or approximation. The need for unanimity on all tax matters meant that little progress was made towards eliminating tax differentials. They contributed to variations of as much as 100 per cent in the price of a car, with the UK maintaining the highest prices in the EU for the most popular models.[9] Eventually, the prospect of EU consumers crossing borders to get the best tax deal, particularly after the launch of the Euro made prices far more 'transparent' (see Table 3.2), created stronger pressures for harmonisation.

In late 1997, ECOFIN agreed an outline agreement on 'poaching', or tax competition, as well as a voluntary code of conduct on business taxation. As is usually the case when the EU carves out new policy territory, unilateral declarations by Member States immediately qualified the decision: for example, Ireland declared that it would need a five-year

Table 3.2   *The price of Coca-Cola (1.5 litre bottle) in 'Euro-land' (1998)*

Member State	Price in national currency	Price in Euro
Austria	14.9 Austrian schillings	1.08
Belgium	48 Belgian francs	1.18
Finland	9 markkas	1.50
France	6.5 French francs	0.98
Germany	3.02 Deutschmarks	1.53
Ireland	0.93 punts	1.18
Italy	2460 lira	1.26
Luxembourg	42 Luxembourg francs	1.02
Netherlands	2.45 guilders	1.10
Portugal	199 escudos	0.98
Spain	125 pesetas	0.74

Source: BEUC.[10] Reproduced with permission of *European Voice*.

phase-out of its (very low) tax on manufacturers. Yet some decision-makers, such as Luxembourg's respected Prime Minister, Jean-Claude Juncker, argued that EMU required much closer co-operation on economic policy, particularly relating to tax and social security standards. After all, EMU meant *economic*, as well as monetary union. Member States continued to defend their anomalous national practices, such as varying rates of taxation, quite fiercely, but the power of market forces within the world's largest capitalist market is daunting, and usually pushes in the direction of uniformity (see Exhibit 3.1).

Competition policy

The policing of the internal market is fascinating in institutional terms. Competition policy is where the Commission has the most autonomy and the EP is weakest. Many important decisions are taken by simple majority votes in the college of Commissioners (not by QMV, since Commissioners are 'neutral' and do not represent 'their' Member States). The Council's role is mainly restricted to granting derogations – opt-outs or implementation delays – to competition rules (on the basis of QMV after consulting the Parliament). Competition policy is highly contentious. EU rules are meant to be applied objectively and legalistically, but politics are rampant.

Competition policy decisions concern anti-competitive practices: monopolistic pricing, cartels, and so on; or public subsidies, known as 'state aids' in the EU's jargon. Two key treaty articles are 81, which prevents actions restricting competition, and 82, which outlaws the abuse of 'dominant market position' by any firm.[14] Both articles are extremely vague, and neither gives EU competition policy real teeth. The Commission was almost powerless in competition policy until the Council delegated powers in 1962 to investigate suspected violations of Community rules and punish offenders. Afterwards, the Commission could turn up at company facilities unannounced to investigate cases and impose fines on offending firms.

Initially, the Commission used its powers sparingly and even meekly. The severity of the recessions of the 1970s meant that governments loathed any action which might reduce domestic employment, even if justified by EU competition rules. The Commission's 1985 White Paper, which was mostly drafted in DG III (Industry) not DG IV (Competition), said very little about competition policy. Yet, the launch of the 1992 project coincided with the appointment of arch-liberals Peter Sutherland (1985–9) and Leon Brittan (1989–91) as Commissioners for competition. First Sutherland and then Brittan used the new 'holy grail' of the internal market to enforce competition policy far more robustly (Swann 1993).

Exhibit 3.1 Alcohol and the Nordics

At the turn of the 19th century, Sweden's rate of alcohol consumption was about five times the EU's rate today. In 1909, more than half of all Swedish adults turned out for a voluntary plebiscite which recorded a 99 per cent vote in favour of absolute prohibition (Scott 1977: 412). The high price of alcohol in Nordic states, and tight restrictions on its sale, are legacies of this period. When Sweden and Finland joined the Union in 1995, concessions on alcohol policy were granted which allowed them to keep their state-owned, retail sales monopolies and to restrict imports of drink from abroad. In Sweden, alcohol (other than light beer) could only be purchased from state liquor stores which closed at 6pm on Friday evenings and did not open again until Monday morning. Public opposition to such restrictions was surprisingly muted, and probably weaker than concerns about 'EU interference' in Swedish alcohol policy. The point was illustrated in 1997 when the Commission ruled that 'alcopops', fruit-flavoured alcoholic drinks, could not be banned in Sweden, prompting the Swedish Green MEP, Ulf Holm, to ask: 'Does the Commission believe there is nothing more sacrosanct than free trade?'[11]

On the day that Sweden entered the EU, a grocer, Harry Franzen, defied Swedish law by offering wine to his customers. The Franzen case went all the way to the ECJ in 1997. Unusually, the Court overturned the preliminary decision taken by one of its Advocates General, a legal 'fact-finder' and advisor, and ruled that Sweden's state monopoly on retail sales could be justified on grounds of public health. However, Franzen won a partial victory when the Court declared that Sweden's law allowing only a small number of licensed wholesalers (nearly all Swedish) to import alcohol *did* constitute an illegal barrier to trade. The Court's decision was decidedly timorous, in the view of many observers, but also politically judged: the ECJ was very reluctant to strike down a swathe of Swedish laws in its very first judgement relating to Sweden.[12] In any event, the ECJ's decision prompted challenges to similar laws in Finland in 1998.

The Nordics face severe difficulties reconciling their alcohol policies with their EU membership. The amount of alcohol smuggled into Sweden reportedly quadrupled after it joined the Union.[13] As this case shows, the forces unleashed by the internal market often overwhelm public power unless it is wielded collectively at the EU level.

More decisions were taken under what became Article 81: 148 were handed down in the 1980s, up from only 27 in the 1960s (see Buiges *et al.* 1995: xv). More industrial sectors became subject to Commission scrutiny (see Allen 1996c). But the Commission was able to walk softly and carry a big stick: about 90 per cent of all cases were resolved informally before the Commission's investigation turned very thorough.

If a government was determined to defend one of its firms from a large fine, a process of bargaining between the government, firm and Commission usually began. The same applied, with few variations, to state aids. The Treaty (under what became Article 88[15]) gave the Commission powers to monitor state aids, but only 'in co-operation' with Member States. When state aid ran out of control in the early 1980s, the Commission put its foot down and announced that henceforth it would require all national subsidies to be 'notified' before being granted, or they would be disallowed. Still, there was little that was automatic about state aid rules. Even with Brittan holding the competition policy portfolio, actions against Renault and British Aerospace resulted in settlements that lowered, but did not totally disallow, large state aid to each. The later case of the French firm Bull, a woeful underperformer in the computer industry, showed how tortured decision-making on competition could become (see Exhibit 3.2).

The 'Super-Systemic' Level: Launch, Lapse, Relaunch

The decisions to launch the 1992 project *and* reform the Treaty via the SEA were inextricably linked, with one justifying the other. Still, it remains a challenge to explain how 'an array of individually dull, technical and everyday items were combined into an overarching programme that attracted such high profile attention' (Wallace and Young 1996: 137). Part of the explanation is that the 1992 project was largely industry-led. It was championed in particular by the European Round Table (ERT), which brought together the chief executives of around 50 of Europe's most powerful multinational companies (MNCs) (see Dekker 1984; Cowles 1995). As large exporters, investors and employers, these firms stood to gain most from a truly internal market. The ERT spoke with a powerful and essentially single voice in support of both the 1992 project and the institutional changes thought necessary to its success.

The Commission helped ensure that the ERT's voice was heard at the highest political levels (see Grant 1994; Ross 1995). In particular, the Commissioner for the Internal Market, Lord Arthur Cockfield, consulted closely the ERT and other industry groups on the precise content of the White Paper. At the same time, Cockfield (1994) realised that European governments needed to accrue political benefit from the internal market and thus encouraged them to claim 'ownership' of the 1992 project.

The success of the Commission–industry coalition highlights two fundamental features of EU decision-making. First, the Commission usually offers leadership at the super-systemic level only when its agenda is supported by a unified constituency of powerful private actors (see Nugent 1995). One of the most striking differences between the SEA and

Maastricht Treaty was that the former was supported by an influential industrial constituency, while the latter – even with its commitment to monetary union – was not.

Second, when advocacy coalitions shift the EU's policy agenda, they usually do so 'from the bottom up' by influencing decision-making within policy networks. Occasionally, however, the EU facilitates advocacy by coalitions which are broad and high-powered, as was the alliance between the ERT, Commission and other supporters of the 1992 project.[20] Such coalitions have the luxury of concentrating on 'whichever level of governance they believe to be the most receptive to their preferences and demands' (Wallace 1996b: 24).

In key respects, the 1992 project's vagueness was an important asset. Despite the Commission's rhetoric to the contrary, not everyone stood to gain from the internal market. Only after it was well in train was the Commission willing to admit that it had little idea which sectors or regions would win or lose (Buiges *et al.* 1990). It also played down evidence that the 1992 project stood to benefit some Member States (Germany) far more than others (Greece) (see Smith and Wanke 1993).

Crucially, the ECJ gave the 1992 project a sort of legal mandate, or apolitical veneer. In particular, the Court provided 'openings' for the Commission to exploit: in addition to the 1979 *Cassis de Dijon* case (see Exhibit 2.4), other Court decisions were used skilfully by the Commission to lay the groundwork for the internal market. For example, the original Treaty of Rome contained no mention of either mergers or acquisitions. For many years the Commission had to rely on case law, particularly the 1972 *Continental Can* case,[21] to establish that a company with a dominant position could be held to be abusing it under Article 82 if it took over a competitor. Yet disagreement about how much power the Community should have over mergers, strong national regimes in some Member States and a weak legal base made the Commission's position a feeble one. In 1987, the *Philip Morris* case[22] provided a breakthrough. The Court decided that an agreement by two competitors (in this case, the purchase of shares by one in another) short of an outright merger might 'distort competition' under Article 81, even if the agreement did not clearly result in a 'dominant position' under Article 82.

The *Philip Morris* case created considerable uncertainty, particularly within industry, about the limits of the Commission's powers. The timing was hardly ideal: the 1992 project was beginning to foster (as was always intended) widespread corporate restructuring and partnership agreements. The Commission deftly played on corporate fears. It also played on the preference of France, which held the Council Presidency in 1989, for the creation of large 'European champions', which were likely to be opposed or even blocked by German competition authorities. Reluctantly, 17 years after

Exhibit 3.2 The Bull state aid case

For most of the computer age, France's Groupe Bull was the second largest European computer manufacturer after Olivetti. Between 1991 and 1994, Bull racked up losses of more than €2.3 billion, a feat matched only by two other French state-owned 'black holes': Air France and Crédit Lyonnais. In all three cases, the French government poured state aid into the companies to avoid bankruptcies and massive job losses. The EU's Article 87 prohibits state aid which 'distorts or threatens to distort competition', yet it (vaguely) allows exceptions for 'certain economic activities' providing aid 'does not adversely affect trading conditions to an extent contrary to the common interest'. In the case of Bull, most aid came in the form of 'capital injections'.

ECJ decisions in the mid-1980s resulted in a strict test for public capital injections: the state had to act as if it were an 'ordinary' investor in the stock market. In 1992, when the Commission challenged plans for a €570 million injection, the French government tried to claim they were 'normal' investments by a 'parent company', and thus not state aid. The case went to the ECJ, which found against the French. Ultimately, however, the Commission approved the aid. Parallel investments by the Japanese firm NEC and America's IBM in Bull clearly paved the way for the Commission's decision.

The decision seemed exonerated in 1993: a new centre-right French government under Edouard Balladur came to power, warning that the days of cash hand-outs to Bull were over. Yet the new EU Commissioner for competition, Karel Van Miert, soon received reports of plans for further aid. In early 1994, the Commission warned the Balladur government against further payments to Bull while DG IV investigated a proposed €1.3 billion injection. Van Miert complained that, 'We are in a completely illegal situation now . . . The Commission is in an impossible position.'[16] However, France could not be *forced* to comply. The Commission could only 'invite' the Balladur government to suspend payments, while threatening action in the ECJ.

In early 1994, after a meeting (held, perhaps symbolically, in Paris) between Van Miert, Balladur and Bull's chairman, the Commission announced that Bull would receive no further unapproved payments. A plan would be drawn up to restore Bull's profitability and, crucially, identify a path towards privatisation. Van Miert insisted that the aid would stop and 'the privatisation prospects of the enterprise are a good guarantee'.[17]

→

→

Within a few days, the French Industry Minister, Gérard Longuet, was in Tokyo urging NEC to take a large stake in what he termed Bull's 'forthcoming capital increase'.[18] The Commission responded by publishing an exasperated letter to the French government in the *Official Journal* of the EU, demanding additional information on Bull's finance plans. The letter noted the long history of state aid to Bull, observed that Bull had fallen to number 13 in world rankings of computer makers and asked for comments from interested parties.

In late 1994, the Commission allowed €1.7 billion as 'one-time, last-time' injection of capital. Van Miert claimed that the decision complied with new Commission guidelines on state aid for rescuing and restructuring companies. The aid to Bull raised fewer objections than Van Miert's earlier decision in 1994 to allow a larger capital injection (of €3 billion) to Air France. Still, the British Trade and Industry Minister, Michael Heseltine, wrote to Van Miert asking for assurances. Van Miert responded that there definitely would be no further aid to Bull.

Perhaps above all, the Bull case highlights how compliance with EU rules is negotiated. Initially, the case prompted a chorus of voices, some within the Commission, accusing Van Miert of being too lax on aids. Yet, Bull became viewed as a personal victory for Van Miert, who went on to become a respected, effective Commissioner for competition.

The case also illustrated how competing firms may be reluctant to complain about state aid for fear of alienating either the Commission or a potential future collaborator (in, for example, the EU's research programmes). Despite the British government's protestations during the Bull case, a spokesman for ICL admitted that the firm had not lobbied the Commission very hard, blandly noting that, 'We have always said that [we] are against state aid because we want a level playing field.'[19] Similarly vague statements from Olivetti and Siemens/Nixdorf revealed how the creation of the internal market sometimes had the effect of making firms more independent of their governments, but also more responsive to the collective interests of the EU policy network in their sector.

Finally, the Bull case shows that state aid is considered far more acceptable if it helps prepare firms for privatisation and global competition. An independent audit ordered by the Commission concluded that privatisation and industrial alliances were crucial for Bull's future viability. French promises of both counted for a lot.

the 1972 Paris European summit first endorsed EEC policing of mergers, the Council adopted the Merger Control Regulation (MCR) of 1989.

The MCR gives the Commission, specifically a Merger Task Force affiliated to DG IV, licence to investigate large proposed mergers. The task force gives its recommendation (after one month) to the Commissioner for competition, who then may clear a merger or decide the MCR does not apply. However, he or she must consult the Commission President before a decision is taken to 'open proceedings' against a merger. Once proceedings begin, the Commission has four months to gather evidence. During this period it must consult an Advisory Committee on Concentrations, consisting of national representatives, while inviting the views of 'third parties', such as competing firms or labour unions. Ultimately, the college of Commissioners sets merger policy by deciding whether to accept, reject or ask for revision of a merger.

The decision to agree the MCR came after years of tough negotiations and only when a brief window of opportunity opened. The MCR shows that history is sometimes made by a *combination* of decisions taken by different institutions: in this case, the Court, Council and eventually the Commission, particularly its own 1990 decision on the Nestlé–Perrier merger which established that a merger could be challenged if it led to 'joint market dominance', or too much power in the hands of a *number* of firms (Armstrong and Bulmer 1998: 112–13). Still, the decision to create the MCR touched the highest political levels: it would have been unthinkable were it not for the political commitment of (what became) the European Council to an EU merger policy, as well as the burgeoning momentum behind the 1992 project.

There is no shortage of debate about why this momentum emerged when it did in the 1980s. Advocates of both neo-functionalist models (Sandholtz and Zysman 1989; Cowles 1995) and intergovernmental models (Moravcsik 1991; Garrett 1992) could probably agree that a new, neo-liberal policy consensus *and* a relatively healthy, growing economy were both necessary, if not sufficient, conditions for the relaunch of the Union. Cockfield's White Paper was tabled when European leaders were still seeking new solutions to the problem of the deep recession of the early 1980s. By the time the legislative programme to create the internal market was in train, the Community had entered a period of relative prosperity. The connection between the 1992 project and renewed economic growth was dubious, but pressures on governments to keep protectionist measures in place were relatively weak. The neo-liberal consensus surfed on a wave of prosperity.

Then, in the early 1990s, the broad environment in which the EU operated changed quite radically. Geopolitical changes in Central and Eastern Europe, war in the Balkans and the Union's new commitment to

EMU distracted attention from the considerable distance still to travel before a truly 'internal' market existed. Perhaps above all, the EU fell into a serious recession: as unemployment rose (to 11.4 per cent in the Union as a whole by 1994) the internal market was sucked dry of its symbolic potency. The President of the European Parliament (EP), Klaus Hänsch, hinted starkly at how much perceptions had changed: 'More and more people associate the EU with social breakdown and the destruction of jobs. We must link it again with the creation of jobs and social progress.'[23]

The Santer Commission was installed in 1995 with a pledge to make the internal market's consolidation the cornerstone of its activities. The Internal Market Commissioner, Mario Monti, promised to clamp down on violations of internal market rules and unveiled the SLIM ('Simplification of Legislation in the Internal Market') programme in response to complaints that EU rules were complicated and sometimes contradictory. Yet by this time the fire had gone out of the internal market as a political project. Measures such as SLIM were practical, but hardly stoked political imaginations.

If neo-functionalist treatments seemed convincing between 1985 and 1993, intergovernmentalist explanations of EU decision-making seemed more plausible in the post-Maastricht period. In a period of rising unemployment, domestically insecure EU governments were less willing to embrace new initiatives (particularly in the face of pre-EMU austerity) which traded short-term economic pain for long-term economic gain. What is often the earliest stage of EU decision-making, the endorsement of new, broad policy goals by the European Council, yielded few new proposals. In debates about extending the internal market to public utilities, decision-makers such as the French Industry Minister, Franck Borotra, openly argued that, 'in certain sectors, the opening of the market to competition has been a grave mistake'.[24]

Momentum appeared to shift again in late 1996. First, the continental recession of the early 1990s finally began to ease. Second, the Commission tabled the first exhaustive survey on the impact of the internal market.[25] It struck a clever balance between celebrating good news, such as the creation of up to 900 000 jobs, and insisting that proper enforcement of existing rules had to become a major priority. Third, it began to appear that EMU would be launched on time. EU governments were reminded that the maximum benefits of the Euro could be realised only if remaining barriers to internal trade were eliminated.

Monti moved quickly to develop an *Action Plan for the Single Market* and had it endorsed twice by the European Council. As a member of Santer's *cabinet* put it, 'Monti started slow, but he's tenacious. He roughs them up.'[26] The *Action Plan* scolded governments for fully implementing only about two-thirds of all internal market directives. Recalling the 1992

deadline which had earlier concentrated minds, and looking forward to
EMU, the Commission (1997a: 2) 'identified . . . specific *actions aimed at
improving the functioning of the Single Market by 1 January 1999.*'[27] Just
in case EU governments did not see the neo-functionalist logic of
completing the internal market before creating the Euro, the Commission
(1997a: 1–2) added:

> The third stage of EMU represents a critical juncture. The Single Market will
> provide underlying economic support for Monetary Union and the Euro will
> provide added value and efficiency to the Single Market.

The EU's most tangible achievement, the internal market, thus became
linked to its most audacious project, the Euro. EU governments were
reminded that past decisions had failed to 'make history' because the
policies they mandated were not enforced or implemented properly. For
the second time, a mainly dull and technical set of measures attracted
attention from the highest political level, with the Commission cleverly
linking them to dawn of the Euro.

The Systemic Level: Institutions and 'Path dependency'

The 1992 project transformed EU decision-making in two related ways.
First, it gave the EU a coherent policy programme with a clear deadline.
Second, it fundamentally extended QMV as a decision rule. After many

Table 3.3   *State aid to the manufacturing sector (€ million)*

Country	1988	1992
Belgium	1 244	975
Denmark	361	342
France	7 394	5 860
Germany	7 843	12 230
Greece	1 555	1 047
Ireland	379	293
Italy	9 410	10 708
Luxembourg	39	64
Netherlands	1 125	844
Portugal	183	418
Spain	4 213	928
United Kingdom	3 945	1 964
EU 12	37 691	35 673

Source: Commission (1995c).

years of 'decisionmaking gridlock' (Keohane and Hoffmann 1991: 8), the Community underwent a revolution of sorts, particularly in its ability to set policies quickly.

The internal market as a policy sector is far broader than Lord Cockfield's White Paper. Still, the general momentum behind the 1992 project gave political licence to decisions outside the scope of the White Paper which otherwise would have been unthinkable. For example, the Commission boldly wielded Article 86,[28] which allows EU competition rules to be applied to 'revenue-producing monopolies', to pry open protected telecommunications markets. It clamped down hard on state aid: leaving aside Germany, which offered massive subsidies to the former East Germany, state aid to manufacturing fell by about one-fifth during 1988–92 (see Table 3.3).

In competition policy, the Commission used the Merger Control Regulation (MCR) to set policy where it had been unable to before. By 1996, the Commission had handed down decisions on nearly 150 cases under the MCR, blocking only a few (see Exhibit 3.3). However, the EU merger regime was far from toothless. Firms usually offered concessions to ensure that the Merger Task Force and Commissioner for competition were satisfied that proposed mergers should go ahead.

Exhibit 3.3 The de Havilland case

After the 1989 Council decision to create the MCR, Leon Brittan began to look for an appropriate significant merger to use as a test case to establish the Commission's new authority (see Ross 1995: 132–5; Allen 1996c: 174–5). He found himself at odds both with Delors, whose *cabinet* prevented several potential cases from being put to the Commission, and with Martin Bangemann, the Industry Commissioner, for whom industrial policy considerations justified many mergers.

It was not until 1993 that the first merger was blocked under the MRC when a Franco-Italian alliance called ATR sought to buy up a Canadian aircraft manufacturer, de Havilland. Despite the vigorous efforts of a Franco-Italian alliance, Brittan managed to squeeze nine votes (a bare majority) in the college in support of his recommendation to block the merger (with Delors abstaining).

The de Havilland case revealed the 'purposeful opportunism' of the Commission (Cram 1994). However, if the Commission seems naturally and constantly to seek the expansion of its powers, in line with public choice theory (Niskanen 1973), its efforts are often complicated by *internal* battles, as well as resistance from Member States. Despite its image as a unified, power-hungry bureaucracy, the Commission is really a political system in itself, where nearly every interest in the Union at large is represented.

A range of ECJ decisions reinforced the Commission's authority. The mere threat of being hauled before the Court in 1990 led the Danish government to pay costs and damages to a British–French consortium whose bid to build the enormously expensive Great Belt Eastern Bridge was cheaper than that of the winning Danish firm. However, compliance in this case, as in most others, was negotiated: the Danes were unwilling to reopen tendering for the contract (Garrett 1992: 555–6).

Moreover, the Commission began to reveal itself as a highly fragmented bureaucracy and really a political system in itself. Despite their oaths of neutrality, individual Commissioners often found themselves supporting their own Member States when decisions had to be taken as to whether internal market rules were being violated. In 1995, the Greek Commissioner, Christos Papoutsis, blocked a move to take Greece to court for an illegal ban on toy advertisements. The Commissioner from Ireland, Padraig Flynn, foiled an attempt to haul Dublin before the ECJ to challenge laws requiring Irish radio stations to play 30 per cent Irish music.

The Commission also seemed incapable of taking clear, timely decisions of the kind needed, for example, to create a single market in financial services (McHugh 1996). Poor internal management hampered the introduction of the 'CE mark', a guarantee that products met EU health and safety standards. The result was long lags in the development of standards, largely due to 'inadequate co-ordination and long-range planning within the Commission' (Dinan 1994: 341). Part of the problem was that the Commission took on an enormously expanded range of responsibilities in the late 1980s without a commensurate increase in resources (see Metcalfe 1992).

For its part, the Internal Market Council evolved into a lively, active decision-taker after its creation in 1983. It convened more often (10 times) than any other Council besides General Affairs or Agriculture in 1990 (Westlake 1995: 60). However, by 1994, the Internal Market Council had become a far less busy, dynamic body, meeting only three times in a year (Hayes-Renshaw and Wallace 1997: 30). As one of the most liberal Councils, its primacy in internal market decision-making had never been unchallenged: even in the late 1980s, the highly conservative Transport Council managed to keep Internal Market ministers from 'poaching' deregulation of the EU's transport industry. Liberalisation of road haulage was thus long delayed, and one-in-three lorries (trucks) continued to return home empty after delivering their loads in other EU countries. The Internal Market Council also saw new, interesting areas, such as audio-visual and telecommunications policy (see Chapter 8), become the prerogative of other, newly created Councils (Culture and Telecoms). As its grip on the internal market weakened, Ludlow's (1992) contention that a strong Commission actually *requires* a strong Council was validated.

In contrast, the European Parliament's role in internal market decision-making expanded incessantly. The SEA's co-operation procedure made the Parliament a 'conditional agenda-setter' on many internal market questions (Tsebelis 1994; Earnshaw and Judge 1997), even if the frenzied pace of new legislation sometimes overwhelmed it. After 1993, the co-decision procedure gave the EP unprecedented powers actually to veto Council decisions on the internal market. In the first 18 months after the Maastricht Treaty was ratified, approximately 130 proposals for 'co-decision acts' were sent by the Council to Parliament, most of which concerned the internal market.[29]

The ability of the EP to force its agenda on the Council varied considerably, yet the post-Maastricht experience of co-decision prompted three broad conclusions. First, as long as its relevant committee chairs and *rapporteurs* showed sufficient political nous, the EP showed it could wring significant concessions out of the Council – usually on stronger consumer rights (see Exhibit 3.4) or environmental protection (see Exhibit 7.4) – before policies were set (see Corbett 1994). Second, the Parliament became less dependent on the Commission, whose support was required under the co-operation procedure, but *not* under co-decision, when the EP sought amendments. Third, the Amsterdam Treaty's extension of co-decision was indicative of a general consensus that the procedure was working well, and in fact better than many anticipated. One Deputy Ambassador observed that 'co-decision has made [the Council's] life tedious, not overly difficult . . . But sure, we can work with it and we do take more account of the EP's amendments now'.[30]

How would a 'new institutionalist' analysis make sense of systemic decision-making on the internal market? First, by highlighting the 'path dependency' of EU policy: the internal market is, in many respects, the common market by a new name and modified means. It certainly was not 'complete' by the end of 1992, but it retained just enough forward momentum for the Commission to recharge it by linking it to EMU and shifting emphasis away from taking new decisions to delivering on ones already made. By the late 1990s, the Internal Market Council had again become a busy, buzzy forum that tackled heavy agendas. The number of internal market measures not implemented by all EU Member States was cut in half in less than a year in 1997–8. The success of Monti's *Action Plan* strategy was reflected in extraordinary scenes of the Commission being 'showered with praise' by ministers after Council debates.[43]

Second, an institutionalist treatment would highlight the policy impact of the evolving balance of power between EU institutions. As the case of motorbikes shows, the enhanced role of the EP has raised the profile of consumer concerns. Third, institutionalists would note that diverse decision-making arrangements for 'setting' internal market policy persist,

Exhibit 3.4 The power of motorbikes: a 'Triumph' for the EP

Two directives on motorbikes agreed in 1994–5 saw the EP come of age in the co-decision era. They also produced vivid spectacles: the barracking of industry ministers by leather-clad bikers; a march on Brussels by 25 000 motorbike enthusiasts; the sight of Bangemann, a portly man, riding on the back of a motorbike driven by his arch political opponent (and keen biker), Roger Barton, Socialist MEP for Sheffield.

The first directive[31] proposed to limit the power of motorbikes while offering an exemption to the UK, the home of a leading manufacturer of powerful 'super-bikes', Triumph. Bangemann justified the proposal on safety grounds, citing evidence from a 1989 German study linking motorbike power to traffic deaths. If agreed, the directive would have allowed Member States to refuse to register as many as 20 per cent of all existing bikes in the EU. One lobbyist who followed the directive closely claimed that, 'Bangemann basically waves the German flag and the German industry in this case was BMW.'[32] The German MNC already manufactured within the proposed restrictions according to a 'gentleman's agreement' with the German government.

The Council endorsed the proposal in June 1993 (with the UK abstaining). The EP signalled its opposition by an overwhelming margin of 262 votes to 76 (with eight abstentions). For its part, the European motorbike industry continued to press for harmonised standards, with Walter Hasselkus of BMW Motorcycles complaining that 'the legal framework which would allow us to operate in a truly European way simply does not exist'.[33] Bangemann thus tabled a fresh proposal, now under the provisions of the Maastricht Treaty. Again, in February 1994, the Parliament rejected the Council common position, this time by 300 to 24, with 13 abstentions, thus triggering conciliation.

The battle over the power limits directive pitted Bangemann against Barton and Peter Beazley, a British Tory, and *rapporteur* for the EP's Economic Affairs Committee. Bangemann repeatedly cited grim statistics on road fatalities and once read out a letter to an EP plenary from an association for the victims of accidents. Barton dismissed the linkage between motorbike power and accidents as a 'stupid idea, a totally discredited idea' and urged MEPs to reject the directive 'on behalf of bikers, on behalf of the manufacturers and on behalf of democracy itself'. In one memorable exchange, Bangemann asserted that bikers were a minority who had to accept majority rule in a democracy, with Barton retorting: 'it ill behoves a

→

→

non-elected Commissioner to lecture this Parliament on democracy'. A furious Bangemann blustered, 'it is true that I am not elected; but I am a member of a democratic system, and the Commission is an organ in a democratic institution, namely the European Union'.[34]

Other key players in the motorbike story included Yiannos Papantoniou, the Greek Industry Minister, who chaired the Industry Council in early 1994 and facilitated progress by encouraging 'all informal contacts with MEPs',[35] thus producing a compromise in conciliation. Another was the flamboyant Federation of European Motorcyclists (FEM), described by one industry lobbyist as 'an aggressive group of Easy Rider types'.[36] FEM's leader, Simon Milward, tirelessly campaigned against 'anti-bike Nazism'[37] and even attended some conciliation meetings (in theory as an assistant to Barton) before being banned. BMW was a crucial actor, particularly when it shifted to opposing the directive. A manufacturer of a diverse range of vehicles, BMW clearly feared the regulatory precedent the directive might set: 'after the horsepower ceiling, what will be next?'[38]

In the end, the Commission agreed to shelve the power limits pending the results of a fresh study on the relationship between power and safety. The study's results, published in 1998, showed virtually no link between the power of superbikes, which tended to be driven by older, more experienced riders, and road accidents, which mostly involved younger, inexperienced bikers. Bangemann was placed in the position of having to tell France, the only EU Member State where superbikes were outlawed, to lift its restrictions on internal market grounds. With visible glee, Barton recalled, 'the Commission told me in private discussions: "look, we will make gestures, but the EP can't win". But I wouldn't back down, and the EP won, completely'.[39]

In a survey of theory-based work on the EU, Caporaso and Keeler (1995: 49) ask: 'How would increasing the power of the European Parliament alter decisionmaking procedures in the EU?' Part of the answer is that new types of transnational citizens or consumer groups are finding a voice in EU decision-making. By nature, bikers are more 'transnational' than are most social groups. The power limits directive was unusual in the way it united what a British official called 'the three EPs: the consumer rights types, the industry MEPs, and the ones who love institutional struggle'.[40] Industry did not lobby hard for the directive, and a senior Commission official recalled, 'the more serious people in DG III knew we had a weak case and were on a hiding to nothing'.[41] But the directive also brought a kind of 'people power' to EU decision-making rarely seen outside of agriculture, leaving a member of Bangemann's *cabinet* spluttering, 'it just shows that those who shout the loudest get the most out of the EP'.[42]

ranging from supranational control of mergers to tax harmonisation, which is quite purely intergovernmental. The internal market programme was mostly in place by the late 1990s, but the regulatory environment was 'confused, more multi-faceted and potentially contradictory' (Armstrong and Bulmer 1998: 317).

The Sub-Systemic Level: Policy Networks Galore

Given the vast sweep of the internal market, there could never be a single 'internal market policy network'. Most European industrial alliances remain narrow ones that tend to form up around economic sectors (pharmaceuticals) or interests (retailers). Particularly as part of a drive to enhance the 'transparency' of EU decision-making (Peterson 1995c), the Commission has tried to construct broad networks, sometimes offering formal representation to a diverse array of interests as it formulates new initiatives. Moreover, collective action at the sub-systemic level has become more nuanced as the EU has shifted towards broad or 'horizontal' policy initiatives, such as company law, consultation with workers (see Exhibit 3.5) or public procurement, which tend to cut across industrial sectors.

The policy network that emerges to shape one major internal market initiative often has quite a different membership from the one that arises for the next. Cross-sectoral lobbies, such as the ERT or EU Committee of the American Chamber of Commerce (Peterson and Cowles 1998) are advantaged by their 'more comprehensive expertise and [ability to] marshal the main argument across a broad swathe of topics' (Wallace and Young 1997: 245). But so may broad consumer and environmental interests, which sometimes link with business interests in what Aspinwall (1998: 201) terms '*ad hoc* collaboration, a sort of disposable collective action'. The generally consensual atmosphere that envelops EU decision-making facilitates such collective action between apparently strange bed-fellows.

In some sectors, the EU does feature routinised bargaining within relatively integrated policy networks. A good example is pharmaceuticals, one of the EU's only world-class advanced technology industries. European firms tend to speak with a single voice, and are supported by close ties to DG III of the Commission and national industry ministries. The result is that the European Federation of Pharmaceutical Industry Associations (EFPIA) is responsible for a significant amount of self-regulation of the industry. What Greenwood (1995b) describes as a 'European business alliance that works' is at the centre of a tightly-integrated policy community which keeps a tight grip on the policy agenda (see Exhibit 3.6).

The energy sector also features a relatively stable and cohesive policy network. Despite a weak legal basis for an 'internal energy market', the Commission has managed to make the EU the primary arena for regulation of the energy industry. Its agenda has been served by the existence of 'an identifiable and small network of people in the EP and the Energy Directorate [DG XVII] that interact between themselves and the key interest groups' (Matláry 1997: 126)

Pharmaceuticals and energy are exceptions more than the rule. Most EU networks are less stable or single-minded and have less grip on the policy agenda. For example, the European air transport industry is made up of (mostly) loss-making airlines, yet many (such as Air France) are symbols of national pride and maintain close ties to their home governments. The ECJ's landmark *Nouvelles Frontières* judgement in 1986 gave the Commission licence to take more robust measures to create an internal market, eventually leading to a significant increase in competition (Westwood Digital 1998). But the EU's aviation policy network features intense rivalries between DGs IV and VII (Transport), and between liberal voices (many British or German) and the Association of European Airlines (AEA), which has worked to preserve the privileges of its members vis-à-vis non-European carriers (Armstrong and Bulmer 1998: 172–4).

Over time, aviation markets have become increasingly globalised but a national champion ethos lives on in many European capitals (Kassim 1995, 1996; Staniland 1995). Neil Kinnock's quest, as Commissioner for Transport, for a mandate to negotiate air transport agreements on behalf of the Union with non-EU states was fiercely contested, and ultimately a failure. EU aviation policy was shaped in weakly-integrated *issue networks*, which featured little capacity for collective action.

Cohesive EU policy networks – particularly ones which link up national networks – sometimes seem to be a prerequisite for effective measures to create a truly internal market. The professions are a good example: the mutual recognition of professional qualifications remains a huge problem. By the mid-1990s, only seven states had laws facilitating the free movement of professionals such as doctors and lawyers. The weakness of the professions in EU decision-making is attributable to their rigid divisions along both sectoral and national lines (Greenwood 1998). Here, as elsewhere, it is striking how little interest representation has shifted to Brussels.

In particular, the sheer pace of EU decision-making after the launch of the 1992 project often overwhelmed national policy networks, with many finding themselves unable to influence decisions which affected them. The decision-making logjam which had long precluded attempts to free trade in some sectors (see Exhibit 3.7) was broken even as the Union's competence was being extended to new, unexplored sectors. Many interest groups

Exhibit 3.5 The 'social dimension': the Works Council directive

The Single European Act brought worker health and safety rules under the internal market, with decision-making on the Council by QMV. It also committed the EC to developing a dialogue between the 'social partners' (industry and labour) at the Community level. Afterwards, EU social policy became a distinct sector in its own right, and certainly one of the Union's most controversial. But it came of age only because of the perceived need to 'flank' the internal market and curb the excesses of mobile and footloose capitalism.

The European Council's adoption (with the UK dissenting) of a Social Charter of Fundamental Social Rights for Workers, in December 1989, seemed a history-making decision at the time. However, little subsequent legislative progress was made, particularly given the need for unanimous Council decisions. To short-circuit British intransigence, the Maastricht negotiations yielded the institutionally messy 'Social Protocol', allowing Member States to legislate in the social arena (by QMV[44]) *without* the participation of the UK, thus establishing a significant precedent for flexible, à la carte decision-making. Maastricht also institutionalised a 'social dialogue': agreements would be sought within a purpose-built series of rolling negotiations between trades unions and employers' representatives, before being ratified by the Council.

The first measure to come under the social dialogue was the long-stalled Directive on Information and Consultation in the Workplace, or the 'Works Council' directive. It aimed to give workers stronger rights to information and consultation about their firms' investment and planning decisions. At one point late in negotiations between the social partners – the European Trades Union Congress (ETUC), the European Centre of Public Enterprises (CEEP) and Union of Industrial and Employers' Confederations of Europe (UNICE) – a deal seemed within reach. However, UNICE came under intense British pressure to withhold its agreement and the talks collapsed (Greenwood 1997: 106). Afterwards, the Social Affairs Council picked up the pieces by passing the Works Council directive in June 1994 (unanimously, with Portugal abstaining). The next measure tabled under the Social Protocol, on parental leave, was successfully agreed by the social partners in late 1995 and nodded through the Social Affairs Council (as an 'A' point) in March 1996.

The social dialogue clearly has the potential to push EU social legislation forward. In particular, it creates a coherent, sub-systemic bargaining arena, which truly deserves the title 'policy network'. The social partners are granted a formal role in shaping legislation as well as the chance to agree measures that political actors, for whatever reason, cannot (see Geyer and Springer

→

→

1998). Of course, policy-shaping decisions mean little when policies cannot be 'set' by the Council and, by all accounts, the switch to QMV was crucial in moving the Works Council directive and subsequent social measures forward.

In key respects, EU social policy has developed along a neo-functionalist path at the super-systemic level: it may be viewed as a result of spill-over from the internal market and incremental steps forward in institution-building. Yet, sharp disagreements remain about whether reinforced capacity for decision-making, via innovations such as the 'social dialogue', can translate to stronger social policies. Streeck (1997) castigates the Works Council directive for its modest ambitions and predicts that it will actually erode relatively high standards for workplace representation in northern Member States. For example, Renault's decision in March 1997 to close down its factory in Vilvoorde, outside Brussels, was taken without consulting its 3100 employees.[45] Afterwards, 40 000 workers from eight Member States marched on Brussels wielding banners with slogans such as 'This Europe – No Thanks'.[46]

EU social policy continues to be mainly voluntaristic and far less developed than national social policies, particularly those in Germany or Sweden. Writing in the early 1990s, Majone (1993: 115) observed that 'the Community remains, and will very possibly remain, a "welfare laggard"'. Yet, he also marvelled at the Union's legislative progress on quality of life issues left relatively untouched at the national level, such as consumer protection and gender equality. His optimistic vision of a 'natural division of labour' in social policy between the EU, national and other levels of government (Majone 1993: 168) was certainly not uncontested. By the end of 1998, the social dialogue process had produced legislation only twice, with employers rejecting the invitation to negotiate four times.

But the Works Council directive at least offered the prospect of a more transnational labour movement in Europe (see Falkner 1996; Greenwood 1997: 160–61; Marginson and Sisson 1998). The election of left-of-centre governments in the UK, Germany and France in 1997–8 boosted the prospects of EU social policy, with the President of UNICE, Zygmunt Tyszkiewicz, complaining that (under QMV) the Council had gone from 28 'pro-employer' votes to only eight.[47] Meanwhile, EMU promised more transparency in levels of pay: one survey suggested that a majority of European multinationals expected that the Euro eventually would lead to pan-European pay agreements (Towers Perrin 1998).

The Works Council directive may prove to be a turning point in the development of EU social policy. Alternatively, its legacy may be that weak EU agreements, after long and complex machinations, are no match for the power of global markets. The 'European model' of capitalism (Ross 1995; Atkinson 1997) hangs in the balance.

Exhibit 3.6 Pharmaceuticals: a policy community with muscle

The EFPIA, or European Federation of Pharmaceutical Industry Associations, is a 'superfederation' of national federations. It is also one of the most powerful, well-resourced and single-minded industrial lobbyists in Brussels. Formed in 1978, it defused the threat of transnational regulation of the European pharmaceuticals industry by the EU. It now acts as a sort of self-regulating agency for the industry as a whole.

To some extent, the EFPIA reproduces long-standing corporatist patterns at the national level (see Greenwood and Ronit 1991). However, its success also is a product of its unique internal decision-making mechanisms. The main producer states – the UK, France, Germany, Italy and Switzerland – form an executive committee and thus wield more power over EFPIA than do national associations from the Netherlands or Portugal. The EFPIA works on the basis of consensus whenever possible, but majority decisions are taken if necessary. A considerable amount of discretion is delegated to the Federation's secretariat in Brussels, which has a 'fast-track' procedure for making decisions when they are needed quickly (Greenwood 1995b: 40–1).

The EFPIA has had several notable successes, which mostly have involved talking the Commission *out* of proposing new regulations. When a restrictive pricing directive was mooted in the mid-1980s, the EFPIA persuaded the Commission that it should be more concerned about the overall health of the industry than with prices. Perhaps the 'greatest testimony to the EFPIA's influence' (Greenwood 1995b: 43) was its ability to agree a self-regulatory code of practice on medicine selling, which operates with the sanction of the Commission.

By no means does the EFPIA always get its way. But the pharmaceuticals industry employs nearly half a million EU citizens and generates a collective trade surplus for the Union of around €8 billion per year. The EU is home to five of the world's 10 largest spenders on R&D in the sector: Glaxo Wellcome, SmithKline Beecham and Zeneca (UK), Astra (Sweden) and Schering (Germany). The European industry as a whole has generated more than half of all new chemicals patented since 1970 (Greenwood 1995b: 42). In short, the pharmaceuticals industry is one of the EU's few clearly 'world-class' high-tech industries. Its power is structural in nature. Given its ability to speak (usually) with a single voice, it would be surprising if it wielded any less influence in EU decision-making.

scrambled to try to find a voice in Brussels, particularly groups which feared that a 'policy network detrimental to their interests was hardening' (Aspinwall and Greenwood 1998: 24).

Being 'out of the loop' when policies were formulated carried higher potential costs after the mid-1980s. Most post-SEA Council presidencies, at the urging of the Council's General Secretariat, went to great lengths to avoid having to put internal market questions to a vote. Nonetheless, when QMV *was* applied, decisions were rarely unanimous: by one count, 91 out of 223 Council decisions taken between 1989 and 1993[52] (most of which concerned the internal market) saw Member States outvoted in ways that caused them considerable difficulties. Thus stopping a proposal meant lobbying much more widely than in the past.

Meanwhile, the legislative hyperactivity of the 1992 project made all EU institutions (especially the Commission) and many private actors more reliant on consultants to provide specialised expertise and help stay on top of very rapid developments. An elite of established lobbyists began to emerge as 'Overlapping groups of consultants worked for the Commission, member governments and firms . . . [and] the conventional delineation between public policy-makers and private influencers became blurred' (Wallace and Young 1996: 142). The combination of QMV and the rush to complete the internal market meant that new policies were often 'set' without the traditional long delays and fastidious scrutiny. More important decisions were taken at the sub-systemic level, when proposals were first formulated, than ever before.

Afterwards, particularly during the recession of the early 1990s, decision-making became more routinised, national positions more defensive and scrutiny of proposals more finicky. In particular, it became harder to forge agreements which appeared to extend the EU's authority. The memberships of many policy networks stabilised, with several experiencing an outright 'shake-out' (Mazey and Richardson 1993a).

Then Maastricht brought the co-decision procedure. It clearly empowered the Parliament, but not *only* at the latest stages of decision-making. At the sub-systemic level, policy networks became far more open to MEPs and their supporters at the early stages of the policy process. Council presidencies often went to great lengths to consult key MEPs informally after a Commission proposal was tabled. The Commission had powerful new incentives to be sure that key MEPs were 'on board' as proposals were formulated and shaped.

The application of the co-decision procedure has enhanced the importance of policy networks as arenas for informal bargaining on most internal market questions. The procedure is complex and potentially time-consuming. Above all, co-decision is not tied to 'a raft of consensus-based legislation or an overall deadline, such as "1992"' (Westlake

Exhibit 3.7 The politics of chocolate

'Why must Eurocrats regulate our chocolate?' Such sentiments were widely aired in the 1980s when one (failed) proposal sought to relabel milk chocolate, of the kind produced by most large UK confectionery firms, as 'vegelate' to highlight its inclusion of vegetable fats instead of cocoa. The case of chocolate shows that the EU often cannot win when it tries to create a single market in the face of rival industrial pressures and divergent national tastes.

The chocolate war began in 1973, when the Community enlarged from six to nine. In the original six, only 'pure' chocolate made using cocoa butter was licensed for sale. Many producers in the new Member States substituted vegetable fats for cocoa butter. Consequently, the 1973 Chocolate Directive (73/241) exempted these manufacturers from existing licensing rules while banning exports of their products. Similar exemptions later had to be granted to chocolate-makers in Portugal, Austria, Finland and Sweden. Thus there was no single market in chocolate: if a producer, such as Nestlé, wished to produce chocolate in France, it had to use cocoa butter, thus altering the recipe for popular brands such as Kit Kat.

In 1996, the Commission began shaping a fresh proposal to create an internal market for chocolate. It deemed that Member States themselves could allow 'their' producers to use vegetable fats up to a limit of 5 per cent of all ingredients. The proposal encountered stiff opposition in the college of Commissioners: representing development interests, João de Deus Pinheiro protested that the directive would hurt African cocoa producers. The French Commissioners, Yves Thibault de Silguy and Edith Cresson, joined forces with Belgium's Van Miert to press the case for favouring 'pure' chocolate. Santer and the Consumer Affairs Commissioner, Emma Bonino, expressed misgivings about sanctifying different market standards.[48] Finally, Bangemann brokered agreement on a compromise: labels would list all ingredients, and draw attention to the presence of any 'vegetable fats other than cocoa butter'.

After the Parliament waded in under co-decision, its Development Committee recommended outright rejection of the proposal. So did continental manufacturers of 'pure' chocolate, who argued that producers

$\longrightarrow$

1994a: 91). Co-decision has made the EU a more pluralistic system of government, but has also increased its reliance on informal deals and backroom bargaining.

Furthermore, the Union remains almost wholly dependent on policy networks for effective implementation. The use of the directive as a main legislative tool of EU decision-making means that many decisions, including many which determine policy content, often still need to be taken *after* the EU itself decides. Enforcement of EU rules remains patchy: by the late 1990s the Commission (1998d) was receiving nearly 1000 complaints a year

→

such as Nestlé or Cadbury were likely to go beyond the 5 per cent limit since it was impossible to measure the amount of vegetable fat in chocolate. The 'pure' chocolate advocacy coalition warned: 'if we are not careful the building of Europe will consider the requirements of the multinationals over those of developing nations and consumers'.[49]

In contrast, the EP's Environment Committee (whose remit stretched to consumer affairs) recommended acceptance of the proposal, but only if 'warning labels' appeared on the front of all chocolate bars made with vegetable fats. The EP's Paul Lannoye, a Belgian Green, said 'the right of the consumer to correct information'[50] was the key, especially because chocolate was often purchased on impulse.

On its first reading, the EP voted through the labelling provisions as well as (amongst others) an amendment requiring a study of the directive's impact on cocoa producers. The Commission agreed to make some changes to the directive, but rejected the 'warning label' requirement, and denied that the directive would 'modify the economic situation' of cocoa producers.[51] The 1998 British Council presidency worked hard to get a deal on the directive, but were unable to shift any members of a blocking minority which included France, Spain and the Benelux countries.

The politics of chocolate were a microcosm of much broader struggles over food policy. Bangemann intended the draft chocolate directive to be one of the last 'vertical' directives, containing specifications on individual products (or 'foodstuffs'). However, Bangemann's efforts to draw together most EU legislation into a horizontal 'framework directive', setting out basic definitions and principles, ran aground owing to opposition from the Agriculture Commissioner, Franz Fischler and DG VI (Agriculture). The CAP policy network rallied behind a broader 'stable to table' approach, encompassing animal welfare, the environmental impact of farming, and so on, thus preventing Bangemann and DG III from 'poaching' food policy. Few other areas of EU policy are more bitterly fought over, and none affects European citizens more directly.

about violations of the internal market, with a majority aimed at Germany, France or Italy, and only about a quarter discovered by the Commission through its own investigations. Member States occasionally tabled proposals to make penalties tougher for violators of EU rules (see Poncet and Barbier 1989; Lamassoure 1995). Yet, as the Commission (1997a: 3) admitted in its *Action Plan*, the internal market could only be preserved through concerted action by 'networks of national and Commission officials dealing with individual areas of regulation' (Wallace and Young 1996: 144).

Conclusion

The Single European Act made history because it made the internal market possible despite the many highly contentious decisions that had to be taken to complete it. The internal market programme, presented as a single package, prevented governments from 'defecting' even when compromises were difficult to find (Fligstein and Brantley 1995). Nearly all of the 282 proposals contained in the Commission's White Paper yielded EU legislation. A range of EU 'flanking policies' – including new cohesion, environment, social and research policies – were constructed to enhance the internal market or compensate for its negative effects. In many respects, the 1992 project was a raging success, and one of the most important achievements of post-war Europe.

Still, the internal market is a fragile achievement. 'Path dependency' may apply to most EU policies, but the internal market has the potential to unravel through *non-decisions* as much as through conscious choices. Accelerating rates of technological change mean that product standards change quickly, thus threatening to erode the gains of the 'new approach'. EU Member States often create fresh barriers to trade by over-regulating at the national level. In 1996, Bangemann pointed out that the EU had been the source of 415 internal market measures in 35 years, while Member States had notified the Commission of 1136 new technical rules in the three years after 1992.[53] The internal market's durability depends on continued vigilance, exhortation and political commitment.

In many sectors the EU still lacked a 'single' market even as it prepared to launch a single currency. Public procurement remained a big problem: even after 1992, less than 5 per cent of public contracts in the Union were awarded to firms in countries outside the Member State where contracts were tendered. A single market for insurance remained a distant ambition. A long, bloody effort to develop a Europe-wide electrical plug and socket system collapsed in 1995, leaving Europe with about 20 different systems, most of them incompatible with one another. The Commission (1998b: 1) warned that the 'gradual downward trend' in state aid had apparently 'come to an end'.

Above all, whatever additional economic growth was fostered by the internal market, it failed to cure the 'European disease': high unemployment. The US economy created around 30 million new private sector jobs between 1974 and 1994. The net total for the EU was zero. Global competitiveness league tables, which generally showed wide disparities between EU countries (see Table 3.4), seemed to expose the notion of a 'Europe without frontiers' as a fantasy. One such study's main author noted that EU countries assigned very different priority to market

Table 3.4 *Global competiveness league table (1998)*

1	United States	14	Germany
2	Singapore		
3	Hong Kong	17	Sweden
4	Netherlands	21	France
5	Finland	22	Austria
6	Norway	23	Belgium
7	Switzerland		
8	Denmark	27	Spain
9	Luxembourg	29	Portugal
10	Canada	30	Italy
11	Ireland		
12	UK	36	Greece

Source: *World Competitiveness Yearbook 1998*, Institute for Management Development, Switzerland.[55] *Reproduced with permission.*

mechanisms or social consensus, 'in flagrant contradiction to the Maastricht criteria' for EMU.[54]

The prevailing wisdom of the post-Maastricht period was that the 1992 project had failed to deliver on its promises. European voters became increasingly sceptical of economic liberalisation, and even began to associate the EU itself with rising unemployment. In fact, popular views of the internal market remained surprisingly stable and public support had 'reached some sort of equilibrium' by the mid-1990s (Anderson 1995: 127).

Yet falling public support for the EU as an institution may have been a consequence of the way in which the internal market was constructed in the post-SEA period. While the internal market was (and remains) extremely broad as a sector, the representation of interests was often narrow and restricted in the frenzy to create a 'Europe without frontiers'. Although the EU embraced more 'horizontal' policy initiatives over time, many key decisions after 1987 were taken in closed circles of ministers, officials and policy networks. Internal market directives were often transposed into national law using subordinate legislation which attracted little debate in parliaments or the press (Wallace and Young 1996). One plausible explanation for declining public support for the EU, despite apparently solid support for the internal market, was that the 1992 project at least promised benefits, of one kind or another, for virtually all (in a way, for example, that EMU never could). Decision-making to construct the internal market, however, was often the domain of remarkably few.

Chapter 4

External Trade Policy

The external face of the internal market
Making history in trade policy
Setting EU trade policy
Policy networks and trade policy
Conclusion

Civilian superpower? Economic giant? Political pygmy? Much controversy surrounds the question of how the European Union should be characterised as an international actor (see Peterson and Sjursen 1998a). There is no question that the EU is a major trading power.[1] The Union accounts for about 40 per cent of all global trade. More than half of all EU trade is internal 'trade' within the internal market, but the Union is the single largest trading bloc in the world. For Sir Leon Brittan (1996: 20), the Trade Commissioner for most of the 1990s, trade policy 'has been perhaps the finest advertisement for the pooling of national sovereignty since the European Community came into existence'.

At first glance, EU decision-making on trade seems dominated by a small number of mainly technocratic actors. A second glance reveals that external trade policy has become increasingly politicised and thus contested: a diagram showing how and by whom EU trade policy is influenced ends up looking like felled power lines after a hurricane (Woolcock and Hodges 1996: 303). A third glance exposes very deep divisions – particularly between the Adam Smith-inspired British and Colbertiste French[2] – that emerge almost every time a trade policy decision is taken. Two veteran EU trade negotiators concede that 'negotiations between the Member States can sometimes be far more gruelling than negotiations with third countries' (Paemen and Bensch 1995: 95).

Naturally, the question arises: is the Union a force for global free trade or for protectionism? Many economists, including Krugman (1991, 1994), insist that all trade blocs, including the EU, cause 'trade diversion' – diverting trade from 'natural' patterns in a truly free market – and thus distort the global economy. Yet, once the EU has agreed its own internal position, international trade negotiations become far more efficient. The Union facilitates 'side-payments' of various kinds that can induce Member States to forgo protectionism (see Jacquemin and Sapir 1991; Devuyst 1995). Hanson (1998: 56) claims that 'the institutional context in which trade policy is made' gives the EU 'a systematic bias toward liberalization over increased protection'. In any case, the EU's contribution to the international trading order can only be gauged after a close examination of trade policy decision-making.

The External Face of the Internal Market

As a customs union, the EU *must* be a single entity in global trade or the internal market cannot function (see Eeckhout 1994). For example, there can be no truly single European market for motor cars if individual member states, such as (say) Italy, maintain import quotas on Japanese cars (see Exhibit 4.1). In the absence of internal EU border controls, a Japanese company could avoid the quotas simply by importing cars into France and transporting them to Italy.

EU external trade policy is built on two girders: the Common External Tariff, a common tax applied to all foreign products entering the EU's market, and the Common Commercial Policy (CCP), which obliges Member States to negotiate and sign deals as one with non-EU states. These measures, negotiated under Article 133,[7] must be compatible with international trade rules by dint of the Community's collective membership of the World Trade Organisation (WTO).

Article 133 is a unique, interesting and – by common consent – badly-drafted section of the Treaty (Devuyst 1992). It gives the EU exclusive competence in commercial policy, but never defines commercial policy. The Commission is granted sole rights to negotiate on the behalf of the EU, within the limits of Council 'mandates' and in consultation with a 'special committee' of the Council, but the scope of such mandates is left unspecified. In any event, the 'Article 133 Committee' is one of the most powerful and active of all Council committees. Its role is particularly significant because Council decisions to conclude trade agreements are taken by qualified majority voting (QMV), at least according to Treaty. In practice, few major agreements are concluded without consensus on the Council, although the 'shadow' of QMV encourages compromise.

Two other articles of the Treaty help the EU use its economic power as a political tool. Article 300 allows the EU to conclude trade and economic co-operation agreements that offer a foreign state (or a group of them) a privileged trade relationship. The EU now has so many co-operation agreements that foreign signatories often find that their 'privileges' are also offered to many other third countries. Still, most agreements also contain some type of special concession or aid (see Exhibit 4.2).

Sometimes the Union goes further and concludes 'association agreements', on the basis of Article 310. Highly prioritised states receive a variety of prizes – political dialogue, technical assistance, aid – of which

Exhibit 4.1 Cars: 'Elements of Consensus', lots of dissension

The automobile sector may well be the most politically sensitive industry in Europe. The Union's industry and all of its offshoots employ more than 4 million workers, accounting for as much as 15 per cent of industrial employment (Holmes and McGowan 1997: 160). The car industry is dominated by 'national champion' producers that have relatively low sales outside their home markets.[3] It is also plagued by chronic overcapacity: even after Daimler-Benz and Chrysler announced the biggest industrial merger in history in 1998, one commentator noted 'there are [still] 20 significant manufacturers in an industry which does not really need more than half-a-dozen'.[4] Europe's car-makers face extremely stiff foreign (especially Asian) competition.

The so-called 'Elements of Consensus' agreement, signed between Japan and the EU in 1991, may well be 'the most important quota arrangement in the history of global trade'.[5] The deal was clearly needed after the 1992 project made national import quotas on Japanese cars (especially those maintained by France and Italy) unsustainable. 'Elements of Consensus' and the decision-making process that gave birth to it are both fascinating, and have been amply treated elsewhere (see McLaughlin 1994; Mason 1994). Here we highlight three features of this very strange agreement.

First, 'Elements of Consensus' reveals how the EU is often forced to resort to informal understandings to settle its own internal differences, since formal agreements usually create clear winners and losers. 'Elements' was never published or formally adopted by the Council. The Commission has even stated that the Union has no agreement that restricts Japanese car imports (Holmes and McGowan 1997: 164).

Second, 'Elements of Consensus' reveals that car politics are high politics: nothing very important is likely to be decided unless a way is found to depoliticise decision-making. In 1991, the political split on the Council was a familiar one, with southern Member States (led by France) opposing primarily

→

special trade concessions are usually only one. Often association agreements will hold out the prospect of an eventual free trade area with the EU. They may even promise eventual EU membership, as in the case of the 'Europe agreements' with most Central and East European countries (CEECs).

Association agreements require unanimous Council decisions and are subject to the assent procedure, requiring a majority vote by the EP. As such, they are usually agreed only after long, painful struggles, which feature plenty of opportunity for EU producers to demand protection from

→

Germany, whose producers – Mercedes, BMW and Volkswagen – were competitive globally (even in Japan) and feared retaliation from a protectionist agreement. A finely-balanced compromise, brokered largely by Jacques Delors' *cabinet*, had to be sold to France, whose position was split between its liberal Minister of Industry, Roger Faroux, and *Colbertiste* Prime Minister, Edith Cresson. Caught between them, the French European Affairs Minister, Elisabeth Guigou, appealed directly to President Mitterrand who put 'the imperative of Community consensus' (Mason 1994: 445) above his concerns for Renault and Peugeot, and accepted 'Elements'.

After the deal was done, further decision-making was delegated to twice-annual negotiations with Japan's Ministry of International Trade and Industry. Holmes and McGowan (1997: 164) argue that 'it is these that set trade policy with Japan, not the wording of what was said or written in 1991'. The Commission clearly leads the negotiations from the EU's side, as it often does in trade policy when the Council is so split that it cannot effectively or coherently challenge existing EU policy.

Third, and finally, the 'Elements of Consensus' shows that bargaining within policy networks is usually crucial when informal deals are struck in EU decision-making. The 1992 project forced the European automobile industry to engage in considerable collective action, while avoiding collusion, to identify and defend their collective interests. A critical step was the reconstitution in early 1991 of the industry's primary association, the *Comité des Constructeurs du Marché Commun* (CCMC), which took all decisions by unanimity. The CCMC was superseded by a new Association of European Automobile Manufacturers (ACEA), which adopted a 75 per cent majority voting rule, thus isolating Jacques Calvet of Peugeot in his opposition to anything but the (highly protectionist) status quo. Calvet became a rallying voice for Eurosceptics in France and elsewhere during the recession of the early 1990s. Despite his frequent attacks on 'Elements of Consensus' as 'unacceptable and suicidal for the European car industry',[6] the agreement proved as durable as it was vague, and it held.

low-cost eastern imports. In the case of the Europe agreements, most eastern governments emerged disappointed, bewildered and feeling as if the EU's rhetorical commitments to assist them were betrayed by its protectionist instincts (see Saryusz-Wolski 1994).

Besides co-operation and association agreements, the EU also operates a 'Generalised System of Preferences' (GSP), a relic from the early 1970s when the Community granted tariff concessions on selected manufactured imports from certain developing countries. The GSP has never worked very well: only the most advanced developing countries have benefited very

Exhibit 4.2 The EU and the developing world: more trade, less aid

The EU emerged at the end of the 20th century as one of the world's most important donors of development aid, committing about 0.51 per cent of its GNP each year to aid, compared to Japan's 0.32 per cent and the United States' miserly 0.15 per cent (Piening 1997: 190). However, the EU was hardly a 'single actor' in aid policy (see Grilli 1993). Europe accounted for more than half of all aid donated by industrialised countries, but the Community's own budget was the source of only 15 per cent of the combined total offered by the EU and its Member States.

Nonetheless, the Union presents an ostensibly single face to much of the developing world via the Lomé convention, the most developed of all EU co-operation agreements. It offers special aid and trade privileges to former European colonies, earmarking nearly €15 billion for the European Development Fund (EDF) for 1996–2000, to be split amongst 71 signatories to Lomé, known as the ACP (African, Caribbean and Pacific) states. Lomé is unique in terms of its extensive (and perhaps wasteful) institutional structures for promoting 'partnership' between EU and ACP states: its own bilateral Council of Ministers meets at least once a year, and its Committee of Ambassadors and Joint Assembly of MEPs and ACP parliamentarians meet twice annually (see Nugent 1994: 408). Lomé is not without critics (see Babarinde 1995), but it is certainly more long-term in focus and offers aid with fewer strings (such as 'tied' contracts, which require recipients to buy

⟶

much, with the EU often allocating quotas late and arbitrarily, and sometimes punishing exporters for being successful (Brenton *et al.* 1997: 329). By the late 1990s, tariffs on most manufactured goods had been cut so low by successive global trade rounds that the GSP had become an anachronism. More generally, non-tariff barriers, resulting from 'behind the border' public policies such as health standards, business taxation or public procurement, had become a far more important focus for all trade policies. One study even suggested that the administrative cost of collecting duties on imports into the EU would exceed their value by the year 2000 (Federation of Swedish Industries 1996).

The policy instruments available to the EU, and rules governing how they are used, conspire to create an EU trade policy that often defies economic logic. Trade theory tells us that the best way to fight a market distortion is to eliminate it at its source. In principle, international trade rules are meant to do away with such distortions where they occur. In practice, EU instruments such as safeguard clauses (which limit foreign imports) or anti-dumping measures (which make imports more expensive)

→

from donors) compared with other western aid policies. Its defenders insist that 'many other regions of the world are seeking to emulate' the Lomé relationship (Lowe 1996: 28).

Yet, with Lomé IV set to expire in 2000, the EU signalled its desire to give less aid to Lomé governments and to work towards new free trade agreements with ACP states. Proposals for Lomé V departed from the existing mixture of aid and trade concessions and focused instead on encouraging structural economic reforms in Lomé states and measures to attract inward investment. Fears that the EU was abandoning its poorest southern partners to the rigours of globalised markets were partially appeased when the 1998 British presidency of the Council tabled a compromise extending 'equivalent treatment' to the existing position under Lomé of states which proved unable to join new free trade agreements with the EU.

In weighing up the EU's contribution to North–South relations, it is impossible not to notice that the Union's share of world trade – 7 per cent in 1970, but 25 per cent by the late 1990s (excluding internal EU trade) – has expanded primarily at the expense of less-developed countries. Even if Lomé is more progressive than other western aid programmes, it does not compensate for the damage done to poorer, southern countries by other EU policies (particularly the CAP) and it did little by itself to alleviate grinding poverty, particularly in Africa. The Lomé of the 21st century is difficult to foresee.

continue to be deployed frequently. They do *not* eliminate market distortions at their point of origin (Vosgerau 1994).

A hallmark of the EU's neo-liberal consensus is an acceptance that 'trade policy's broad objective is to progress steadily towards free trade' (Buiges *et al.* 1995: xii). Yet EU trade policy is often schizophrenic, with one decision rewarding consumers and another punishing them. Some sectors are liberalised as others receive increased protection. Progress towards free trade is thus unsteady and sometimes subject to setbacks, particularly when specific trade issues become politicised, as frequently occurs in a post-Cold War world where trade and investment have taken on higher political salience (see Peterson 1996a; Smith 1998).

When EU trade policy becomes politicised, the result is often French leadership of an alliance of mainly southern Member States that opposes trade liberalisation almost instinctively. France is usually joined by Italy, Spain, Portugal and Greece – as well as Austria and Belgium – in a coalition which wields 47 votes on the Council: more than enough for a blocking minority. Usually in opposition, the 'free traders' are led by

Germany and the UK, with support from the Netherlands, Sweden and Denmark. However, this split between Member States simplifies considerably. For example, Germany often has been nearly as reticent as France on proposals to liberalise trade in agriculture, as evidenced by German support for French moves in 1998 to remove agriculture from a proposed free trade accord with *Mercosur*, a customs union including Brazil, Argentina, Paraguay and Uruguay.

At the national level in Europe, most parliaments play a minor role in trade policy. The EU mirrors national practice: the European Parliament must give its assent to association agreements and most other important international agreements (see Corbett *et al.* 1995: 216–17), but it is otherwise something of a bystander. The real push and pull of trade policy decision-making is between the Commission and the Council. All trade policy decisions must begin with a proposal by the Commission. Generally, a decision to reject a Commission proposal leaves the status quo ante in place, without adding to the EU's *acquis*, or its rights and obligations, in trade policy. This result may often suit national ministers, but leave the Commission powerless and without a policy to uphold vis-à-vis the Union's trading partners. Thus the Commission naturally seeks compromise, even a weak one, and is often accused of adopting the positions of the most protectionist Member States and generalising them in somewhat weakened form over the EU as a whole (see Winters 1994). The Commission's rationale is often that highly protectionist national policies are avoided and the Union's unity is maintained. The strong will to speak with one voice in trade policy has led to radical liberalisation rarely, and mildly attenuated protection far more frequently.

Making History in Trade Policy

The development of the EU's competence in trade policy seems relatively easy to explain in theoretical terms. For neo-functionalists, the emergence of an integrated EU trade policy is a clear case of 'spill-over' from the internal market.[8] For Moravcsik (1994: 27) and other intergovernmentalists, Member States and the European Court of Justice (ECJ) have been allies in placing 'all international agreements under exclusive Community competence'. Doing so 'strengthens the state', and helps free national executives from domestic political and sectoral pressures. The ECJ acquiesces because it is generally predisposed to closer European integration. The resulting system of trade policy decision-making is dominated by technocrats. Even important revisions to the system, such as those mandated by the Maastricht Treaty, have been relatively uncontroversial (see Devuyst 1992).

This cosy consensus was shattered in the mid-1990s, for three fundamental reasons. First, the wider international framework was transformed, as the General Agreement on Tariffs and Trade (GATT) yielded a major dose of liberalisation and was superseded by the new, stronger World Trade Organisation (WTO). Second, the Commission and Council clashed vigorously over whether the EU had exclusive competence over new trade issues, such as services. Third, trade policy became 'high politics', as international competitiveness became increasingly identified with 'security'.

The Uruguay Round

The trade policy story of the 1990s was the Uruguay Round of the GATT (see Exhibit 4.3), which exposed the EU's institutions as ill suited to highly politicised trade negotiations. Eight years of tough dealing finally yielded agreement, but the inclusion of agriculture in the Round and US insistence on substantial CAP reforms provoked combat between the Council (particularly the Agriculture Council) and the Commission. As a major trading power, the EU's interest in a GATT deal was clear, and the Commission was determined to get one, even if it meant concessions on agriculture.

One upshot was the US–EU 'pre-agreement' on agriculture, named after the building in Washington where it was signed in November 1992. 'Pre-agreement' meant that the 'Blair House' accord required ratification by the Council. With considerable understatement, Devuyst (1995: 452) found 'that communication between the Commission and the member states [was] not always optimal' during the Uruguay Round. The Blair House accord was initialled by the Commission after virtually no consultation with the Council. After repeatedly denouncing Blair House during his 1993 electoral campaign, the French Prime Minister, Edouard Balladur, insisted 'there is no European position until the Council of Ministers decides'.[9] Balladur even threatened to invoke the Luxembourg compromise 'to see off intolerable pressure'.[10] France was the most vocal critic, but Blair House was also condemned by Ireland as well as Belgium's Prime Minister, Jean-Luc Dehaene, who described the Commission's offer of concessions as a 'tactical blunder', which had to be 'corrected'.[11]

The Blair House accord emerged only after repeated, brutal, behind-the-scenes clashes *within* the Commission. In June 1990, Ray MacSharry, the Commissioner for Agriculture, lashed out publicly at Frans Andriessen, insisting that he, not the Commissioner for Trade, was 'in charge of agricultural negotiations'.[12] Two years later, MacSharry dramatically (if temporarily) resigned his post after accusing Delors of meddling on the side of France in the negotiations on agriculture. The more general point is

Exhibit 4.3 The Uruguay Round

The Uruguay Round was the most ambitious set of international trade negotiations in history. The EU had much to gain or lose, as a global trading power with powerful export industries in areas central to the Round (especially services). The Round's successful conclusion in late 1993 was probably as significant for global trade as was the original creation of the GATT. The Union's role as instigator, facilitator and (nearly) spoiler of an agreement, was crucial. Leaving aside agriculture (see Exhibit 5.3), the EU was an effective negotiator on most matters of substance (see Woolcock and Hodges 1996). Yet, there was little evidence of any clear, overall EU strategy and the Union was severely wounded by the negotiations.

Part of the problem was that the Commission repeatedly 'got ahead' of the Council as it strained to find a basis for agreement. In particular, it overstepped its mandate at the 1990 GATT summit, held near the Heysel football stadium in Brussels, which was meant to produce a final agreement to end the Round. With the negotiations deadlocked, the Commission began making informal offers (particularly on agriculture) in exchange for desired concessions. National EU ministers cooled their heels on the margins of the negotiations, with nothing to do but wait for the Commission to emerge. EU ministers only learned of the Commission's tactics from the Australian delegation, sending many into a cold fury. The Council firmly reprimanded the Commission, and even threatened to place an official from the Italian presidency in each negotiating group (Woolcock and Hodges 1996: 315). The summit broke up without agreement, and with the EU shouldering the blame for the 'Heysel bloodbath' (Paemen and Bensch 1995: 177–89).

A separate set of problems arose from the lack of a formal Council of Trade Ministers. The EU sorely needed some intermediary (besides the Committee of Permanent Representatives: COREPER) between the technocratic Article 133 Committee and the General Council of Foreign Ministers, particularly when the latter became distracted by dramatic geopolitical changes in 1989–91. Without such an intermediary, the Council was often unable to take decisions quickly or respond adequately when the negotiations demanded them. One upshot was that EU farm ministers retained effective veto power for much of the Round, even though agriculture accounted for only about 8 per cent of the EU's exports.

For several beleaguered Council presidencies, the only solution was to hold so-called 'jumbo councils', bringing together foreign and farm (and sometimes

→

→

trade) ministers. The record of jumbo councils was decidedly mixed. The session held in 1990 just before the 'Heysel bloodbath' endorsed a mandate so narrow that the Commission could hardly avoid exceeding it. In contrast, a jumbo council convened in September 1993 seemed a masterstroke by the Belgian presidency. Crucially, it was billed as a non-voting 'discussion' of the EU's position,[13] which neither tied the Commission's hands nor isolated any Member State. The Council gave the new Balladur government the opportunity to talk tough in the face of severe domestic pressures from French intellectuals, economists and (especially) farmers who opposed the liberalisation of trade in agriculture, audio-visual products and other sectors (Devuyst 1995: 452). It also gave the French Foreign Minister, Alain Juppé, a relished opportunity to tell Leon Brittan that his views were discountable because the Trade Commissioner was 'only a bureaucrat'. Nonetheless, the French were given just enough political cover – in an agreement to seek 'interpretations, amplifications and additions' to the Blair House agreement on agricultural trade – to placate them. Generally, the shifting of the negotiations from the EU to the GATT, where states are more dominant, allowed high-level French decision-makers to break free of the constraints imposed by the French agricultural policy community (see Epstein 1997).

Formally, the French did not enjoy a veto over the Uruguay Round.[14] However, the Uruguay Round required the EU to take a number of decisions which 'made history', particularly concerning the CAP. Unusually for trade policy, it touched the highest political levels. The 1993 Belgian presidency established the principle (accepted by the Commission) that any Council decision on a final settlement to the Uruguay Round would have to be taken unanimously, and not by QMV.

Perhaps above all, the Uruguay Round revealed that the EU is usually as powerful as it is unified in international trade diplomacy. The final Uruguay Round agreement was broadly favourable to the EU, but only because the Union kept its unity at crucial stages in the negotiations. The Round also seems, in retrospect, a conspicuous illustration of the point that the EU is often less protectionist than the sum total of its Member States. EU enthusiasts were quick to argue that 'Without the European Union, there would have been no Uruguay Round. Had the Member States negotiated individually I cannot believe that in fact global consensus would ever have been achieved' (Sutherland 1995: 9). Even the EU's detractors had difficulty refuting the argument.

that the Uruguay Round put EU trade policy at the very forefront of political agendas in European political capitals. It also strained both the Commission's political neutrality and its collective responsibility.

The Institutional Battleground

The battle for control of EU trade policy did not subside after the Uruguay Round ended. The central question was whether the EU had exclusive competence in 'new' areas of trade, particularly services and intellectual property.[15] The stakes were high, as services accounted for about two-thirds of the EU's total economy. The importance of intellectual property was reflected in the European recording industry's estimate that it lost about €1 billion a year to piracy.

In 1994, the Court ruled that the Uruguay Round Final Act was a 'mixed agreement', and thus the Commission would have to share responsibility with Member States for negotiating agreements on 'new' trade issues. The ECJ decision was full of nuances, such as the proviso that services transmitted electronically across frontiers – including telecommunications and financial services – were like goods, and thus subject to exclusive Community competence. In an extraordinary statement, the Court also predicted that

> interminable discussions will ensue to determine whether a given matter falls within the competence of the Community. . . The Community's unity of action *vis-à-vis* the rest of the world will thus be undermined and its negotiating position greatly weakened.[16]

Still, the Court essentially backed the Council in its battle with the Commission. The ECJ's decision both made history and cast doubt on the thesis that the Court is an ally in creating an integrated EU trade policy that 'strengthens the state'. It also raised thorny questions about how the EU would be represented in the WTO, after many years of the Commission taking the lead in representing the Community in the GATT, often without a clear legal basis (Footer 1998: 321).

The 1996–7 IGC gave the Commission another chance to argue for a clear, exclusive Community competence in 'new' trade areas. The Commission lobbied Member States hard, insisting that all international trade deals in future would involve services and thus Member States would have veto power over virtually all trade negotiations. However, the UK, France, Germany and Spain all feared a backlash from their national parliaments over the preservation of national veto rights generally. The Amsterdam Treaty thus essentially endorsed the status quo: the Common Commerical Policy (CCP) could be extended to services and intellectual property without treaty reform, but only by a unanimous Council decision.[17]

Brittan (1996: 20) protested that in future 'a small national tail could be wagging the large European dog at every turn'.

The refusal of EU Member States to extend the decision-making formula that it traditionally had deployed, with considerable success, was indicative of the increased political salience of trade policy in the 1990s. So, too, was the treatment of so-called 'audio-visual products', such as television programmes and films. For France and other Member States, cultural products became matters of 'security': artefacts of European cultures and languages, which the power of Hollywood (and European appetites for popular American TV and films) threatened to steamroller. In the end, the cultural sector was formally included in a new General Agreement on Trade in Services (GATS) at the end of the Uruguay Round, but was exempted from the GATS' general commitment to progressive liberalisation of trade. Ultimately, the perceived need to protect Europe's cultural heritage resulted in a growing EU competence in audio-visual policy (see Exhibit 8.1), but not in trade policy.

The International Context

The politicisation of EU trade policy was fuelled by dramatic changes in the Union's relationships with its most important trading partners. In particular, the 'privatisation' of US trade policy under the Clinton administration meant that American policy became increasingly responsive to whichever interests lobbied most effectively or, more cynically, contributed most to increasingly expensive US political campaigns. Little attempt was made to aggregate interests in US trade policy, as the EU still struggled to do in the name of the 'Community interest'. US trade policy also lurched towards 'extra-territoriality', or the application of US laws to firms acting beyond American borders, with the practice justified on dubious grounds of national security. The EU reacted with considerable indignation and ultimately even unity (see Exhibit 4.4) in a landmark case before the new WTO.

The EU also had to work hard to ensure that US–Japanese trade relations, marked by American aggression and severe political tensions, did not produce agreements which harmed European interests 'in passing'. Brittan repeatedly sought assurances from Tokyo that Japan would not end up favouring American exporters for political reasons at the expense of European firms. Alarm bells went off in European capitals when Japan Airlines decided in 1994 to purchase Boeing 737–400 aircraft, without even considering the rival Airbus A320.

The Commission eschewed a combative, US-style approach to trade with Japan. Brittan trumpeted the EU's quieter approach as more appropriate to Asia and, ultimately, more successful: the EU's trade deficit

Exhibit 4.4 Helms–Burton: trade policy as foreign policy

After 1989, trade policy became foreign policy, entering the realm of 'high politics' far more often than in the past (see Moon 1996; Peterson 1996a). Responding to the shooting down by Cuba of two Miami-based civil aircraft (which deliberately transgressed Cuban airspace), the US Congress passed the 'Cuban Liberty and Democratic Solidarity Act' in 1996. Better known after its Congressional sponsors as the Helms–Burton Act, it punished EU and other non-American firms for investing in Cuba, or 'trafficking' in property confiscated by Castro's government (largely from organised crime syndicates) after the 1959 revolution. Helms–Burton was clearly 'extra-territorial', in that it applied US legislation to firms acting outside US territory.[18] Yet, in a sign of the ambiguity of international trade law, the bill was not clearly illegal under the GATT/WTO (Labouz 1998). US President Bill Clinton refused to condemn either one, particularly in an election year, and instead repeatedly granted the EU a 'waiver' of the provisions which would have allowed US citizens to sue foreign firms and citizens under Helms–Burton.

Even in a case heralded by the EU as proving its power in trade policy, the Union's position was repeatedly weakened by division. In September 1996, Santer appeared to undercut Leon Brittan's hard-line stance on Helms–Burton by stating that it would be unwise for the EU to retaliate (by lodging a WTO complaint) before the US election. The stakes were high, as Clinton pleaded with the EU not to enrage Congress, promised to continue 'waiving' the worst effects of Helms–Burton and expressed concern about the fragility of American support for the WTO. Ultimately, Brittan appeared to win the argument, convincing the General Council to haul the USA before the WTO dock in October 1996. The decision was a fuelled by indignation at Clinton's failure to invite EU representatives to a Middle East summit. Brittan crowed that 'Respect grows when people think you can stand up for your own interests.'[19]

Then, not for the first time, Denmark threatened to undermine the EU's common front. Countermeasures against Helms–Burton were proposed under Article 308, which allows the EU to 'take the appropriate measures' deemed necessary even if there is no legal justification for them elsewhere in the Treaty.[20] In late 1996, the Danish government faced a domestic court action alleging (among other things) that the overuse of Article 308 had violated Denmark's constitution. The Danish Foreign Minister, Niels Helveg Petersen, thus took the unusual step of blocking countermeasures to Helms–Burton,

→

→

instead of the more usual practice of abstaining and challenging the legislation before the ECJ. In the event, the Commission turned instead to Article 220,[21] which (vaguely) allows Member States to negotiate intergovernmental agreements between themselves to ensure 'the protection of persons and the enjoyment and protection of rights'. Believers in the sanctity of the Commission's trade policy powers swallowed hard at this extension of intergovernmentalism.

The transatlantic war of words moderated somewhat after the 1996 US election, which saw Clinton take electorally important states (Florida and New Jersey) with large Cuban *émigré* communities. It also helped that a conservative government was elected in Spain, which took a tougher stance than its Socialist predecessor on the democratisation of Cuba. The WTO became the scene of a game of cat-and-mouse between the USA and EU on a disputes settlement panel. The USA did not block the formation of a panel in early 1997, but continued to insist that Helms–Burton was legal under WTO rules under which any state could take any trade action 'it considers necessary for its national security interests'. Challenged to explain how Cuba threatened US 'national security', American diplomats recalled that the EU had invoked the same rules during the Falklands War to punish Argentina and had argued that each GATT member 'was – in the last resort – the judge' of its own security interests.[22] By spring 1997, Brittan had tabled a draft text of a six-month 'truce' with the USA, which featured an American offer to limit the application of Helms–Burton to EU firms in return for the dropping of the WTO complaint. Although France, Spain, Italy and Belgium all raised objections, none opposed it outright. Finally, after being suspended for a full year, the EU decided to let the WTO panel lapse just ahead of a USA–EU summit bringing together Clinton and the UK Prime Minister, Tony Blair. The summit sealed a deal trading a tougher European line on Cuba (as well as Libya and Iraq) for a continued waiver of US sanctions against EU firms.

The repeated US claim that Helms–Burton was 'foreign policy, not trade policy', and thus not subject to international trade diplomacy, raised hackles as well as alarm in Brussels and EU capitals. Insofar as it proved a basis for EU solidarity, the Union generally came away with its dignity intact. Sometimes, as in this case, the EU's relative youth as a trading power becomes an advantage in trade negotiations. As they approach key decisions, European decision-makers start to appreciate, sometimes as never before, the Union's enormous strength. Usually, they then realise that it is sand through their fingers in the absence of European unity.

with Japan fell for most of the 1990s, while America's continued to climb. The Union applied much the same formula to its biannual Asia–Europe Meeting (ASEM), launched in 1996, which brought all EU heads of government together with 10 Asian counterparts,[23] mostly to discuss trade and investment. ASEM was heralded as an 'historical turning point' by its advocates (Pou Serradell 1996) and even resulted in over €35 million in EU funding to help Asian states (particularly South Korea) rebound from the financial crisis of 1997–8. ASEM revealed that the Union – a relatively 'young' trading power – had considerable empathy with other new players in the international economy. Like them, the Union often seemed unsure of itself and was sensitive about its dignity, but also went to great lengths to make it clear that it would not be pushed around by more established players, particularly the USA.[24]

Setting EU Trade Policy

Choices in trade policy increasingly are determined by concerns about the EU's status as a diplomatic power. After all, trade (along with aid) is the EU's most potent tool of influence in foreign policy. One logical outcome is a tangled thicket of trade preferences offered to third states on the basis of political rationale, as opposed to economic logic. For example, Russia was offered major trade concessions in November 1993 just prior to a Russian general election, amid rising concerns about the growing strength of neo-fascist and communist parties. Crucially, the proposals included a promise to stop designating Russia a 'state trading country' (along with Cuba and North Korea), a category to which punitive sanctions were more readily and easily applied. However, the EU came under enormous pressure to do far more for Russia after its economy began to collapse following a severe financial crisis in 1998. Barber's (1998: 22) *cri de coeur* was typical: 'Russia, huge, heavily armed, endlessly unstable, demands attention.' But here as elsewhere the EU ran up against the limits of using trade as a political tool.

For one thing, the use of trade policy as foreign policy usually provokes considerable internal controversy. *Colbertistes* were outraged when the Commission tabled proposals in 1998 for preferential trade agreements with Mexico and *Mercosur*. In some respects, the Commission was responding to a wider global trend: 26 free trade agreements (FTAs) were struck in just over a year and a half, in 1994–6, or half of the total agreed since the creation of the GATT in 1949. But the Union had no clear policy on FTAs: they were mostly negotiated on an ad hoc basis by Commissioners between whom the world was divided into regional responsibilities. Each Commissioner defended each subsequent FTA as a means to strengthen the Union's hand in 'their' patch of the globe. Critics included France and the Commissioner for Agriculture, Franz Fischler, who feared that FTAs would disrupt the EU's agricultural markets. But FTAs were also attacked by economic liberals, such as Clinton's first Ambassador to the EU, Stuart Eisenstadt, as corrosive to the idea of a multilateral trading system (see Carnegie Endowment 1996).[25] In the absence of regulation of FTAs (say) within the WTO, it is clear that they will remain a primary tool of the Union's foreign policy, if also a disputed one.

The Commission's geographical division of labour is not counter-balanced by a unified or 'dedicated' Council of Trade Ministers. Ministers for trade carried little weight in European national capitals when the Community was launched in the late 1950s. Thus the General Affairs Council retained overall responsibility for trade policy. With trade often becoming 'high politics' in the 1990s, there seemed no alternative to giving Foreign Ministers ultimate responsibility for setting EU trade policy. Take, for example, the long-running trade dispute over steel-jaw 'leghold' traps, used in the fur industry in Russia, Canada and the USA. The row was fuelled in 1996 by the hard line taken, on grounds of animal rights, by the Environmental Council, before the issue was recaptured and defused by the General Council, which usually is far more concerned to avoid trade disputes (see Chapter 7).

The General Council's attention to trade policy is, however, sporadic and national positions are mostly a product of domestic imperatives and pressures. Thus understanding how EU trade policy is 'set' requires knowledge of *national* trade policies. France's behaviour is rooted in a domestic trade policy process that has always favoured producers over consumers and featured close state–industry links (see Milner 1993). By contrast, the traditional free market orientation of Germany has been encouraged by the aloofness of German federal ministries (particularly its fiercely liberal Economics Ministry) towards producer interests.

The EU's own trade policy process can be a powerful 'leveller' of liberal ambitions. As Winters (1994) observes, it is difficult for any national delegation to accept protection that extends only to other Member States' producers. It is equally difficult for Member States such as Germany or the UK to avoid taking positions that make it clear that protectionism is more acceptable if extended to *their* producers. In trade policy, as much as any sector, it is usually better to be 'inside' a group of Member States which determines the final outcome than arguing on grounds of principle from an isolated position 'outside' an emerging compromise.

This point applies particularly to anti-dumping measures, which impose punitive tariffs on exporters who sell their goods at prices set lower than their production costs. Such measures remain outside the remit of the WTO.[26] Under the Treaty, the Commission has the right to investigate charges of dumping and to take provisional decisions about whether to impose duties, *without* a vote from the Member States. If, after an investigation, the Commission finds that dumping has occurred, it must seek Council approval to impose 'definitive' anti-dumping duties. In short, the Commission acts as judge and prosecuting attorney, even if the Council acts as jury. One study (Hindley and Lal 1994) showed that the Commission found dumping in 95 per cent of all cases: 'a conviction rate rarely matched in other judicial procedures'.[27]

Anti-dumping also offers a clear illustration of the way a 'history-making decision' – the final Uruguay Round settlement – can transform systemic governance. Part of the price demanded by France for its acceptance of the GATT deal in 1993 was new rules making it easier to deploy, by a simple majority vote, rather than QMV, the EU's 'commercial defence instruments', including anti-dumping procedures. Germany, Denmark and Luxembourg considered the changes an acceptable price to pay for French support for the Uruguay Round agreement, leaving the UK and the Netherlands isolated in opposition to them.[28]

For his part, Leon Brittan took advantage of a situation he, as a free trader, did not welcome; using the change in voting rules as an excuse to increase both the speed and inclusiveness of decision-making on anti-dumping. Liberals welcomed Brittan's pledge to strengthen the involvement of consumer organisations in the Commission's investigations and to consider the broadest range of EU interests (consumers and importers, as well as producers). In a sop to *Colbertistes*, Brittan insisted that the number of anti-dumping officials in DG IV, numbering less than 90, had to be increased to levels similar to those of the USA, which had around 500 anti-dumping professionals. Yet Brittan also secured agreement on a more stringent definition of dumping, based on evidence of clear harm done to producers in the importing country.

By this point, globalisation was making it far more difficult to determine whose interests the EU was defending. Used in the 1980s mainly against Japanese exporters (which accounted for 70 per cent of the total value of EU anti-dumping actions in 1993), commercial defence measures in the 1990s were often *requested* by Japanese firms, which produced from Europe, against South Korean imports. In one case, video recorders made in Singapore by the French firm Thomson were the subject of a 1995 complaint by the Dutch MNC Philips. Another saw the Commission impose dumping duties on imported soda ash (used in glass-making) even as DG IV was finding European producers guilty of operating a cartel. Decisions that set EU trade policy were rarely straightforward.

Ultimately, Brittan and the Commission retained the right to pull any proposal for protection of EU producers off the table. However, as the European recession of the early 1990s began to bite, it became harder for the Commission to resist political pressures for the use of commercial defence instruments. A member of Brittan's *cabinet* conceded that 'national officials are getting less room for manoeuvre. Too much detailed stuff is being done by the Council and we're seeing a gradual centralisation of power at the level of Council. We get lots of blockages when ministers paint themselves into a corner'.[29]

Two episodes provide evidence for the point. The first saw the Commission try to close a 1994 investigation into the dumping of gum rosin products by China, particularly shower sandals ('flip-flops'), on the grounds that consumer interests outweighed EU producer interests. In the Article 133 Committee, only Portugal initially raised objections. However, a later meeting saw no fewer than six (of 12) Member States support the Portuguese.

The second case concerned EU quotas on imports of Chinese toys. The Secretary-General of the Toy Manufacturers of Europe, Maurits Bruggink, observed that many European firms had transferred production to China and claimed that there was not a 'shred of evidence to show that the quotas have saved or created one job in the EU'.[30] But the quotas remained in place, in the teeth of British opposition, even though one for stuffed toys (including human likenesses) was increased, leading to the anomaly that plastic figures of Star Trek's Captain Kirk were reportedly allowed in, while those of his colleague Mr Spock (a 'non-human') were not.

In a climate of political twitchiness on trade questions, the Commission tried to smooth the entry of the Union into the WTO era, with its more stringent and binding procedures for settling trade disputes. Brittan announced in late 1994 that the EU would not hesitate to make use of a new set of rules to govern another commercial defence instrument: 'countervailing duties', or the imposition of taxes on foreign goods unfairly subsidised by public funding. In the past, the Union had often been reluctant to resort to such duties for fear of provoking retaliation against the CAP. However, agricultural liberalisation in the Uruguay Round had made such fears less acute. At the same time, Brittan stressed that such retaliation would take place only after all disputes resolution procedures within the WTO were exhausted (see Exhibit 4.5).

Of course, the Union embraced the WTO revolution with great reluctance, and only because side payments were offered to sectors and Member States harmed by the Uruguay Round. Portugal received €400 million through a Community 'special action' to help modernise its textiles industry, which accounted for about one-quarter of all Portuguese industrial employment and faced new competitive pressures from the GATT deal. The measure was indicative of the EU's 'internal compensatory adjustment' system, without which 'several member countries would not have approved the Round's Final Act' (Devuyst 1995: 450).

Exhibit 4.5 Bananas, beef and the WTO revolution

The World Trade Organisation (WTO) superseded the GATT in 1995. The main difference between the WTO and its predecessor was in 'disputes settlement': the WTO was given a stronger, more compulsory mechanism for deciding who was right in international trade disputes and how much remedies should cost. Two of the first WTO decisions held against the EU's banana regime and its import ban on hormone-treated beef.

The Union's banana policy has always been hotly contested (see Read 1994; Borrell 1995; Stevens 1996; Thagesen and Matthews 1997). When the EEC was created, France and Italy were allowed to give special concessions to producers from their former colonies. Germany, where bananas were a prized symbol of post-war prosperity, was allowed to import large, fleshy, 'dollar bananas' from Latin America tariff-free. Other EEC Member States paid tariffs on their imported bananas. The UK wanted import preferences for its former colonies when it joined, so they were enshrined (together with French and Italian preferences) in the Lomé convention in 1975. After Mediterranean enlargement, around one-quarter of the EU's banana needs were met by domestic European producers, which were heavily protected. There was nothing close to a common EU policy. As with cars (see Exhibit 4.1), national import arrangements for bananas were threatened by the freeing of the internal market.

The Commission tabled proposals in 1992 for an external banana trade regime (BTR) and an 'internal' banana policy. Both were broadly favourable to the interests of ACP producers of small, sweet, high-cost bananas. The BTR was adopted by QMV, with the British Council presidency mindful of its former colonies and urging adoption. The 'no' camp found Germany – where bananas were consumed at twice the UK level – joined by Denmark.[31]

A vote on the 'internal' banana regime again saw Germany in opposition, this time with Belgium and the Netherlands. Denmark, as Council president, had the deciding vote, and 'decided in the interests of EU decision-making to vote for the proposal' (Stevens 1996: 345). The case showed how states holding the Council chair would often swallow their own objections to a proposal in order to get a 'deal'. More generally, the new regime effectively extended the most protectionist national restrictions to the Union as a whole (Borrell 1995).

The USA, with support from several Latin American countries, successfully pushed for a WTO disputes settlement panel on the EU banana regime. As the panel was convened in 1995, a group of ACP producers (mostly island-states in the Caribbean) desperately argued that they had no alternative to banana production besides ecologically destructive subsistence agriculture or illegal drugs. A Caribbean trade association bitterly attacked the Americans for their 'cynical and ruthless exploitation' of the WTO.[32]

Nonetheless, the WTO upheld the US complaint, as had two GATT panels in the past. The difference this time was that the EU could not block the

→

→

WTO panel's findings, as it could (and had) under the GATT. As the Union scrambled to decide what to do, old internal splits opened, with Germany leading a nine-state bloc ready to scrap the BTR, and a blocking minority of six (including Britain and France) defending it. The Commission admitted that getting internal EU agreement would be a 'bigger problem' than reaching agreement with the USA.[33] Eventually, after Germany signalled its desire for any solution that was WTO-compatible, the Union agreed to enlarge the quota for Latin American producers, create more competition between ACP producers and give increased aid to the hardest-hit ACP countries. The USA and its Latin American allies attacked the new scheme as inadequate, with the Clinton administration threatening severe retaliation – and risking a trade war – in 1999. Ultimately, it seemed clear that EU banana policy would be 'set' in a way that put respect for WTO rules on a par with loyalties to the ACP states.

Similarly, the EU's ban on the growth hormone BST (*bovine somatropin*) and all cattle products exposed to it caused a long-running row with the USA, where BST was widely used (see Peterson 1989). In 1997, a WTO disputes panel decided that the EU ban was illegal. The Commission said it would pay fines rather than expose EU consumers to BST-treated beef, with its officials gasping, 'The precautionary principle is out. This ruling suggests you can't ban something unless you show people are dying from it.' The Commission was backed by BEUC, a leading consumer organisation, which concurred that 'Under no circumstances should the EU lift the ban.'[34]

After an appeal in 1998, the Union was told that it could set consumer protection standards that were higher than international norms, but could only ban substances which failed scientific tests of 'safety, efficacy and quality'. In other words, it could legally ban hormone-treated beef only by proving the presence of toxins in the meat. Somewhat triumphantly, one EU official declared, 'one molecule is enough'.[35] European scientists set out to find it under a WTO-agreed timetable, although it soon became clear that the final results of tests would not be available until after the deadline, setting the scene for another flaring up of the dispute.

The creation of the WTO was a major step towards strengthening international trade rules, even if its earliest rulings were ambiguous and disputed. The EU was not always a loser in the WTO: another early case saw massive Asian taxes on imported European gin and whisky declared unfair. A senior British trade official remarked, 'it is very important that Leon [Brittan] can now say, "we've won on spirits in South Korea. The WTO is a good thing. We must take our medicine in these two other cases"'. 'Good thing' or not, the WTO was certainly busy: it considered more than 50 cases in its first 18 months, compared with the GATT's handling of fewer than 200 in nearly 50 years. Clearly, the EU's autonomy in trade policy decision-making stood to be cut back considerably in the WTO era.

Yet 'buying' support for free trade becomes less viable as more European producers face more international competition, and more domestic constituencies seek compensation, or at least influence over commercial policy. The point was illustrated clearly in trade with Eastern Europe. The 'Europe Agreements' were unprecedented, offering more trade concessions to CEECs than the EU had ever offered to any non-members.[36] However, the actual extension of concessions was, in many cases, subject to very long delays. To take one example, the General Affairs Council approved an interim accord on trade with Bulgaria in late 1993 to plug the gap until Bulgaria's association agreement could be ratified (in spring 1994). The interim deal was scheduled to be in place more than six months earlier, but became caught up in the internal EU debate over anti-dumping voting rules, particularly given concern about low-cost competition from Bulgarian producers. The Bulgarians repeatedly and furiously deplored the delay.

In this case, as in others, grand political bargains struck at the highest political levels seem to 'set' EU trade policy for years at a time, with the Union extending promises to its trading partners that appear to limit its subsequent room for manoeuvre. Yet all major trading powers retain policy levers, such as commercial defence instruments, which can be used to hedge such promises. The EU, along with most of its trading partners, came under strong pressures to use them as the WTO era dawned.

Policy Networks and Trade Policy

Arguably, the less politicians are involved in trade policy decision-making, the better. Negotiations often hang on points of detail that are beyond the grasp of all but experts. Judgements need to be made, as in one case in 1997, about whether to apply import duties to Chinese-made schoolbags, sports bags or handbags (or all three). At the political level, domestic pressures usually push more in the direction of protection than liberalisation. In contrast, when epistemic communities of specialised officials are given autonomy in trade negotiations, they are often able to craft compromises which liberalise trade and can be sold to both their political masters and negotiating partners. In their analysis of the Uruguay Round, Woolcock and Hodges (1996: 303) are blunt in suggesting that 'the EU was effective . . . when these technocrats were in control'.

The sub-systemic level of trade policy decision-making is highly sectorised and sometimes schizophrenic. It is not uncommon for trade disputes to rage with a third country in one sector even as the EU signs a liberalisation agreement with the same state in another. For example, the

Union agreed a 1997 deal with South Korea on liberalising telecommunications procurement even as it pressed ahead with a WTO complaint against high Korean taxes on spirits.

Moreover, in a sector where the EU, arguably, requires integrated, transnational epistemic communities, we find policy networks that are more *nationalised* in structure than is the case in most other policy areas. Over time, Member States have resisted the Commission's attempts to forge its own, independent links with private sector interests. Witness the General Affairs Council's refusal in 1994 to accept Commission proposals to allow firms *themselves* to request safeguard measures, which would have deprived national governments of their roles as go-betweens. Paradoxically, in some cases the freeing of the internal market may even have bolstered links between national governments and 'their' national firms by making it easier for firms to produce for the entire EU from one or a few locations. Individual firms that consolidated their production geographically found that fewer governments had a political stake in their economic well being. Many producers thus reaffirmed their links with national trade ministries.

In some respects, policy networks structured around national lines persist because Member States value them as a line of defence against the Commission. Occasionally, the Commission finds that it can bypass them and the Council: consider its 1993 decision under the obscure 'anti-absorption' procedure to double (nearly) anti-dumping duties on imported plastic woven sacks from China, after initial duties were simply 'absorbed' by Chinese manufacturers. Generally, the Council was happy to see the Commission out in front in policy vis-à-vis China – the last large 'state trading' country. Many Chinese exporters seemed to have little knowledge of how to set prices and no export strategy beyond 'find a market and flood it'.

However, the Commission's penchant for accruing trade powers by stealth generally united Smithites and *Colbertistes* in opposition. In one case, the French were joined by the Netherlands (and Spain) in successfully arguing before the ECJ that the Council had a right to vote on the 1991 US–European Competition Agreement, which mandated exchanges between American and EU anti-trust authorities. The Agreement itself was less controversial than the Commission's unilateralism in agreeing it with the Americans.

Meanwhile, national trade or economics ministries went to considerable lengths to nurture links to their nationals and like-minded allies in the Commission, particularly during the recession of the early 1990s. A member of Brittan's *cabinet* complained in 1994 that 'in the college we now start with 10 votes [out of 17] against anything liberal. That reflects the drift in the Council, where there are lots more statements in Council minutes about the need to defend European industries. There is just far less giving up with good grace than there used to be'.[37]

Even in an improving economic climate, personnel decisions in DG I of the Commission provoked intense battles, particularly when Rod Abbott, a Briton, was named to head the EU's office in Geneva (home of the WTO) and Hans-Friedrich Beseler, a German liberal, was appointed as DG I's Director-General in 1996. A number of cases after 1995 saw the Council vote 8–7 to impose anti-dumping duties.

The Commission also often found the Article 133 Committee more vigilant and confrontational in the 1990s. In principle, the Committee retains the right to adjust the negotiating mandates given to the Commission on technical issues, but not on political or sensitive issues. When the latter arise, dossiers are passed 'upstairs', first to COREPER and then, if necessary, to the General Council itself. Consequently, the more EU trade policy becomes politicised, the less the Article 133 Committee can 'hold on' to dossiers. In the late 1990s, rising politicisation was accompanied by more fragmentation: trade policy discussions became more specialised and sector-specific over time, inducing greater variance in the membership of the Article 133 Committee. In 1997, a British trade official conceded that the Article 133 Committee was 'becoming a forest' and increasingly incapable of single-minded action.[38]

Fragmentation at the sub-systemic level is rarely a force for liberalisation:

> This decision-making structure tends to lead the Community towards protectionist outcomes. The compromises and bargaining may avoid extreme forms of capture by national interests, but it encourages a drift towards generalised protection and probably strengthens the hands of Community-wide lobbies which can bring pressure to bear not only in Brussels but also in several national capitals – for example, the agriculture and iron and steel lobbies. (Winters 1994: iii)

Textiles offer a particularly good example of the way fragmented decision-making structures can hedge political agreements to liberalise. For most of the post-war period, textiles were subject to the Multifibre Arrangement (MFA), one of the greybeards of international trade agreements, with roots in the early 1960s. The MFA imposed controls on the exports of (mostly) Asian countries, which were progressively tightened. The European industry lobby was spearheaded by COMITEXTIL (the Committee for the European Textile and Clothing Industry), 'a small but highly professional body', backed by the Commission and wielding 'profound influence on the shape of EC textile policy' (Kenis and Schneider 1987: 452).

The Uruguay Round yielded a 'history-making' decision to dismantle all controls on textiles trade gradually until the MFA ceased to exist in 2006. The EU, as the world's largest textiles and clothing importer, seemed finally to have conceded that protecting European producers from low-wage competition, in an industry where labour can account for 30 per cent of costs, was silly. Prior to the Uruguay Round deal, the textiles sector had accounted for nearly one-third of jobs lost in the EU between 1988 and 1994, with imports rising by about 80 per cent. Yet in 1994 the Commission 'implemented' the agreement by lifting controls on products that were mostly *exempt* from MFA quotas anyway, thus resulting in little 'net' liberalisation. The result was described by the World Development Movement, a non-governmental organisation, as 'a travesty'.[39]

The Commission then imposed provisional duties on imports of cotton from India, Pakistan, Indonesia, China, Egypt and Turkey. As the clock began ticking towards a Council committee vote, European fabric weavers, and their association *Eurocoton*, allied with national policy networks from southern EU Member States in a fierce campaign to urge a vote to confirm the duties. A far larger group of European industries, involved in processing fabrics (making them into soft furniture or clothing) condemned the duties as barriers to cheap cotton imports.

Member States were split 6–6 on the issue, with Austria, Luxembourg and Germany undecided. A Commission compromise – to impose the duties for one year instead of five – seemed to resolve the dispute. However, the firmly liberal German Economics Ministry seized control of Germany's position on the issue. The Austrian and Luxembourg delegations followed the Germans in voting 'no', thus killing the proposal (on a vote of 9–5 with one abstention).

Subsequently, the cotton row climbed to the highest political level. Between rounds of the 1997 French parliamentary election, the French President, Jacques Chirac, came under fierce pressure from French textiles producers and their *patron*, Philippe Séguin, the President of the French National Assembly, to table the anti-dumping case at the Noordwijk European summit. In theory, the summit was meant to accelerate negotiations on the Amsterdam Treaty. In the event, it spent considerable time discussing cotton and yielded a typical Eurofudge, endorsing the status quo but ordering a fresh study of the proposed measures.

The row refused to die in 1998 after the provisional duties expired. Eight EU Member States issued a furious declaration attacking the Commission's 'regrettable decision' to renew temporary duties, while a smaller group, including France, Spain and Italy, tabled a counterdeclaration supporting the Commission. With the British EU presidency and its allies accusing the Commission of blatantly flouting the majority will, one senior diplomat commented that 'the Commission is twisting in the wind over this one'.[40]

Its compromise proposal – dropping anti-dumping duties while agreeing minimum prices for non-EU cotton products – was not clearly workable or enforceable. Finally, the General Council put the Commission out of its misery in October 1998 by rejecting five-year duties (by a vote of 8–6, with Belgium abstaining).

The cotton saga showed that the line between what is 'technical' and 'political' is often blurred. The Commission was accused of trying to buy Austria's vote for duties by proposing only a small duty on imported embroidery. It also decided to exempt Turkey from duties, despite finding evidence of dumping, amidst general attempts to 'rescue' diplomatic relations with Ankara.

The cotton case also highlighted three features of post-Uruguay Round decision-making on trade policy. First, the EU's 1995 northern enlargement had tilted the political balance in favour of the Smithites (Peterson and Bomberg 1998: 53). Second, globalisation was making it increasingly difficult to identify clear 'Community interests': the UK and the Netherlands, but also Finland, Sweden and even Ireland, increasingly tended to favour large importing interests over smaller production interests. Third, the EU remained predisposed to 'commercial defence', thus blunting its broad political decisions to liberalise. In this regard, the French were more determined than ever to mobilise their trade policy network, especially what one British diplomat called the 'France–Commission nexus, which really is at its most impressive on trade policy'.[41] French fingerprints were clear on the extraordinary Commission decision to impose provisional duties on cotton imports in early 1998 after only five (France, Spain, Greece, Italy and Portugal) Member States supported the proposal in an advisory committee.

If the trade policy decisions are shaped at the sub-systemic level by national policy networks, what determines how national networks are structured? Katzenstein (1977) suggests the two key questions are: how differentiated is a particular state from its society, and how centralised is each? In France more than most EU Member States, state and society (at least elite society) are not very differentiated and highly centralised. Thus France – like Japan, in some respects – has been effective at promoting exports and limiting imports through co-ordinated public and private actions. The case of cotton in 1997 showed that a French policy network could mobilise to hold a government to ransom even though the cotton weaving industry offered barely more than 10 000 jobs in France. In contrast, British state and society are clearly differentiated, and society – especially producer interests – is not very centralised. British policy networks tend not to be very integrated or single-minded.

Any state's policy networks will have trouble engaging in collective action when national interests are hazy, as they increasingly are in a more globalised economy. Consequently, Brittan managed to push through new rules in 1996 exempting firms from 'state trading' countries and the CEECs from EU trade defences if they respected market economy principles. Thus European firms producing from China or Poland could avoid trade sanctions. These changes seemed minor ones, which did not even require approval by the Council. However, they placed significant limits on the future application of EU anti-dumping actions. For liberals, they showed the wisdom of keeping trade policy, as much as possible, away from the politicians (see Exhibit 4.6). For agitated *Colbertistes*, they suggested an erosion of the EU's resistance to the brutal effects of globalisation.

Conclusion

The question of whether the EU is a force for liberalisation or protectionism continues to provoke debate. The 1992 project was clearly a neo-liberal project. Arguably, however, one of its main effects was to accelerate the growth of internal trade at the expense of EU trade with the rest of the world. By this interpretation, European states decided to *avoid* the rigours of stiff competition in global markets by 'taking in one another's high-cost washing' while claiming to embrace free trade (see GATT Secretariat 1993). Critics of the EU's patchwork of third country trade preferences contend that every country that benefits from a trade preference does so at the expense of another that is hurt by it.

Yet, as late as 1993, EU Member States (numbering 12 at the time) maintained around 6500 different *national* import quotas, some dating from the second World War. Most were eliminated at the end of the Uruguay Round and either abandoned or replaced by less stringent EU-wide controls. Defenders of the EU could argue that the cumulative effect of the trade concessions offered to third countries, via partnership or association agreements, was a net liberalisation of trade.

Many EU trade agreements, including 'Elements of Consensus', are vague enough to be used either for liberal or anti-liberal purposes. During the first year (1993) of the EU's deal with Japan on cars, the Commission insisted that Japanese exports be cut drastically. At the same time, the Commission usually sought 'the most liberal solution from among those that it consider[ed] politically realistic' (Holmes and McGowan 1997: 180). Miraculously, given how coddled the European car industry was before 1991, 'Elements of Consensus' committed the EU to 'full liberalization' of its market for cars before 2000. Ultimately, the EU seemed to be making the best of an impossible job. By the late 1990s, massive overcapacity, combined with falling sales and more aggressive Asian competition, meant

Exhibit 4.6 Maize and 'novel food'

Trade disputes surrounding new genetically modified organisms (GMOs) in food remained mostly the domain of sub-systemic decision-making even as they provoked broad public displays of protest in the late 1990s. Initially, the Environment Commissioner Ritt Bjerregaard sought to require that all food products using genetically modified soya, mainly produced in the USA, be labelled as such in 1995. With a transatlantic trade war looming and US producers saying the idea was impractical, the college of Commissioners refused to back Bjerregaard, and the labelling scheme was dropped.

A subsequent dispute arose in 1996 over imports (again from the USA) of maize (or corn) containing GMOs which protected the crop from a weed-killing chemical. The product, developed by the Swiss firm Ciba-Geigy, had already been approved by the USA, Canada and Japan. Yet, with the 'mad cow disease' affair very much in the news, the Environment Council decided that consumer concerns about the use of antibiotics in GMOs were serious enough to ask the Commission to put three expert committees to work examining the health implications of maize. Environmental groups argued that approving the maize would represent a victory for unelected bureaucrats over democratically elected governments. A consumer boycott was quickly organised, with the anti-GMO activist, Jeremy Rifkin, declaring himself 'amazed by how this has caught fire'.[42] The British Environment Minister, John Gummer, huffed that 'the Americans are trying to force this on Europe without us making our own minds up about it. One of the important reasons for the EU is that we are strong enough to say to the Americans that we decide what we want in our food chain, and not you'.[43] One protest in Hamburg had to be broken up by police, another in Rotterdam blockaded a Unilever plant, and chefs from London's poshest restaurants lent support to an anti-GMO campaign.

In a clear case of buck-passing, the Environment Council pressured the Commission to approve the maize, or ban it, with one official describing ministers as 'fed up. Any decision is better than no decision'.[44] Finally, the Commission took the advice of its experts and approved the maize. Nonetheless, Italy, Luxembourg and Austria (later joined by France) banned imports of US maize. The Austrian government was particularly hamstrung, after a national anti-GMO campaign led by the best-selling tabloid newspaper, *Kronen-Zeitung*, convinced no fewer than 20 per cent of all

→

$\longrightarrow$

Austrian voters to sign a petition condemning the EU's decision. Partly in response, the Commission proposed that a new 'Novel Food Regulation' should require the labelling of *all* new consumer products which 'may contain' GMOs, including, eventually, the maize and soya already approved. However, the measures were supported only by a minority of northern Member States, along with Italy and the EP. Thus the compromise became that foods would be labelled only if the presence of GMOs was proved according to EU-approved testing methods. Still the row refused to die, with the Commission expressing exasperation at the two-faced behaviour of several Member States, particularly France, that supported approval of the new crops but refused to condemn the national bans of Luxembourg and Austria in regulatory committees. The Commission carried the can for the EU's policy on GMOs, while protesting, 'It's France's fault that we are in this mess in the first place.'[45]

Statements by some of the main protagonists gave an indication of how bad-tempered the politics of 'novel food' had become. Gabrielle Zgubic of the Austrian Ministry for Women and Consumer Affairs poured scorn on the Commission's labelling scheme by insisting, 'This is a health issue, not a consumer information issue.'[46] The US Secretary of Agriculture, Dan Glickman, argued that 'sound science must trump passion' and argued that new food products were 'safe and good for the world'.[47] The French Research Minister, Claude Allègre, admitted that he 'would hate French farmers not to be able to grow transgenic maize while American maize is being imported into France',[48] before France itself banned genetically engineered corn seeds. Ciba-Geigy, appearing to defy common sense, opted to run adverts claiming the firm was 'With You for Life'.

The creation of new types of food creates a clear need for science-based regulatory decision-making, largely by experts. Yet even technocratic bodies such as the Standing Committee for Foodstuffs could not always agree when new food properties rendered food 'no longer equivalent' to an existing product, as stated in the Novel Food Regulation. Political agreements were impossible in these circumstances. As Peter Scher, the EU's special trade ambassador put it, 'There is clearly something wrong when the EU takes up to three years to approve products which the USA, Canada and Japan have approved in eight to 12 months'.[49]

that more European car plants were likely to go the way of Vilvoorde, the Renault plant in Belgium that was closed overnight in 1997 (see Exhibit 3.5).

On balance, the EU has become a stronger proponent of freer trade over time, even if it often continues to take a step back for each two forward. Yet it is important to distinguish between different levels of decision-making. At the highest political levels it seems clear that 'in some cases there may be more checks and balances against protectionism [in the EU] than within an individual country' (Woolcock and Hodges 1996: 323). However, the gap is wide between the 'high politics' of negotiations which lead to large liberalisation packages and the day-to-day grind of deciding whether Chinese flip-flops are being dumped on Europe. At the sub-systemic level, national policy networks from southern states frequently pressure the Commission to water down the effects of political decisions which embrace liberalisation. The Commission often seems willing to make what it considers small gestures at the sub-systemic level, such as using commercial defence instruments, to keep issues from being politicised. Its power clearly diminishes as issues ascend to more 'political' levels of decision-making.

However, it does not necessarily follow that actions at the sub-systemic level are always, or even usually, protectionist. At all levels of Council decision-making, northern enlargement in 1995 made the EU more instinctively liberal, while Leon Brittan was about as liberal as any European Commissioner could possibly be. The general 'drift' in EU trade policy was exposed by France's audacious proposal in early 1998 to create an independent anti-dumping agency, which would only consult Member States and cut out the Commission altogether. The French complained that Member States increasingly voted according to their 'national interests' on commercial policy questions, rather than the 'common European interest'. The proposal was a non-starter, but it signalled that France felt increasingly betrayed by EU external trade policy.

In particular, the WTO revolution and the galloping pace of globalisation were difficult for *Colbertistes* to swallow. In a 1998 review of the WTO, the Commission led calls for more transparency at the WTO level and wider access to its decision-making proceedings for the public and non-governmental organisations. Yet the French and several other Member States protested that the settlement of disputes should remain strictly a matter for governments. The WTO's early record of success was an extremely fragile one: no government had rejected a decision against it in its first three years, but most of its decisions were left so vague that it was often unclear what 'compliance' really meant. Many trade specialists believed that most decisions were left deliberately vague to avoid pushing bigger WTO members, such as the EU, into corners, which might lead them to disregard its rulings entirely. Moreover, much ambiguity was clearly 'built in' to the WTO because the Union (and the USA) wanted to hold other countries to account without binding their own hands too tightly. The WTO's development from birth to adolescence was highly contested, not least because EU trade policy remained subject to constant disputes about principles as well as particulars. Caught between globalised markets and national policy networks, the EU soldiered on, trying to remain loyal to both.

By the late 1990s, it was easy to exaggerate, as the French often did, the extent to which the EU trade policy had become 'captured' by Smithites. EU decision-making on external trade was schizophrenic and often unpredictable. It was likely to remain so. A highly contested policy sector in a political system geared so much to consensus means that neither the *Colbertistes* nor the Smithites can ever hope to steal a clear march on the other for long.

Chapter 5

The Common Agricultural Policy

The CAP in context
The high politics of the CAP
Setting the CAP: the 'clubby' Council
The farm lobby, the CAP and policy networks
Conclusion

The Common Agricultural Policy (CAP) seeks to provide an internal market and common prices for agricultural products. It is distinctive amongst EU policies in its complexity, conflicting objectives and status as a 'cornerstone' of the EU. The CAP accounts for large shares of both EU decision-making and spending: about half of the Community's budget, down from a staggering 87 per cent in 1970. Yet agriculture now accounts for only about 2.5 per cent of the Union's gross domestic product (GDP).[1] The CAP is blatantly regressive: it results in food prices that are about 8 per cent higher than in the United States (USA), with the burden falling most heavily on the poorest consumers. Roughly 80 per cent of the CAP's benefits traditionally have accrued to 20 per cent of the EU's (richest) farmers. Why such an elaborate, tortured and controversial policy for such a relatively marginal sector of the EU's economy? There is no simple answer to this question, although this chapter, more than any other in this book, tries to simplify much that is very, very complicated (see Table 5.1).

Unlike virtually all other EU policies, agriculture has been mostly impervious to liberalisation and 'marketisation'. The CAP has never really tried to make European farmers internationally competitive. Instead, it has evolved into a *social policy* to keep them on the land.[3] As with other social policies, the benefits that flow from the CAP have come to be seen as entitlements, which may be reduced only if compensation is offered to 'losers'.

The CAP is neither indefensible nor even all that exceptional amongst agricultural policies globally. The EU is roughly in line with other industrialised states in that about one-fifth of the income of its average citizen is spent on food, thus making the sector politically sensitive. Arguably, the strict application of the laws of supply and demand to

120

Table 5.1   *The basics of the CAP*

- *The Treaty*   Article 33[2] stipulates five objectives for the CAP (summarised here), which are not clearly compatible with one another:

  1   to increase agricultural productivity
  2   to ensure a fair standard of living for farmers,
  3   to stabilise markets,
  4   to assure the availability of supplies,
  5   to ensure that supplies reach consumers at reasonable prices.

- *Target price*
  a price for each agricultural commodity, set during the annual price review, which it is hoped farmers will be able to obtain on markets.

- *Intervention price*
  a set price which triggers a procedure by which national agencies (*not* the Commission) buy produce and take it off the market, so as to reduce supplies and encourage higher market prices.

- *Export refunds* (or 'restitution')
  a subsidy paid so that products may be sold outside the EU at a price lower than the cost of production; intended to ensure that farmers incur no losses, although in fact the payments are made to agricultural traders.

agriculture is implausible, even impossible, in a sector where unstable prices are inherently undesirable (Nugent 1994: 363).

At first blush, the EU seems to have been forced by external pressures to create a 'new CAP' (Swinbank 1996b; Urry 1997). However, the demands of the EU's trading partners for reform sometimes have had the contrary effect of stiffening European resolve to defend the existing CAP. Despite significant reforms in the 1990s, it is remarkable how *unchanging* the CAP has been: no other major EU policy is defined by treaty articles which are essentially the same today as they were in 1957. To a considerable extent, EU Member States have been able to 'hide' behind the CAP, thus avoiding the ' "ugly work" of both satisfying the farm lobby and managing agricultural trade relations in an international environment dominated by liberal multilateralism' (Rieger 1996: 100).

Making sense of the CAP is often 'ugly work' requiring patience and effort. Yet, the story of the CAP is a gripping one in many respects. And it is simply impossible to understand EU decision-making without understanding the CAP.

The CAP in Context

Rieger (1996) offers a powerful case for the argument that the CAP was created in the 1950s to integrate farmers into the European welfare state, by giving them a policy which improved the situation of nearly all of them (although some far more them others). Socially disadvantaged and politically and geographically isolated, farmers tilted towards radical, far-right, even fascist parties in the early 20th century. Mainstream party governments were often unable or unwilling to prevent farm prices from fluctuating wildly, and often collapsing (Milward 1992: 30). The CAP was a way to buy the support of farmers for European integration. Also, more urgently, it gave them a stake in a type of liberal democracy that many traditionally had rejected.

The subsequent story of the CAP has been dominated by four prominent themes. First, the Agriculture Council has always ruled supreme, but the Commission has played a crucial role as, first, a 'foreman' in the construction of the CAP, then as honest broker amidst intergovernmental deadlock, and finally as an agitator for reform. Second, the power of farmers as a political force in the EU – while still disproportionate – has gradually declined. Third, the 'politics of food', particularly measures to ensure its safety, have increasingly encroached on the CAP. Fourth, the impact of the CAP on other EU policies, and other policies on the CAP, has become more conspicuous over time.

The Council, Commission and the CAP

The first Commissioner for Agriculture, Sicco Mansholt, was one of the longest-serving and most-respected Commissioners in the EU's history. A former Dutch agriculture minister with an intimate knowledge of farming, Mansholt played a crucial role in rallying farming groups to support a truly common EEC policy. He also brokered tough and sometimes bitter negotiations on prices and financing (Griffiths 1995: 52). After the CAP was in place, agricultural surpluses appeared almost immediately, and became increasingly uncontrollable. In an act of considerable political courage, Mansholt tabled a plan in 1968 to radically restructure the Community's farming sector. The Mansholt Plan's demise, amidst violent opposition, reinforced the Council's dominance over the CAP.

The Council jealously guarded its powers to fix prices, determine quotas on specific products, and generally decide the CAP's price support policy. However, the application of qualified majority voting (QMV) after 1982 enhanced the importance of policy-shaping decisions taken primarily by the Commission. Over time, responsibility for many day-to-day decisions needed to manage markets for specific products were delegated to the Commission.

Moreover, the Commission often had to step in to break political impasse and essentially 'make' decisions on fundamental CAP issues in the 1980s. Massive surpluses led to stopgap measures, such as 'automatic stabilisers', which cut support prices or restricted intervention measures when CAP spending or production breached certain limits. Most such mechanisms acted to empower the Commission (Swinbank 1989; Swinbank and Tanner 1995).

The CAP exposed many tensions within the Commission, particularly between DG VI (Agriculture) and other services (such as DG I). Generally, however, the Commission highlighted the spiralling costs of the CAP and the damage done by the policy to the EU's international credibility. The Commission did not go unheard, just (mostly) unheeded: reforms in the 1980s amounted to 'rearranging the deck chairs on the Titanic' (Fennell 1987). But the CAP was enshrouded in an atmosphere of crisis almost from its origins and became gradually more politicised by world trade tensions. The Commission, after taking many decisions for which governments wished to avoid responsibility, became a leading advocate of reform.

The Decline of the Farm Lobby

Despite popular mythology to the contrary, the power of farmers has diminished over time. Soon after it was launched, the CAP became a political albatross, particularly because it severely distorted international markets. The argument that the CAP was a symbol of European unity, and deserved support for that reason alone, wore thin as it began to eat up an increasingly large share of the EU's budget. In the late 1970s and early 1980s, the problem of surpluses became so acute that the EU was forced to adopt measures such as 'producer co-responsibility', which required that farmers themselves help pay for part of the cost of getting rid of their unwanted produce.

By 1986, pressures from the EU's trading partners had become so strong that the farm lobby was unable to stop agriculture from being included in the Uruguay Round of global trade talks. A few years later, principled concern to shoulder the EU's new responsibilities in Central and Eastern Europe merged with practical fears of mass economic migration unless the Central and Eastern Europe countries (CEECs), which included several agricultural exporters, were integrated into western markets and, eventually, the Union itself. In late 1995, the Commission presented a report on the (daunting) implications of eastern enlargement for the CAP. At an informal dinner following the report's unveiling, the German Agriculture Minister (not, as might be expected, the French or Spanish!) bluntly told

Exhibit 5.1 The CAP and eastern enlargement

The agricultural sectors of the 12 countries that had applied for EU membership by the late 1990s were marked by enormous diversity. Of those closest to membership, Poland, a country of nearly 39 million with more than a quarter of its workforce in agricultural employment, posed the greatest challenge to the CAP. Poland had far too many small farms and relatively barren soil. Many Polish farms were certain to become unviable after Poland joined the EU, thus creating a rural crisis requiring urgent (and expensive) regional development funding. Yet Poland's northwestern region looked likely to become Europe's lowest-cost milk production area, posing stiff competitive challenges to western producers.

In contrast, the Czech Republic's agricultural sector was small and promised few problems for the CAP. Hungary, on the other hand, was equipped by climate and geography to be a major, successful agricultural producer, particularly in 'southern' EU product sectors (wine, olives). By the late 1990s, more than 20 per cent of the CEECs' workforce – about 10 million people – were employed in agriculture. The totals for the EU were about 5 per cent of employment and 8 million farm workers.

Agricultural prices generally were far lower in the CEECs than in the EU and bringing them up to CAP levels would be massively expensive. Eastern enlargement seemed unlikely before 2005, but it threatened to bankrupt the CAP without fundamental reforms. Even as EU agricultural ministers took turns trashing the proposals for CAP reform in *Agenda 2000* (Commission 1997b), the Polish Agricultural Minister, Jacek Janiszewski, rejected the idea of an interim period after accession during which full EU subsidies would not be extended to new Member States: 'Polish farmers must be treated exactly the same as their western counterparts.'[5] Very difficult, politically unpopular decisions were unavoidable if the CAP and enlargement were going to be reconciled.

his colleagues that the only conclusion to be drawn was that enlargement had to be delayed.[4] But, as enlargement became increasingly inevitable, it became more difficult to defend the privileges enjoyed by the EU's farmers (see Exhibit 5.1)

The Politics of Food

The CAP mainly supports food production, as opposed to ensuring its safety. In contrast, consumer protection is the focus for much EU legislation on 'foodstuffs', which has accumulated over time according to a style of decision-making distinctly different from that which governs the

CAP (see Exhibit 5.5). In important respects, food law was and remains an element of the internal market more than agricultural policy (see Exhibit 3.7).

The Franco-German alliance that has been so fundamental to the CAP simply has never existed in decision-making on food law. Arguably, Germany lacks a 'food policy': it remains caught between the inclination of its Health Ministry to take a maximalist, 'Scandinavian' position on all matters of food safety, and the considerable stake of large German firms in the food industry, whose interests are looked after by the German Industry Ministry. For their part, the French tend to oppose stringent food law, particularly because many French foods are produced by artisanal methods. The French line became challenged by concerns about consumer safety, particularly after the 'beef crisis' of 1996 (see Exhibit 5.2), which began to encroach on the CAP more generally.

The End of CAP Exceptionalism

In spite of the enormous budgetary costs of the CAP, the Union still managed to develop formidable new responsibilities for environmental protection, regional development and research in the 1980s. In each of these sectors (as well as trade policy), new policy networks emerged and pursued objectives which clashed fundamentally with those of the CAP. For example, the incentives built into the CAP to encourage increased production meant that farmers sometimes used large quantities of pesticides or fertilisers, often with devastating environmental consequences. A 1980 directive on nitrates – a by-product of agricultural waste and fertilisers – posed little threat to existing practice as it specified standards so strict that they were largely ignored or unenforced across the Community. Yet a 1991 directive on the protection of water against nitrate pollution marked a turning point (Johnson and Corcelle 1995: 104–8). Months later, Member States voted through a section of the Maastricht Treaty which became Article 174,[12] and mandated that 'environmental protection requirements must be integrated into the definition and implementation of other Community policies'.

Meanwhile, the EU's structural funds became serious money. In important respects, the EU's cohesion policy served the cause of keeping farmers on the land, particularly given high unemployment levels across the EU. Yet rising rural poverty and unemployment spurred proposals for an EU 'rural policy'. The Commission's (1997b) *Agenda 2000* proposals, designed to prepare the EU for enlargement, highlighted the need for a 'coherent rural policy' and the integration of the EU's various rural initiatives and budgets. Because such ideas posed a clear challenge to the CAP status quo, they encountered substantial resistance.

Exhibit 5.2 The beef crisis

In March 1996, the British government shocked its EU partners by announcing that scientists had established that a link might exist between the disease BSE (bovine spongiform encephalopathy: 'mad cow disease') in cattle and a new variant of Creutzfeld-Jakob disease (a degenerative and ultimately fatal nervous disease) in humans.[6] The announcement was made in a short statement to the House of Commons which was preceded by virtually no consultation of any other EU Member State or institution. The Agriculture Commissioner, Franz Fischler, described the result as the 'biggest crisis the EU has ever had'. The CAP suddenly entered the realm of 'high politics' (see Grant 1997a).

Initially, at least, mad cow disease was viewed as a British problem, resulting from the practice of feeding cows 'offal', or feed made from the remains of other (including diseased) animals.[7] Once the possibility of an animal–human link was established, the Commission responded by placing a ban on the export of British beef – an industry worth more than nearly €750 million per year – on the advice of the Standing Committee of National Veterinary experts. The British government (led by John Major) retaliated by adopting a 'non-co-operation policy', blocking about 100 different measures which required unanimous votes.

The beef crisis arose from a very unusual set of circumstances in which public health, animal health and market support all became mixed. Still, the episode illustrated three fundamental characteristics of CAP decision-making. First, the UK is an outlier on virtually everything to do with the CAP, which remains highly German- and (especially) French-dominated. Few in Brussels believed that there would have been any 'crisis' had the culpable Member State been France (or Germany): some sort of solution would have been quietly cooked up together with the Commission before the possible link between BSE and the disease in humans was announced.

Second, the beef crisis showed how quickly technical issues can become politicised (and vice versa) in agricultural decision-making. The previously obscure Standing Committee of Vets was given responsibility for most decisions concerning the export ban on British beef. Although Major received political assurances from Portugal and the Netherlands that their vets would vote to lift the ban on British exports of beef derivatives – gelatine, tallow and bull semen – both voted in favour of keeping the ban intact. About a month after the crisis broke, Major called Helmut Kohl and Jacques Chirac to the British residency in Moscow at midnight in the margins of a summit on nuclear security and insisted that they help find a way out of the crisis. In the

→

→

words of one official at the meeting, 'To call them in at that level at that time of night for that sort of issue was unbelievable. What could they decide?'[8] By this point, BSE had been defined as a scientific problem requiring a scientific solution.

Third, the beef crisis showed that many CAP policy networks are powerful veto groups. Although the Union's beef market initially collapsed, the export ban later appeared to serve the interests of the beef policy community (leaving aside British producers), as beef from other EU states began to turn up on markets traditionally supplied by the UK. By late 1996, the Commission decided that the ban could be lifted on certain British products or BSE-free herds, but only after specific proposals were endorsed first by the Scientific Veterinary Committee, then a newly-created multidisciplinary committee on BSE, then by the Standing Veterinary Committee, and finally by the Commission itself. Once a policy (such as an export ban on British beef) is 'set', CAP policy networks usually have multiple hurdles they can manipulate to thwart attempts at policy change.[9]

In 1997, a European Parliament (EP) Committee of Inquiry uncovered evidence that key actors in the beef policy network – particularly in DG VI – had earlier argued that a campaign of 'disinformation' was needed to protect the beef sector from the BSE threat.[10] An angry European Parliament threatened a motion of censure against Santer and the Commission for its handling of the beef crisis. A visibly nervous and shaken Santer promised the EP's Agricultural Committee 'nothing short of a revolution in our way of looking at food and agriculture', including much greater EP influence over EU animal plant and health rules. Without consulting Fischler, and in defiance of legal advice, Santer took the extraordinary step of agreeing that export labels for beef (indicating which country it came from), proposed initially under the traditional CAP Treaty article (37 after Amsterdam), would be withdrawn and tabled again under a separate article (95) for proposals concerning health or safety, which 'take as a base a high level of protection'. The upshot was that the EP would be given powerful rights to scrutinise and amend under co-decision, even though the phrase 'public health' never appeared in the Commission's original proposal.[11] Predictably, agricultural ministers (not to mention Fischler) were outraged. The Council pulled the equally extraordinary manoeuvre in March 1997 of voting through the directive under Article 37. Santer pledged to back the Parliament in its effort to take the Council to court on the grounds that the move was illegal. Regardless of the Court's eventual decision, the beef crisis provided grounds for scepticism about any 'revolution' in the way the CAP worked.

Research policy also became entangled with the CAP, as the EU's Framework R&D programme began to fund research into biotechnology and other agriculturally relevant technologies. Some promised 'greener' farmer methods, reducing the need for fertilisers and pesticides. Others, such as the cattle growth hormone bovine somatotropin (BST), threatened to increase yields (such as milk produced by dairy cattle) and thus exacerbate the problem of surpluses (Peterson 1989).

Finally, the Uruguay Round's (1986–93) focus on agriculture drove a wedge through a previously cosy policy consensus on the CAP. It was also indicative of a more globalised and technologically advanced agricultural trading system which raised new questions about whether EU farmers – and the CAP itself – could be protected from threats emanating from new genetic engineering techniques (see Exhibit 4.6). Traditionally, the CAP's problems had always been solved by spending more money. By the late 1990s, ceilings on overall levels of support, agreed during the Uruguay Round, removed that option. More generally, as the EU became a more developed, ambitious system of governance, the CAP became less of a policy island.

The High Politics of the CAP

The CAP stands out as a classic example of the way pursuing political objectives – integrating farmers into European welfare states – can have unintended policy consequences. There was no single decision taken at the birth of the CAP to coddle farmers. Despite food shortages and even outright starvation in parts of post-war Germany, there was no decision to increase food production at all costs. But early choices *were* informed by recent and unhappy memories of wartime food shortages, even as surpluses were already emerging in several product categories.

The familiar assumption that the CAP was created as a trade-off between German industrial interests and French farming interests is not uncontentious (see Milward 1992; Rieger 1996). What is clear, in line with liberal intergovernmentalist theory, is that the CAP was 'hatched' as a way to satisfy the converging preferences of the largest original EU Member States (plus the Netherlands; Moravcsik 1998: 152–8). Many early decisions were driven by complementary French and German interests, thus leading to 'log-rolling' which ensured high prices in product sectors of importance to France or Germany.

In particular, decisions taken between 1958 and 1962 made history by establishing the fundamental principles that underpinned the CAP. Other important policy instruments were tacked on later to cope with a rolling series of crises sparked by production surpluses and financial shortfalls. Of course, the biggest crisis in the EU's history occurred partly over the construction of the CAP. De Gaulle's 'empty chair' policy was a response to (inter alia) plans tabled by the Commission in March 1965 for common financing of the programme. Agreement on the Luxembourg compromise (see Exhibit 2.5) cleared the way for a five–year deal on fixed national contributions to the CAP.

Even before the financing arrangements had run their course, the CAP began to generate huge surpluses. The Commission's response was the 1968 Mansholt Plan, which proposed to consolidate small farms into larger, more efficient units and reduce the amount of farmland under production. The plan called for a substantial short-term increase in CAP spending in exchange for long-term savings.

Most European farmers opposed the Plan and many marched on Brussels, hanging Mansholt in effigy and provoking violent riots, one of which led to the death of a Belgian policeman and nearly 150 serious injuries.[13] Most EU governments were instinctively sceptical of the Mansholt Plan either because it proposed to increase CAP spending (West Germany) or because it gave the Commission too much power (France) to shut down farms. No Member State wished to be seen to be 'selling out' Western Europe's small (mainly family-owned) farms in the interest of 'efficiency'.

No single decision was ever taken to reject the Mansholt Plan. Instead, it simply faded away as the Community became preoccupied with exchange rate crises in 1969, and then the oil crises of the early 1970s. The CAP's emphasis shifted to propping up poorer farmers, instead of restructuring agriculture, as governments had no incentive to encourage farmers to leave the land in a climate of rising unemployment. The demise of the Mansholt Plan showed the power of 'non-decisions' in EU governance: the Plan died a quiet death of neglect, even though some of the structural changes it proposed occurred 'naturally' from economic forces.

Meanwhile, the CAP became prone to what economists call the 'restaurant bill' problem: the dilemma faced by individual diners who agree to pay equally for the cost of a shared meal. When one diner orders an outrageously expensive delicacy, other diners may choose to order their *own* favourite high-priced morsel rather than urge restraint on the part of others, and thus risk putting a damper on the evening. Similarly, EU Member States, particularly 'liberal' ones, frequently found themselves in the awkward position of arguing: 'we oppose this CAP measure as damaging to the Union, but if you persist and win we want a share of the loot' (Winters 1994).

The CAP imposed the costs of high prices on consumers and was also a drain on the EU's budget. Thus its expense was borne in rough proportion to Member States' GDPs. Meanwhile, its benefits were distributed between

Member States roughly in proportion to their share of production. Each state thus had incentives to seek high prices for any commodity for which its share of EU production exceeded its share of GDP. Nearly every country had such a candidate.

For West Germany, natural (and politically powerful) candidates were cereal producers. Most initial CAP prices were set extremely high, but a common EU price for wheat could be agreed only after several years of hard bargaining because it had to be set *below* the (exorbitantly high) West German price. Crucially, an early decision was taken to protect EU cereals producers from cheaper imports by instituting a 'variable levy', or sliding scale tax, which ensured that no imports could be sold at a price below the EU's set price. The effect was to establish 'Community preference' (discrimination against imports) as one of three pillars of the CAP, along with market unity and financial solidarity.

Afterwards, the CAP sometimes entered the realm of 'high politics' during annual price reviews, when a range of different farm prices was set for each product (see Table 5.1). Usually, working on the basis of carefully prepared proposals from the Commission, the Agricultural Council managed to decide prices themselves. However, choices taken during the 1982 annual price review truly 'made history' and marked a watershed in EU agricultural policy-making in two respects.

First, the 1982 annual price review was the first ever to be settled (essentially) by a majority vote. Here, as elsewhere, the formal rules had not previously been applied: the EEC Treaty made QMV possible, but applying it to decisions on farm prices was politically unthinkable. What made 1982 different was that Belgium, one of the staunchest critics of the Luxembourg compromise, held the Council Presidency. In a dramatic move, the Belgians called for a vote on the package, despite British protests. France, the traditional defender of the Luxembourg compromise, voted with the majority which supported the Commission proposal while Denmark and Greece abstained.

Second, intergovernmental conflict over the UK's (large) net contribution to the Community budget came to a head. Earlier, the reaction of most EU leaders to Margaret Thatcher's famous injunction, 'I want my money back', was incredulity at the 1979 Dublin summit. British attempts to invoke the Luxembourg compromise to scupper the deal agreed at the 1982 price review met with a similar response. Yet it became clear to all that the EU would be unable to make meaningful progress, particularly on new ideas that evolved into the 1992 project, without resolution of the 'British problem'. A final solution did not come until the 1984 French presidency (see Taylor 1989), but the wheels began to turn in May 1982.

The episode marked a distinct break in CAP decision-making. Afterwards, QMV took on far more prominence in the EU generally and the

CAP specifically. Far more votes were taken on individual elements of Commission proposals as well as whole packages. Member States had to get used to being outvoted: for example, the 1987 annual price review was agreed by a majority vote in which Greece voted against the entire Commission package, with Germany and Ireland opposing elements of it (Swinbank 1989: 310).

In key respects, the shift to QMV empowered the Commission. When it tabled proposals in 1985 to cut cereals support prices, West Germany voiced strong objections and even threatened to invoke the Luxembourg compromise, even though it had previously denied its existence in principle (see Vasey 1985). After months of deadlock, an Italian Council presidency – as disdainful of the Luxembourg compromise as the Belgians – put the cereal proposals to a vote. Most Member States agonised about isolating the Germans and refused to take part in the vote. In the end, only Italy, Belgium and the Netherlands voted at all. Yet, the Commission emerged out of the smoke of one of the unhappiest Council meetings in history with a solution: it simply imposed its cereals plan, using its treaty-based prerogative to do so, satisfied that the mere fact that the Council had voted at all gave it sufficient political cover (Swinbank 1989). In subsequent years, annual price reviews tended to produce 'close alignments between the original Commission proposals and the final settlement' (Nugent 1994: 384), particularly after the margins for manoeuvre were reduced by agreements on multi-annual 'financial perspectives' (see Laffan 1997a).

Nonetheless, most measures to reduce the costs of the CAP amounted to tweaking at its margins. 'Stabilisers' and budget ceilings, as well as favourable global market trends, sometimes gave the appearance that costs were under control, but the long-term trend was inexorably upwards. In the seven years after 1987, CAP spending per head of population soared by more than 40 per cent (Rieger 1996: 112).

One effect was to allow new players to find a voice in the CAP decision-making process. DG 1 (External Economic Relations) raised its profile in response to the insistence of the Reagan administration that agriculture *had* to become subject to multilateral trade rules. EU Finance Ministers actually welcomed US pressure as a lever to secure approval of the so-called 'MacSharry reforms' of 1992, which represented the most significant amendment of the CAP since its origins (see Exhibit 5.3)

The MacSharry reforms were enough to get a GATT deal *only* because the USA backed down considerably from its ambitions for agriculture in order to get a wider trade deal (Skogstad 1994). Pressures continued to build for further CAP reform, particularly after the American 'Freedom to Farm' Act was passed in 1996. It weakened the link – always far more tenuous in the USA than the EU anyway – between subsidies and

Exhibit 5.3 The MacSharry reforms

In the first years of the Uruguay Round, it was easy to dismiss as a joke the so-called 'zero option': the US proposal to eliminate all agricultural subsidies globally by the year 2000. One of its primary effects was to encourage a *laager* mentality in CAP circles. Nonetheless, strong pressure from the USA, as well as the 'Cairns group' of other agricultural exporters,[14] gave impetus to the decision to adopt the reforms tabled by the Agriculture Commissioner, Ray MacSharry. Logically, we might assume that the MacSharry reforms were driven mainly by the EU's internal budgetary crisis (see Rieger 1996: 114–15; Nugent 1994: 376–7). Yet, bilateral pressure from the USA was probably a more crucial factor (Paarlberg 1997), as evidenced by the fact that the MacSharry reforms were *more* expensive than the status quo. The MacSharry reforms' main provisions were:

- price cuts of 15 per cent for beef and 30 per cent for grain, with a new cereals regime fixing support prices until they were deliberately changed, thus making the annual price review less crucial;
- direct compensation to farmers to soften the blow of lower prices and discourage overproduction;
- compulsory 'set-aside' requiring large farmers to take some of their arable land out of production;
- flanking measures to encourage early retirement, afforestation, environmentally friendly farming methods and so on.

production and made American farmers more dependent on foreign (especially Asian) markets just before the 1998 Asian financial crisis. The Cairns group of agricultural exporters prepared to renew its alliance with the USA in pushing for further liberalisation of global agricultural markets in the next round of trade talks set to begin in 1999. And, of course, eastern EU enlargement hung over the CAP like a cold, thick fog.

Santer's Agriculture Commissioner, Franz Fischler, tried to seize on these pressures, as well as the budgetary squeeze caused by the beef crisis (see Exhibit 5.2), to develop the notion of a 'European social space' in which small farmers would be supported through a new 'rural policy'. EU aid would be shifted from larger to smaller farms through 'modulation', or setting an overall limit on the amount that any single farmer could receive, while integrating other EU policy instruments: linking farm aid to environmental services, using the structural funds to modernise rural telecommunications links, and so on.

The 1996 Irish Council presidency tried to run with rural policy, but did not get very far. The end result of a major conference on Europe's rural problems in Cork was a declaration that endorsed a confusing mix of principles, such as uniformity and subsidiarity. French and German reservations about the very idea of rural policy, shared by the Spanish, led a statement from the Cork conference to be dropped from the official conclusions of the December 1996 European Council meeting in Dublin.

The problem was not just one of vested interests: it was difficult to imagine an effective rural policy that was also not very expensive. The political upshot was that German backing was unlikely. The typical German farm remained considerably smaller than the average French farm, thus making an EU rural policy potentially attractive. Yet farm policy in Germany remained more sensitive to the votes of farmers than was the case in France. The CAP status quo reflected even more closely the preferences of the German farmers' association, the *Deutsche Bauernverband* (DBV), than the closest French equivalent, the *Fédération Nationale des Syndicats d'Exploitants Agricoles* (Hussain 1992). Any German government (prior to 1998) was likely to approach root and branch CAP reform with great reluctance. In assessing the prospects for an EU rural policy, or the CAP more generally, 'the single most important actor is Germany' (Grant 1997c: 161).

Moreover, an EU rural policy would require co-ordinated actions across EU policy sectors – particularly agricultural and environmental – and cohesion. Making it work would mean eliminating 'fire walls' which divide EU policy sectors. A history-making shift towards rural policy, while desirable in theory, was made difficult in practice and perhaps even precluded by the established power and autonomy of EU policy networks.

Setting the CAP: the 'Clubby' Council

'Setting' EU agricultural policy has often required high-level intervention to break a total impasse on the Agricultural Council. In 1988, for example, the European Council had to set annual farm prices at a long, ill-tempered meeting during which the French Prime Minister, Jacques Chirac, responded to remarks made by Margaret Thatcher by using an obscenity not often heard in diplomatic settings. Sometimes (although rarely), the EP has played a role in setting policy: in 1980, it dramatically rejected the EU's draft annual budget, thus paralysing CAP decision-making. By the late 1990s, a significant percentage of farm policy business was being 'kicked upstairs' to the General Affairs Council or European Council.

However, in normal times the Agriculture Council rules supreme on most CAP questions. Traditionally, it has met more frequently (about 15 times a year) each year than any other Council besides the General Affairs Council (Hayes-Renshaw and Wallace 1997: 30). In its early days, the Agriculture Council often saw certain ministers – such as Josef Ertl of West Germany from 1969 to 1983 – remaining in their posts for long periods of time, dominating the Council, and acting at odds with the rest of their domestic cabinets. The familiarity of Agriculture Ministers with each other helped to facilitate complex package deals, to which the Agriculture Council has always been more prone than any other version of the Council. It has always been willing to go to enormous lengths, in bargaining sessions which sometimes last for days, 'to find its own solutions, rather than passing any agricultural dossiers to the higher "cross-sectoral" General Council, where agricultural interests might be traded off against quite different ones' (van Schendelen 1996: 541).

Few industries in Europe have their own ministerial department as farmers do. It is little wonder that the ministers who head them tend to adopt the priorities of the industry as their own. The relative seclusion of agricultural ministries from the mainstream of governing most EU Member States also helps explain why it has been so difficult to reform the CAP to suit other EU policy priorities.

The autonomy of the Agriculture Council is accentuated by the fact that most of its decisions are prepared, not by the Committee of Permanent Representatives (COREPER), but by the Special Committee on Agriculture (SCA). The SCA was created on the grounds that the technical complexity of the CAP required a negotiating forum for specialists. The political reality was that farmers' interests were viewed as best served by a completely separate machinery for preparing CAP decisions. In practice, the SCA became more of a talking shop than a decision-making forum, and it was deciding less and less by the late 1990s. Asked why the SCA passed the buck so often, one national agricultural official replied:

> First, anything remotely politically controversial needs to be put to ministers. That is just the ethos. Second, it traditionally has always been that way, and there is just not that much scope for liberal thinking. Third, of course, is the money problem: even minor and technical decisions can have huge cost implications.[15]

Most members of the SCA do not hold ambassadorial rank, as do nearly all members of COREPER. The SCA simply lacks the authority to decide much that is very important.

The Commission has considerable autonomy to manage the CAP. Still, it sometimes finds its proposals watered down beyond all recognition by the Council, particularly when the country holding the chair strains to polish off agreements in June or December before passing the presidency to another Member State. The President-in-Office usually draws up an alternative proposal to the Commission's during the annual price review, even though it can only be accepted (by QMV) if the Commission also agrees to it (Swinbank 1996a). However, unity of purpose between national agricultural ministries and DG VI of the Commission is considerable. DG VI has benefited enormously from the Commission's prominent agricultural management role and the status of CAP as one of the EU's only common policies. It is the second largest Commission service, after DG IX (Personnel, which has no specific policy remit).

The EP's influence over the CAP is minimal. Its desire for a voice in the policy process, and repeated failure to achieve it, was symbolised by the Council's brushing aside of the EP's bitter condemnation of its behaviour during the 1996 beef crisis (see Exhibit 5.2). The EP remains a stubborn advocate of the consumer, and the Commission sometimes seeks alliances with it: a proposed ban on 'offal', a cattle feed linked to the BSE crisis, was rejected by farm ministers but then reintroduced as an internal market measure under co-decision. An advisor to the Commissioner for Consumer Affairs, Emma Bonino, described the switch as a 'tactical move. National governments will have to explain, under the glare of democratically elected representatives, why they are holding up a vital consumer protection measure'.[16] Yet consumer protection is by no means a hallmark of the CAP, and its 1997 budget for promoting olive oil consumption – considered 'compulsory spending' and thus untouchable by the EP – was more than the Union's entire consumer budget.[17]

In short, the Agriculture Council dominates the 'setting' of agricultural policy in the strongest sense of the term. Once the Council decides to grant support to a certain product or scheme, a qualified majority is usually needed to abolish support.[18] As a consequence, the CAP is extremely path dependent. To illustrate the point, the Council 'rescued' agricultural policy from the threat posed by floating exchange rates after 1971 by creating 'Monetary Compensatory Amounts' (MCAs) which 'in effect renationalized the common market with regard to agriculture' (Rieger 1996: 108). Like customs duties, MCAs insulated national markets from the effects of exchange rate changes. They required extensive border controls, and thus MCAs had to go when the 1992 project was launched. However, a system of artificial 'green currencies', set by agriculture ministers and fixed regardless of changes to 'ordinary' exchange rates, were still needed to keep agricultural markets, incomes and prices stable. MCAs and 'green currencies' are amongst the real exotica of the CAP. The important point is that the policy's mechanisms for coping with exchange rate changes (see Exhibit 5.4) provide yet another mechanism to pursue national interests despite the common financing of the CAP.

Even after the advent of the European Council in 1974, the Agriculture Council usually remained the overlords of the CAP. For example, the MacSharry reforms – after being watered down in various committees – were adopted by the Agriculture Council in May 1992 after a marathon, four-day meeting. The reforms had three main effects: they imposed new supply controls, reduced subsidised prices (by nearly 30 per cent for

Exhibit 5.4 Agrimonetary aids[19]

Before it was abolished in 1993, one of the CAP's most criticised elements was its so-called 'switch-over mechanism', which adjusted agricultural prices across the EU in response to changes in currency values. The effect of the mechanism was to create the equivalent of a 'Deutschmark zone' in agriculture and inflate farm prices – by as much as 20 per cent – because of the strength of the D-mark. A new system created to replace 'switch-over' was even more complex than its predecessor and complicated management of the CAP during the post-Maastricht currency crises of the mid-1990s (Grant 1995: 159).

In particular, exchange rate changes in 1995 led France to allege that other Member States (particularly Italy and Spain) had engaged in 'competitive depreciation' of their currencies, hurting French farmers. A proposal to allow the French to compensate their farmers was opposed by the UK, Italy and Sweden, which together wielded 24 votes under QMV: less than a blocking minority, but enough to trigger the so-called 'Ioannina compromise' (see Chapter 2) at the request of the UK. Italy offered to switch its vote, but sought concessions on citrus fruit, which were considered too expensive by other Member States and the Commission. The Spanish presidency refused British demands for changes in the actual proposal, thus focusing attention on Sweden. In the words of one participant, 'Sweden just kept asking for changes in the text, which showed that they are not used to dealing across issue-areas. In the end, they got state aids to their northern regions allowed, but it wasn't really their idea.'[20] Leaving aside Italian grumbling, all came away satisfied with the deal, except the UK. By this time, the Major government had isolated itself with its hard-line position concerning QMV in an EU of 15. Most Member States took pleasure in demonstrating that the Commission and Council presidency normally would seek to deal with whichever member was the cheapest to 'buy off', and not the one which invoked the Ioannina compromise, as the UK had intended.

The final decision on 'agrimonetary aids' was fascinating, for at least three reasons. First, France's pull within the CAP was abundantly illustrated, with many observers concurring that no other Member State could have secured the right to grant the (national) aids. Second, after joining the EU only months before, Sweden held a swing vote but had enormous difficulty wielding it to Swedish advantage, revealing how difficult it is for any newcomer to adjust to the cut and thrust of EU negotiations. Third, the episode showed the apparent emptiness of the Ioannina compromise.

cereals) and compensated farmers for lost income. The Council adopted the reforms only because of two crucial contingencies, without which they probably would have been rejected: first, farm ministers were pushed hard by their heads of government and cabinet colleagues to bite the bullet; second, it was conceded by the Agriculture Commissioner, Ray Mac-Sharry, as well as by national finance ministers (particularly Germany's), that no significant reforms were possible without generous compensation for farmers. The total budgetary cost of the CAP actually increased, with no prospect of altering the compensation scheme in future without a decision by QMV to do so.

The 1993 price round marked a return to 'business as usual'. Spending plans to offer extra compensation to farmers – French-inspired and with a price tag of around €1 billion over three years – were adopted (Grant 1995: 168). By 1995, the MacSharry Plan's provisions for 'set-aside', or the amount of arable land which farmers were compelled to leave fallow each year, had fallen from its original 15 per cent to 10 per cent after being reduced twice in two years.

The ability of the Agriculture Council to keep a grip on the CAP depends in large measure on who chairs it. Traditionally, major changes to the EU's regimes for sensitive products have required an honest broker in the chair. For example, sorely needed proposals for reforming the EU's wine and fruit sectors made little progress under the French, Spanish and Italian presidencies of 1995–6.[21] Enormous expectations built up in advance of the 1999 German presidency, during which Germany, as expected, moderated its domestic interests and brokered reforms crucial to eastern enlargement, while also linking CAP reform to reform of the EU's finances (see Exhibit 10.1).[22]

Major innovations in EU farm policy usually require individual Council Presidents-in-Office who are political heavyweights. It was difficult to imagine that milk quotas could have been adopted as a crisis measure to cope with massive surpluses in March 1984 had the Council's chair not been held by Michel Rocard, a prominent member of the French Socialist government (Avery 1984: 491–2; Swinbank 1989: 306). The operation of the milk quota system, which carves up dairy markets between Member States, is of interest mainly to true CAP aficionados, but it illustrates three general features of the CAP clearly. First, the EU sometimes 'strengthens the state' (Moravcsik 1994) by giving governments supranational policy instruments which they can control to suit their own agendas. Milk quotas were justified in 1984 on the grounds that they protected small farmers, but the Conservative British government permitted a 'market' to develop for quotas, which contributed to increased concentration in the British milk industry (Rieger 1996: 109).

Second, fines slapped on Italy in the early 1990s for vastly overstepping the limits of its milk quota demonstrate how meaningless the EU's formal rules often are. Italy managed to have its fines reduced considerably by trading them off against concessions in other, unrelated policy sectors. Concern about the precedent set by such Machiavellian deal making was outweighed by widely held concern to solve the problem and make a deal.

Third, the milk sector became one of the CAP's most hotly contested battlegrounds in advance of eastern enlargement. Proposals to scrap milk quotas after 2000 met with furious opposition, despite support from the UK, Sweden, Denmark and Italy. Fischler conceded that the plans would cause massive disruption to milk markets and producers but insisted that reform was essential, particularly in light of evidence that Poland's accession would bankrupt the existing system (see Exhibit 5.1).

Past EU enlargements and more frequent changes of government in long-time Member States have combined to make the Agriculture Council less 'clubby' over time. The entry of Greece, Spain and Portugal to the EU in the 1980s brought new categories of Mediterranean products that had never been subject to the CAP. Package deals had to become even more finely balanced to ensure that all ministers left the Council at least 51 per cent happy. After 1995, the accession of Austria, Finland and Sweden made bargaining even more complicated, with more CAP issues finding their way to meetings of foreign or prime ministers. But the CAP was often defended at the highest political levels, particularly by Helmut Kohl and Jacques Chirac.

Generally, however, the Agriculture Council is *the* key decision-maker on the CAP. It has managed to sustain the ethos that farmers should be compensated whenever any reduction in their 'entitlements' is mooted. The Council takes a broad range of decisions, including some which make history, and others that would be taken by far less 'political' levels in any other EU policy sector. It is the Agriculture Council, more than anything else, which sets the EU apart as a system for agricultural decision-making.

The Farm Lobby, the CAP and Policy Networks

The 'byzantine complexity' of the CAP is legendary (Neville-Brown 1981: 509). Technocratic specialists are empowered by the fact that the CAP is understood by so few. Even recent reforms have contained such complicated provisions that they have made the CAP less comprehensible to non-specialists (see Grant 1993, 1997c).

The complexity of the CAP may help explain why recent studies of EU lobbying have neglected farm lobby groups (see Greenwood *et al.* 1992; Mazey and Richardson 1993b; Greenwood 1997). The power of the farm lobby has declined but it still plays a crucial role. Given the weakness of the EP on agricultural questions, national and transnational farm groups have played the role – played by parties in national polities – of mediating between the interests of farmers and of the EU (Rieger 1996: 105).

Since the Council fixes most CAP support prices, farmers have tended to concentrate their lobbying on national capitals. Intimate, even incestuous, relationships between national agriculture ministries and farmers' groups have manifested themselves in quite insular and integrated national policy networks (see Smith 1990; Hussain 1992; Daugbjerg 1998). However, the autonomy of the CAP decision-making process and the power of farmers as a pressure group are separate matters: 'the influence of the farm lobby *per se*, as distinct from the existence of a separate decision-making network for agriculture, has been exaggerated in the past' (Grant 1993: 38).

Still, the complexity of the CAP helps tightly integrated farm policy communities to keep a grip on decision-making. In other industrialised countries, such as the USA, farmers are supported mainly by direct payments from public budgets. Such a system is far more transparent than is the CAP, which relies on market support and thus spreads the burden of paying for the policy to consumers as well as taxpayers. Although the post-MacSharry Plan CAP relies more heavily on direct payments, farming groups in the EU remain opposed to direct payments in principle because they are perceived as a one-way street to 'increased economic insecurity and a sharpened political dependence' (Rieger 1996: 117).

The main goal of the EU farm lobby thus is to preserve the CAP status quo. The transnational, Brussels-based peak-level association, the Committee of Professional Agriculture Organisations (COPA), has traditionally been one of the EU's most successful veto groups. Its influence is mainly limited to 'policy-shaping' decisions and its predominance has declined since the 1960s. Yet COPA and the rest of the farm lobby have been remarkably effective in protecting the privileges of its members:

> They shape agricultural policy-making by pointing out the likely economic and social consequences of decisions. But they are not able to influence the parameters of agricultural policy-making – which derive for the most part from welfare statism – nor are they in a position to formulate *positive* statements and proposals. (Rieger 1996: 117)

Highly fragmented decision-making mechanisms at the sub-systemic level are a significant barrier to sweeping policy change. There are far more Council working groups and various types of Commission committee in agriculture than in any other policy sector. The product-specificity of these committees is striking: there is no group of EU policy-makers whose eyes light up more than CAP-involved officials when the concept of 'policy networks' is explained to them. The use of labels such as 'the beef people', 'the milk people' or 'the wheat people' is commonplace in Brussels. At the sub-systemic level, at least, 'in practice there are several agricultural policies rather than just one' (Nugent 1994: 370).

At the core of CAP policy networks are approximately 20 management committees which are chaired and serviced by the Commission and exist for all individual products. They are preoccupied with decisions concerning measures such as export refunds that are, in most cases, delegated to the Commission and needed to manage agricultural markets on a daily basis. Each Member State sends one delegate, usually a civil servant based in a national capital, to each management committee and votes are distributed in the same way as on the Council under QMV. Management committees give their opinion on most Commission decisions before they are formally taken: a qualified majority is needed to give a 'favourable opinion', a negative opinion results from the same number of votes *against* a proposal, and no opinion is registered if there is no qualified majority either for or against.

Management committees thus provide a bridge between national imperatives and sectoral interests in CAP decision-making. Crucially, however, the Commission can do as it wishes unless there is a qualified majority *against* its proposed course of action. The Council can review and reverse (within a month) any decision that has received a negative opinion from a management committee. Management committees thus may 'limit the power of the Commission' (Rieger 1996: 108), but unfavourable opinions are rare and the Commission remains the crucial player in the day-to-day management of the CAP. Its status as 'ring-leader' of CAP policy networks is revealed by the way in which it (primarily DG VI) used COPA as a foil for asserting its prerogatives in the 1970s, only to 'sell out' the farm lobby quite blatantly when the Commission's overall priority became CAP reform in the early 1990s.

By this time, COPA and national farmers groups no longer even bothered lobbying the Commission very much. The Commission *was* lobbied heavily by the food industry (as opposed to farmers), which generally sought lower prices for agricultural products. In particular, food and drink interests continued to complain about the grip of producers on national agriculture ministries, the 'farmer-driven' nature of CAP decision-making, and specifically the management committee procedure. Usually, the agendas of management committees were either kept secret or only made available to food and drink industry representatives just before they were convened, thus allowing them little opportunity to influence decisions (Swinbank 1989: 318). The Commission generally remains the guardian of the policy agenda within specific CAP networks. But it is important to acknowledge that there is no clear, simple alliance between the Commission and farming interests.

In particular, the policy analyst must distinguish between DG VI and the Commission as a whole. DG VI's power as the Directorate-General *for* Agriculture has become increasingly subject to challenge by other arms of the Commission, particularly DG I but also DG III (Industry), which tends to defend the interests of the food industry and is a key agenda-setter in 'foodstuffs' policy (see Exhibit 5.5). In the face of such challenges, DG VI has been impressively resilient. Witness its success in co-ordinating the farm lobby's successful attempts to block or shape plans for new free trade agreements with the USA, South Africa and Mercosur in 1997–8, in the latter case amidst charges from COPA that liberalising farm trade with Latin America was 'incomprehensible' and 'disastrous' in the view of a spokesperson for French farmers.[23]

DG VI also was effective in perpetuating the myth of the CAP as a 'cornerstone' of European integration. In 1994, it effectively buried DG II's (Economics and Finance) so-called 'Munk Report' which questioned the wisdom of a 'common' agricultural policy and asked whether renationalisation might facilitate reform (Grant 1997: 216–17). In nearly all cases, DG VI was firmly backed by France. Proposals in 1998 to reform the EU's finances by transferring a large chunk (up to one-quarter) of CAP spending to national budgets were curtly dismissed by the French Finance Minister, Dominique Strauss-Kahn, as 'not in the spirit of Community action'.[24] No Directorate-General is purely the *domaine réservé* of any single Member State (see Peterson 1997), but DG VI comes close: virtually all of its internal communications are in French, and its Director-General is always a French national.

At all levels of decision-making, including the sub-systemic level, the CAP closely resembles no other EU policy sector. Yet the CAP has quite a lot in common with farm policy decision-making processes in *other* industrialised states, nearly all of which result in high food prices, regressive income redistribution and high costs both domestically and internationally (Grant 1995). The CAP's complexity is almost impossible to overstate, and in many respects is an anathema to coherence or centralisation. At the sub-systemic level as much as elsewhere, 'The CAP is not quite as common or as integrated as it is often thought to be' (Nugent 1994: 384).

Conclusion

The CAP is expensive, wasteful (see Exhibit 5.6) and regressive. It also persists as a symbol of European unity. It has proved remarkably resilient in the face of pressures for reform. The CAP has endured largely unchanged and its decision-making mechanisms remain relatively isolated from and impervious to non-agricultural influences. Above all, the CAP is

Exhibit 5.5 'Foodstuffs': regulating Europe's culinary riches

EU foodstuffs policy, designed to ensure food safety and a single market for food products, is more decentralised, technocratic and 'nationalised' than the CAP itself. Decentralisation is a natural consequence of both the logistical impossibility of harmonising so many diverse national rules – up to 120 000 on food additives, for example – across the EU as well as the cultural imperative summed up in a Commission (1985a) communication: 'it is neither possible nor desirable to confine in a legislative straitjacket the culinary riches of . . . European countries'. Prior to the European Court of Justice (ECJ)'s landmark *Cassis de Dijon* decision (see Exhibit 2.4), the most common approach to foodstuffs legislation was to harmonise national laws using what became Article 94,[25] which required unanimous voting and meant very slow progress. The 'new approach' was applied to foodstuffs beginning in 1985.

Most decisions about foodstuffs are made within highly technocratic policy networks. All Commission proposals involving food safety must be preceded by consultation of the Scientific Committee for Food (SCF), established in 1974. It consists of eminent scientists drawn from a variety of disciplines concerned with food safety, and is often 'helpful in overcoming politically constituted preferences by relying on the fiction of objective science' (Joerges and Neyer 1997: 619). A plethora of working groups operates under the SCF, with scientists sometimes drawn from outside the EU. The SCF sits at the top of a structure of individual networks – many of which are tightly integrated – corresponding to different categories of food. The Committee's opinions have been judged to be 'prima facie' evidence of safety in the eyes of the ECJ in a

→

the way it is because most Member States want it that way. It is hard to imagine that any other 'common' policy could serve the national interests of so many individual EU Member States.

In analytical terms, policy network analysis may be more apt as a method for understanding the CAP than for any other EU policy sector. However, the same could be said for virtually any western system of support for farmers: 'Exclusivity, specialised institutions operating privileged arrangements, and policy complexity serving as a political entry barrier have been among the distinctive features of agricultural policy communities across a number of countries' (Grant 1995: 168). The CAP reveals that the most powerful EU policy networks are those which are able to operate as veto groups and prevent policy change. Inertia remains a powerful force in EU decision-making, and the CAP illustrates this point better than any other sector.

⟶

number of cases. The primary emphasis of comitology in foodstuffs appears not to be defending national interests so much as 'identifying areas of interdependence and common interest with the aim of ensuring the coherence and reliability of the European management network in the foodstuffs sector' (Joerges and Neyer 1997: 609).

The EP plays an important role in food policy. Most decisions are taken under internal market procedures and the Parliament usually presents itself as the defender of consumer rights. The EP was an important catalyst behind the EU ban on cattle hormones in the late 1980s (see Exhibit 4.5). It was the prime focus for lobbying on a later directive regulating the use of sweeteners, which featured major disputes involving industrial and national interests (Earnshaw and Judge 1993).

A centralised, American-style system of food safety regulation has been resisted by the EU. An EU equivalent of the 1993 US Nutrition Labeling and Education Act, which required detailed information on product labels at an additional annual cost of around $50 per household, was rejected on the grounds of 'adverse social effectiveness in bringing the least benefit to those [presumably the poor and uneducated] for whom the relative cost is the highest' (Gray 1993: 6). At the same time, pressures built up for stronger EU consumer protection, particularly after the EP began calling for the creation of a US-style Food and Drug Administration (FDA) in 1990. New demands mounted on the back of the 1996 beef crisis (see Exhibit 5.2). The eventual creation of a Euro-FDA became imaginable for the first time as institutions (such as DG VI and the British Ministry of Agriculture, Fisheries and Food) with responsibility for food safety *and* close ties to food producers faced widespread accusations of conflict of interest.

Recent reforms reflect, to a considerable extent, widespread consensus on the need to 'save' the CAP. In retrospect, external pressures for reform, which were such an important feature of the Uruguay Round, appeared actually to increase resistance in Europe to globalisation and the threat it poses to the CAP (Grant 1997b). The Commission's *Agenda 2000* proposals called for quite deep cuts in support prices, but the 1999 Berlin summit yielded agreement on far less radical reforms. Those who argued that the CAP was not worth 'saving' faced the burden of proving that steps towards the renationalisation of agriculture would not impose even higher costs, while damaging and dividing the EU.

Eastern enlargement puts the CAP, as we know it, under threat as never before. Fischler insisted that his 1998 reform package provided a 'much-needed example to Eastern candidates for EU membership. The European model of agriculture no longer justifies artificially high prices'.[27]

Exhibit 5.6 Fraud and the CAP[26]

Even the CAP's staunchest defenders cannot deny that it is riddled with fraud. All CAP-watchers have their favourite tale of scam: for example, in 1993 the Court of Auditors reported that €50 million had been spent over five years to subsidise rice exports to Réunion, even though the French island supplied more than its own consumption of the product.

The problem of fraud is mostly a result of three factors: first, near-total national control over the detection and reporting of fraud; incentives built into the CAP to cheat; and the policy's ultra-complexity. As the CAP is, in many respects, the EU's only truly common policy, most cases of Commission maladministration – the incorrect application of administrative rules – concern agricultural policy. Yet the amounts lost in this way are tiny compared to those lost through fraud at the national level. Although most actual decision-making takes place in Brussels, the CAP is almost entirely implemented by national bodies. The Commission is unlikely ever to have enough monitors to police the CAP and the (nearly 5 million) farmers who benefit from it. Member States have weak incentives to turn in their own farmers if the result is likely to be reduced national receipts from the CAP.

The complexity of the CAP makes it a fraudster's dream. Around 400 new sets of provisions, or rules, are issued every year for about 1400 different product groups. Until the early 1990s, the beef regime divided the world into 11 different zones with different rates of export refund for each, and further variances for different types of beef (such as chilled or frozen). Advance knowledge of expected changes in levels of export refunds, which are discussed in management committees, can bring large commercial benefits. Thus a 'mini-industry has evolved in Brussels, garnishing information from the Commission services and Member State delegates about the proposals placed before management committees', and faxing information to commercial clients (Swinbank 1989: 318). The 'green money' system encouraged 'roundabout', or the practice of repeated crossing of frontiers (such as the border between the Republic of Ireland and Ulster) by the same goods to secure 'compensation'.

The MacSharry reforms, particularly their provisions for cutting back export subsidies, had important anti-fraud effects. The Santer Commission, dogged by EP allegations that it was soft on fraud, endorsed the idea of creating an independent anti-fraud investigations office and insisted on higher-than-usual 'clearances of accounts' for detected fraud cases. A total of nearly €1 billion in fines were either levied or made subject to conciliation in 1996, with about three-quarters involving four Member States: Italy (a staggering €416 million alone), Spain (€206 million), Greece (€165 million) and Ireland (€87 million).

CAP fraud may be less rife now than ever before, but agriculture remains the single most important source of waste in EU governance. It will remain so unless a massive (and thus far unimaginable) shift from price support to income support takes place.

This line of argument justified EU plans *not* to offer compensation payments to east European farmers until 2006 at the earliest.

Yet, the 'European model of agriculture' has been built around the idea that farms, farmers and rural life are essential cornerstones of European culture and society (see Coleman 1998; Skogstad 1998). As Nugent (1994: 362) argues,

> The view that there is something special about agriculture, something that distinguishes it from other sectoral activities and merits it receiving special advantageous treatment, whilst not commanding such strong support as in the early days of the EC, still strikes a chord with EU decision-makers.

This view – or sentiment – will not soon disappear. It will continue to narrow profoundly the range of policy options for the EU of the 21st century.

Chapter 6

Cohesion Policy

Cohesion policy in context
Cohesion policy and intergovernmental bargaining
The systemic level: who sets policy?
The sub-systemic level: how networks shape
  decisions
Conclusion

Cohesion policy marks out one of the most ambitious, complex and misunderstood areas of EU decision-making. It is important in budgetary terms – consuming over a third of the EU budget – but also in its sheer ambition, unintended consequences and wider influence on EU governance. Cohesion policy refers to a set of activities designed to reduce disparities and promote a more even pattern of economic development across the EU. In its broadest sense it means applying cohesion objectives to a range of EU policies (such as competition) and high-level co-ordination of macroeconomic policy. But its primary tools have been the *structural funds*, aimed primarily at helping regions suffering from low gross domestic product (GDP), high unemployment, or industrial or agricultural decline (see Table 6.1), and the *Cohesion Fund*, which reserves funds for infrastructure and environmental projects in four countries – Greece, Ireland, Portugal and Spain – whose GDP is less than 90 per cent of the EU's average. These policy tools are not designed only to aid 'regional development' narrowly defined. By promising solidarity and 'harmonious development',[1] they also work (in principle, at least) to create a 'social space' or a 'European wide socioeconomic and political fabric' (Hooghe 1996b: v).

The cohesion policy decision-making process is complex. It is marked by a blurring of stages (formulation/implementation) and a conscious attempt to bring together policy actors across different levels of governance. This exercise in multi-level governance has fired the imaginations of EU scholars, but has left open the question: is cohesion policy a 'one-off', unlike any other area of EU policy, or does it reflect a wider transformation of EU governance?

146

Table 6.1   *EU structural funds: the basics*

The Funds
In 1988 three separate funds were brought under the same framework to form the 'structural funds':

- the European Regional Development Fund (ERDF),
- the European Social Fund (ESF) and
- the European Agricultural Guidance and Guarantee Fund (EAGGF).

A fourth instrument, the Financial Instrument for Fisheries Guidance (FIFG), was established in 1993. By the late 1990s the four funds amounted to around 35 per cent of all EU spending.

The Regulations
The 'structural fund regulations' stipulate the overall design of the structural funds, including the priority objectives of the funds, the principles under which they will operate (see below) and the role of various actors in their operation and implementation.

The Operating Principles

Concentration
The funds are concentrated on priority 'objectives' for lagging regions, declining industrial areas, unemployment, worker adaptation and rural development. Despite the goal of concentration, over 50 per cent of the EU's population was covered under one or more of these objectives in the period 1994–9.

Programming
'Structural programming' refers to the design of specific economic programmes for the expenditure of EU structural funds in particular regions or Member States.

Partnership
The principle of partnership requires the involvement of relevant actors from EU, national and sub-national levels at all stages of the planning and implementation of programmes.

Additionality
Additionality is the often controversial requirement that any funds received from Brussels should be additional to national spending and not just a substitute for national funds.

Source: Commission (1996d).

Cohesion Policy in Context

The growth of EU cohesion policy has spurred the development of models of 'multi-level governance' (MLG) which emphasise the decreasing importance of central governments, the 'existence of overlapping competencies among multiple levels of governments and the interaction of political actors across those levels' (Marks *et al.* 1996a, 1996b). Going further, some claim that a 'Europe of the Regions' has begun to emerge, with power being usurped from national governments both 'upwards' to the EU level and 'downwards' to sub-national actors (see Anderson 1990; Harvie 1994; Hooghe 1995; Jeffrey 1996).

Critics of these approaches underline the continuing dominance of national actors and interests. Allen (1996a: 210) argues that cohesion policy is best seen as a series of side payments designed to facilitate intergovernmental package deals related to the advancement of the European integration. Pollack (1995) demonstrates how the essential framework of cohesion policy has been determined by a process of high-level intergovernmental bargaining, assisted by the Commission but primarily resolved by the central governments of the Member States. Intergovernmentalist accounts assume that decision-making related to the formulation of cohesion policy remains dominated by high politics and is not indicative of new pattern of multi-level governance.

Clearly, Member States still dominate the history-making decisions which guide cohesion policy. Yet, decision-making concerning the management of cohesion policy guarantees a strong role for the Commission and sub-national authorities (SNAs). For their part, advocates of MLG recognise that national state actors still command overwhelming relative power compared to both European transnational and sub-national actors: 'National state sovereignty has not been replaced by a European sovereign state' even if non-state actors have become more influential over time (Hooghe 1996c: 16). The complexity of EU cohesion policy provides grist for both these theoretical mills. But this chapter argues that the real question is not 'who determines' cohesion policy. Clearly, different actors dominate different tiers and stages of decision-making. The more important question for understanding cohesion policy is how, and with what effect, decisions taken at one tier affect those taken at another.

A multi-tiered examination of cohesion policy suggests that it has been above all a political rather than an economic exercise. Spending on cohesion policy has increased remarkably since the 1970s. Constituting less than 5 per cent of the budget in 1975, cohesion policy was set to take more than one-third of total EU spending by 1999. The sums involved are massive: €27.4 billion in 1999 up from €7 billion in 1987 (Commission 1996a). The economic rationale for cohesion policy usually hinges on factors such as efficiency (the EU can improve the efficiency of national regional development by ensuring that spending is concentrated where it is most needed); 'common economic interest' (depressed regions harm the entire EU on economic and social equity grounds); and 'dynamism' (regional disparities may be a barrier to smooth functioning of the single market) (Armstrong and Taylor 1993; Wishlade 1996). In short, structural funds are a tool to reduce economic disparities by contributing to the development of the poorest regions, but in the general 'Community interest'.

Yet it is clear that, even at their present levels, the funds are not large enough to make a significant difference either to regional disparities or to convergence, even though income from the fund is significant for poorer states (Tsoukalis 1993). Moreover, while the gap between the EU's richest and poorest Member States (in terms of per capita gross domestic product: GDP) has narrowed, regional disparities within individual countries have actually increased. Measured by certain criteria such as unemployment levels, the gap between regions is wider than ever (Commission 1999).

The development of cohesion policy thus requires a political explanation (see Wallace 1977; Allen 1996a; George 1996). Put simply, cohesion policy *means* have been more important than policy *ends*. The funds have had the political effect of binding together the Union, even though they are far too small to have their desired economic effect. Cohesion policy is the primary reason why several Member States are net contributors to the EU's budget (see Chapter 10). But paradoxically, because of this imbalance there is a will on the part of the Commission, and a desire on the part of Member States, to distribute the benefits of cohesion policy widely, to the extent that over half the EU's population was covered by funds by the late 1990s.

Throughout the EU's development, cohesion policy has been used as a bargaining tool, side payment, or inducement to get (especially poorer) Member States to go along with more general integrative moves (Allen 1996a; Wishlade 1996). Cohesion policy's role as a lubricant was underlined by the Director General for regional policy, Eneko Landaburu, in 1997. Explaining the Commission's proposal for the forthcoming round of structural funds reforms, he voiced reassurance that there would be measures for the poorer countries, for the new entrants, but also aid for the poor regions in the richer countries: 'There is something for everybody'.[2] Cohesion policy is thus a political tool: without it, package deals would be harder to broker and poorer Member States less willing to bear the harsh economic sacrifices that certain economic policies (such as EMU) may require.

Cohesion Policy and Intergovernmental Bargaining

This use of cohesion policy as a side payment in larger bargains may be seen in a series of history-making decisions which have determined the overall distribution of funds and direction of cohesion policy (see Table 6.2). These decisions have included treaty revisions, agreeing multi-annual budgets, as well as more specific choices concerning 'Objective 1' regions, in particular determining which regions qualify for the largest slice of structural aid.

In 1974, Member States agreed unanimously to the establishment of the European Regional Development Fund (ERDF). Wallace (1977) and Allen (1996a: 212) illustrate how the creation of the Fund was essential to the brokering of consensus between Member States on enlargement and further integration. The basic ERDF deal set up a fund, agreed a budget for 1975–8 and established a set of national quotas to determine the division of funds amongst Member States. The Commission was cast as little more than an administrator, with overall decision-making dominated by national governments working under the quota system.

The Single European Act (SEA) inserted in the Treaty a new title which mentioned the goal of cohesion and explicitly linked it to reducing economic disparities between regions. The SEA provided a constitutional base for the set of far reaching reforms in 1988 which dramatically altered the content and process of cohesion policy. The Delors I budget package, adopted at the Brussels summit in February 1988, doubled the budget of the structural funds and revamped decision-making surrounding cohesion policy's formulation and implementation.

The impetus for this historic package of reforms was the interplay between Iberian enlargement and completion of the single market. Fears that the single market would make rich regions richer and poor regions poorer led to an explicit linkage between cohesion policy and the 1992 project. More to the point, the doubling of funds was required to secure

Table 6.2   *Cohesion policy: history-making decisions*

1974	Paris summit: European Regional Development Fund established
1986	Single European Act : new title
1988	Brussels summit: Delors I/1988 reforms
1991	Maastricht Treaty: EMU/Cohesion Fund established
1992	Edinburgh summit: Delors II/1993 reforms
1997	Agenda 2000 proposed

from the four poorest Member States a commitment to the single market project. The result was presented as a contribution to solidarity, but best understood as a traditional package deal (Allen 1996a; George 1996: 238; Pollack 1995).

Changes in decision-making rules were far reaching. The three existing funds (ERDF, European Social Fund and the EAGGF) were brought under the same framework. New operating principles were also introduced (see Table 6.1).

The impact of these reforms on decision-making was as dramatic as it was unforeseen. In particular, the 1988 changes enhanced the position of the Commission, which now had the power to designate the regions that would be eligible for assistance under the different objectives. The Commission was also given central control over 10 per cent of the structural funds budget set aside for specific EU-wide measures. Moreover, the 1988 reforms widened the circle of participants considerably, in particular by giving a more explicit role to sub-national authorities in the design and implementation of funding programmes.

The Maastricht Treaty and Cohesion Fund (see Exhibit 6.1) again illustrated the importance of cohesion policy in high-level intergovernmental bargaining. Felipe Gonzalez, Spanish Prime Minister and poor countries' standard bearer, fought tenaciously and successfully in the run-up to the Maastricht summit to win a greater commitment to cohesion (see Dinan 1994: 409). Article 161[3] stipulated that the Council, acting unanimously on a proposal from the Commission and with the assent of Parliament, would set up a Cohesion Fund. The unanimous decision in 1992 to establish the Cohesion Fund was a prize given to poorer Member States in return for their endorsement of further enlargement, integration and acceptance of the Danish opt outs from the Maastricht Treaty.[4]

In 1992, the Commission also presented its proposed 'Delors II' budgetary package for 1993–7. The Commission proposed improving structural funds operations (through, say, closer monitoring) and increasing spending for Objective 1 regions. Marathon negotiation sessions in July 1993 over the budget package in general, and designation of Objective 1 areas in particular, were even more intense than usual. First, Member States competed to portray their own underdeveloped regions as the most desperately poor, thus making them eligible for Objective 1 funding (see Exhibit 6.2). Several Member States threatened to block any agreement on dispersing funds unless they received guarantees on the share they sought. The prize for being most obstructionist went to the Irish government, who had made the sum of I£8 billion in structural aid part of a crude pro-Maastricht ratification domestic campaign. Only a dramatic intervention by Jacques Delors secured a deal on the budget. Summoned from his bed at 5.30 am and suffering from sciatica, Delors savaged the ministers present

Exhibit 6.1 The Cohesion Fund: Intergovernmental Hardball

While often controversial, the notion of 'cohesion' seldom made headlines before 1991. In the IGC of that year, however, Spain led the poorer countries in a well-orchestrated, well-publicised campaign for the inclusion of a special protocol which would supplement the Maastricht Treaty's cohesion provisions. Acrimonious negotiations over money were averted by a decision at the Maastricht summit to leave decisions on actual sums until later. The protocol agreed at Maastricht restated the EU's cohesion objectives, linked them to EMU, and specified that a Cohesion Fund be established which would benefit Member States with a per capita GDP less than 90 per cent of the Community average. The real bargaining came in later negotiations at the 1992 Edinburgh summit when precise sums were agreed. The Spanish Prime Minister Felipe Gonzalez led the cohesion countries in fierce negotiations. Their strategy was threefold: insist on the need for more financial help in meeting EMU criteria; link the Cohesion Fund to more general demands for increased structural funds; and threaten to veto other agreements already reached, such as the EU's handling of Denmark's opt-outs or the opening of accession talks with European Free Trade Association (EFTA) countries. In an early morning meeting at the close of the summit, Kohl and Mitterrand finally agreed to endorse the budget increases sought by the cohesion countries (see Laffan and Shackleton 1996: 84). In addition to the 'need to get something done' in the aftermath of Maastricht ratification troubles, Kohl also wanted to show his gratitude for Spanish support for early German unification. One German participant explained: 'Our Chancellor felt obliged to demonstrate [he was] still a good European, but it was also a "thank you" for support of unification.'[5] The UK presidency was fiercely averse to higher spending, but the Major government was soothed by the assurance that the

→

for being 'anti-community' and threatened to expose their greed to assembled reporters.[7]

Second, Member States took decisions which clawed back some of the power lost to the Commission and SNAs in the 1988 reform. While the extent to which power was 'renationalised' is debated (see below) the new rules agreed in 1993 did ease requirements on additionality and partnership, and gave Member States a greater role in determining eligibility.

Later changes resulted from similar package deals. In the mid-1990s, new Nordic entrants were able to secure a new category of funding to favour sparsely populated areas as part of their accession package (see Peterson and Bomberg 1998). More monumental was the tabling of

⟶

UK would be able to keep its budget rebate (see Exhibit 10.1) despite earlier opposition from Germany and France.

The four beneficiaries of the Cohesion Fund – Greece, Ireland, Portugal and Spain – together received €15 billion over the period 1993–9 to help finance transport, infrastructure and environmental projects. Spain was the clear winner: the new Cohesion Fund, combined with increases in its structural funds, effectively doubled Spanish receipts of EU money for regional development.

On one hand, the considerable resources pledged under the Cohesion Fund appeared a remarkable display of 'Community solidarity', enabling the wealthiest countries to aid their less prosperous partners (Commission 1996a). Yet the Fund was an even more graphic display of the by now familiar role of cohesion policy as a lubricant. Put another way, the funds were intended to create the economic *and* political conditions necessary for EMU and further integration more generally. One senior Commission official summed it up this way: 'Let's be clear, the Cohesion Fund was the price for EMU, just as structural funds were the price for the single market.'[6]

The Cohesion Fund was also the result of a familiar two-staged bargaining process. First came agreement in principle for establishment of the Cohesion Fund by 1993. The precise funding levels were left undecided until the 1992 Edinburgh summit. Similarly, Member States agreed at Edinburgh to increase the size of the structural funds, and altered the criteria governing the allocation of funds to different objectives. But a decision on how the prize would be divided up between Member States was left for another day. This two-stage bargaining process illustrates a wider tendency in EU decision-making: a basic deal is agreed, but 'sequentially implemented for reasons of decision-making efficiency' (Allen 1996a: 219; see also Majone 1994, McAleavey 1994). Put more bluntly: EU decision-makers will seldom make tough choices today if they can be postponed until tomorrow.

proposed structural fund reforms arising from *Agenda 2000* (Commission 1997b). In 1998, the Commission presented its proposals for a financial framework for the period 2000–2006, including new regulations governing the structural funds (Commission 1998e). In many respects, these reforms marked the most fundamental overhaul of structural funding ever. The proposed changes were part of a much larger package which included reform of the CAP and pre-accession agreements with East European countries. In its section on structural fund reform, Agenda 2000 suggested a tighter concentration of resources, a simplification of monitoring procedures and a greater role for Member States in the day to day administration and monitoring of the funds (see Table 6.3).

Table 6.3   *What is new under Agenda 2000*

Agenda 2000 altered each of the four key principles guiding the operation of the structural funds:

Concentration
The proposed regulations for 2000–2006 promised to reduce the percentage of the population covered from 50 to around 40 per cent, and limit the number of objectives to three:

- Objective 1 criteria remain the same: regions whose economic performance is under 75 per cent of EU average;
- Objective 2 covers areas of industrial decline and urban deprivation (which would include measures for rural and fishing communities);
- Objective 3 aims at the development of training and 'employability'. It takes as its starting point the new title on employment introduced in the Amsterdam Treaty.

Programming
The programming requirements are redesigned to ensure a clearer division of responsibilities: the Commission will set broad strategic priorities (from a list including competitiveness, innovation, employment and sustainable development), but leave to the Member States the management and monitoring of programmes.

Partnership
In the proposed regulations, SNAs are not necessarily the primary 'partner'. In addition to local and regional governments, the principle is broadened to include private and social partners and other relevant organisations, such as environmental non-governmental organisations.

Additionality
The proposed regulations relax this requirement by limiting and simplifying the procedures by which 'additionality' is verified.

Source: Commission (1998e).

Although it included no increase in overall budget contributions,[8] the Commission's blueprint was still controversial for financial and political reasons. Agenda 2000 was presented at a time of intensified controversy concerning Member State contributions, and a more fundamental debate concerning the future of the structural funds in the context of enlargement. By late 1997, Spain had again cast itself as the standard bearer for cohesion countries by arguing that the accession of new members should not mean cuts in cohesion funds for current recipients. In November 1997, Spain's State Secretary for Europe warned that altering the current patterns of spending on cohesion 'would imply such an injustice that Spain would not be willing to accept it'.[9]

Richer states also felt threatened. Under the Commission's figures, the UK looked set to lose hundreds of millions from the nearly €2.3 billion it received annually in the period 1994–99. Two regions (Northern Ireland and the Scottish Highlands and Islands) were set to lose their Objective 1 status, and several recipients of the Objective 2 fund no longer looked likely to qualify. By March 1998, the UK had already won a concession when the Commission announced that no country would lose more than one third of its current support (in terms of the percentage of population covered) in areas of industrial and rural decline. Nonetheless, Britain campaigned for further concessions and sought to broaden the eligibility criteria which it believed were too heavily based on unemployment.

In the past, cohesion policy had been used to convince poorer countries to accept further integration and enlargement. This time, however, seduction of this kind was far less plausible. In particular, the EU's main paymaster, Germany, voiced its intention in early 1998 to reduce significantly its contribution to the EU's budget. At the Cardiff summit in June 1998 Chancellor Kohl, facing a domestic selection later that year, pushed for a special rebate (not unlike that secured by the UK in 1984) which would reduce Germany's disproportionate net contribution to the EU budget. While backed by the Austrians, Dutch and Swedes, Germany's bid met fierce opposition, not least from the French, who feared they would be the loser in any budget carve-up. Clearly, securing the financial resources for expansion would continue to prompt serious clashes between Member States.

Much can be learned from studying intergovernmental bargaining and package dealing at the super-systemic level. Member States clearly do set the 'budgetary envelope' (Marks 1996b) which broadly determines 'who gets what'. Decisions at this level are driven more by politics than by economics. Intergovernmentalist accounts tend to assume that only this stage matters very much. For instance Allen (1996a: 222) argues that, once the budget is set, essentially everything else is implementation which 'does not constitute a significant stage in the policy process . . . because of the restrictive parameters set by the basic or "historic" agreements'. But this argument misses two important points. First, stages are blurred: in cohesion policy, implementation and formulation co-exist (see Exhibit 6.2) and there is no clear demarcation between them. Second, Allen's argument neglects an important reverse dynamic: namely, the ways in which decisions and bargains struck at lower tiers restrict or shape intergovernmental bargaining.

Exhibit 6.2 Bargaining to be poor: the coveted Objective 1 status

Objective 1 regions receive the biggest chunk of structural aid, accounting for two-thirds of the structural funds budget in the 1994–9 period. Eligibility is meant to be restricted to those regions whose GDP is less than 75 per cent of the EU average. However, the intergovernmental nature of these decisions requires lots of room for fudge. The precedent was set in 1988 when, partially as an effort to make the funds more attractive to the UK, ministers agreed to give Objective 1 status to Northern Ireland even though its GDP was closer to 79 per cent of the EU average. Eligibility decisions in 1993 continued the trend. The unofficial benchmark became 79 per cent, and the economic criteria adopted by the Commission under Delors II (and agreed at the 1992 Edinburgh summit) were watered down accordingly. In addition to the 'Cohesion Four' (Spain, Portugal, Greece and Ireland) and Northern Ireland, which were covered in their entireties, several new regions received the status: in the UK, Merseyside and the Scottish Highlands and Islands; in Belgium, the Hainaut region in Wallonia. The inclusion of Hainaut prompted vociferous complaints from the French who claimed Hainaut's inclusion would lead to a distortion of competition with the neighbouring French region, Nord–Pas-de-Calais (which the French made a point of labelling 'French Hainaut'). For its part, the Netherlands pressed for the inclusion of Flevoland, a 'godforsaken piece of reclaimed soil complete with resident hippies'.[10] Italy pressed for the continued inclusion of Abruzzi even though its GDP was close to 90 per cent of the EU average. In the end, everyone was a winner: the Cohesion Four, Merseyside, the Scottish Highlands and Islands, Nord–Pas-de-Calais and Flevoland were included, and Abruzzi was allowed to continue its Objective 1 status until the end of 1997.

→

The Systemic Level: Who Sets Policy?

History-making decisions determine the broad direction of cohesion policy as well as the multi-annual budget allocations amongst Member States. They provide the framework of cohesion policy for a five- to six-year period. But between these history-making decisions, cohesion policy is 'set' by a broader and more diverse set of actors motivated by different interests. Policy setting in cohesion policy refers primarily to decisions which establish the 'institutional design' (Marks 1996b) of cohesion policy. More specifically, these decisions concern the establishment of eligibility and the drawing up of formal regulations (see Table 6.1).

→

Commission representatives decried the triumph of 'political over technical' criteria: 'Even though ground rules were set in Edinburgh, all we saw [on the Council] was political decisions and dealing. The technical criteria were all but abandoned.'[11] A German representative conceded: 'What finally came out of the Council meeting stood the notion of "rational" criteria on its head: it was a pure bargaining process.'[12] During all-night bargaining sessions in July 1993, a miffed Commissioner for Regional Policy Bruce Millan refused to commit the Commission to specific figures, provoking a revolt among Member States who accused him of displaying a 'Scottish accountant's mentality'.[13] Unflustered, Millan later remarked of the bargain: 'I dare say when you're talking about money lots of people get disappointed.'[14] He argued that 'It's not a question of being pedantic or bureaucratic, it's just that the more you dilute the thing, the less valuable it is.' The Scot even conceded that the Scottish Highlands and Islands was a 'very marginal case . . . the figures the previous time the area was looked at showed that they actually had a gross domestic product of 90 per cent of the Community. But these are ultimately political decisions'.[15]

Similarly, in the run-up to Agenda 2000, the head of DG XVI, Eneko Landaburu, again urged that the Commission's 'non-political' criteria be applied. He pleaded: 'We must be vigilant. In some countries there may be pressure to include regions for political reasons. We must not have a political list.'[16] But Objective 1 decisions will always be political decisions. Moreover, the Commission's virtuous insistence on 'non-political' technical criteria is itself somewhat misleading: the Commission ultimately is concerned with its own institutional power which lies, not least, in its ability to apply 'neutral' criteria.

At this level, institutional rules, norms, muscle flexing and bargaining go some way towards explaining the shape and character of cohesion policy. A 'winning coalition' (Hooghe and Keating 1994: 372) of actors spanning EU, national and sub-national institutions has shaped cohesion policy into one of the most financially important policy sectors. But the broad, tri-level (EU, national, sub-national) support base for an expanded cohesion policy has also expanded opportunities for institutional conflict. The systemic level is characterised by competition between institutions over who controls cohesion policy, but success in setting cohesion policy is determined above all by the extent to which actors can build broad, interinstitutional coalitions.

The central importance of the Commission in setting cohesion policy has been widely studied. Advocates of multi-level governance in particular have emphasised the central, even dominant, role played by the Commission. Hooghe (1996a) portrays the Commission as an essentially autonomous actor in this sector. Conzelmann (1995: 139) argues that cohesion policy is 'one of the rare examples of an EU policy in which the European Commission is able to directly influence the structures of policy formulation and implementation'. Even state-centric accounts concede the central importance of the Commission at the agenda-setting and management stages (Allen 1996a; Pollack 1995: 374–5).

The Commission owes much of its strength to what other institutions do not or cannot do. Cohesion policy (like external trade) lacks a dedicated Council. Cohesion policy is covered by a variety of councils and it thus lacks the regular routinised collaboration enjoyed by ministers and officials in other sectors (Hayes-Renshaw and Wallace 1997: 30). For instance, the structural funds reforms presented in Agenda 2000 were discussed in the General Affairs Council, Social Affairs Council, Informal Council of Regional Ministers, Agriculture Council and the Council of Economic and Finance Ministers (ECOFIN). Sometimes the result is that Council members are not terribly well informed about cohesion policy. A member of the Regional Commissioner's *cabinet* complained that ministers on the various councils 'know very little about cohesion, about Objective 1 . . . although they might know about money'.[17] Arguably, once overall funding is set, the Council has played a primarily reactive role, responding to institutional designs drawn up by others, especially the Commission.

Moreover, the decision rule of unanimity on structural fund decisions arguably has limited the Council's flexibility. In his examination of the 1993 round of structural fund reforms, Marks (1996b: 397) claims that unanimity 'was probably enough to thwart renationalization because the Commission had the support of the Belgium government' plus two cohesion countries. The point is that rolling back integration under unanimity is often no easier than pushing it forward. Underlining the point, a representative from a large 'donor' Member State complained: 'The smaller Member States have a tendency to latch on to the Commission. . . . It's my impression that the Commission always has some kind of ally on the Council [which means] the Council is not as strong as it could be institutionally.'[18] The Council can fight the Commission's institutional designs, and can even win power back from the Commission (see Pollack 1995) but it must act unanimously.

The European Parliament's role in cohesion policy is also circumscribed. The EP's role in budgetary decision-making is strong, but overall it plays a relatively weak part in cohesion policy, especially when compared to its role in environmental or internal market policy. One DG XVI official remarked that, once the budget is set, 'there's really very little for the Parliament to do. . . This means they're only actively involved once every six years or so' and even then 'the relationship between us is pretty consensual as long as everyone gets a slice of the cake'.[19] However, the EP's role in cohesion policy grows with each treaty revision and budget reform. For instance, the Agenda 2000 package and its implementation had to be negotiated with the EP. Members of the European Parliament (MEPs) accepted major reform in the last round primarily because it included a large increase in non-agricultural spending (spending in the EP's area of budget competence) (see Laffan 1997a). Because no such increase was planned in the Agenda 2000 package, the EP's approval had to be 'won', not assumed. The dynamics of interinstitutional competition suggested the EP would use its approval of the package as a lever to strengthen its own budgetary influence in other areas.

Less established institutions play an even weaker role. The Committee of Regions and Local Authorities (CoR), established by the Maastricht Treaty, would seem to be an obvious institutional player in cohesion policy. The Maastricht Treaty endowed the CoR with purely advisory status, but it must be consulted on all cohesion policy matters and the structural funds regulations in particular. Thus far, the CoR's impact has been muted (see Bomberg and Peterson 1998). In particular, it has suffered from internal divisions between strong regions and weak localities. German, Belgian and Austrian regions are far more powerful and autonomous than those of other Member States, although the Basque and Catalonian Spanish regions and (to a lesser extent) some Italian regions are partial exceptions. The very different constitutional powers enjoyed by regions in different Member States means that a coherent institutional position is unlikely. While still a young institution, the CoR thus far has been a disappointment, even for its supporters. Early hopes that the Amsterdam Treaty would extend its competence were dashed. Proposals for the CoR to become a kind of second chamber of the EP sank without a trace. The CoR certainly does not counterbalance the Commission's power.

The most dramatic advance by the Commission came with the 1988 reforms. Previously, the Council, Commission and Parliament decided the budget of each of the three funds annually. After Delors I was agreed in 1988, the Commission had significantly more control over the designation of regions and allocation of funds. In addition to legitimising the Commission's role in drawing up plans, the partnership principle gave a voice to sub-national authorities who often acted as potential allies of the Commission against national governments (George 1996: 239). Finally, the 1988 round set aside 10 per cent of the structural funds budget for innovative projects and Community Initiatives (CIs). In practice, CIs

Exhibit 6.3 The 'CIs': empowering the Commission (without noticing?)

The 1988 structural funds reforms introduced Community Initiatives as a special financial instrument to address specific problems of EU-wide concern. By the late 1990s, these initiatives numbered 13 and consumed 9 per cent (€13.5 billion) of the structural funds budget. Each initiative was given its own budget, task and (sometimes) catchy acronym: the PESCA initiative supported economic diversification in areas heavily dependent on the fisheries sector; KONVER did the same for regions heavily dependent on the defence sector; INTERREG II facilitated cross-border co-operation in energy networks, regional planning or the management of water supplies; URBAN promoted the regeneration of urban areas; EMPLOYMENT NOW promoted equal employment opportunities for women.

The Initiatives were launched in 1989 as a means to cover specific cross-national regional problems which slipped through the cracks of projects covered under other structural programming. They were agreed by the Council without much fuss or concern about relinquishing power to the Commission. Yet the Commission has used the CIs to increase its own visibility and influence. The Commission is ultimately responsible both for designing CIs and for setting the conditions for eligibility. Its power derives principally from its ability to present Member States with a given sum of EU funding on a take-it-or-leave it basis. Moreover, because CIs are focused on specific problems rather than areas of general economic decline, the Commission can tailor the programmes to appeal to regions or Member States who otherwise might resist its plans. Some of the most successful (or least opposed) initiatives benefit several of the wealthiest regions in Europe. The inclusion of German regions in the KONVER and INTERREG programmes was no coincidence but rather a 'clear and successful attempt to extend the Commission's connection to regions in the biggest, richest Member State' (Ansell *et al.* 1997: 362–3). More generally, the Commission has used the CIs to strengthen links with sub-national authorities (SNAs). Unlike other types of structural funds spending, the shape and form of CIs tend to be almost exclusively determined by the Commission working with

$\longrightarrow$

proved to be a notable boost for Commission autonomy and power. Not only did the Commission draw up the Initiatives, they also determined the conditions for eligibility. In its deliberations the Commission could choose to consult – or not – sub-national authorities (SNAs) and national governments (see Exhibit 6.3).

The 1993 structural fund reforms clearly represented an attempt by the Council to 'claw back' powers lost to the Commission and SNAs in 1988.

→

SNAs. The Commission is keen to garner SNA support for CIs partly because they offer useful information, but also because alliances with them help fend off criticisms from central governments.

Finally, the CIs are also amongst the most visible instruments of the EU. They finance distinct projects, often high-profile which target recipients with specific needs. One senior member of the Commission's Secretariat General gave this candid assessment: 'The popular base for the EU is spending. Regional policy "speaks to the people" and gives the impression of building things together. The funds are good visibility for the Commission'.[20]

The use of the CIs as an advertisement for the Commission has not gone unnoticed. CIs regularly incite heaps of complaints from national governments,[21] although their budgetary significance relative to overall structural fund spending is slight. As part of the 1993 reforms, the Commission's own autonomy was curtailed through the creation of a new management committee of national representatives to oversee the Initiatives. In the Agenda 2000 proposals, the CI budget was cut to 5 per cent of overall structural fund spending, the number of Initiatives reduced to three, and the role of monitoring committees increased (Commission 1998e). Yet, while the relative importance of CIs has declined, their formulation remains mainly the prerogative of the Commission working closely with SNAs.

The establishment and development of CIs reveal how intergovernmental decisions frequently have unintended consequences. Member States' negotiators assumed a small percentage of structural fund spending could be put under the Commission's control without prompting a transfer of decision-making power. But the CIs represent the Commission at its most autonomous. It is not surprising that CIs feature in most accounts which stress the importance of the Commission's role in cohesion policy (Conzelmann 1994; Hooghe 1996a; McAleavey 1993). Finally, CIs suggest that *process* can be more important than *outcomes* in EU decision-making. The CIs' actual impact is insignificant: they comprise only a sliver of the EU's budget, and their effect on regional disparities is marginal (Begg 1997: 16). Their real importance is as a football in the battleground of tri-level, interinstitutional bargaining.

The reforms enhanced the power of central governments over EU cohesion policy in several ways. First, new streamlined programming options simplified the process in Member States' favour by reducing the number of access points for the Commission and SNAs. Second, the 'partnership' principle could now include 'social partners' (chambers of commerce, development corporations, enterprise councils) chosen by the Member States. Third, the principle of additionality was maintained but mitigated by a provision that a Member State's 'macroeconomic circumstances' (arising from, say, a slump in the business cycle or the pains of privatisation) be taken into account. Finally, Member States reasserted influence over the selection of eligible regions. Previously, regions eligible for Objective 2 (declining industrial areas) and Objective 5b (rural areas) funding were chosen unilaterally by the Commission, essentially on the basis of economic criteria. Afterwards, determining who got what from the structural funds became far more a matter of intergovernmental bargaining between Member States (Pollack 1995).

However, the reforms did not produce a straightforward 'renationalisation' of cohesion policy. In some respects, they enhanced the Commission's role as an arbiter. Under the 1993 regulations, Member States forwarded proposed lists of regions to be funded, which then became the basis for bilateral negotiations with the Commission (Marks 1996b). Most governments put forward far more regions than they realistically expected to be eligible for funding. The result was bargaining between the Commission and Member States to decide which regions actually received funding, thus still leaving the Commission considerable discretion to influence choices concerning eligibility.

More generally, decision rules strengthen the Commission's lead in setting cohesion policy. First, the Commission enjoys a monopoly of initiative on the institutional design of cohesion policy. It 'sets' cohesion policy by drawing up the regulatory blueprint (structural funds regulations) of the policies for spending money. Its agenda-setting powers put it in a strong position to 'define the cohesion problem and lay down the rules for a cohesion policy' (Hooghe and Keating 1994: 374). While it cannot have its way without Member States' support, it does enjoy a first mover's institutional advantage.

Second, the Commission is always strongest when it can be shown to be carrying out its treaty obligations. The Treaty's combination of an explicit reference to cohesion (Article 2) with vague wording as to what cohesion constitutes allows the Commission flexibility to fill in the details of cohesion policy. Similarly, intergovernmental agreements are concerned with overall funding and thus leave open the question of how precisely funds are to be structured. In short, whereas fundamental reforms are agreed at the highest level, the blueprint for reforms is drawn up by the Commission. Cohesion policy is set when a broad interinstitutional coalition drives it forward.

Even within the Commission itself coalitions must be formed, because cohesion policy crosses sectoral divisions. Disputes over the direction of cohesion policy between different Commissioners are incessant. For instance, in 1997, the Commissioner for Regional Policy Monika Wulf

Mathies rejected calls from Agricultural Commissioner Franz Fischler to use EU regional aid to help farming communities cope with reductions in agricultural subsidies. Wulf Mathies objected to the possible dilution of regional aid as well as the encroachment on her institutional territory: 'I don't want structural policies linked to the CAP. . . Rich farmers [already] get 80 per cent of the EU farm subsidies.'[22] She found an ally in social affairs Commissioner Padraig Flynn, who complained that the regional aid budget was already overcomplex, inefficient and spread over too many EU initiatives. His intervention was primarily a defence of his 'niche', the European Social Fund, but it provided Wulf Mathies with useful support for her campaign to prevent regional aid being skewed towards rural development. Battles over the shape of cohesion policy are rife within the Commission, and are often manifested in thinly disguised turf wars.

Even when the Commission itself is united, it must win over allies from other institutions. Thus it encouraged the EP's full participation in and support for its Agenda 2000 proposals[23] and was careful to respond to concerns of the Committee of the Regions even though its approval was not legally required. The Commission also was quick to respond to Member States' concerns about the status of 'their' regions under the Agenda 2000 proposals.[24] In short, the Commission succeeds only when it can construct a broad, inter-institutional coalition. But institutional bargaining alone does not give us the full picture. Much of the grit of cohesion policy (shaping regulations and structural programming) is decided or moulded by networks of actors prior to the adoption of rules at the systemic level.

The Sub-Systemic Level: How Networks Shape Decisions

The sub-systemic level features two types of decisions. First, and most widely acknowledged are decisions about 'structural programming' or the 'creation, negotiation, implementation and monitoring of regional development plans' (Marks 1996b: 389). Many of these are unspectacular, often mundane decisions about the specific details of the regional development spending (for instance, drawing up the co-financing arrangements for a waste water treatment plant). Second, decisions taken at this level can sometimes 'shape' how policies (financial and institutional) are ultimately decided at higher levels.

Cohesion policy networks typically include Commission officials, SNA representatives, national civil servants within COREPER, MEPs, interest groups and private actors involved in the 'partnership' programmes. Actors which may pull little institutional weight (the Economic and Social

Committee,[25] CoR) can play a more meaningful role within networks. For instance, despite the CoR's *institutional* weakness, its members and staff are potentially important members of EU policy networks. Many possess the valued resources of legitimacy, information and contacts.

Actors within cohesion networks shape policy behind the scenes. For instance, once big budget decisions are agreed, Member States delegate to COREPER the 'nitty gritty' detail, where, according to one participant 'the real work is done . . . it's amazing how many technical, specific documents emerge from one general plan'.[26] These technical documents go far towards determining precisely how EU money is spent 'on the ground'. Key players during this stage are specialist groups within the Councils such as the '*Groupe des Amis*' involved in the 1993 reforms. The group, which included government representatives and senior Commission officials, met beforehand to help smooth the way for formal meetings and negotiations. Decisions taken here are far removed from the dramatic, highly publicised negotiations on setting the budget. Said one close observer: 'What you have to remember about COREPER is their informality and intimate nature. These guys work with one another every day, they know their problems, their limits. [It is] very intimate precisely because it's closed to the public'[27] (see also Lewis 1998).

Cohesion networks vary enormously, in form, size and influence, across and within Member States. Some take the form of domestic horizontal networks or 'territorial communities' which centre upon sub-central governments (Rhodes 1988; Bomberg 1994). Scotland or Wales in the UK, the Länder in Germany and the autonomous communities in Spain all give rise to such networks. These communities are usually tightly knit and can mobilise within their Member States, across Member States or across government levels to shape EU policies. For instance a network of territorial actors, led by the Belgian regions and German Länder, had considerable success in shaping their governments' general negotiating positions on the Maastricht Treaty. Working together with the Assembly of European Regions, the Länder and Belgian regions may legitimately take credit for the Maastricht Treaty's creation of the Committee of the Regions, as well as its article on subsidiarity. Their lobbying was also instrumental in the inclusion of Article 203[28] of the Treaty, under which a Member State can send sub-national (or 'regional') ministers to act as its delegate on the Council of Ministers (Bomberg and Peterson 1998).

Other cohesion networks spring up around specific projects or objectives. These are likely to be truly tri-level, involving (and often led by) Commission officials, and individual state executives alongside country-specific sub-national actors. The dynamics of structural programming invite the formation of such vertical networks: when the elaborate development programmes are designed, a whole range of resources (information, money expertise, legitimacy) is required. 'Hence each player needs to exchange resources with other actors in order to exert power' (Hooghe 1996c: 17). Advocates of MLG have argued that the way the structural funds are managed has led to a situation in which the autonomy of central governments is challenged by the Commission and by subnational authorities. Decision-making competencies in cohesion policy are more dispersed among national, supranational and sub-national levels than in other policy sectors. 'State-challenging' actors (in particular, the Commission and SNAs) play a key, if not dominant, role in policy shaping because state actors alone are unable to muster all the resources necessary.

To illustrate the point, decisions concerning Objective 1 eligibility are ultimately intergovernmental, but Member States cannot 'win' in the negotiations without support and information from their SNAs. In the case of the Scottish Highlands and Islands, participants in the negotiations highlighted the important roles played by the Highlands and Islands Council and their liaison office in Brussels in obtaining the coveted status in 1993. More generally, a SNA lobbyist underlined the critical role of a broad coalition of Scottish actors, which included Scottish MEP Winnie Ewing, officials in Whitehall, the Scottish Office and the Council, in shaping the decision:

> I certainly think [the SNA's European office] played a large part in the award, but so did a lot of others. . . . Having Bruce Millan, a Scot and ex-Secretary of State for Scotland as Regional Commissioner, and having Sir John Kerr [UK's ambassador to the EU at the time and a Scot] in UKREP didn't hinder the case. If you were to ask any of these players they would all say that they were the decisive ones in bringing Objective 1 to the Highlands. Ian Lang [the then Secretary of State for Scotland] has also claimed this. And the truth is that they all were [decisive].[29]

Most scholars applying policy network analysis emphasise the importance of the partnership principle established in the 1988 reforms. Partnership has spawned a 'dynamic web of networks, communication exchanges and patterns of influence' stretching from Brussels to the remotest community (Hooghe 1996c: 14). Because SNAs are directly involved in cohesion decision-making alongside national and EU actors, 'the fixed territorial boundaries of the national state are permeated by EU partnership' (Hooghe 1996c: 14). Similarly, Benz (1988: 121) argues that the partnership principle 'implies that hierarchical control structures are removed'.

However, two caveats are in order. First, policy networks represent more than the 'institutionalisation' of the partnership principle. The influence of a broad range of actors (public, private, national, suprana-tional, sub-national) in shaping cohesion policy is determined not by this principle but by the value of resources (information, legitimacy, constitutional, and so on) these actors can bring to the table. Put another way, partnership is valuable only when translated into a resource to be exchanged. The notion of partnership confers on SNAs a certain legitimacy they lacked before the principle was adopted, but it is not granted in every case and is, in any event, only one of many resources actors can exchange.

This point is illustrated by the fact that, in spite of the partnership principle, decision-making in practice 'has been determined primarily by existing [national] structures and responsibilities' (Wishlade 1996: 44). Indeed, 'partnership' is virtually non-existent in Member States which lack any tradition of strong regional mobilisation (Hooghe and Keating 1994; Marks 1996b; Le Galés and Lequesne 1998).

The variation of SNA involvement invites another caveat. For every instance of assertive SNAs (as in Belgium and Germany) there is an instance in which Member States and their central institutions retain significant if not exclusive control over cohesion policy, despite the efforts of individual SNAs (Bache *et al.* 1996).[30]

To influence cohesion policy, SNAs must gain access to informal bargaining within EU policy networks (see Exhibit 6.4). Information, legitimacy and other resources held by SNAs can serve as their 'entry card' to policy networks concerned with the formulation of cohesion policy. Their influence (on, say, the precise wording of Objective 2 eligibility criteria) may be determined more by their informal bargaining skills than by formal rules (including partnership). But structural con-straints remain: SNA networks, like any other, remain embedded in a larger constitutional setting.

Analysts reluctant to attribute much significance to the role of sub-national or non state actors argue that the policy networks they inhabit are, in any case, primarily involved in implementation. But whereas most policy sectors are characterised by a relatively clear demarcation between formulation and implementation, this line is blurred in cohesion policy. Commission, national and SNA officials involved in the drawing up of cohesion proposals are also in charge of implementing them on the ground (see Heinelt 1996: 16–17).

This blurred distinction is critical. To sideline as 'mere implementation' the actions of networks is to miss their role as policy *shapers*. Policy networks are involved in the implementation (actual spending of funds) and monitoring on the ground, but they are also involved in decisions prior to implementation, such as shaping the structural fund regulations and drawing up development programmes.

Moreover, in certain cases, decision-making within networks can facilitate or constrain later decisions made at the highest level. First, domestic networks made up of territorial actors can shape significantly the negotiation positions and subsequent decisions of central governments. Conversely, domestic networks can foster co-operation between sub-national and national actors to force the Commission's hand.[35] The expansion of partnership to include private actors in the 1993 regulations is explained by Rhodes *et al.*, (1996: 374) as a result of central government bypassing local authorities in favour of private sector and special purpose bodies. In short, a domestic network of national and private actors was able to shape the Commission's proposed regulations.

Similarly, commercial networks have forced the Commission to rewrite regulations to prevent abuse of structural fund regulations. For instance, in 1997, the French car maker Renault shut down its plant in Vilvoorde near Brussels while standing to gain from Objective 1 funds for opening a factory in Spain (see Exhibit 3.5). Although Wulf Mathies deplored the move as a violation of the spirit and rule of cohesion policy,[36] her objection may have stemmed from a perceived violation of the Commission's dignity. In this case, action by commercial networks forced the Commission to introduce measures to prevent companies from 'shopping around' for aid or benefiting from aid more than once within a certain timeframe. Specific revisions were proposed in Agenda 2000.

Finally, networks involved in the implementation of cohesion policy, that is the actual spending of the funds, can also shape intergovernmental negotiations. The inability or unwillingness of those at lower tiers actually to spend money despite agreements made at super-systemic level means that the next round of budget talks is affected. The mid-term review figures released by the Commission in 1996 revealed that the UK, Netherlands, Italy, France and Belgium had spent less than 40 per cent of funds allocated to them for the 1994–6 period. Weak or non-existent implementation networks help account for the failure.[37] In sum, at the sub-systemic level, decisions are made within a variety of policy networks. These networks influence day to day decision-making regarding structural programming, but can also shape decisions taken at other levels of governance, sometimes in ways that are crucial.

Exhibit 6.4   Do SNAs matter?

The 1990s witnessed an explosion of activity by sub-national authorities in decision-making related to cohesion policy.[31] The introduction of the partnership principle in 1988 gave an explicit role to SNAs in the formulation and execution of structural programming. The number of SNA information and lobbying offices in Brussels increased dramatically (Jeffrey 1995). Similarly, a plethora of regional coalitions mobilised to push forward regional demands on the European level. The mobilisation of sub-national actors was a key factor leading to the exposition of multi-level governance and the thesis that a 'Europe of the Regions' might be emerging (see Marks *et al.* 1996b; Jeffrey 1996).

But what role do SNAs really play? It is difficult to generalise. The power and influence of SNAs vary tremendously between (and at times within) Member States. As a starting point, a clear correlation may be drawn between the domestic distribution of power between central government and SNAs, and the ability of central governments to control national decision-making concerning cohesion policy. The constitutional privileges afforded German Länder and Belgium regions, for example, include the right to scrutinise proposed EU legislation and even to serve as their nation's delegate in the Council of Ministers in sectors where they have competence. These privileges remain distant dreams to regions in Greece, Denmark and England. But domestic constitutional positions are not the only determinant of SNA influence at the EU level. Influence in EU decision-making derives largely from effective coalition-building with other like-minded actors, with Commission officials and also, inevitably in the case of sub-national authorities, with central governments.

Coalition-building with other like-minded regions is a growth industry, and a number of formal regional alliances have emerged in the past 15 years (see Ansell *et al.* 1997; Hooghe 1995). The direct decision-making impact of these alliances is negligible, but they do promote information exchange and help to create aggregated views which are more likely to be received sympathetically by EU decision-makers. Working sometimes alone, but usually through such coalitions, SNAs can liaise directly with the Commission in attempts to shape policy independently of their Member State. The Commission is not shy about nurturing such contacts. In a widely cited example, British SNAs appeared to play a more important role than Whitehall in the design of the RECHAR initiative to promote the reconversion of declining coal-mining

→

→

areas. In the ensuing conflict over 'additionality', the Commission threatened to withhold RECHAR funding when it became clear that the British central government was not intending to make additional (national) spending provisions. British SNAs gave their full support to Commissioner Millan in defiance of central government (see McAleavey 1993).

In general terms, however, SNAs fare best when they work with their central governments. As one representative from a large state warned: 'Bargaining on regional policy can get emotional, but alienating your Member State is not smart.'[32] SNAs' real impact depends on their ability to influence their own Member States as well as Commission officials. SNAs hold crucial information which is useful both to their Member States and to the Commission. Moreover, as a layer of government 'closer to the people', SNAs can confer on the decision-making process a certain legitimacy that central governments, and certainly the Commission, are keen to nurture. A national government representative responsible for cohesion policy explained: 'We try to get regions to speak for us, because the Commission listens more to regions than to Member States who have a more predictable position. . . . SNAs keep us informed. We need their involvement. We can use them, well, not "use" them, but make use of them and their views.'[33]

To illustrate the point, SNAs formed effective coalitions which shaped certain elements of the 1993 structural funds regulations concerning Community Initiatives. In the case of the KONVER programme, SNAs persuaded the Commission to expand the eligibility criteria to include regions not previously eligible. The change was, according to a senior Commission official, a result of 'being bruised and battered by the German Länder and British local authorities'.[34] German and British governments, like most central governments, remained uneasy with CIs. But their SNAs were able to convince them not to do anything to jeopardise their chances of getting a 'share of the loot', regardless of how ill-conceived such initiatives might be.

SNAs can thus take part in informal bargaining by building alliances among regions and across Member States, but especially by pushing their central governments to act on their behalf. Where the Commission has flexibility, such as in the definition of CI criteria, SNAs can work with their Member States or other SNAs to shape the details of policy. Sub-national authorities alone do not matter much in the formulation of cohesion policy, but the networks they populate might.

Conclusion

Cohesion policy provides ample evidence to sustain both state-centric and multi-level governance approaches to understanding the EU. Clearly, intergovernmental bargaining determines outcomes when the big decisions are taken which shape the overall direction of cohesion policy. National governments and national interests, moreover, are powerful at other levels of decision-making as well. But the state-centric view underestimates the role of SNAs by assuming they matter only when they work through their national governments, and only at the implementation stage.

Multi-level governance, on the other hand arguably hits its height of explanatory power in this policy sector. While it may overestimate the influence of SNAs and the autonomy of the Commission, its emphasis on tri-level 'power sharing' is critical to understanding how cohesion policies are shaped and set. There is no denying that the design of cohesion policy between 1988 and 1998 had important political effects, particularly by involving sub-national authorities in EU decision-making to an extent never before seen. Yet cohesion policy is unique in both its rationale and its decision-making process. It is not clear that the MLG findings from this sector can be applied to other EU policy sectors. In particular, a meaningful role for 'third level' actors remains conspicuously absent from most other arenas of EU decision-making. The extent to which cohesion policy represents a wider transformation of EU governance has to be questioned.

In any event, understanding EU cohesion policy means going beyond the question of who dominates, and exploring the ways in which decisions taken at one level, within networks of different actors, influence others. Cohesion policy is rich in examples of the way decisions taken at one level can have intended and unintended consequence at other levels. Exploring the linkage between levels is particularly helpful as cohesion policy undergoes the most radical change in its existence. Arguably, the stated 'ends' of cohesion policy – solidarity and the reduction of territorial inequalities – have always been more symbolic than real. Future decisions on cohesion policy, especially those related to Agenda 2000, suggest a fundamental redefinition of both the ends and means of cohesion policy. This redefinition has three components.

First, Member States are unlikely to commit themselves to a larger budget for cohesion. German largesse, the lubricant which greased the wheels of cohesion consensus, is not likely in post-unification Germany. Net contributors to the EU budget have become far more vocal in their opposition to future cohesion spending. When, in late 1998, the Dutch government slammed the Commission's proposed spending on cohesion policy as 'unnecessary and undesirable',[38] it signalled the budgetary fights ahead. Even leaving aside questions of enlargement, the fundamentally redistributive nature of cohesion policy is being questioned as never before. Accession talks with the Central and Eastern Europe countries (CEECs) may stretch the already wavering commitment to cohesion to its breaking point.[39]

Second, in the past 'means' have mattered more than 'ends' in cohesion policy: the political process of redistributing money has been more important than the actual effect on economic convergence. But this equation is shifting as questions of efficiency, effectiveness and 'value for money' enjoy increasing resonance both amongst Member States and within EU institutions. The shift is seen especially in scrutiny of the 'cohesion deficit': the extent to which disparities have *not* appreciably narrowed since 1988 (McAleavey and De Rynck 1997). These short-comings did not matter much before because cohesion policy's main function was to facilitate wider bargains concerning integration or market liberalisation. This function is less important now not only because of budgetary constraints but also because poorer members, especially those in the first wave of EMU, are no longer in a position to demand side payments in return for market liberalising projects or the more general institutional advancement of the EU.

Third, the rules of cohesion policy are likely to undergo significant change under Agenda 2000 (see Table 6.3). In particular the partnership principle has come under increased attack, and not only by national governments, as laborious to administer, and vulnerable to clientelism and corruption (Hooghe 1998: 465). Agenda 2000 implies a less explicit partnership role for SNAs and emphasises instead closer co-operation between national and local actors to meet established targets.

Within the Commission the debate about cohesion policy's future has become enmeshed in wider debates about internal Commission reform. Reformers pushing for 'simple and effective management' advocate a radical restructuring of cohesion policy, whereas others, not least those in DG XVI, remain fiercely opposed to such wide scale reform and continue to favour a 'grand vision' of cohesion policy. While sharpest in the Commission, these fault lines run through other EU institutions (see Hooghe 1998: 461).

Whatever the outcome of the institutional debate, the Commission's internal discussion of cohesion policy reform reveals a shift in cohesion policy. Agenda 2000 implies a reduction in the scope of EU cohesion policy and the Commission's role within in it. The emphasis has shifted towards alleviating practical problems (unemployment) and encouraging new innovative technologies. In short, visions of solidarity and cohesion have given way to concerns about practicality and efficiency.

Policy networks, too, are fundamentally affected by this shift. Territorial or multitiered networks have emerged to take advantage of existing structures and principles of cohesion policy. Most have responded to EU cash, or the 'pork barrel effect' of cohesion policy (see Wallace 1977; McAleavey and De Rynck 1997). But several territorial networks have used cohesion policy to strengthen their own bargaining hand in political relationships with their central government (see Anderson 1990; Conzelmann 1995; Hooghe 1996c).

New types of networks are now likely to emerge, made up of different constellations of actors and emphasising priorities which match the new demands of efficiency and innovation. Already, several local authorities in the UK have shifted the emphasis of their proposed programmes away from large infrastructure projects (roads, bridges and so on) towards employment training, telecommunications and education. According to one British observer, the old cohesion policy was about opening roads; the new one was 'about opening minds'.[40]

But there are limits to such adaptation. A policy which consumes a third of the budget has invariably yielded powerful political constituencies. In many cases, the institutions setting policy, and the networks shaping it, will resist change. High-level intergovernmental bargaining will in part be constrained by resistance on the part of actors reluctant to forgo the financial prizes or institutional power enjoyed under the existing cohesion policy framework. In short, radical change in cohesion policy may be inevitable, but it will not occur without a fight, and one not just between Member States.

Chapter 7

Environmental Policy

The development of EU environmental policy
History-making decisions and national diversity
The systemic level: intra- and interinstitutional bargaining
The sub-systemic level: messy networks
Conclusion

Environmental policy is one of the EU's most diverse and crowded policy realms, populated by a staggering array of actors and interests. By its very nature, decision-making on environmental issues is highly technical and driven by scientific expertise. Yet growing public concern for the environment has politicised environmental issues and rendered them susceptible to wider pressures, debate and scrutiny. Moreover, the broad scope of most environmental issues means they have become increasingly intertwined with other sectoral issues, especially those surrounding agriculture, cohesion, transport and the internal market. This chapter examines patterns of decision-making across a range of environmental issues and considers how the crowded and diverse character of environmental policy reveals itself at different levels of analysis. It argues that, although the EU has developed a strong regulatory regime in environmental policy, its success in integrating environmental concerns into other policy areas remains limited.

The Development of EU Environmental Policy

The EU's involvement in environmental policy is relatively recent. The Treaty of Rome made no reference to the environment or environmental policy. Yet today the EU's environmental policy *acquis* is substantial and wide-ranging (see Table 7.1). It includes over 200 pieces of legislation related to environmental quality or to environmental aspects of internal market measures.[1]

This expansion in the EU's environmental remit occurred in response to pressures both from above (international negotiations and treaties) and from below (public opinion and Member States). The post-war economic boom brought with it environmental costs: increased energy consumption, pollution and urban development into natural landscapes. Concern about the consequences of economic expansion was piqued by a series of

173

Table 7.1   *Key areas of EU environmental legislation*

Controlling air pollution
- vehicle and industrial emissions; ozone-depleting substances; climate change

Controlling water pollution
- bathing water; urban waste water treatment; nitrates use

Health and safety, consumer protection
- eco-label; chemical and nuclear hazards; noise pollution

Waste management
- packaging and packaging waste; hazardous waste; landfill waste

Wildlife and countryside protection
- biodiversity; habitat protection; wild bird protection

industrial and nuclear accidents such as the Chernobyl accident and the Sandoz chemical spill into the Rhine in 1986. Increasing awareness amongst the European public was reflected in a series of public opinion polls (see Commission 1992a) growing demand for environmentally sound consumer products and services (see Elkington and Hailes 1988) and rising electoral support for green parties on the local, national and European level. For instance, in the 1989 European Parliament (EP) elections, green parties doubled the number of Members of the European Parliament (MEPs) they sent to Strasbourg and increased their percentage of the popular vote in every Member State (Bomberg 1998a). In short, the environment became politicised.

A second force behind the EU's expanding remit was a growing recognition of the transnational nature of environmental degradation. Acid rain stemming from industrial emissions in one Member State crossed national borders and harmed forests and eroded buildings in another. Pollution of rivers such as the Rhine affected all countries along its banks. It became a truism to state that, because EU Member States shared air, rivers and seas, environmental problems and solutions had to be found at the European level.

Meanwhile, global environmental problems such as climate change, deforestation and depletion of the ozone layer captured the attention of European publics and governments. Efforts to address these problems widened further the EU's environmental remit. The United Nations Conference on the Human Environment held in Stockholm in 1972 was widely seen as sparking the EU's interest in global environmental problems, and highlighting the necessity for global action (Weale 1996; McCormick 1998). The 1992 United Nations Conference on the Environment and Development (or Rio summit) underlined the EU's contribution to both the causes and solutions of global environmental problems (see Baker *et al*. 1997; Sbragia 1998). Most Member States were too small individually to play a decisive role in global negotiations, but the EU was a powerful transnational actor able to respond to environmental as well as economic global challenges, or to push others to do so. The need for global solutions to global problems expanded the EU's environmental policy beyond European borders.

Yet perhaps the most important reason for the increased activity of the EU in environmental issues had little to do with rising green awareness or the salience of global environmental issues. EU environmental legislation was necessary to eliminate trade distortions between Member States in the single market. Widely differing national rules on industrial pollution could distort competition, allowing 'dirty states' to profit economically (Lodge 1989: 320). In sum, ecological, political and economic factors combined to cause the EU's environmental policy role to expand.

The Union's rising concern with environmental issues can be traced through successive Environmental Action Programmes (EAPs). These multi-annual programmes set objectives, state key principles, select the priorities and describe measures to be taken in different policy sectors related to the environment. The first, approved in 1973, was quite modest in scope. By the Fifth EAP (1992–2000) the EU's comprehensive remit in environmental issues was apparent. Entitled *Towards Sustainability*, the 5th EAP brought the term 'sustainable development' into EU parlance.[2] At the heart of the concept was the idea that each generation should not close off options for the next. To be sustainable, development had to meet 'the needs of the present without compromising the ability of future generations to meet their own needs' (see Baker *et al*. 1997). It implied new strategies to secure 'continued economic and social development without detriment to the environment' (Commission 1992c: 3). The notion of sustainable development thus underlined the EU's commitment (in word if not often in deed) to incorporate environmental concerns into other EU activities.

Although these action programmes expressed an increasing EU commitment to environmental protection, they were only guides to action and did not carry the same force of law as treaty articles or legislation. Until 1987, environmental legislation had to be passed either under the Treaty's internal market provisions or under the general catch-all provisions of Article 308.[3] This legal base meant that the pace of environmental protection had to be directly related to the objective of economic harmonisation, and had to be unanimously agreed. Even by the mid-

1980s, the EU thus lacked the legal means to deal effectively with many environmental problems.

The Single European Act (SEA) was a watershed in the development of the EU's environmental and related policies. In particular, the SEA added to the treaties a special title on the environment which gave legal force to certain principles already set out in earlier EAPs (prevent pollution rather than simply control it; introduce the 'polluter pays' principle; rectify environmental degradation at the source when possible; and integrate environmental protection into other Union policies). The Treaty now explicitly stipulated that 'environmental protection must be a component of the EU's other policies'. Finally, the title contained the treaties' first expression of the subsidiarity principle for deciding whether action should be taken by the EU or by Member States. In one sense, the title did no more than provide a clear legal base for principles which had been developing since the early 1970s. But its symbolic importance was considerable: following the adoption of the SEA, it finally was possible to speak of an EU environmental policy. The Union's environmental policy competence was secure and not restricted to measures related to trade.

The EU's environmental remit was furthered by the Maastricht Treaty, which gave the EU legal licence to promote 'measures at the international level to deal with regional or world wide environmental problems'. The Maastricht Treaty also reasserted the principle of subsidiarity invoked earlier by the SEA in its Title on the environment. The principle itself is double-edged. On the one hand, it provides a powerful justification for the EU to develop policies where it has never done so before. Clearly, many environmental policy objectives can be better attained at the EU level than at the national level. On the other hand, the Maastricht Treaty leaves wide open the question of precisely where EU policies bring advantages over purely national ones. For instance, after difficulties surrounding ratification of the Treaty in Denmark and the UK, fears arose that this principle would be used to 'repatriate' environmental policies back to the national level as a way to mitigate fears about the growing powers of the EU (Peterson 1994). Although little if any such repatriation occurred, several proposals (on water quality, noise pollution and dumping) were withdrawn 'in accordance with the subsidiarity principle' (Golub 1996a: 700). One implication of the EU's new commitment to subsidiarity was that its competence in a range of environmental policy areas remained a major source of conflict.

By the time the Maastricht Treaty was finally ratified in 1993, public interest in environmental issues had begun to wane. In a climate of severe European recession, environmental concerns appeared to become less salient as the state of the economy became the most pressing issue for many voters. Support for ambitious new environmental legislation diminished. Moreover, new popular doubts about the European project was one important factor motivating the Santer Commission to try to 'do less but do it better'.

The effect was a considerable shift in the quality and quantity of the EU's environmental legislation. First, whereas dozens of new proposals were introduced annually during the 1980s and early 1990s, only two new proposals were introduced in 1996. Second, the Commission put far greater emphasis on the potential economic benefits of environmental protection. The Commission's (1993) White Paper, *Growth, Competitiveness and Employment*, touted the possibility of improving the EU's global competitiveness by means of cleaner technologies, energy efficiency and other measures (Liberatore 1997: 109). Similarly, in an effort to simplify administrative procedures and improve relations with industry, the Commission's Environment Directorate (DG XI) placed a new emphasis on 'voluntary negotiations' and 'cooperative corporatism', or directing governments to set targets, but allowing industry to help determine what those targets should be and how best to meet them. The EU's 'auto–oil programme', which featured close co-operation between Commission officials and industry representatives, embodied this new strategy (see Exhibit 7.1). The new ethos of restraint was reflected again in the 1997 Amsterdam Treaty which restated the EU's commitment to Rio-inspired 'balanced and sustainable development' (Article B) but featured no significant advances in the EU's overall environmental remit.

Overall, the development of EU environmental policy has been marked by a steady expansion of EU competence, punctuated by short, sharp surges of activity. An upsurge of activism followed the SEA, partly reflecting the politicisation of environmental issues, but primarily as a consequence of the need to harmonise environmental measures in the context of the single market. By 1993, the scale and pace of development had slowed. Harmonisation flagged, the political saliency of the environment waned and enthusiasm for the European project more generally became muted. This pattern of development suggests that, more than other sectors, EU environmental policy is susceptible to changes in the wider political and economic climate.

History-Making Decisions and National Diversity

History-making decisions in environmental policy usually must accommodate a striking array of different national interests and styles. In broad terms, it is helpful to categorise Member States into three tiers (Haas 1993; Sbragia 1996). A 'greener' tier of Member States (Germany, Netherlands, Denmark) traditionally have acted as leaders in pushing the EU towards

Exhibit 7.1 The auto–oil programme: new discourse in DG XI

The auto-oil programme began in 1992 as a series of consultations between Commission officials and representatives of the oil and automobile sectors. It was launched to develop proposals for cost-effective action to reduce motor vehicle emissions by the year 2000. A DG XI Commission official described the initiative as a move away from old regulatory-style environmental policy towards a 'structured dialogue, a shared responsibility approach: agreeing what the problem is, what the solution is, and then trying to agree in policy terms how best to deal with it. It's not enough just to look at the legislative approach'.[4]

Unlike most earlier proposals emanating from DG XI, the auto–oil programme did not feature input from environmental non-governmental organisations (NGOs). Their initial exclusion made these groups suspicious of the entire process. A high-ranking Commission official in DG XI suggested that groups such as Friends of the Earth or Greenpeace would have difficulty accepting the talks: 'These radical groups find it very hard to accept that we should be consulting industry because they say "You don't consult the polluter about pollution, you consult us."' Yet, for many environmentalists, the exclusion was unwarranted. One of their lobbyists complained: 'We were willing to sit down and talk with the polluters but were not invited.' [5]

The consultations between industry and the Commission yielded a draft set of measures in June 1996. The Commission sought to reduce the level of auto emissions over the next 10 years by requiring vehicle manufacturers to introduce 'cleaner' technology. From the year 2000, the Commission would require the proportion of key pollutants (such as carbon monoxide) to be reduced by between 20 and 40 per cent from their present levels. After 2005, emissions would be reduced by a further 30 per cent. The proposal also required the oil refining industry to reduce levels of the pollutant sulphur in diesel and petrol, and to phase out leaded petrol by the year 2000 (poorer Member States would be exempt until 2003).

These standards represented a significant tightening of current emission limits, but they did not, in the view of many MEPs and most environmentalists, represent a serious effort to reduce emissions. The standards fell far short of standards in the USA and Nordic countries. Moreover, environmentalists claimed that the stricter standards would allow industry to duck responsibility. European Environmental Bureau[6] secretary-general Raymond Van Ermen criticised the provisions as 'too weak: the companies are seldom monitored and bad behaviour is never punished. That

→

→

is why they are, on the whole, ineffective'.[7] Even the plan to phase out leaded petrol was described by one Greenpeace lobbyist as a mere tactic 'to keep the European Parliament happy'.[8] If so, it was not entirely successful: the European Parliament pushed for more stringent targets than were sought by the Council. The disagreement triggered conciliation talks in 1998, which resulted in a typical compromise. The Council delegation agreed to the EP's demand that targets for sulphur content in fuel be made mandatory, but the EP relaxed its demands concerning other gases. The agreed legislation, which did not differ fundamentally from earlier drafts, was greeted with predictable ambivalence by environmental constituencies. Several critics argued that the Commission proposal was accepted with only minor modifications, thus illustrating 'how unambitious this project was overall' (Friedrich *et al.* 1998). Yet the programme was marked, not only by a predictable conflict between industry and environmental interests, but also by disputes between the fuel industries and automobile manufacturers. Both sectors had invested considerable time, energy and money in the programme, but tension surfaced repeatedly over who was carrying the bigger burden, and who was shirking responsibility. A Commission official involved in the programme remarked: 'most of the struggle takes place behind closed doors, but there's quite clearly a tension between these two industries . . . The car industry would tell you that they are being asked to pick up the bill for this, for that and forever, while the oil industry got away [unscathed]'.[9]

The auto–oil programme illustrated clearly the EU's new approach or 'discourse' (see Weale 1996) in environmental policy. Instead of a 'command and control' approach based on imposing industry standards, the EU encouraged more direct industry input in the design of policies, and a more explicit assessment of economic benefits and costs. As summed up by a key Commission participant: 'To get the expertise, resources and dynamism of leading industries in the auto–oil programme is not only innovative, it has been very, very constructive.'[10]

But the programme also illustrates the inherent difficulties of this strategy. The NGO 'shut-out' left behind an embittered cluster of environmental groups which consistently criticised the programme and were able to mobilise opposition within the Parliament. In 1998, the Commission conceded that the subsequent 'Auto Oil II' consultations beginning later that year would involve a 'cast of thousands', including several environmental NGOs.[11] Finally, the auto–oil case revealed deep splits between the automobile and oil industries, who often undercut each other as well as their new allies in DG XI. It appeared that attempts to appease different sectors of industry could prove every bit as difficult as reconciling environmental and economic goals.

higher environment standards. This coalition of 'pioneers' (Andersen and Liefferink 1997) was strengthened considerably by the accession in 1995 of Sweden, Finland and Austria. Leader states tend to adopt a strategy of 'first mover' in which 'the initiator seeks to widen the scope of European policy-making according to its own preferences' (Héritier 1996: 151). By raising European environmental standards to their own national level, greener states seek both to avoid the costs of legal adjustment caused by European legislation, and to establish favourable competitive conditions for their own industry. For instance, Member States which have already introduced some sort of energy tax on the national level are keen to see these adopted at the European level (see Exhibit 7.2).

The next tier includes France, Belgium and Luxembourg. These 'fence sitters' may push for fundamental change to environmental policy on one occasion but not on others, depending on the specific issue and circumstance. Finally, several countries might be termed environmental 'laggards' because of their reluctance to legislate on environmental matters or their opposition to stringent EU-wide regulation. This tier features the poorer cohesion countries (Spain, Portugal, Greece and Ireland) as well as the UK.[12] Arguably, Member States of this tier would have only minimal domestic environmental legislation if the EU did not exist (Sbragia 1996). This three-tiered distinction is somewhat crass, as the preferences of Member States vary across time as well as across issues,[13] but the categorisation does highlight sharp variations in levels of environmental protection and awareness across the EU's Member States.

Member States also differ in their preferred approach to meeting environmental protection goals. Following a 'precautionary principle', Germany and the Netherlands have tended to favour standards which measure pollution levels at the point or source of emissions. They also tend to favour the application of controls which are as stringent as available technology permits (Haigh 1992). By contrast, the UK favours ambient or quality standards which measure the pollution's 'sink' (that is, the body of water, land or air where the pollution is absorbed) rather than levels of contamination at their source. According to the British view, emission standards may vary from place to place, and need be no more stringent than required to meet agreed ambient standards.[14]

These contrasting views have had to be accommodated in the history-making decisions defining the broad direction of environmental policy. The inclusion of an environment Title in the SEA was the result of a tacit bargain between northern states (leaders) seeking higher environmental standards, and southern states (laggards) seeking more aid and less onerous environmental requirements. The resulting bargain involved both a commitment to high standards of environmental protection and the use of the structural funds to aid southern countries in meeting them (Weale

1996: 597). The bargain had to appease both those Member States favouring 'legitimating and possibly expanding' the EU's environmental powers and those seeking to place limits on the EU's legislative prerogative (Golub 1996a: 689). In these negotiations the principle of subsidiarity was inserted to reassure both leaders and laggards. For Member States pushing for more EU action, subsidiarity enforced the belief that most environmental issues could be better addressed at the EU level, thereby setting the stage for further consolidation of EU-wide action. For Germany, the inclusion of subsidiarity was also necessary to meet the demands of its Länder who, in the warm-up to the Maastricht negotiations, had begun in earnest their efforts to shape the negotiating position of their 'mother state' (see Jeffrey 1996).

For laggards, such as the UK, however, subsidiarity represented a 'formal safeguard for British sovereignty and Britain's unique environmental policy style' (Golub 1996a: 689–90). Describing the UK's position during the SEA negotiations, a senior member of UKREP remarked that the UK 'would from time to time say that [Britain] did not think that a particular piece of legislation needed to appear before the Council at all. This was sort of the first germs of the subsidiarity idea'.[16] The UK certainly played a role in pushing for the principle's inclusion in the environment Title. Yet to assert that the principle 'bears all the marks of British influence' (Golub 1996a: 690) is probably to overstate the case. First, the principle's ambiguity meant it appealed to (and could reflect the interests of) both leaders and laggards. Second, British resistance to further EU action on the environment was by now so well known that it had ceased to carry much influence. A member of the German Permanent Representation described the British position on most environmental matters as 'certain to be a line of resistance, certain as the Amen in the church'.[17] Nonetheless, the case illustrates why subsidiarity has become an accepted norm of EU decision-making: in the environmental sector at least, it can unite Member States with opposite positions on environmental protection in general and the EU's role in particular.

Attempts to accommodate environmental laggards were also linked to later history-making decisions. At the 1992 Edinburgh summit, the Spanish government insisted on (and received) a healthy slice of the Cohesion Fund (see Exhibit 6.1) in exchange for agreeing to extended qualified majority voting (QMV) on environmental and other measures. The EU often relies on such 'pay-offs' or side payments (often in the form of increased regional funding) as an incentive for laggard Member States to sign on to ambitious environmental decisions.

Accommodating 'leaders' has also led to fundamental change. For instance, at Denmark's and Germany's insistence, the SEA included a clause allowing greener Member States to adopt tougher environmental

Exhibit 7.2 The carbon/energy tax: intergovernmentalism rules?

The idea of some sort of EU energy tax was first floated during the oil crisis of 1973 (Matláry 1996). Following the release of several strategy and working papers in the mid-1980s, the Commission presented an ambitious draft proposal for a carbon/energy tax on fossil fuels and most 'major' sources of electricity (including nuclear and hydropower). Initially, this relatively radical proposal faced only mild opposition, not least because of the belief that it would never make it through the Commission (Zito 1995: 440). Yet opposition grew and by the mid-1990s, in the face of sustained opposition from a minority of Member States, the Commission was forced to do what it seldom does: withdraw a proposal.

The carbon tax measure was initially pushed by 'leader' Member States (Netherlands, Germany and Denmark) who wanted Europe-wide measures to match taxes already introduced at the national level. The robust character of the Commission's first draft was attributable also to the active role of several DGs (especially XI) and their Commissioners. External factors, such as the Commission's desire to play a global leadership role in the 1992 UNCED summit, also played a part. Finally, the tax signalled a move away from regulation and towards voluntary instruments which fit the EU's new flexible approach to environmental policy (see Exhibit 7.1).

But opposition was also strong and sustained. For energy intensive industries, the fuzzy threat of a tax became real when the Commission released its formal proposal for a tax in 1992. By the mid-1990s, industry's relatively relaxed approach had shifted to frenzied lobbying. Eventually, the industrial lobby successfully convinced EU decision-makers to adopt the principle of 'conditionality': that is, implementation of the tax was made conditional on other western countries adopting similar taxes or measures. Member States with energy-intensive industries pushed for a graduated reduction in tax for industries disadvantaged by rising imports from countries that had no such tax. Individual Member States also weighed in with particular objections: cohesion countries claimed exemptions because of their relatively low level of emissions and their need for economic development. France objected to the taxation of nuclear power. The UK opposed any extension of taxation powers by the EU.

→

⟶

As a fiscal measure, the tax needed a qualified majority on the Environment Council but unanimous agreement on the Council of Economic and Finance Committees (ECOFIN). Despite majority support for the introduction of a tax, Member States in favour of the tax eventually buckled under at the 1994 Essen summit. An embarrassing failure for its Council presidency, Germany conceded at Essen that the proposal for an EU-wide tax would be replaced by the far more modest establishment of guidelines under which individual Member States could choose – or not – to adopt their own taxes.

The carbon/energy tax case illustrates clearly the EU's intergovernmental backbone. Strong intergovernmental constraints still exist which limit the range of measures that can be adopted, as well as the scope and character of environmental policy (Weale 1996: 602). But decision rules are crucial in this respect. Environmental measures which involve fiscal considerations have to be agreed by unanimity, thus reducing incentives for the majority of states to push forward in the face of minority but entrenched opposition. The case also highlights the continuing North/South and leader/laggard divide amongst Member States in environmental matters. The divide is not simply one of rich v. poor but also between those Member States favouring more EU-wide action on the environment, and those resisting such a move.

Finally, this case illustrates how issues remain on the EU's agenda for years, dormant but not dead. Although considered finished in 1994, the tax re-emerged in different guises in subsequent years. One UK representative involved in the negotiations lamented the 'inevitability' of the tax: 'Once several Member States have a tax on the national level the Commission will have more incentive (and power) to introduce a European-wide one. Pressure will build for one. It will be back.'[15] Indeed, by 1996, five Member States (Austria, Denmark, Finland, the Netherlands and Sweden) had introduced a carbon/energy tax on the national level and pushed for resumption of the debate. The Commission began exploring a new approach combining the carbon/energy tax with excise duties on mineral oils. This approach received a push in 1998 under an Austrian Council presidency, which sought a compromise deal allowing long transition periods and concessions for domestic consumption. The Germans, taking over the Council presidency in 1999 and led by a red–green coalition, made a Europe-wide energy tax one of their top policy priorities. Decision rules matter: when unanimity applies, intergovernmentalism rules. Yet, even under these circumstances policy initiatives may be easy to shoot down, but nearly impossible to kill.

standards, even if they restricted trade, as long as the goal was truly environment protection and not simply protectionism. The distinction is tricky and often has to be adjudicated by the European Court of Justice (ECJ). A well known example is the Danish bottle case. In the 1980s, Denmark passed legislation to the effect that all beer bottles sold in Denmark had to be recyclable. The law was challenged by non-Danish brewers on the grounds that it acted to restrain trade, since foreign brewers had more difficulty than Danish brewers in retrieving and reusing their beer bottles. In a truly history-making decision in 1988 the ECJ upheld the Danish law on the grounds that, while the law did restrain trade, it had legitimate environmental protection aims and thus should be allowed to stand.

Under pressure from the Nordics and Austrians, the Amsterdam Treaty strengthened the provision by permitting governments to introduce more stringent environmental measures if based on new scientific evidence specific to the Member States concerned. This provision helped to offset the disappointment of greener states like the Netherlands which, during their 1997 Council presidency, had fought hard for an extension of QMV to all aspects of environmental policy, including taxation. Germany had been a traditional supporter of increased QMV in environmental policy (at least verbally), yet, in the intergovernmental conference (IGC) which culminated in the Amsterdam Treaty, Kohl was under severe pressure to resist such a move. The pressure came principally from the German Länder which held exclusive or shared jurisdiction in environmental matters. Kohl was expected to override domestic opposition, but surprised his European partners by opposing the broad extension of QMV (see Exhibit 1.2). In the end, only Belgium, Italy, Austria, Portugal and Finland actively supported the Dutch proposal, and unanimity on the Council was retained for all taxation questions. Thus, at the highest level of decision-making, environmental policy has been marked by the need to accommodate pressures from below (the German Länder) as well as the widely varying orientations of its Member States.

Finally, environmental policy accommodation is sometimes achieved through 'burden sharing' and flexible targets. While overall standards are agreed, the precise targets may vary across Member States. Less developed Member States are often given less stringent targets than those borne by their more developed counterparts (see Liberatore 1997: 119; Golub 1996b: 328–9). This strategy has become especially common when the EU tries to present a common position in external environmental negotiations (see Exhibit 7.3). The 'burden sharing' approach inevitably requires hard bargaining because it allows for unequal standards. In particular, the approach meets with tremendous resistance from northern states. A member of UKREP put it thus: 'We don't want to let other Member States do bugger all while we spend billions to meet standards.'[18]

Despite such accommodation measures, intergovernmental bargaining continues to reflect basic disagreements over not only the importance of environmental protection, but also the means – the 'best' policy solution. This disagreement will become more severe after eastern enlargement because of the catastrophic environmental situation in most applicant countries, and the Central and Eastern Europe Countries' (CEECs) general priority of wealth creation and economic development. In environmental policy decision-making, as much as in any other arena, the EU's ability to accommodate diversity will be severely tested.

The Systemic Level: Intra- and Interinstitutional Bargaining

Decisions taken at the highest political levels have determined the overall framework for making environmental policy. But history-making decisions in the environmental field are rare, and the dynamics of their negotiation tell us little about the day to day decisions which set policy. Understanding these decisions requires examination of institutional rules and bargaining norms both within and between institutions.

At the systemic level, bargaining on the Council is again marked by attempts to accommodate diverse environmental interests. QMV is the dominant form of voting on the Environment Council and this rule informs bargaining on most (non-fiscal) environmental matters by encouraging coalition building between leaders or laggard Member States. 'Fence sitters', committed to neither camp, occupy an enviable bargaining position. Their ability to deliver decisive votes under QMV gives them strength well beyond their size or voting weight. However, there are no fixed coalitions on environmental policy. Allies on issues of, say, water quality legislation often oppose one another on issues related to biotechnology or nuclear energy.

Fundamental differences in environmental preferences mean that it is often easy to end up with clear winners and losers on the Council. In the EU's consensual system, enormous efforts are made to ensure that no one comes out a clear loser. A variety of tools for consensus building are deployed (see Weale 1996: 606; Hayes-Renshaw and Wallace 1997). Laggards are often allowed exemptions or extended periods in which to comply with legislation. Typical is a 1997 directive which set limits on the benzene and sulphur content of fuel. Poorer southern Member States were allowed to apply looser standards if they could prove that their limited

Exhibit 7.3 The EU as a global environmental actor

The EU is unique amongst international organisations in that it has a substantial environmental policy of its own, but also participates in a wide array of international agreements. It has been an important player in international negotiations to halt the increasing emissions of greenhouse gases, especially carbon dioxide, and negotiations to protect the ozone layer by reducing ozone-depleting substances such as chlorofluorocarbons (CFCs).

The EU's global role expanded considerably in the 1970s when the European Court of Justice ruled that, where the EU had passed *internal* legislation in a particular area, it had the right to handle *external* affairs relating to that field. Still, ambiguity remained regarding the proper division of labour in negotiating international environmental agreements, and precise competencies and roles often were not decided until negotiations were under way. This ambiguity, enormously frustrating to EU actors as well as third country negotiators (see Benedick 1991; Sbragia 1998), meant that in environmental affairs, as in other fields, the perennial question remained: who speaks for Europe?

Part of the EU's difficulty is that it must negotiate a common line internally before entering multilateral talks. Increasingly, the EU has relied on 'burden sharing' or differentiated targets internally, as a way to present a common position externally. For example, the EU put forward one common position in the run-up to the climate convention talks in Kyoto, Japan in December 1997. The EU's common pledge was to reduce a basket of greenhouse gases by 15 per cent by 2010, though individual Member States had their own targets (based on energy use, pollution levels, economic development, and so on).

$\longrightarrow$

crude oil supplies made it difficult to respect the agreed rules.[22] Similarly, on several occasions the UK has been allowed longer periods for complying with EU water directives (Richardson 1996d: 162).

Another consensus mechanism is the use of package deals, which have been used to secure adoption of several air pollution directives. In a typical example, two separate directives on emissions were linked: German ministers made concessions on auto emission standards to secure agreement on large industrial plant emission standards (see Golub 1996c: 11; Arp 1995: 238). However, focusing exclusively (or even primarily) on bargaining amongst Member States makes it easy to neglect the unintended or unexpected consequences of EU environmental decision-making. Intergovernmental theorists have difficulty explaining why EU environmental

→

Environment Commissioner Ritt Bjerregaard considered this agreement no mean feat, yet the exhausting negotiations to agree a position internally did her little good in the actual Kyoto discussions. First, the Commission found itself constrained in the negotiations precisely because the EU's 'common' position was so tenuous and internally complex. The EU's position was attacked as inflexible, not only by other countries, but by well-known experts on climate change.[19] Its inflexibility meant it could be outmanoeuvred by other countries. One critic commented, 'The EU went to Kyoto a lion and returned a lamb. US negotiators overwhelmed the slow moving Europeans on virtually all issues.'[20] In the end, the USA did not feel compelled to emulate the EU by accepting tough reductions. Its willingness to agree only significantly weaker reductions meant Bjerregaard had to return to Brussels with a new target, and thus new internal negotiations. In June 1998, the burden sharing targets carefully constructed in 1997 disintegrated when over half the EU Member States demanded and won further relaxation of their national targets to limit or reduce greenhouse emissions. The deal was further threatened when several Member States attempted to make national commitments conditional on the introduction of EU-wide emission control measures. Ignoring the British Council chair's confident announcement that 'There is no conditionality, there never could be',[21] a new Dutch government announced in July 1998 that their target would be conditional on EU countries agreeing to introduce an energy tax by 2002.

In global negotiations, flexibility internally equals coherence externally. But, clearly, wide variation in Member States' interests and preferences often weakens the EU position. The Kyoto negotiations and their aftermath illustrate the limits of EU global action on the environment, even when internal compromises can be reached.

policy sometimes creates standards well above lowest common denominator outcomes or pre-existing national environmental policies. For instance, the EU nitrate standards agreed in the 1970s (even before QMV) were significantly tougher than those in effect at the national level, including those in Germany or the Netherlands. Similarly, Weale (1996: 604) demonstrates how integrated pollution control, pushed initially by the UK, took a far more stringent, ambitious form than originally intended or desired by the UK.[23]

In short, environmental decision-making is not simply a process which reflects dominant coalitions of Member States (leader or laggard) pushing their own national style of regulation. National concerns are 'displaced' onto a higher level (Weale 1996), but in the process become mediated by institutional bargaining between the Council, Commission and, increasingly, the EP. In environmental policy the institutional balance of power is constantly shifting, and decisions rules are manipulated in the struggle. Three institutional factors are particularly important in determining how policies are set: the increase in 'veto players' (Tsebelis 1995), the growth in the EP's power and the Commission's enduring role as agenda-setter.

Previous to the SEA, the setting of environmental policy was dominated by the bilateral relationship between the Council and the Commission. The policy-making process provided little formal access through which 'third' actors such as the EP or oppositional groups could exert influence. The number of 'veto players' – actors whose agreement is required for a change in policy – was small. The SEA expanded the use of QMV in nearly all sectors related to the internal market (including much environmental policy). The SEA's introduction of the co-operation procedure also increased the powers of the EP, in which environmental concerns tended to be better represented than in other institutions. Under co-operation, the EP had a second chance to table amendments and bargain. The EP's more robust role affected decision-making on a range of legislation. The best known example is the 1989 auto emissions directive in which the EP was able to force the Council to accept standards well above those preferred by most EU Member States (see Exhibit 7.4).

The EP's influence over policy-setting decisions increased with the enactment of the Maastricht Treaty. The new co-decision procedure gave the EP the right to veto legislation related to environmental strategy, consumer protection and public health. Whereas under the co-operation procedure, the EP required the Commission's backing in order to get its amendments through the Council, co-decision gave the EP the right to negotiate directly with the Council the changes it wanted and ultimately to reject bills that did not contain them. In particular, co-decision required much greater sensitivity on the part of the Commission to the policy aspirations of the EP (Judge and Earnshaw 1994: 269). One senior member of a Commissioner's *cabinet* argued that the co-decision has made an 'absolute difference. The Commission just can't ignore Parliament anymore. It's much more of an interchange now'.[24] By extending co-decision to virtually all non-fiscal environmental measures, the Amsterdam Treaty further enhanced the Parliament's bargaining position.

Treaty changes after the mid-1980s increased the EP's institutional powers generally, and its role in environmental policy-making particularly. As the EP's own visibility and influence grew, conflict among the EU's institutions became a much more common feature of EU politics. The EP's 'hardball' strategy on the biotechnology patenting directive (see Exhibit 8.5) illustrated its potential role as 'veto player'.

More generally, the EP's influence (or, even more specifically, that of the EP's Environment Committee) clearly has contributed to increased stringency in EU rules on bathing water, urban waste water treatment and stationary air pollution (Judge 1993b; Judge and Earnshaw 1994; Collins and Earnshaw 1993). The EP's overall role in policy-setting is sometimes exaggerated (see Golub 1996b), but its bargaining has led to important changes in environmental policy on the margins. 'And that,' at least according to one MEP, 'is where it counts.'[25]

Although both Member States and the EP participate in setting the environmental agenda, the main initiator remains the Commission. The precise origins of its ideas are usually unclear, but its formal prerogatives give it obvious agenda-setting powers vis-à-vis the Council: 'The Council can instruct the Commission to prepare a text, but cannot command its contents' (Hayes-Renshaw and Wallace 1997: 180). Similarly, Sbragia (1996: 244) argues that, while the Commission 'may indeed propose regulations which are inspired by the green laws of one of the leaders', it often 'acts as a policy entrepreneur when it comes to the substance of the proposed legislation'.

Even before enactment of the SEA, the Commission massaged existing rules to widen its competence in the environmental field. Using its prerogative to select the treaty articles under which legislation is introduced, the Commission applied Articles 94 and 308[26] to justify EU action in environmental policy long before Member States agreed to have an environmental policy in principle. The Commission's boldness helps explain why the EU had a significant body of environmental legislation even before the SEA was enacted.

The Commission's power of initiative is critical because the content of early drafts is essential in shaping the final text. But the Commission is not a monolithic actor. First, the services or Directorates-General feature fierce rivalries, particularly on environmental matters. As Bulmer notes (1994: 361) 'Commission administrators may see their loyalty as being to "their" director-general or "their" Commissioner rather than to a more collegiate notion of the Commission.' More specifically, DG XI's priorities and loyalties are often at odds with those emerging from other services, especially DGs III (internal market) and VI (agriculture).

Similarly, individual Commissioners compete to get 'their' policy proposals adopted. In the late 1990s, the outspoken Environment Commissioner Ritt Bjerregaard often locked horns with other Commissioners responsible for issues related to trade or industry. Typical was the dispute in 1997 between Bjerregaard and Sir Leon Brittan, Commissioner for Trade. Bjerregaard sought a ban on imports of furs (from the USA and elsewhere) from animals caught using 'inhumane' leghold traps. However,

Exhibit 7.4 Auto emissions: the EP flexes its muscles

The 1989 directive on auto emissions standards for small cars is widely cited as an example of the EP's growing influence in environmental policy. Although intended to promote environmental protection, the directive's primary purpose was the removal of non-tariff barriers (such as differing national environmental standards) to trade in automobiles. In 1987, the Commission issued a draft directive standardising emission limits for small cars. The emission standards initially specified in the draft directive were significantly weaker than standards enforced in the USA, and much weaker than standards advocated by environmentalists, the European Parliament and 'leader' Member States such as Denmark and the Netherlands. In its first opinion in September 1988, the European Parliament proposed far stricter ceilings and advocated the mandatory introduction of catalytic converters, which reduce the emission of carbon monoxide and other harmful gases. The Council of Ministers ignored the first opinion of the EP. Voting by qualified majority (QMV) in November 1988, the Council adopted the weaker standards in its common position. The Netherlands, Denmark and Greece opposed the position but were outvoted.

Because the directive was proposed under Article 95,[29] the EP was granted a second reading as well as the right to reject the common position by majority vote. Environmentalists took the opportunity to mount an awareness campaign directed at the public and potential allies within the EP. They lobbied hard for drastic amendments or a complete rejection of the Council's position. However, according to a Commission official (Hull 1993: 89) the real pressure came from within the Parliament where the strength of green feeling was especially strong.

Responding to green concerns, the EP amended the common position, insisting that norms which were 'at least as strict' as US standards be obligatory from 1 January 1993. The EP threatened that, if its amendments were not accepted, it would reject outright the norms proposed by the Commission and agreed by the Council. Had the Parliament done so, the Council of Ministers would have had to act by unanimity (an unlikely prospect) to overturn the position.

→

her efforts were stymied, with Brittan warning that a ban would leave the EU open to attack within the World Trade Organisation. In the end the Commission presented a much diluted proposal to the Council in summer 1997.[27]

Fragmentation and rivalry within the Commission are more acute in the environmental field than in other sectors. Most environmental issues cross over several policy areas and Directorates-General. Extensive discussions must take place within the Commission itself to determine which policies

→

The Commission and Council were forced to reassess their positions. The Commissioner for the Environment, Carlo Ripa di Meana, convinced the Commission to recognise the EP's preference for stricter standards and to accept them in its draft directive. In return the EP's Environment Committee dropped two amendments unacceptable to the Commission (Judge 1993b: 202). In April 1989, one week before the EP's threatened vote, the Commission announced that it was set to propose stricter small car emission standards in the near future. The Council either had to approve this revised position by a qualified majority, amend it by unanimity or see it fail. The latter option effectively was no option: it would have divided the internal market and caused chaos in the automobile industry.

In June 1989, the Council adopted the stricter legislation by QMV. The resulting EU directive introduced mandatory standards for exhaust emissions and required the introduction of catalytic converters. The EP's muscle flexing had produced an EU policy which set a minimum level of environmental protection which was higher than could have been achieved at a domestic level in most EU Member States. The directive was a political triumph for the EP because it signalled its growing institutional power. But the auto emissions directive was agreed at a time of exceptionally high environmental awareness and concern. David Grant Lawrence, a member of the Environment Commissioner's *cabinet*, explained that the vote 'came just before the European elections. It was becoming clear that the Greens would do well everywhere. No minister could afford to be seen to sabotage a good decision'.[30] Moreover, Ripa di Meana was particularly sympathetic to environmental concerns and later became a Green MEP. Above all, environmental actors working within the EP enjoyed a rare moment of unity on auto emissions. The auto emissions case signalled the EP's growing influence on EU environmental decision-making: as the EP's power increased, so the EU, too, became greener. But 'greenery' has its limits in the EU. Both it – and the EP's power – remain contingent on situational, often fleeting, circumstances.

should be allocated to which Directorates. To illustrate the point, the Commission's formulation of EU climate policy (including energy efficiency measures and a carbon/energy tax) initially involved 10 separate DGs (Skjaerseth 1994). Ambiguity concerning 'ownership' of policy means that the content of environmental proposals often reflects turf battles and competing agendas. DG XI officials guard their environmental portfolio jealously, especially from DG III intruders. One DG XI official insisted: 'The bottom line is that in an ideal world environmental legislation should be managed by us . . . we are not entirely convinced that the area of the Commission whose vocation is to promote industrial interests is necessarily the best place to set environmental emission standards.'[28]

DG XI is clearly a junior player in many of these turf wars. Its status is reflected in the seemingly minor matter of venue. When, in the early 1990s, the Commission moved out of the Berlaymont building in central Brussels, DG XI was pushed literally to the furthest corner of Brussels, the suburb of Beaulieu on the outskirts of the city. By contrast, DG III was relocated almost across the road from the Berlaymont. DG XI's relative weakness puts it at a disadvantage when it seeks to push its proposals through inter-service negotiations.

The effect of its stature is most often reflected in the dilution of DG XI's proposals even before bargaining with the Council begins. Fierce opposition from DGs XXI (taxation) and III (internal market/industry) weakened considerably the ambitious climate package initially prepared by Commissioner Ripa di Meana and DG XI in the run-up to the Rio summit. Divided internally, the Commission (with Ripa di Meana as its putative but now peeved spokesman) could hardly act as an effective counter to a Council reluctant to agree to any but the most marginal of targets. In sum, the Commission retains important powers to set environmental policy, but the influence of DG XI is highly circumscribed. Moreover, the Commission must share its power to set policy not only with the Council but, increasingly, with the EP, whose influence in environmental policy has expanded steadily.

The Sub-systemic Level: Messy Networks

One of the most conspicuous features of environmental decision-making is the influence of a wide array of non-institutional members and interests, particularly in the early 'shaping' stages. In addition to national and EU officials, the formulation of environmental policy usually brings together scientific experts, business interest groups and environmental non-governmental organisations (NGOs). The crowded nature of the environmental policy-making process means that policy-shaping usually takes place within loose 'issue networks' (see Mazey and Richardson 1993b; Bomberg 1994, 1998b). These issue networks often feature a range of actors who have radically different views of the policy problem as well as the desired policy outcomes. Memberships change frequently and sometimes dramatically when new issues arise or as they are transformed. Environmental policy networks are messier than most.

Technical expertise is an important entry card to most policy networks, but the role of scientific and technical expertise is especially important in environmental policy. The prominent position of temporary scientific experts was underscored by Ken Collins, Chairman of the European Parliament's Environment Committee, who described EU policy-making as 'curious in that it is made up of the normal political folk but is also made up scientists of various kinds. They might be biochemists, biologists, or physicists . . . but they're all mixed up with the political types and this makes for a very disparate network'.[31]

The importance of such experts stems from the highly technical character of environmental policy and the Commission's dependence on a wide variety of sources for information. The European Environmental Agency (EEA), which came into operation in 1993, can provide the Commission with comparable information at the European level on the state of the environment. But the EEA's limited resources, as well as its independence from the Commission, accentuates the Commission's need for additional outside experts. Given the restricted size of its permanent staff,[32] DG XI depends on experts and officials on secondment from national capitals, other EU institutions, private organisations and foundations.

The dense web of expert committees and technical working groups which prepare dossiers allows allied groups of specialised technicians or technocrats – epistemic communities – opportunities to control the policy agenda (Haas 1992). In the formulation of climate change policy, for instance, the Council set up working groups to prepare dossiers and keep ministers well informed, but these groups were soon dominated by scientific experts. As one participant explained: 'Member States are expected to send senior representatives who have the direct ear of ministers. But often what happens is that the first meeting of the group is well attended [and has an] impressive membership, but then attendance and seniority drop off; delegates are sent, etc.'[33] On the other hand, 'non-political' specialised technicians who attend these meetings regularly are in a strong position to shape Member States' early responses to Commission's proposals.

Normally, epistemic communities exhibit considerable complicity due to a shared sense of causal understanding and technocratic rationality on the part of their members. Yet a more recent development in environmental policy is the emergence of rival epistemic communities which offer different interpretations of problems and solutions. To illustrate the point, considerable scientific debate surrounds the methodology used for testing the quality of bathing water as required in the reform of the EU's bathing water directive (begun in the mid-1990s). Commission officials complain that scientific experts from different Member States often provide contrasting advice 'not [only] as to what is technically feasible but as to what is technically effective'.[34] For their part, national representatives protest that the Commission is not above choosing 'tame experts'. One British representative claimed: 'In the case of bathing water, the Commission didn't choose mainstream scientists but someone known to be pushing for very low ceilings.'[35] The point is that environmental policy debates are not simply about the political practicality of standards (where one would expect to find disagreement), but also about ostensibly 'neutral' questions concerning measurements and scientific methodology.

The highly technical nature of most environmental policy also makes it difficult for many environmental NGOs or elected representatives to play a meaningful role in the scientific debate which surrounds policy formulation. In the case of the auto–oil programme, NGOs and MEPs complained early on about the insular process of policy formulation and its effective exclusion of non-experts. Yet a Commission official closely involved in the programme retorted that MEPs expected technical briefings 'to be reduced to a ten minute cartoon job'.[36] The prevalence of comitology – whereby committees of national civil servants scrutinise the Commission's implementing measures – reinforces the exclusion of MEPs or NGOs. For example, in legislation related to pesticide residues in food, it is frequently up to the Commission to decide the precise limit of pesticides per kilogram. The Commission's actions are monitored by committees of national civil servants and experts, but the Parliament's role is circumscribed, and consumer and environmental groups barely get a look in (Corbett *et al.* 1995: 253–4).

In addition to ostensibly neutral actors, more overtly political actors seek to forward the aims of their members by combining resources and sharing information within advocacy coalitions. Made up largely of lobbyists and politicians, as opposed to the technocrats who dominate epistemic communities, advocacy coalitions span the EU's institutions and compete for control of networks shaping environmental policy. In EU environmental policy, opposing coalitions have formed around divisive issues such as the biotechnology patenting directive or packaging waste. Coalitions may be based on 'families' of European political parties – the Christian Democrats, Socialists or Greens – while Member States encourage their own nationals in the EU's institutions to uphold national goals and priorities. Actors often must decide which of the different identities – national, party, institutional – should determine their position. On issues such as packaging waste or biotechnology, for instance, MEPs may defy the interests of their party group or Member State to side with their particular coalition.

In environmental policy, advocacy coalitions usually feature lobbyists representing either industry or environmental NGOs. Generally, the most successful lobbyists are those who can 'pool their resources' by sharing information and the 'ear time' of a Commission official or EP Committee chair. An assistant to the chair of the EP's Environment Committee noted that 'ear time' is most likely to be offered to lobbyists who represent an EU-wide association with a unified position. 'Then we'll say "We will give you 15 minutes, give us your amendment." Otherwise you get 50 different proposals.'[37]

DG XI is generally considered to be more open to lobbyists than any other Commission service. Some have described environmental policy-making as a pluralist balancing game with varying interests enjoying similar access and influence. This view, particularly prevalent in the early 1990s, is underlined by two DG XI officials who describe access to the service as something of a 'free for all' with the 'door open for any groups wishing to contact Commission officers' (quoted in Mazey and Richardson 1992: 111).

Yet it is easy to exaggerate the pluralist character of environmental policy issue networks. Compared to other sectors, environmental policy networks are relatively accessible, but openness should not be confused with equal influence. Clearly, resource imbalances occur within even fairly accessible networks. For instance, a senior Commission official responsible for waste management policy insisted that, for DG XI, apart from contacts with national administrations, '90 per cent of the contacts are with trade and industry'.[38] Moreover, many environmental activists argue that DG XI's tradition of openness was watered down in the mid-1990s by a desire to dispel its image as a 'nest of green radicalism' (Ehrlich 1996: 18). In short, environment policy does not represent a pluralist paradise. The uneven resource base of different actors within networks is illustrated by the development of the 1994 packaging waste directive, in which the initial influence of environmental advocates was soon overshadowed by the superior resources and access of industry representatives (see Exhibit 7.5).

Whatever their composition, the ability of policy networks to shape environmental policy is uneven. The case of packaging waste shows how the policy-shaping process can be captured by networks dominated by a coalition opposing tougher environmental measures. Alternatively, 'green' advocacy coalitions can seize control of policy networks which cohere temporarily, using them to exploit fleeting, but favourable political circumstances or policy windows and achieve unexpected results. In the case of emission standards for small cars (Exhibit 7.4), an issue network dominated by environmental interests managed to unite across EU institutions and take advantage of the rising (if temporary) salience of green issues to push successfully for relatively stringent standards in 1989.

Moreover, it is possible for policy networks to move one step beyond shaping EU policies and even influence history-making decisions. Although rare, this can occur when networks are led by agents who seek a rewriting of the rules, or a new 'grand bargain' in their sector: take the mobilisation

Exhibit 7.5 Packaging waste: 'capturing' issue networks[39]

The 1994 directive on packaging and packaging waste introduced a harmonised waste management policy designed to reduce the impact of packaging waste on the environment. Following over a year of consultation, negotiation and several drafts, the Commission published a formal proposal in late 1992. The proposal stipulated that 90 per cent of packaging would have to be recovered within 10 years, 60 per cent of which was to be recycled.

At its first reading in June 1993, the EP adopted *rapporteur* Luigi Vertemati's report and several amendments which sought to strengthen the draft directive by, inter alia, introducing a hierarchy of preferred treatment (that is, prevention, reuse, recycling, incineration, landfill disposal) and measures to prevent production of unnecessary packaging. Although the Commission's amended proposal, presented in late 1993, adopted several of the EP's amendments, many of its tougher amendments (including those listed above) were rejected by the Commission as inappropriate or incompatible with the aims of single market.

At the end of 1993, following further consultation and negotiations, the Environment Council adopted a Packaging Waste Directive which was considerably weaker in content and tone than were earlier drafts. The Council agreed that within five years of the directive's implementation not less than 50 per cent, nor more than 65 per cent of packaging waste should be recovered rather than dumped. Minimum recycling targets were dropped to 25 per cent, although within 10 years the Council would have to agree a 'substantial increase' in these percentages. Several concessions were made to cohesion countries because of their peripheral status and comparatively low consumption of packaging. Although the Council's decision received a cautious welcome from packaging organisations, it was harshly criticised as regressive by several NGOs and three Member States (Germany, Belgium and the Netherlands). Indeed, the Dutch Environment Minister complained the directive was so weak that it had 'nothing to do with the environment'.[40]

Under the co-decision procedure, the Council's decision was subject to a second reading by the EP in 1994. It was widely believed that the EP would insist on its earlier tougher amendments, including the imposition of a hierarchy and prevention of unnecessary packaging. However, the

$\longrightarrow$

→

environmental coalition within the EP failed to secure the parliamentary majority (260 votes) needed to pass the more stringent amendments. In the end the directive was adopted with virtually the same targets and stipulations.

The policy network shaping the legislation featured a varied and fluid membership. Even within the Commission itself, 16 different DGs were involved with the proposal at different stages of its formulation (Porter and Butt Philip 1993: 17). Scientific experts were needed to help clarify technological uncertainty as to the most effective means of treating packaging waste. Lobbyists representing over 50 Euro-level interest groups were active at different times during the directive's development. Several dozen environmental NGOs lobbied separately or under the auspices of SPAN (Sustainable Packaging Action Network). SPAN, Friends of the Earth and the European Environmental Bureau formed the core of a green advocacy coalition which was especially active early in the process. A plethora of trade and industry groups (such as INCPEN, ERRA and EUROPEN)[41] also became active early on to prevent stringent new packaging legislation on the national level.

The exchange of resources between these lobbyists and the Commission was loose, informal and open. It was also uneven. By the early 1990s, industry coalitions had seen environmental networks push Member States towards increased QMV on environmental issues, and towards adoption of more stringent environmental measures. Industry responded by becoming more active and effective lobbyists of all institutions, but especially the Parliament. In the packaging waste case, manufacturers and industry interests clearly had a resource advantage in terms of more sophisticated lobbying techniques, more lobbyists and more extensive access to scientific and technical data. One of Vertemati's aides underscored the power of actors representing the packaging industry: 'They had consultants, scientists and lobbyists in every corridor . . . and that is where decisions are made.'[42]

Packaging waste, like most environmental policies, was subject to bargaining between a vast and varied array of actors over both the definition of the problem and the desired solution. Yet this case illustrates that, despite the fundamental unpredictability of the EU's environmental policy agenda, issue networks are not merely pluralist politics by another name. The issue network may have been loose but it was still 'captured' by those opposing stringent measures regulating packaging waste.

of 'greener' Member State governments, green parties (including those in the EP), non-governmental organisations and other actors with interests in environmental policy which pushed a critical mass of Member States to embrace increased QMV for environmental policy in the Maastricht Treaty (Sbragia 1996; Corbett 1998). Generally, however, most EU environmental policy networks remain loose and ad hoc, and their policy impact is seldom decisive.

Conclusion

The environment marks an especially dynamic policy area in the EU. Unlike more entrenched policy areas such as agriculture, patterns of EU decision-making in the environmental arena are still relatively new and fluid. The open and experimental character of decision-making on environmental policy has several broad implications. It means that there is no single pattern to environmental decision-making. Not only does decision-making reflect the diverse goals and means of 15 Member States, it also reflects a set of institutional rules with its own form and logic (see Weale 1996). Finally, decision-making reflects the *informal* politics of bargaining and resource exchange across and within loose issue networks.

The lack of established patterns means that outputs (environmental legislation) remain unpredictable. Legislative outputs reflect bargaining and resource exchange among Member States, institutions and a wide variety of public and private actors who often disagree about the nature of the problem as well as the solution. Certain features of environmental decision-making – its crowded pattern of interest representation and reliance on varying, sometimes conflicting, scientific advice – can result in policies which are difficult to follow and harder to implement. The most oft cited example is water quality (see Bomberg and Peterson 1993; Ward 1998; Jordan 1999), but other cases, such as the packaging waste directive, reveal EU regulations that are rich in incongruities and ambiguities (see Bomberg 1998b). In environmental policy, the complex bargaining required to reach decisions can produce results that are as tortured as the decision-making process itself.

The cross-sectoral character of environmental issues complicates decision-making. The overlap between the environment and other spheres such as the internal market, agriculture or cohesion policy is widely recognised. So, too, is the need to integrate environmental policies into these other areas. Constitutionally, the link is well established. The inclusion of environmental factors in other EU policies was made explicit in the SEA. The 5th Action Programme, *Towards Sustainability*, expressed the need to integrate environmental policies more explicitly into other policy areas.

The Amsterdam Treaty made this link stronger in its new Article 6, which insists that environmental protection requirements *must* be integrated into the definition and implementation of EU policies and activities. The massive budget reform package, Agenda 2000, makes 'a top priority' the linkage of the structural funds to environmental protection and the promotion of sustainable development (Commission 1997b).

Yet the idea of sustainable development is not yet a norm of EU governance. Whereas environmental policy has become more stringent in its own traditional domain (air pollution and water quality), the impact of environmental considerations on other EU policies remains weak. The non-integration of environmental criteria is particularly visible in areas related to cohesion, agriculture and internal market policy. The CAP not only fails to incorporate environmental criteria; in many instances it violates them. The conflict between EU environmental directives and decisions on EU cohesion funding for peripheral regions is widely documented (see Court of Auditors 1992; Baker *et al.* 1994; Baker *et al.* 1997). Much internal market policy, beginning with the framing of the 1992 project itself, ignores or contradicts environment considerations (see Weale and Williams 1992; Liberatore 1997).

Constitutional or formal changes, in other words, do not alone bring about change. Whereas environment policy is informed by agricultural or internal market imperatives, the 'environmental imperative' is comparatively weak. As long as powerful neo-liberal ideas about free trade and limited government remain entrenched in EU governance, environmental policy will remain one of the Cinderellas of EU policies, despite its popular appeal.

Chapter 8

Research and Technology Policy

The development of European RTD policy
Making history and setting budgets
The systemic level does it matter?
Policy networks and the politics of expertise
Conclusion

Before the 1980s, EU activities designed to promote research and technological development (RTD)[1] were pretty small beer. By the mid-1990s, funding for research was the third largest item of policy expenditure in the EU's budget. Moreover, the Union had become the most important source of policy affecting a range of high-growth, technology-intensive European industries. It had entered the highly politicised realm of broadcasting and 'audio-visual policy', where common interests were illusive even as technological advance made national borders increasingly meaningless. The EU became the horse that Europe rode in the race to create the vaguely explicated 'information society'.

The EU's policy role arises from the new challenges to the nation-state posed by technological change, which itself often makes national borders more porous and less effective in controlling flows of people and information. The rapid establishment of the Internet as a primary mode of communication for millions by the late 1990s, after few had even heard of it five years before, illustrates the point. Meanwhile, any region's competitiveness in global markets, its capacity to generate good jobs and its general quality of life increasingly are a product of its relative ability to innovate or, at least, to absorb or adopt innovations developed elsewhere. The vast costs and risks involved in research into the next generation of core technologies, such as computer chips, computers and modes of transport, virtually dictate that European firms must collaborate in the face of daunting competition from America and Asia. The need to diffuse new technologies quickly to remain 'in the game' in global competition makes logical the EU's role as a promoter of technology transfer. The Union is unlikely to see its RTD policy role diminish even as it enlarges. However decision-making on goals and priorities – already highly contested – is likely to become far more laborious as the Union becomes a political unit that incorporates wildly varying levels of technological development.

The Development of European RTD Policy[2]

In the EU, as in most systems of government, public actions to promote RTD fall under the rubric of *industrial policy*. Johnson (1984: 7) defines industrial policy as a 'summary term for the activities of governments that are intended to develop or relieve various industries in a national economy in order to maintain global competitiveness'. Note that industrial policy is considered, by definition, a *national* activity that involves intervention by governments in an economy. The idea of an 'EU industrial policy' is quite novel: no other international organisation in existence can be said to have one. In particular, no other has anything close to the RTD policy power possessed by the Union.

Of course, the 1992 project was built on the assumption that governments should stop intervening in their national economies so that market forces would take hold and a truly single European market would emerge. However, the crisis which beset Europe's steel sector in the early 1980s was still a fresh memory when EU Member States turned to the Commission – particularly the Industry Commissioner Etienne Davignon – for a solution to lagging European technological competitiveness. The steel crisis had given the EU a track record in solving industrial problems which national governments shared but could not solve on their own. Industrial policy, including its RTD elements, became an accepted means of 'flanking' the internal market, even if its content remained highly disputed.

The EU's flanking policies all either cushion the harsh effects of the internal market or hasten its construction. Increased EU competence in industrial policy was justified on both counts in the early 1980s. First, new collaborative research programmes could help ensure that the primary beneficiaries of the 1992 project were not large, integrated Japanese and American firms that were used to selling in large, foreign markets. Large R&D investments by the Americans via the Strategic Defense Initiative and the Japanese through the 5th Generation Computer Project led to a new acceptance that similarly ambitious projects were needed in the EU and that they could only be organised on a European scale.

Second, RTD programmes became a way to convince firms to treat the single market as a 'home' market. The Commission insisted that only projects involving firms from at least two different Member States would be eligible for EU research subsidies. Firms would thus learn about new market opportunities beyond their national borders, in some cases by osmosis or mere contact with 'foreign' partners. Moreover, as collaborative projects led to new processes and products, pan-European technical standards would be created through the back door.

Third, industrial policy was a favoured sector for advocates of closer European integration because it offered considerable scope for leadership by the Commission in areas where national policies no longer worked (see Sandholtz 1992). Audio-visual (AV) policy illustrates the point. The explosion of new cable and satellite channels foreseen for the 1990s promised to open up huge new markets for programming which could only be met by increased foreign imports unless Europe's own film and TV industries were nourished and expanded. After having virtually no AV policy role, the EU became a battleground for the highly controversial 'Television Without Frontiers' directive which tried to promote Europe's AV industry in the face of daunting American competition. AV policy was marked by intense cultural sensitivities, a common external threat, and rapid technological change. It seemed ripe for a European 'solution' (see Exhibit 8.1).

The EU's mandates for competition and industrial policy often clash with one another, but they *appeared* complementary when crucial decision points were reached in the development of an EU research policy in the 1980s. For example, the initiatives launched by Davignon in the late 1970s to subsidise research by Europe's electronics industries, leading to the European Strategic Programme for Information Technologies (ESPRIT), added momentum to the 1992 project. Later, the EU had to reconcile its programme of liberalisation with calls by Member States (particularly France) for active measures to promote the global competitiveness of European firms. Signing on to the 1992 project meant that national governments committed themselves to stop protecting and subsidising their 'national champions'. For the French and others, the argument became: if the Commission is going to police national state aids more strictly, it must compensate by using EU funds to support the emergence of 'European champions' which can compete with large and powerful American and Japanese firms (see Hayward 1995).

The main architect of an EU industrial policy was Martin Bangemann, the Commissioner for Industry for most of the 1990s. A former German economics minister, Bangemann found a middle ground between the fierce liberalism of Leon Brittan and the interventionist sympathies of Delors. For Bangemann (1992: 24–51), 'competition and industrial policies are not opposites', and the internal market itself is 'the best example of an industrial policy'. In other words, EU industrial policy should consist mainly of 'horizontal measures', instead of industry-specific ones, to create a favourable business environment, promote structural adjustment and open markets. For political as well as practical reasons, it should not 'pick winners' or give public aid to oligopolistic European champions.

By 1991, Member States had agreed a new (Maastricht) treaty article (157)[9] which committed the Union to ensure 'the conditions necessary for the competitiveness of industry'. Known colloquially as the 'Cresson clause', after the French Socialist Prime Minister of the day, Edith Cresson, it did not even contain the term 'industrial policy'. The provision that any actions taken would require unanimity on the Council seemed to guarantee that the Cresson clause would be little used.

By the mid-1990s, Cresson held the research portfolio in the Santer Commission. The EU was spending serious money, close to €3 billion per year, subsidising research. The Union's support for the information technology (IT) sector, for example, equalled about 10 per cent of total EU investment in the sector. Yet, despite Cresson's best efforts, the Maastricht industry title remained unused. Her affinity for large, strategic, *dirigiste* projects was effectively nullified by Bangemann's 'horizontalist' ethos. It remained possible to argue about what principles should inform policy choices, but RTD policy had become established as a sector where the Union's *acquis* and spending were considerable.

RTD policy illustrates that a very large share of what the EU does springs from the internal market, which itself was 'a patchwork full of derogations, exceptions, missing links, transitions, and anomalies' well into the 1990s (Dinan 1994: 360). But its 'creation' led to a vast expansion of the EU's reach and power. This process of expansion was particularly rapid on policy matters concerning technological change.

Making History and Setting Budgets

Prior to the early 1980s, the Community's RTD policy role was negligible outside of energy research and scattered regulations that affected some high-tech industries. A series of robust proposals by the Commission, beginning with the 1970 Colonna Report, sought to create new EU programmes to try to halt Europe's perceived decline in technology-intensive industries. If anything, they backfired. The Commission was lambasted for being 'excessively preoccupied with the pursuit of an executive power which itself really presupposes a political unity' (Williams 1973: 139). European collaboration in RTD took place intergovernmentally, when it took place at all (see Sharp and Shearman 1987: 27–41; Peterson 1993a: 49–55).

An important breakthrough came after Davignon tried to encourage middle-level managers from Europe's 12 largest electronics firms to identify their collective needs and design collaborative projects which met them. The lack of enthusiasm for a Community initiative at this level convinced Davignon to go straight to the top and invite the top executives of each firm to discuss the future of IT in Europe. By 1981, the 'Big 12 Roundtable' of large European electronics firms held its first meeting and issued a joint communiqué which highlighted Europe's paltry 10 per cent share of global markets for IT and (declining) 40 per cent share of its own

Exhibit 8.1 'Television Without Frontiers'

Probably no single legislative act did more than the 1989 'Television Without Frontiers'[3] (TWF) directive to promulgate the notion of a 'Fortress Europe', or one which constructed new protectionist barriers to *external* trade as it tore down barriers to *internal* trade (see Hanson 1998). The directive created an internal market for broadcasting while harmonising rules on advertising. But it also reserved a majority of broadcasting time ('where practicable') for programmes of European origin, thus provoking outrage in the USA, whose annual exports of TV programmes to the EU were worth billions of dollars (see Collins 1994).

The economic stakes were high, with global audio-visual (AV) markets worth more than €250 billion (Commission 1993: 120). Audio-visual policy also provoked cultural sensitivities (see Fraser 1996). Technological advance (leading to expanded satellite, cable and pay-TV systems) meant that demand for programmes was set to double in the 1990s. The French led calls to restrict the influx of American 'cultural products', notably by insisting that AV be excluded from global trade rules at the end of the Uruguay Round (see Exhibit 4.3). Afterwards, the French Minister for Culture, Jacques Toubon, insisted 'now we must go further and build a protection system and a system for promoting the sector in the framework of the European Union'.[4]

The French view on AV policy was not universally shared, but the case for updating the TWF Directive became overwhelming. Advances in technology made it possible for, say, a Dutch satellite channel to broadcast pornography to the UK (circumventing British restrictions) and a British channel to televise toy advertisements to Sweden (where adverts aimed at children were banned). New media, such as shopping channels and 'video-on-demand' from the Internet, were not covered by the original Directive. The European Federation of Audiovisual Producers (FERA), an effective and truly pan-European lobby, demanded a tighter definition of 'European works' and a scrapping of the loophole requiring quotas only 'where practicable'.[5]

The Commission took its usual first step of tabling a green paper in early 1994. DG X (communications) took the lead, in the face of merciless criticism from DG III (industry) for being 'exclusively defensive', DG XV (internal market) for ignoring the economic effects of quotas, and DG XIII (telecoms and IT) for neglecting the impact of new technologies.[6] When the dust cleared, the Commissioner for AV policy, João de Deus Pinheiro, proposed closing the loophole on quotas *and* extending them to new, electronic, screen-based services (such as cable and pay-TV). However, Leon Brittan demanded that a decision by the college be postponed until after the Delors Commission's term had formally expired. Despite fierce lobbying from the French government, which raged at Jacques Santer's comment that quotas were 'always something artificial',[7] the Commission's legal service confirmed that the Delors 'caretaker' Commission could only take decisions on urgent matters, and thus the dossier passed to the Santer Commission.

→

→

Finally, a draft text was agreed by the college in mid-1995. It removed the words 'wherever practicable', but proposed that quotas should expire after 10 years. New 'thematic' channels (such as shopping or movie channels) were allowed to invest 25 per cent of their programming budgets in European productions as an alternative to observing quotas. The battlelines were drawn for a two-year punch-up: the French, Belgians, Spanish, Greeks and Irish confirmed their strong support for quotas on the Culture Council, while the German, British, Dutch, Swedish, Austrian and Danish delegations expressed strong opposition. Eventually, France became isolated as the only Member State favouring broad and unrestricted quotas, and began to threaten a veto.[8] Finally, in November 1995, the French accepted an informal political agreement (negotiated by the Committee of Permanent Representatives: COREPER) that the words 'wherever practicable' would stay in the directive and its scope (such as to video-on-demand) would not be extended. Basically, the deal endorsed the status quo, adding new provisions for a study of the Directive after five years and a 'Contact Committee' of national representatives to facilitate its implementation.

The Council reached political agreement even before the Directive went to the EP for its first reading. MEPs reacted with indignation and voted through a host of amendments, including one which replaced the 'where practicable' clause with 'by legally effective means'. The Commission rejected nearly all of the proposed amendments, as did the Council, which held firm behind its earlier compromise. Conciliation became inevitable.

In the event, the EP was bought off, rather cheaply, with a Council commitment to the principle of broad public access to major sporting events. The EP thus could claim to be protecting the interests of average sports fans from large media giants with pay-TV interests. But its proposed amendment to require all TV sets to carry 'v-chips', which enable parents to protect their children from violent programming, was a non-starter which cost the EP political capital (although the Council conceded a fresh study on TV violence). In the end, the TWF was voted through, with Germany voting no and Belgium abstaining.

The TWF case shows why EU legislation is often vague. The loophole in the original TWF made it legally shaky, but murky language helped all Member States to live with the Directive. The negotiations also revealed that two steps tend to be taken when EU decision-making requires a lubricant: first, launch a study; second, convene a committee. In addition to the Contact Committee, a new high-level 'think tank' of the great and good from Europe's audio-visual industries was created, which became the source of a 1998 proposal to create European versions of Hollywood's Academy Awards. Sensing a prized opportunity to promote itself and the EU to a wider public, the Commission seemed initially to embrace the idea, yet it backed away quickly when few Member States expressed support for it and several expressed concern about overshadowing existing (mostly national) awards. AV policy was a minefield, where it was almost impossible to tread without setting off explosions.

markets (Guzzetti 1995: 76–7). Crucially, Davignon decided to form a new 'Information Technology Task Force' within the Commission, but independent of any DG, to work with the 'Big 12'.

The result was the ESPRIT programme. Unlike the Commission's past RTD policy initiatives, this one was firmly backed and even largely designed by industry. Davignon's strategy worked: some of Europe's most politically powerful firms identified their collective problems and needs and joined the Commission in lobbying Member States for collaborative EU initiatives. ESPRIT's pilot phase only cost €11.5 million. However, it established important principles which were applied to virtually all later EU initiatives. First, projects involving research organisations from at least two different Member States were eligible for EU funding of up to half of the total costs of research. Second, ESPRIT funded only 'precompetitive' projects, concerned in principle with generic research, not research specific to a particular product or process. This proviso ensured that the EU would not violate its Article 81[10] Treaty obligation not to take any action which might favour one competitor over another, and 'effect the prevention, restriction or distortion of competition'. Yet the *results* of EU-funded projects would be jointly shared by all of its participants. Moreover, research organisations participating in other ESPRIT projects would have privileged access to the results, thus promoting the 'horizontal' objective of diffusing new technology.

Third, and probably most importantly, industry was involved intimately at all stages of ESPRIT's design and operation. More than two-thirds of projects initially funded through ESPRIT included participation by at least one 'Big 12' firm. Over time, RTD policy networks expanded and decision-making concerning ESPRIT (and most EU programmes generally) became less dominated by a small number of large firms. But EU-level collaborative initiatives encouraged the emergence of unified Commission–industry axes in a range of technology sectors.

After its pilot phase was complete, the Council agreed to a €750 million budget for ESPRIT for 1984–8. Member States did not endorse ambitious and expensive new EU-level actions without careful scrutiny. The Commission's initial proposal for expanding ESPRIT, at a price of €1.5 billion over 10 years, reawakened old suspicions about the Commission's political agenda. Moreover, when the US Reagan administration announced in 1985 that the Strategic Defense Initiative, with its staggering initial price tag of €26 billion, would reserve a share of its funding for European researchers, the Commission overplayed its hand in response. Karl-Heinz Narjes, the new Commissioner for Research, called for an immediate tripling of EU spending on RTD, to reach nearly €3 billion a year.

The reaction of the French President, François Mitterrand, was to propose a new *intergovernmental* European framework to promote and fund collaborative research projects: EUREKA (the European Research Co-ordinating Agency) which would draw on national RTD budgets. EUREKA allowed participation by non-EU states (such as Sweden and Austria) and promised to give Europe a more immediate competitive boost by avoiding the pre-competitive restrictions on EU-funded research. Suspicions immediately arose that EUREKA was a device by which Paris could channel large amounts of funding to primarily French projects, which would take place in nominally European frameworks and thus evade inspection by the Commission's competition authorities (see Peterson 1993a).

Nonetheless, EUREKA was launched successfully, with three important effects on EU decision-making. First, EUREKA became an alternative to the EU's own programmes, and one which carried no obligatory budgetary commitment. In practice, EUREKA became a sort of 'catch-all' initiative incorporating a wide range of different types of research, as opposed to a framework specifically for 'near-market' research. One result was that net contributors to the EU's budget, particularly Germany and the UK, could argue that any new collaborative research should be funded through EUREKA rather than the EU.

Second, EUREKA's existence, and its domination by Europe's largest, most technologically advanced states within it, rigidified battle lines in debates about EU research policy. The Commission's general disdain for EUREKA was manifest in a troubled relationship between it and the EU's initiatives. EUREKA became dominated by France, Germany and the UK, which was unsurprising given the fact that the 'big three' accounted for more than three-quarters of total national spending on civilian research in the EU (Peterson 1996c).

Above all, if EUREKA had not existed, the EU's programmes probably would have continued to function, in political terms, as initially intended: as a way to compensate the big, technologically advanced Member States for their large net contributions to the Union's cohesion programmes. With EUREKA, decision-making concerning the EU's programmes became far less driven by the perceived need to ensure that large Member States received disproportionate benefits, since their firms dominated collaborative projects undertaken within EUREKA.

Thus cohesion objectives increasingly shaped RTD policy, particularly after the Maastricht Treaty added a new treaty Article – at Spanish insistence – which mandated that the goal of greater economic and social cohesion should inform decision-making on *all* EU policies.[11] The Union's RTD programmes became an essential component of the research efforts of poorer Member States. By the mid-1990s, the EU accounted for 10 to 35 per cent of total civil R&D expenditures in Greece, Ireland and Portugal, which participated in relatively few EUREKA projects.[12] The 'cohesion countries' became a solid bloc in support of increased EU funding for research, while the 'big three' became increasingly sceptical about the Union's role in RTD.

Third, from its origins, EUREKA incorporated a wider Europe than the Union itself and promoted links between EU and non-EU research organisations.[13] The effect was to complicate the Commission's job as the manager of the EU's programmes, as consortia of firms from both inside and outside the Union sought EU funding and had to be accommodated with tricky 'rules of origin' governing the participation of each. EUREKA opened up western research networks to eastern participants, thus forcing the Commission to confront very difficult questions about incorporating relatively backward national research communities into the Union's RTD policy.

By 1997, the total value of nearly 1200 current or finished EUREKA projects had grown to €16.7 billion. However, the Union's Framework programme expanded at roughly the same rate. In the 10 years following its launch in 1984, the Framework programme more than tripled in size (see Table 8.1). By the late 1990s, it equalled a research effort even larger than that of EUREKA in terms of money and project numbers.

Institutional jealousies did not preclude a considerable amount of co-operation between the Commission and EUREKA on specific, high-profile projects, including the ill-fated high definition television (HDTV) EUREKA project (see Exhibit 8.2). A rather more successful attempt to strengthen Europe's hi-tech position was a project to develop the next generation of computer chips: the Joint European Silicon Structures Initiative (see Peterson and Sharp 1998: 170–1). JESSI cost nearly €3 billion, but assumed 'strategic importance out of proportion to the fact that it represent[ed] only a small part of European microelectronics R&D expenditure' (EUREKA secretariat 1996: 6). JESSI illustrated, first, that Europe lacked the 'critical mass' to conduct ambitious and expensive research without pooling national and EU efforts and, second, that the Union had success stories as well as tremendous disappointments in RTD policy.

At the super-systemic level, the European Council frequently heaps praise on the EU's research programmes for their contribution to the enhancement of European competitiveness. The Commission's 'think

Table 8.1   *EC/EU research spending, 1984–98 (million €)*

1984	1986	1988	1990	1992	1994	1996	1998
848	1 140	1 374	1 947	2 842	2 637	3 066	2 801

Note: Constant prices, 1992.

Source: Commission (1994a), Peterson and Sharp (1998).

piece' documents, such as its 1994 communication on industrial policy, usually exalt the Framework programme as an important policy tool for modernising and stimulating the EU's economy (see Commission 1994c). The Union's lead role in the pursuit of a global agreement with Japan and the USA on trade in semi-conductors or the emergence of the 'Information Society' are generally uncontroversial. In both cases, the nature of the technologies makes national borders in Europe meaningless and national policy efforts ineffective.

Yet decisions concerning multi-annual budgets for EU research often preoccupy the highest political levels and are never easy to make. The budgetary politics of RTD policy have become increasingly hard-fought and bitter over time. The Single European Act (SEA) made the Framework programme's budget and broad outline subject to a unanimous vote on the Council. Then the 'implementation' of specific programmes – approval of detailed proposals for specific programmes such as ESPRIT – required another Council vote, this time by qualified majority voting (QMV), with the Parliament involved under the co-operation procedure. Despite the galloping pace of technological development, research thus was subject to a long and time-consuming 'double legislative procedure'.

A decision on the budget and broad outline of the second (1987–91) Framework programme was held up for almost a year, mostly by the intransigence of the UK under Margaret Thatcher. Framework III (1990–94) was agreed with slightly less difficulty, but only after a special meeting of the Presidents of the Council, Commission and EP dedicated *exclusively* to finding a compromise (Elizalde 1992: 320), in a clear case of determined agency overcoming a structure and process designed for stalemate. Subsequently, the Commission took the dramatic step of withdrawing its proposals for implementing several individual programmes, claiming that the Member States, via management committees, had amended them beyond recognition. The Commission eventually relented to avoid delaying the onset of research under Framework III, but the clear message was that it expected to be given substantial new autonomy over RTD policy by the Maastricht Treaty.

The Commission's hopes were dashed at literally the final minute of the Maastricht summit in December 1991. The Dutch Council presidency tabled a proposal under which decisions taken on the multi-annual budget and outline of the Framework programme would be subject to co-decision with the EP. Mindful of the enormous difficulties of agreeing past Framework programme budgets, the Dutch also proposed that *all* Council decisions on research should be made by QMV. With so many other, more politicised, issues at stake, particularly Economic and Monetary Union (EMU) and the Social Chapter, few delegations expected that the proposals on research would meet with objections, or even merit discussion.

Exhibit 8.2 The HDTV project: 'A Nice Try'

Europe's failed attempt to develop a home-grown standard for high definition television (HDTV), the 'next generation' of TV with wider and clearer pictures, is now well-documented. By some estimates, it was the second most expensive industrial project in European post-war history (after the Channel Tunnel) and involved nearly 1700 European engineers and researchers (Cawson 1995). Launched as a EUREKA project in 1986, the HDTV initiative featured Thomson and Philips as the leaders of an all-out European effort to prevent a consortium of Japanese firms from cornering the market for consumer TVs. The rhetoric of its promoters was shrill, with Japanese developers of a rival standard accused of seeking to 'dominate tomorrow's economic world'.[14]

The Commission provided considerable support to the HDTV project, particularly by forging agreement on a 1986 directive which mandated that all new European satellite broadcasters use the EUREKA project's standard. However, EU policy could not keep pace with technological developments. An important nail in the HDTV project's coffin was Rupert Murdoch's decision to use an alternative standard for his new Sky TV channel in early 1989. This option was available only because new reception technologies made it possible to broadcast using low-powered satellites not covered by the EU directive. The Research Commissioner, Filippo Pandolfi, went to great lengths to try to get Murdoch on board. But, as a former official recalled, 'there was a night in 1989 when Pandolfi and I stayed in the office late waiting for Murdoch to return his call. Finally, I had to leave and Pandolfi stayed on alone. The call never came'.[15]

Eventually, the Commission changed tack. In 1991, it rallied a broad range of satellite broadcasting interests behind the HDTV standard and proposed an expensive (€850 million) 'Action Plan' to develop the standard. The UK, with Murdoch influencing its position, essentially vetoed the Action Plan, and the ensuing dispute went all the way to the European Council in late 1992 (Peterson 1993b: 509). In the end, none of it mattered: Bangemann took the HDTV 'portfolio' in early 1993 and announced that the Commission would no longer support the European HDTV standard or project, primarily because a more advanced digital standard had emerged in the USA. In a textbook example of the way politically sophisticated firms often hedge their

$\longrightarrow$

→

bets, Philips and Thomson were involved in the US digital standard's development, while insisting that Europe had no choice but to pursue the less sophisticated European analogue standard.

According to Bangemann, the HDTV project showed that it was impossible for the EU to support specific economic sectors because of disparate national interests in nearly all of them. For example, the Dutch and French interests in supporting the European HDTV project were much clearer than the interests of Portugal or, especially, Luxembourg, which became the headquarters for satellite broadcasters using a competing and incompatible standard. Bangemann consolidated his gains by dismantling parts of DG XIII, the highly interventionist and French-dominated Commission service for information technology, and transferring some of its duties – including the ultimate prize of ESPRIT – to DG III (Industry).

Bangemann also played an important role in ensuring that Framework IV (1994–8) embraced more 'horizontal measures', such as exploiting generic technologies across industrial sectors, and played down *grand projets* such as the HDTV project. Meanwhile, the advanced television services sector showed the EU shifting away from supporting producers and enforcing technical standards, as was done with HDTV, and instead promoting demand for new technologies and strictly applying competition policy rules (Cawson and Holmes 1995).

Europe's HDTV project *did* help European producers to acquire technical expertise which allowed them to become players in the development of the new, American, digital standard. However, the Commission (particularly DG XIII) showed an alarming disdain for the interests of the consumer. More generally, the project could be seen as a classic example of 'group-think' (see Janis 1982), as a range of national and EU protagonists refused to shut off the spigots of effort and money even after it was clear that the project would fail. Dai *et al.* (1996: 161) conclude that 'Politicians and bureaucrats will find it hard to escape responsibility for delaying until 1992 a review of the decisions taken in 1986 which were threatened by developments in 1990.' Even Dutch officials, whose loyalties to Philips encouraged a 'no surrender' policy on HDTV, were admitting quite early on that the project was likely to fail, while insisting that 'it was a nice try'.[16]

As is now well known, the Maastricht summit nearly ended without a final agreement, with the British government insisting that it could not sign up to either the Social Chapter or EMU. Eventually, the UK was granted 'opt-outs' from both. After so many concessions had been made to the British, the Dutch presidency, with the Prime Minister, Ruud Lubbers in the chair, wearily asked for approval of its proposed text on research. One national ambassador who was a participant at Maastricht later recalled:

> There was a final *tour de table*. Every Member State said they supported QMV on R&D: 11 for, one against and that was John Major. Lubbers said, 'We've given you so much already. It's 11 against 1, so you're going to have to accept that QMV will apply to R&D.' Major replied: 'This isn't the Council of Ministers, it's the European Council. We do not decide by majority votes in the European Council. I refuse to allow QMV to be applied this time.' There was a short silence and then [Helmut] Kohl just fell about laughing and said 'Ruud, you've got to admit, he really does have you on that one.'[17]

The essential difference between the super-systemic and systemic levels of EU decision-making was made clear to all. And yet another new and anomalous decision rule was created. First, setting a budget for the Framework programme would continue to require a unanimous vote. Second, and bizarrely in the eyes of many Member States, decision-making on multi-annual budgets and broad programme outlines would be subject to co-decision. Research thus became the only case, besides culture, where unanimity was required on the Council and yet co-decision applied. Co-decision was designed generally to promote the negotiation of compromises between the EP and Council. However, unanimous Council positions usually could be shifted only marginally before they collapsed. Thus the Maastricht Treaty's procedure for R&D 'effectively neuter[ed]' co-decision (Corbett 1994: 208).

Moreover, the 'double' legislative procedure was retained. Specific EU programmes still required Council adoption by QMV, but with the EP only *consulted*. Thus MEPs were given strong incentives to play hardball and negotiate tenaciously on multi-annual budgets under co-decision. Pointedly, whenever Santer argued for simplification of the EU's Treaties in the run-up to the 1996 IGC, he inevitably mentioned research as an area where existing decision rules made little sense (see Peterson and Sharp 1998: 173).

Even before Santer became President, the Commission complained repeatedly about the Maastricht Treaty's provisions for research. Its extraordinary 1992 communication, *Research After Maastricht*, lambasted Member States for agreeing decision rules which inevitably would lead to delays and a less focused EU effort (due to the involvement of the EP). In the event, the budgetary negotiations on Framework IV (1994–8) were long and bloody. They featured fierce intergovernmental bargaining, spirited intervention by the EP and a 'widening' of the technological areas on which the Commission proposed to focus (see Exhibit 8.3). Similarly, Framework V (1998–2002) took a long time to agree, with the Research Council endorsing a budget of €14 billion in its common position – *less* than under Framework IV – only after a marathon, 12-hour negotiation. At its end, Cresson declared that it had been 'a black day' for European research.[18] A member of her *cabinet* complained that Member States wanted to add more programmes to the Commission's (tightly-focused) proposal, and 'not always for the right reasons', but because research ministers wanted programmes which reproduced their own, national schemes.[19] The EP sought a budget of €16.7 billion, before settling for 14.96 billion under co-decision. It was accepted by all that Framework V would not get under way until 1999.

In short, budgetary decisions on the Framework programme remained highly politicised and bore some of the hallmarks of 'history-making' decisions. It was difficult to argue that outcomes at the super-systemic level were not best explained by intergovernmentalist theories, especially given the Parliament's somewhat marginal impact in the Framework IV negotiations (see Exhibit 8.3).

Yet neo-functionalists could counter that the EU's budget for research climbed steadily from the early 1980s. Above all, they could point to the decision at the Amsterdam summit to extend QMV (finally) to future budgetary negotiations, thus raising at least the hypothetical possibility that the two perennial budgetary sceptics, Germany and the UK, might be outvoted in future. Even joined by Sweden, as they were on the Framework V negotiations, the sceptics still fell short of a clear blocking minority, wielding only 24 votes (although enough to trigger the Ioannina compromise, for whatever it was worth). Thus in RTD policy it was certainly possible to argue that integration continued to beget more integration.

The Systemic Level: Does it Matter?

If further proof of the intricacies of Maastricht's new decision-making procedures for RTD was needed, the negotiations on the Framework IV (1994–8) programme provided it. The Council appeared at first to be irretrievably split on its budget. Ultimately, research ministers were unable themselves to sanction what appeared to be a substantial increase in the EU's budget for research. The decision on the budget for Framework IV thus had to be 'kicked upstairs' to the European Council, which endorsed a compromise figure at the Brussels summit of December 1993, albeit without discussion. Thus the EU's five-year budget for R&D had become

Exhibit 8.3   The Framework IV negotiations[20]

The negotiations on the Framework IV (1994–8) programme marked a unique and even historic episode in EU decision-making. Not only were the Maastricht Treaty's new provisions for agreeing an RTD budget employed for the first time, but the budget and broad parameters of Framework IV were agreed after the first-ever application of the co-decision procedure.

As the Commission (1992b: 24) had predicted in *Research After Maastricht*, the rogue version of co-decision that was applied to R&D, combined with a double legislative procedure, did 'inevitably result in long delays', with negotiations taking nearly a year to complete. They almost certainly would have taken even longer if the EP's will to make its mark in the first test of co-decision was not tempered by the need to finish all legislative business quickly in spring 1994 to prepare for the European elections in May. In the end, the EP's influence on the outcome, even after conciliation, was marginal (see Peterson 1995b: 395–9). Although the Council and EP bickered long and hard over the budget, the broad content of the Framework IV programme was little changed from the Commission's original proposal.

The Commission acted with considerable autonomy in the second stage of the 'double legislative' process, even tabling proposals for 20 specific programmes before agreement was reached on a final budget for Framework IV. In the words of Antonio Ruberti, the Commissioner for Research, the intent was to send a 'political signal' of the Commission's strong will to get programmes 'implemented' quickly, and for their content to reflect Commission preferences.[21]

Yet decisions about multi-annual budgets for the Framework programme are big, expensive decisions which 'make history' in some respects. For example, it took the European Council itself to decide a common Council position on the overall budget for Framework IV in late 1993, after research ministers simply could not agree despite the proddings of a resourceful

$\longrightarrow$

sufficiently large at a time of general budgetary austerity for it to require a mandate from the highest political level.

After receipt of this mandate, the Council behaved as a generally unified actor in negotiations with the EP. It held firm behind its common position, especially its compromise budgetary figure, even as the Parliament pressured for more R&D spending. Clearly, many MEPs felt obliged to make the Framework IV negotiations 'a test case to show that the [Maastricht] treaty really did increase parliament's powers' (Adam 1994).[23] However, the EP's inability to 'pick off' Member States from the Council's hard-fought and unanimously agreed common position weakened the Parliament's hand. The EP faced the same difficulty, with similar results, in the negotiations on Framework V (1998–2002).

→

Belgian Presidency. Moreover, deliberations within the Commission – for instance, *before* it tabled its proposal for Framework IV in early 1993 – were hard-fought and 'intergovernmental' in fundamental respects. According to insiders, *cabinets* approached the proposal on a 'Christmas tree basis, as you'd have in the US Congress. Every *cabinet* stuck on what it wanted',[22] in line with national priorities. When this practice occurs, 'compromises almost always operate in the same direction – that of the widening of the field of action' (Commission 1992b: 21). It is little wonder that the EU has trouble ensuring that its research effort is 'focused'.

At the same time, the Framework IV negotiations gave one of the first hints of the way pre-EMU austerity would effect EU decision-making. For the first time, the perennial budgetary sceptics – Germany and the UK – were joined by the French in opposing a large increase in spending on Framework IV. In the end, these 'Big Three' would not be shifted by the EP's insistence on a budget of €13.7 billion, with an eventual compromise on 12.3 billion plus a possible 'reserve' of €700 million to be committed later. Cresson, who took over the RTD portfolio from Ruberti in 1995, organised 'Task Forces' to design large, ambitious projects with a view to spending the reserve, particularly in sectors of interest to the 'Big Three' (see Peterson and Sharp 1998: 166). Yet, by the time Cresson's plans were tabled in 1996, the Union had three more net budgetary contributors (Austria, Finland and Sweden) and all Member States were clamping down on public spending – some desperately – to try to meet the convergence criteria for EMU. The EP's insistence that at least €200 million be mobilised from the reserve was appeased by a (weak) compromise to spend €115 million on research into BSE, landmine detection and renewable energy. The importance of research to innovation and economic growth was undisputed by the late 1990s. Yet, in the run-up to EMU any proposal to spend more money, for R&D or anything else, was virtually a non-starter.

Still, the post-Maastricht period showed the Parliament to be a more important force in RTD decision-making. MEPs could claim, with justification, that the EU was spending far more on technological co-operation with Central and Eastern Europe because of the EP's pressure on the Commission and Council. In AV policy, the Parliament became a primary channel of influence for the European film industry, which pushed governments hard for money and protection from their oligopolistic American competitors. Even on decision-making related to the liberalisation of telecommunications, where the Commission wielded considerable independent power, the EP was successful in insisting on changes to key proposals. Here, as on the internal market more generally, the co-decision procedure had the effect of making consumer protection a higher priority, with the EP presenting itself as the voice of the consumer in EU decision-making (see Exhibit 3.4).

However, decisions taken at a systemic level generally have far *less* impact on final outcomes in RTD policy (leaving aside AV policy) than is the case in most other policy sectors. Hard bargaining over the Framework programme's budget reflects, to a considerable extent, the inability of Member States to control much *else* about EU research policy. The nature of the RTD sector is such that many policy decisions must be taken by experts or scientists. Generally, the Commission's autonomy in research policy is unmatched in any other sector besides (arguably) agriculture. Significantly, from the Council's point of view, research (like telecoms – see Exhibit 8.4) is mainly the domain of COREPER I, not COREPER II, and thus is considered a technical, more than a political, arena for decision-making.

In AV policy, the Council has been the scene of very hard bargaining between Member States with diametrically opposed views of the proper role of the state in influencing what people watch or listen to in the media. However, as one British official dealing with the sector argued, 'there are only a few Member States with very strong feelings about AV policy. So the key debate really takes place within the Commission itself'.[27]

More often than in other policy sectors, systemic level decision-making on RTD policy tends to ratify, with relatively minor changes, the Commission's proposals. In some cases, as in AV policy, very divergent preferences on the Council mean that its debates begin with the outcome crucially 'loaded' by the Commission's proposal in one direction (such as on the continuation of quotas). In the case of EU research programmes, the parameters of schemes such as ESPRIT are usually changed very little when decisions are taken by QMV on 'implementing' Commission proposals. Far more important decisions are taken in the first round of the 'double legislative procedure', when general budgets and technological priorities are set. Even after Commission texts on specific programmes are 'implemented', plenty of room still exists for discretion on how EU funds will actually be spent, with most distributive decisions taken later in a series of technocratic committees. As a lead Commission official in the Framework IV negotiations put it:

> To be cynical, at the end of the day the Framework programme is not reality. The reality is the individual projects and proposals that come in. They are of course chosen by the Commission together with the committees, who have experience in adjusting things to suit the priority projects. The scientific and technical content agreed by the Council is so wide that you can make it fit a very large diversity of projects.[28]

Exhibit 8.4 Telecommunications: The power of Article 86[24]

When the Thatcher government privatised the national phone company, British Telecom (BT), in the early 1980s, the prevailing view in continental Europe probably was 'that this was a rather strange Anglo-Saxon experiment which began in the US, drifted over the gulf stream, but was not coming across the channel'.[25] However, the nearly total liberalisation of the EU's telecoms sector by 1998 was indicative of the way radical neoliberal ideas had become mainstream ones. The key lever in prying open an industry worth well over €500 billion globally was (what became) Article 86, which allows treaty rules to be applied to state-owned firms or ones maintaining some type of special relationship with the state. When the Commission sought to liberalise the telecoms sector using Article 86, which essentially cuts the Council out of formal decision-making, a number of Member States (particularly France) were horrified. However, a series of ECJ decisions to uphold the Commission's use of Article 86 marked a historic step forward in the Union's emergence as a force for liberalisation (Sandholtz 1998: 153–7).

The path to liberalisation was by no means a smooth one. Only the UK, Finland and Sweden met a deadline of 1 July 1996 for the full liberalisation of telecoms infrastructure, which allowed railway, energy and water companies to lay fibre-optic cable and set up hardware needed to compete with traditional phone companies. Germany missed the deadline and found itself in the tricky position of seeking to privatise Deutsche Telekom (DT) while removing its monopoly over the provision of infrastructure. The Commission watched DT carefully and quashed the company's offer of large discounts to business customers which seemed designed to stitch up the profitable German business market before privatisation. More generally, the Commission's telecoms agenda was resisted fiercely by the French, who sought an actual (Amsterdam) Treaty commitment to the principle of 'universal public service', or the idea that consumers had a right to certain minimum public services.[26] The Commission also was forced to grant poorer Member States an additional five years to meet its deadlines for liberalisation.

Still Bangemann and Karel Van Miert, the Commissioner for Competition, jointly insisted on full competition in the EU's telecoms market, including basic voice telephone service, by 1998. They argued that increased competition with regulatory safeguards would guarantee universal service at lower prices to the consumer, while noting that the Union was in step with the USA, which passed similar telecoms legislation in the 1996. Above all, the Commission (1996b: 2) insisted that 'it is demonstrable that telecoms employment by new service suppliers offsets jobs shed by incumbent [public telecoms operators] as they take on the productivity gains of new technology'. Enormous job cuts undertaken by operators such as BT and DT during a period of considerable economic insecurity made telecoms liberalisation a tricky task, which clearly would have been impossible in the absence of Commission determination and Article 86.

Exhibit 8.5   The biotechnology directive

In March 1995, a directive on the patenting in biotechnological inventions became the answer to the trivia question: what was the first measure to be vetoed by the EP under the co-decision procedure? The directive sought to establish common rules on patent protection, which clearly were needed given the existing legal patchwork in the Union and biotechnology's status as an important 'sunrise' industry. It seemed certain to pass when a 'yes' vote was recommended by both the EP's *rapporteur* on the measure, the German Socialist Willi Rothley, and the Legal Affairs Committee.

However, the directive ran into trouble when MEPs were lobbied by environmental groups (allied with Green MEPs) who opposed the measure. The main stumbling block was the directive's provisions for patenting the use of genes in specific biotechnological processes. Without such protection, argued Rothley and others, European firms would not be willing to make the massive investments (averaging €300 million) needed to discover new medical treatments because of fears that other firms would steal the benefits. Yet many MEPs remained uneasy about the notion of 'patenting life'. In the event, the measure failed by a vote of 242 to 188, with 23 abstentions (Bomberg 1998a: 160).

An attempt to pass the directive in modified form was made in 1996. Both industry and Rothley promised to support separate bioethical legislation in future if the current directive could be passed. This time, the Commission's draft explicitly stated that 'germ-line' gene therapy, – that is, altering a human's genetic identity by in vitro fertilisation – could not be patented. The

———→

Thus a 'new institutionalist' view of RTD decision-making sheds considerable light. The notion of path dependency comes alive in this sector as much as any other. The Commission's RTD policy role is now well-established, but it has enormous difficulties changing the priorities of existing programmes or proposing new activities. To propose unstitching the Council's original compromise on 'Television Without Frontiers' was always risky. As for EU-funded research, in many cases R&D only produces results after a considerable period of time and experimentation. When attempts were made at a political level to change the goals of a certain initiative or cut off funding for existing activities, the beneficiaries usually respond with alacrity. As a Commission official put it, 'As long as we build on existing experience, our proposal doesn't get attacked. We can count on sufficient support from the scientific community to help converge national positions towards an agreement. If

directive also confronted the tricky issue of animal patenting, applying proportionality to questions about whether an animal's suffering was worth the invention which resulted.

The biotechnology directive illustrated three fundamental points about EU decision-making. First, the EP's political groups remained ill-disciplined and amorphous compared to national parties. Members of the Socialist Group later admitted that Rothley failed to communicate sufficiently with the rest of his group on the measure, while officials from the Council and PermReps complained that the weakness of party groups made the EP an unreliable negotiator under co-decision. Second, the directive highlighted the EP's general lack of expertise and technical support. Lacking a US-style Office of Technology Assessment, one industry expert asked, 'How can the Parliament decide what is safe? They have no expert advice and don't honestly know what they are doing.'[30] Third, and finally, the directive illustrated the powerful pressures that exist in many high-tech industries for uniform, EU-wide legislation. The EP eventually buckled under such pressures and voted through a modified version of the biotechnology directive in 1998, after one of the most animated lobbying efforts in the EU's history. Similarly, the Commission was forced to take decisions on its own concerning genetically modified organisms, such as pesticide resistant maize (see Exhibit 4.6), because it was simply unacceptable that such products could be available across the Union on the initiative of only one Member State. The EU's role in regulating complex new technologies is unlikely to diminish in the 21st century, nor are its difficulties in making decisions in this realm.

we try to enter into new areas, then the Commission is much more vulnerable.'[29]

Yet by the late 1990s the Commission – and the EU more generally – needed a sea change in its RTD policy: a shift in focus to *users*, as opposed to producers of technology, and the *diffusion* of innovations, as opposed to the production of technology. The key factors in promoting technological competitiveness had become skills and infrastructure. Arguably, oligopolistic European technology producers no longer needed R&D subsidies or inducements to collaborate in exclusively European consortia. They needed collaborative links to non-European firms at the leading edge of technology as well as market shares beyond the Union itself. In short, the ESPRIT model was out-of-date but EU technology policy remained highly path-dependent, particularly given widely-held affinity for the creation of 'European champions' in specific sectors (see Peterson and Sharp 1998: 211–34).

Policy Networks and the Politics of Expertise

As we have seen, the Commission has strong incentives to refrain from proposing entirely new RTD activities or trying to regulate fast-developing technologies (see Exhibit 8.5). Its power in budgetary decision-making is clearly limited. Otherwise, it enjoys considerable autonomy in RTD policy, but only when it acts as the ringleader of policy networks whose members include industrial and scientific elites. Most decisions about which projects are funded through specific research schemes such as ESPRIT or BAP (the Biotechnology Action Programme) are made within policy networks led by the Commission and populated by various types of experts and industrialists. Because relatively little of importance is decided at the systemic level, decision-making within policy networks is crucial in determining who gets what, when and how from the EU RTD policy.

In some sectors, the Commission faces apparently irreconcilable divisions between different types of firm or research actor as it seeks to make policy. For example, the EU's research programmes in biotechnology have been the scene of quite acrimonious feuding between rival associations of firms. Representation of the biotechnology industry is more developed in Brussels than in national EU capitals because the industry – and gene-splicing technologies more generally – matured as the EU's internal market was being created. However, the industry has had considerable difficulty speaking with a single voice. The Senior Advisory Group on Biotechnology (SAGB), a direct membership association which offers the Commission policy advice, has traditionally been dominated by large firms and was once described by Jacques Delors as the most influential Eurogroup in Brussels (Greenwood and Ronit 1995: 81). Meanwhile, the European Secretariat of National Biotechnology Associations (ESNBA) became the voice of smaller biotechnology firms and struggled to uphold their quite different interests. The relationship between the SAGB and ESNBA was hostile: for years, neither would attend meetings with the Commission to which the other had been invited.

The structure of biotechnology as an industry is reflected in the links which different types of firm have to different parts of the Commission. For example, the SAGB enjoys excellent links to DGs III (Industry), IV (Competition) and XII (Research). Meanwhile, the ESNBA, whose members often focus on 'greener' ways of making products, is allied closely to DG XI (Environment), whose officials attend ESNBA board meetings. Signs that biotechnology policy networks were beginning to cohere emerged in the mid-1990s (see Peterson and Sharp 1998: 183). The Commission's urgings were an important factor: it tried to give the industry incentives, as in the form of expanded R&D programmes, to speak with a single industry voice because it made it far easier to design effective EU programmes and establish the Union's policy role in the sector.

Using much the same methodology, the Commission's track record in telecommunications was remarkable: it succeeded 'in mobilizing a network of supporters not only at the European but also at the domestic levels' while 'neutralizing' the stiff opposition of several Member States, including Germany and France, to deregulation and liberalisation (Schneider *et al.* 1994: 494). The Research in Advanced Communication for Europe (RACE) programme, which offered large EU subsidies towards the development of a new integrated digital telecoms network to span the entire Union, was an important source of leverage for the Commission (Peterson and Sharp 1998: 73–7). Schneider *et al.* (1994) argue that the emergence of an EU telecoms policy network (or, as they put it, 'actor network') was crucial since hierarchical decision-making was impossible in a sector marked by widely-dispersed power.

Of course, what unites actors in RTD policy most of all is technical expertise. The 'politics of expertise' (Peterson 1995b) which characterises RTD policy-making empowers epistemic communities of experts and strictly limits the degree to which generalist politicians, even research ministers, can scrutinise sub-systemic outcomes. At the same time, Member States pay careful attention to their receipts from EU spending on RTD, and do so mainly through programme committees which bring together national experts to sift through project proposals and generally monitor the Commission's management of initiatives such as ESPRIT. These arrangements do allow Member States a 'check' on who gets what, with most receiving a broadly similar share of funding from *each* individual EU programme (see Peterson and Sharp 1998: 179–81).

In 1998, the Commission proposed to boost its independent decision-making powers at this stage by reducing the scope for national experts in the project selection process. Its rationale was the need to cut delays (four to five months between 'calls for proposals' and actual selection of projects to be funded), focus assessment on fewer proposals (a total of 24 000 were submitted in 1996) and reduce the cost of technical assessment (nearly 7 per cent of the Framework programme's budget). However, the suggestion was rebuffed by Member States, who clung to programme committees as one of their only levers (along with Commission *cabinets*: see Exhibit 8.3) for ensuring national influence in sub-systemic decision-making.

In the face of such influence, one of the Commission's favoured methods for maximising its autonomy was seeking the endorsement (and thus legitimation) of its general RTD strategy by respected and 'independent' experts. The European Science and Technology Development Committee

(CODEST), consisting of 24 leading 'personalities from the world of science nominated by the Commission', was an important player in general policy development (Commission 1994a: 210). It often acted as a counterfoil to the Committee for Scientific and Technical Research (CREST), consisting of senior officials from national science ministries. CREST was unusual in that it advised both the Commission and the Council on general policy matters, thus pointing to the blurred line between the national and supranational at the sub-systemic level of RTD policy.

A particularly important institution for linking EU-funded research to the needs of industry is the Industrial Research and Development Advisory Committee (IRDAC), created in 1984 at the same time as the Framework programme. IRDAC's members are industrial experts who are nominated on a personal basis by the Commission. The Committee has been crucial in promoting the steady movement of the BRITE programme (Basic Research in Industrial Technologies for Europe) towards research with immediate and practical industrial applications, regardless of the 'precompetitive' restrictions on EU-funded research. Together with its sister programme, EURAM (European Research in Advanced Materials), BRITE is generally considered the Union's most important initiative after ESPRIT and, by many analysts, its most successful. Its role in helping small firms, such as those which dominate the Italian textiles industry, to apply new technologies and modernise has been considerable (see Peterson and Sharp 1998: 78). In political terms, virtually every EU Member State has firms which benefit from BRITE/EURAM, and there has been relatively little dispute about its virtues.

In contrast, the ESPRIT programme has faced criticism from Member States which do not have large, integrated, 'Big 12' IT firms. In ESPRIT's earliest days, it was no exaggeration to argue that the programme was as much managed by industry as by the Commission itself. ESPRIT's Executive Committee, which included representatives of most 'Big 12' firms, became the core actors in an IT policy network which kept a firm grip on EU decision-making within the initiative (Peterson 1991: 277). Later, ESPRIT's technological focus was broadened and the initiative became less clearly dominated by large firms. A senior representative of Philips claimed:

> The idea for the Framework programme really came from Philips. But there are more people involved all the time: more committees, more working groups, more bureaucracy. And now the role of the Parliament is especially increasing. . . The main problem is that the Commission wants to do everything for everybody. We at Philips want large projects that are targeted. We are beginning to wonder about the wisdom of participation in the Framework programme at all. The need to accommodate Eastern Europe and enlargement acts to water down the original strategic objectives.[31]

Such arguments reinforced many of Cresson's preconceptions after her appointment to the Commission in 1995. Faced with considerable resistance to the use of the 'Cresson clause' on industrial policy, the Research Commissioner decided to treat the €700 million 'reserve' created as part of the budgetary compromise on Framework IV as a window of opportunity to mount large, strategic projects with EU funding. Since the funds were not automatically available and Member States had to be sold on the idea of spending them, Cresson decided that the money should be spent on specific, selected and ambitious projects developed by a series of 'task forces'. Each was designed to bring together all European research efforts into large, co-ordinated, ambitious projects with EU funding acting to catalyse ongoing efforts. The themes chosen for work by the task forces – the 'car of the future', the 'train of the future', educational software and viral vaccines – were designed to fire public imagination, demonstrate the social value of EU-funded research and directly enhance European competitiveness in technology-intensive industries.

Perhaps above all, the task forces were designed to give the Framework programme more focus and to prevent its 'widening' to include the pet technological priorities of each Member State. As a member of Cresson's *cabinet* observed:

> [Cresson's predecessor, Antonio] Ruberti did a lot of good work in only two years. He tried to insist on 10 priorities for Framework IV and ended up with 21. So Cresson decided to start with six – so she might end up with 10.[32]

In the end, under the strictures of EMU-induced austerity, Member States refused to spend more than €115 million from the 'reserve'. Still, the task forces helped Cresson set the agenda for the negotiations on the Framework V programme. In response to Commission requests for new ideas from Member States on the future of EU research policy, France, Germany and the UK all broadly endorsed the work of the task forces. All of the 'big three' opposed large budgetary increases, but each acknowledged the need for a tighter focus on industrial competitiveness, more involvement of the users of new technologies, streamlined management structures and fewer and more specific programmes. As it formulated plans for Framework V, the Commission made it clear that it would build on the work of the task forces, and 'spin off' advisory groups from each to inform the development of work programmes, which identified priorities for individual R&D schemes such as ESPRIT or BRITE. Claude Allègre, the French Research Minister, described the approach as 'forward-looking'.[33] Even the (Conservative) British Research Minister, Ian Taylor, agreed on the 'clear need for a further programme of research and technological development at European level to address questions of industrial competitiveness'.[34]

Exhibit 8.6   The 'Information Society'

The so-called 'Information Society' became one of the Santer Commission's big ideas, analogous in some ways to the 1992 project during the Delors years. The Commission (1994b) had long been keen to be a force for the modernisation of European economies, but the sweeping changes foreseen in the transition to 21st century capitalism provided a new rationale for EU-level action (see Reich 1991). The Information Society was developed as a general framework for measures to promote the diffusion of new information technologies, and became a touchstone for EU policies on growth and employment. Generally, Member States 'bought' the initiative: for example, the Commission's proposed thematic programme for Framework V on 'a user-friendly information society' was the *only* programme (out of five) which sailed through the Council without debate in 1997–8.

Sometimes the Information Society seemed as much hype as substance. The Commission insisted that a rapid transition to advanced communications infrastructures was desirable because it promised to generate competitive advantages for firms, greater flexibility in employment, more jobs and new economic growth (see Peterson and Sharp 1998: 130–5). Asked for specific evidence to justify these claims, the Commission (1996b: 9) could only plead that 'it is extremely difficult to substantiate [them] . . . in quantitative terms. Much of the change . . . is structural and simple extrapolation of past trends is not a reliable guide to the future'. However, the initiative at least encouraged governments to think beyond the short-term and prepare for a 21st century economy. There were tangible signs that it was encouraging growth in European markets for telecoms and IT, which were growing faster than the world average for the first time in 10 years by the late 1990s.

The Information Society was also translated into concrete action on two other fronts. First, the Commission acted as the EU's voice in international diplomacy concerning information infrastructure issues. The Bangemann Group of high-level experts (see Table 8.2) was created to develop a coherent European strategy in telecoms, and acted as an important line of communication to the US Clinton administration. To illustrate the point that the Information Society was supported at the highest political levels, all members of the Bangemann Group acted as the personal representatives of members of the European Council. The Group illustrated the general trend in EU decision-making towards more formal and systematic consultation at the policy formulation stage, through purpose-built policy networks. Some, such as the Bangemann Group, operated at the very highest political level.

Second, the Commission used the 'cloak' of the Information Society initiative to legitimate specific programmes that promoted information skills enhancement, usually by involving private or non-governmental organisations. The strategy usually worked: a good example was the 'Schools Adopt Monuments' programme, initiated by Bangemann in 1996 at a cost of nearly half a million Euro. The programme encouraged students to learn how to use

→

→

Table 8.2   *The 'Bangemann Group' on European information infrastructures (1994)*

Martin Bangemann (chairman)	European Commission
Peter L. Bonfield (UK)	Chairman and Chief Executive, ICL
Eurico Cabral da Fonseca (Portugal)	President, Campanhiua Comunicacaoes nacionais
Etienne Davignon (Belgium)	President, Société Générale de Belgique
Peter J. Davis (UK)	Chairman, Reed Elsevier
Carlo de Benedetti (Italy)	President, Olivetti
Brian Ennis	Managing Director, IMS
Pehr G. Gyllenhammer (EFTA)	Former Executive Chairman, AB Volvo
Hans Olaf Henkel ('European Union')	Chairman and Chief Executive Officer, IBM Europe
Lothar Hunsel (Germany)	Chairman-Designate of Geschaeftsfuehrung DeTeMobilikfunk
Anders Knutsen (Denmark)	Administrative Director, B&O
Constantin Makropoulous (Greece)	Former Managing Director, Hellenic Information Systems
Pascual Maragall (Spain)	Mayor of Barcelona, Vice President of POLIS
Romano Prodi (Italy)	President Director General, IRI
Andre Rousselet (France)	Former President Director General, Canal Plus
Pierre Suart (France)	President, Alcatel
Gaston Thorn (Luxembourg)	Président du Conseil d'administration du CLT
Jan D. Timmer (Netherlands)	Voorzitter, Philips Electronics
Candido Velazquez (Spain)	President, Telefonica
Heinrich von Pierer (Germany)	Vorsitzender des Vorstandes, Siemens

new multi-media technologies in the production and dissemination of materials related to historical European monuments that they 'adopted'. The Commission's decision to allow the programme to be co-ordinated by Pegasus, a group formed by the EP to promote a 'European identity' through actions in education, was shrewd. The programme was interinstitutional, youth-focused, 'Europeanist' and – above all – conducted under the banner of the Information Society. It was hard to imagine how anyone, other than diehard Eurosceptics, could oppose it.

Yet such calls inevitably prompted responses from actors which benefited from precompetitive restrictions on EU-funded research. For example, the European Science and Technology Assembly, yet another advisory
body of experts created by the Commission in 1995, passed a motion
urging that no less than 10 per cent of the Framework V programme be
earmarked for basic science. Thus RTD decision-making is *not* uncontested at the sub-systemic level, but the Commission enjoys a strong
position as a broker of different ideas and interests. Most outcomes in
the sector are determined mainly in the details of the Commission's
proposals.

More generally, the gap between the 'high politics' of budget-setting for
the Framework programme and sub-systemic decision-making is very wide
in RTD policy. Very different rationalities guide dominant actors at each
level. The Commission's power to determine budgetary choices at 'higher'
levels of decision-making is limited, but it has considerable power to
determine the parameters of debates about the detailed content of the
Union's RTD policy. Put another way, the Commission wields considerable power *in between* the 'big' decisions. A key source of its power is its
capacity, originally nurtured by Davignon, to induce Europe's industrial
and research communities to identify their collective interests, after which
the Commission often joins them in lobbying their governments for an EU
policy with resources and teeth. The policy which results gives the
Commission not only a considerable autonomy but also *money* to spend.
One need not be a cynic to conclude that the Commission's power at the
sub-systemic level allows it to 'buy its own political constituency' in RTD
policy (Peterson and Sharp 1998: 182).

Conclusion

In important respects, RTD decision-making appears to be a law unto
itself. The EU's forays into new areas, such as AV policy, have provoked
quite severe clashes between national philosophies and policies. The EP's
role has expanded in a range of RTD areas, despite questions about its
competence to judge on such issues. Yet the most striking feature of RTD
policy is the general power of the Commission, wielded mainly through
close alliances with industry and research communities.

Clearly, the Commission has been guilty of highly questionable judgements, as illustrated by the case of HDTV, particularly ones which have
elevated the interests of producers over those of consumers. Generally,
however, the Commission has performed an almost impossible job quite
well. It has encouraged independent evaluation of its research programmes
and made enormous efforts to promote European excellence while

respecting the principle of *juste retour*. In telecommunications, it has acted with foresight and considerable boldness in pushing liberalisation on reluctant Member States. Its recent attempts to demonstrate the value of technological development for ordinary Europeans, as illustrated by its 'Information Society' initiative (see Exhibit 8.6), have shown both imagination and pragmatism, given that the relative technical proficiency of Europe's workforce will be crucial in determining its future competitiveness.

Despite the technocratic nature of the 'politics of expertise', the Commission clearly brings political motives to its RTD policy role. Perhaps above all, the Commission has tried to use RTD policy to demonstrate the benefits of European integration. In research policy as much as any other, there were clear and sensible arguments in the 1980s for combining European efforts to achieve the critical mass needed to innovate in the development and production of very expensive and sophisticated new technologies. In the 1990s, the EU's role shifted – albeit far too slowly – towards a more user- and diffusion-oriented approach designed to upgrade Europe's technological skills and infrastructure. The rationale for a strong EU role in this type of strategy was more ambiguous, as it did not lend itself to the EU model of subsidising collaborative R&D projects in programmes designed by the Commission and its allied policy networks. Most policy measures arising from a diffusion-oriented strategy 'are best designed and delivered at the regional or even subregional level of government' (Peterson and Sharp 1998: 233).

At the same time, advancing technology tends to shrink the power and importance of the nation-state. The regulation of biotechnology, telecommunications and other fast-growing, technology-intensive sectors clearly demands EU-level measures. In RTD policy, as in others, if the Union did not exist, European states would have to invent something like it.

Chapter 9

The Common Foreign and Security Policy

The CFSP in context
The high politics of CFSP
Setting the CFSP: the 'single' institutional framework
Policy networks: the 'Brusselisation' of foreign policy?
Conclusion

To non-specialists, the European Community and European Union are interchangeable terms for the same organisation. To the serious student of decision-making, they are entirely different animals. The EC is a system for legislating according to the 'Community method' of decision-making (Devuyst 1999), which carefully weights Member States and EU institutions. In contrast, the EU is a symbolic construct, created by the Maastricht Treaty, which itself made the EC 'just one pillar of a grander edifice called the European Union'.[1] Two separate 'pillars' created for justice and home affairs policies (pillar III) and the Common Foreign and Security Policy (CFSP, pillar II) produce 'legislation' relatively rarely. Decision-making within both is effectively intergovernmental and almost always requires unanimity.

In the post-Maastricht period, pillars II and III often produced stalemate and, effectively, indecision. The malaise which beset European integration, at least until the final drive to EMU, was in large part a product of the creation of something 'new', a European 'Union', which did not work as well as the old European Community. In 1997, the Union was presented with an opportunity, in the form of the Amsterdam Treaty, to make amends. The particularly inauspicious record of justice and home affairs decision-making prompted the 'communitarisation' of a large slice of pillar III, or its incorporation into the EC. The CFSP, in many ways a more visible failure of the European Union, was not 'communitarised' in any important respects (see Exhibit 9.1).

This chapter focuses on the CFSP: a realm of decision-making that is distinct from the EC, but also inextricably linked to it. Our central argument is that foreign policy co-operation is fundamentally different from market integration, insofar as the same decision-making rules and methodology cannot practically be applied to both. It is tempting to judge the CFSP harshly, particularly given its performance in the Balkans (see Exhibits 9.2 and 9.4). Yet the CFSP is best understood not as a 'policy', but as a process: an evolving entity which has reached no final stasis, nor is likely to do so any time soon (see Peterson and Sjursen 1998a). As a means of making foreign policy decisions which bind (at least most of the time) 15 sovereign nation-states, as well as the EU's institutions, the CFSP works surprisingly well. Yet, as we argue below, the ability to make foreign policy *decisions* is by no means the same as having an effective foreign policy.

The CFSP in Context[2]

In important respects, the CFSP was unveiled in 1991 as an entirely new policy. Certainly, European leaders sold it to the media and public as a bold and unprecedented step forward towards creating a European 'Union'. Most European opinion leaders bought the sales pitch. *The Economist*, normally a taciturn newspaper, described the new Maastricht treaty generally as a 'super-deal that may eventually make the European Union a superpower'.[3]

By this time, the EU had 20 years of accumulated experience of foreign policy co-ordination. Something like a common European foreign and defence policy had been mooted as early as the 1960s as part of the still-born Fouchet Plan (Dinan 1994: 49–50), but the first tangible steps were taken in 1969 when the European Political Co-operation (EPC) mechanism was created. It became a sort of 'gentlemen's club' (M. E. Smith 1997) for low-key exchanges between European foreign ministries, at a time when bipolar politics dominated international relations. Under the Nixon administration, the USA often sought to expropriate western foreign policy. EPC became a form of self-defence to try to ensure that the Community's preferences were not discounted, or even ignored.

The EPC mechanism allowed the Community to seize on the 'politics of scale' (Ginsberg 1989) or the simple reality that the Community was far more powerful when it spoke with one voice, instead of between six and 12. The 1980 Venice Declaration, recognising the right of the Palestinians to self-determination, or the Community's independent stance on the declaration of martial law in Poland in 1981 were illustrative examples. Both showed that, by taking collective decisions, the Community could draw a politically significant line between its preferences and those of the Reagan administration, whose attitude towards the Community was perhaps even more loathsome than Nixon's.

Yet EPC had no pretension of aiming for a 'common' foreign policy. It simply sought to co-ordinate the foreign policies of its Member States on selected issues where European solidarity seemed possible and promised benefits. In few cases did the EPC facilitate any kind of 'action'. Decision-making usually focused on common declarations of one kind or another.

Exhibit 9.1 The Amsterdam Treaty and CFSP: ratchets or gadgets?

The Amsterdam Treaty gives the European Council enhanced CFSP responsibilities. Heads of government will lay down 'guidelines' for EU action, as well as adopt 'strategies' that define the goals and means of a joint action. No hard-and-fast distinction exists between 'guidelines' and 'strategies', thus making it likely that the European Council will be the scene of bickering about which of its decisions constitute one or the other. In any event, guidelines and strategies are to be implemented by the Council of Foreign Ministers, which will operate on the basis of three basic methods of decision-making:

- Unanimity applies when votes are taken on the implementation of guidelines, although up to one-third of Member States may abstain without blocking a decision. The upshot is that increased scope for flexibility, or the formation of 'coalitions of the willing', is built into the CFSP.
- QMV (qualified majority voting) is used when votes are taken on proposed action related to agreed strategies. Here, any Member State may indicate that, 'for important and stated reasons of national policy', it will oppose the adoption of a decision taken by QMV. In this case, the Treaty states that a 'vote shall not be taken', although Foreign Ministers may agree (by QMV) to 'kick back' issues to the European Council for a decision (by unanimity). When votes are taken on the CFSP, qualified majorities must include at least 10 Member States.
- All decisions with military implications must be taken unanimously.

Two other institutional innovations contained in the Amsterdam Treaty may have important effects on pillar II decision-making. The first is the creation of

→

EPC certainly was not revolutionary and was even described as 'an updated version of old-style alliance diplomacy' (Pijpers 1991: 31). It had no institutional or treaty base until 1987. At that point, the Single European Act (SEA) foreshadowed Maastricht by stating that EC Member States (or 'High Contracting Parties') would 'endeavour jointly to formulate and implement a European foreign policy'. Yet the SEA made it clear that the Community was engaged in an 'endeavour', and not committed to a new 'policy'. The foreign policy section of the SEA (Title III) was not incorporated into the treaties, as was done with new articles on the environment and research.

In contrast, Title V of the Maastricht Treaty 'established' the CFSP, which would cover 'all areas of foreign and security policy'. Member

→

a new 'High Representative' for the CFSP, who also will serve as the Council's Secretary-General. The post was created against the strong wishes of the Santer Commission, and symbolised the ascendance of the Council as foreign policies were being 'Brusselised', with more and more important decisions taken in Brussels-based Council institutions, but *not* 'Communitarised' (see Allen 1998). Potentially, at least, the High Representative gives the EU's partners 'one phone number to call' on pillar II matters. On the other hand, the gap between the EU's capabilities and the outside world's expectations (Hill 1998) could well be widened by the personification of the CFSP without any shift of executive power from the Council.

The second institutional innovation is the creation of a new 'Policy Planning and Early Warning Unit', consisting of members of the Council Secretariat, the Member States, the Commission and the Western European Union (WEU). It is probably naïve to think of the new unit as a 'nascent EU foreign ministry'. However, it does promise to give the CFSP what it sorely lacked in the post-Maastricht period (particularly as regards the former Yugoslavia, see Wiberg 1996; Kintis 1997): the capacity for analysis which is 'independent' of national views or priorities, or at least a reasonable amalgam of them.

In short, the Amsterdam Treaty may lead to a 'significant extension' of QMV within pillar II (Roper 1997: 2), particularly given its new forms of flexibility. How the Treaty is implemented will determine more than what the Treaty says: whether the new Policy Planning Unit and High Representative 'ratchet up' foreign policy co-operation, or end up being institutional gadgets, remain open questions. On balance, however, it is difficult to resist the argument of the former Belgian Prime Minister, Leo Tindemans, that, 'Although it makes a number of technical improvements, the Amsterdam Treaty will not make any substantial difference' to the CFSP (EP 1998: 12).

States promised to support it 'actively and unreservedly in a spirit of loyalty and mutual solidarity'. A far more formalised system of decision-making was agreed. Acting unanimously and on the advice of the European Council, the Council would take 'joint actions'. It could agree (again unanimously) to implement joint actions by QMV, with Member States' votes weighted as in pillar I. Article J.2 offered the alternative formulation of 'common positions', or the alignment of national policies (agreed unanimously). Nowhere did the Treaty actually define 'joint action' or 'common position', but it appeared that the former would involve actual action (as opposed to declaration) and possibly the expenditure of resources. In contrast to EPC, the CFSP promised to revolutionise foreign policy decision-making in Europe, even if it did not endow the Union with new policy instruments, such as increased foreign aid or a military capability, which remained concentrated at the national level. Above all, pillar II remained distinctly different from pillar I in terms of decision-making and dominant actors, with the European Parliament (EP) and Commission far weaker in the CFSP than in the EC.

In the event, the EU developed an acute 'capability–expectations gap' (see Hill 1993). In international relations, perceptions often matter more than objective 'facts' (see Janis 1982; Jervis 1976). In the eyes of the world, the EU began to be viewed after 1989 as a new 'superpower', a perception encouraged by the rapid decline – and eventual collapse – of the Soviet Union. Yet, even before Maastricht was fully ratified, the EU appeared

> [in]capable of fulfilling the new expectations already (and often irrationally) held of it. . . . The Community does not have the resources or political structures to be able to respond to the demands which the Commission and certain Member States have virtually invited through their bullishness over the pace of internal change. (Hill 1993: 315)

Arguably, the 'bullishness' of the Commission and 'certain Member States' – usually Italy, Germany and the Benelux states (see Hill 1996a) – arose from the mistaken belief that the 'Monnet method' of promoting market integration could be applied to foreign policy. According to Monnet (1978: 93), integration was a piecemeal process: 'starting with limited achievements, establishing *de facto* solidarity, from which a federation would gradually emerge' (see also Wallace 1996a: 42–7). The essence of the Monnet method, according to Edward Heath, the Prime Minister who took the UK into the EC, was 'governments giving a remit to experts and leaving them to get on with it' (quoted in Featherstone 1994: 160). Monnet's preferred method of decision-making was by 'a small and powerful committee able to make far-reaching decisions'(Milward 1992: 336).

The Monnet method has proved to be an effective means of promoting market integration, but it remains impractical as a means of foreign policy co-ordination for at least four fundamental reasons (see Pijpers 1997). First, market integration is driven by an 'expansive logic'. Decisions taken within pillar I are often functionally interrelated. For example, many internal market decisions have external trade policy considerations: creating a single market in automobiles made national quotas on Japanese car imports unsustainable and a common EU policy essential (see Exhibit 4.1). In contrast, pillar II issues and decisions are rarely interrelated in the same way.

Second, social or interest groups often play an important role in market integration. European firms, particularly those of the European Round

Table of Industrialists (ERT) (Cowles 1995), were forceful lobbyists of the Commission and national governments in support of the 1992 project because barriers to trade were costly for them. In contrast, 'though some argue for the political benefits that CFSP would bring, few societal transactors find its absence costly' (Stone Sweet and Sandholtz 1997: 309).

Third, formal rules and institutions are far more effective in facilitating market integration than foreign policy co-operation. Comparing the Maastricht Treaty's provisions for the CFSP and EMU illustrates the point (see M.E. Smith 1997). EMU involved a clearly defined goal and clear criteria to achieve it. The treaty contained a timetable for EMU, sanctions for defectors (who ran excessive budget deficits) and provisions for a new central institution to govern EMU. The Common Foreign and Security Policy had no clearly defined goal and thus the treaty offered no timetable for achieving it. There were no sanctions to punish Member States who did not respect pillar II agreements and no new central institutions to govern the CFSP.

Fourth, and finally, issues of market integration are usually 'elastic' enough to allow for derogations or transition periods without undermining the (eventual) goal of a common EU policy. For example, Spain and Portugal were granted quite long transition periods when they joined the Community on many internal market directives because otherwise their national producers would have been overwhelmed by new competition. Issues that preoccupy the CFSP usually are *inelastic*. For example, when economic sanctions are applied to an outlaw regime such as Iraq or a decision is taken to recognise a new 'breakaway' state such as Croatia, policies are often completely ineffective unless applied with equal rigour by all EU Member States. In foreign policy, as Alfred Pijpers (1997) has argued, there is not much in between a genuinely common policy and no EU policy at all.

In a backhanded way, the impracticality of the Monnet method in the realm of foreign policy co-operation was acknowledged in the Maastricht Treaty. In place of technocratic gradualism it employed a 'big bang' approach, creating a new European foreign policy from scratch (albeit without new institutions) and imposing it 'top-down' from the highest political level. The one overt nod to the Monnet method resulted from a fierce and inconclusive struggle prior to the 1991 Maastricht summit over the EU's relationship with the defence alliance, the West European Union (see Exhibit 9.2). Unable to reconcile deep differences between Franco-German proposals for a new EU 'defence identity' and a more circumspect UK–Italian plan, the treaty stated that the CFSP would extend to the 'eventual framing of a common defence policy, which might in time lead to a common defence'.

Exhibit 9.2 The EU, the WEU and NATO

Signed in 1991, the Maastricht Treaty created a Common Foreign *and* Security Policy, and made the WEU 'an integral part of the development of the Union'. In practice, the EU did not develop a 'security policy' in the military sense. In Bosnia, it was widely argued that 'it was simply the EC's inability to take effective (i.e. military) action that brought its efforts to nothing' (Piening 1997: 62).

Despite German and (especially) French affinity for the idea of a 'European Security and Defence Identity' (ESDI), the vast, unthinkable expense of giving Europe a truly independent military capability led to the 'fudge' of Common Joint Task Forces (CJTF), or coalitions of the willing assembled from within NATO. Such coalitions might not include the USA, but could still have access to American military assets, such as sophisticated command and control systems or heavy air transport, which Europe lacked. According to the US Ambassador to NATO, the CJTFs gave the WEU 'for the first time . . . a true capacity to act. . . . But whether that will actually happen remains problematic, for a simple reason. The US considers itself to be a European power and is ready to take part in any significant challenge to security on the continent. If this were the case, NATO would go into action and not the EU' (Hunter 1997: 14).

The USA under Bill Clinton wished to encourage the EU to do more to defend itself, but remained touchy about America's status in Europe. A Republican-controlled US Congress harassed Clinton (a Democrat) on matters of foreign policy, and seemed poised to insist that US troops come home from Bosnia as scheduled in mid-1998, despite clear indications that the West had much unfinished business left there. Eventually, in a reaffirmation of American power in Europe, Clinton declared that US troops would stay on past the deadline in Bosnia. EU leaders showed little enthusiasm for making Bosnia a test case of CJTFs, and even stated that their troops would leave when the Americans did.

The Union's sluggish 1998 response to the repression of ethnic Albanians by government forces in the Yugoslavian province of Kosovo led to a startling turnaround by the British government under Tony Blair. After insisting that the Amsterdam Treaty acknowledge the primacy of NATO in European security, it considered proposals less than a year later to make the WEU a '4th pillar' of the Union.[4] The first-ever (informal) EU meeting of defence ministers was convened under the 1998 Austrian Council presidency. It no longer seemed certain, as it did for most of the 1990s, that the CFSP would continue to lack a military dimension for a very long time.

In the event, the EU still lacked a defence identity by the late 1990s. The CFSP did *not* cover 'all aspects of foreign policy'. Few 'joint actions' or 'common positions' changed the world very much. Meanwhile, national foreign policies certainly did not disappear. To illustrate the point, French *national* foreign policy decisions to test nuclear weapons in the Pacific, send troops to Bosnia or propose a French candidate to head the European Central Bank were far more momentous and consequential than anything agreed within the CFSP between 1995 and 1997. It was possible to dismiss the CFSP – in the sense of either a truly 'common' or a comprehensive foreign policy – as a myth (see Peterson and Sjursen 1998b).

Yet the CFSP became an important reference point for national foreign policies. While never hesitating to highlight the CFSP's shortcomings, Hill (1997) acknowledged that it had become one of three strands in a European 'external relations system' by the late 1990s, comprising national foreign policies and the EU's (or EC's) pillar I, as well as the CFSP. This system was a product of accident as much as design. Yet, sometimes it proved capable of effective foreign policy decision-making and even 'strategic action' in the pursuit of European interests (see Smith 1998). On many specific questions, such as preventing nuclear proliferation or support for Central and Eastern Europe, foreign policy co-operation was becoming institutionalised, even if decision-making powers remained mainly in the hands of national (as opposed to supranational) actors. The CFSP was easy to criticise, but it was hard to deny that Europe was more united in foreign policy than ever before in the post-war period.

The High Politics of the CFSP

For Stanley Hoffmann, one of the most perceptive of all post-war political scientists, foreign policy was the ultimate expression of 'high politics'. In contrast to 'welfare' sectors where market integration was a viable policy goal, foreign policy marked out 'areas of key importance to the national interest [in which] nations prefer the self-controlled uncertainty of national reliance, to the uncontrolled certainty' of policy integration (1995: 84; originally published 1960). Hoffmann's analysis seemed as prescient in the 1990s as when it was first written more than 35 years earlier. Decisions taken in 1991 appeared to 'make history' by creating a truly common European foreign policy. In reality, foreign policies remained primarily national in orientation and widely perceived as the one of the ultimate expressions of national sovereignty.

For Hoffmann (1995: 85), the Monnet method of integration constituted 'a gamble on the possibility of substituting motion as an end in itself, for agreement on ends'. In other words, even in the absence of widespread agreement on what the goals of European integration should be, gradually closer co-operation could be viewed by all as a desirable good in itself. However, this gamble was untenable in the realm of 'high politics': 'Decisions on foreign policy and membership and defence cannot be reached unless the goals are clarified' (Hoffmann 1995: 85). To a considerable extent, the simple desire to be *heard* in international affairs, in an era of superpower dominance, was enough of a 'goal' to allow the EPC to function effectively. In particular, smaller Community states, whose international voices were virtually non-existent outside the EC, had powerful incentives to be parties to common EPC positions.

Yet the CFSP, like the EPC before it, has been seriously hindered by very considerable discrepancies in power between its Member States. The most obvious contrast is between Germany, France and the UK, on the one hand, and all other Member States on the other. Italy's leadership of the 'coalition of the willing' that dispatched a military force to Albania in 1997 and Spain's advocacy of the Barcelona process to create a comprehensive EU policy towards the Mediterranean region after 1995 (see Gomez 1998) were both impressive, yet neither state could claim to be first division international powers in the same class as the 'big three'.

After unification, Germany became by far the largest EU Member State and occupied critical geopolitical space as a bridge between the EU and the East. Germany remained a major military power despite restrictions on its ability to wield it. As the EU's biggest net budgetary contributor by far, Germany's sway over the CFSP increased in line with decisions taken in the post-Maastricht period, usually after long and tortuous discussions, to pay for CFSP joint actions out of the European Community's budget (Monar 1997).

Meanwhile, the UK and France remained the EU's only nuclear powers. In advance of a permanent German seat on the UN Security Council (which seemed imminent by the late 1990s), the British and French were privileged members of a powerful club restricted to China, Russia, the USA and themselves. No major diplomatic or (particularly) military initiative under the CFSP was likely without large British and French contributions.[5]

In practical terms, the discrepancy in power between big and small Member States is larger and more consequential on CFSP matters than it is in any other EU policy sector. Voting weights assigned to Member States under QMV in pillar I do not accurately reflect power disparities in pillar II. From time to time, ideas are floated for the creation of a *directoire* at the core of the CFSP, with institutionalised privileges for the 'big three'. Ideas for decision-making by 'double majority' with some type of population criterion[6] were discussed seriously in the run-up to the Amsterdam Treaty, with Jacques Chirac signalling that France might accept some sort of QMV with a recalibration of voting weights (more votes being given to larger states). The accepted need for unanimity on all CFSP matters, to avoid the politically unthinkable act of obliging one of the 'big three' to support a joint action against their will, was gradually being eroded. When asked what surprised her most about CFSP decision-making, a senior French official responded: 'It must be the power of the small states. In formal terms, Luxembourg is as powerful as we are. More actual voting would be a good thing if there were more equilibrium and more weight for the more powerful states.'[7]

In practice, French support for closer foreign policy co-operation has been mostly rhetorical. In 1991, 'as far as decision-making was concerned, there was no real French pressure to go beyond the provisions of the Single Act, since the timid introduction of qualified majority voting with respect to the implementation of common actions was not really restraining' (de la Serre 1996: 33). The distance between the position of the UK, the most vocal and reticent opponent of the 'communitarisation' of foreign policy (see Hill 1996b), and that of France has always been far wider in rhetoric than in practice.

When the CFSP did achieve success in the post-Maastricht period, it was often because France took a strong lead and others followed. The so-called 'Balladur Plan', designed to prevent 'new Yugoslavias' emerging in Central and Eastern Europe, was a good case in point (see Exhibit 9.3). By the same token French unilateralism – in the testing of nuclear weapons in the Pacific (condemned by most other EU Member States) and on policy towards the troubled Great Lakes region of Africa or Algeria – sometimes made a mockery of the CFSP. At the level of 'high politics', the CFSP (like the EPC before it) allowed opportunities for 'France to dress up its own national interest in European clothes, without imposing any real constraints on what was left of her international ambitions and will to independence' (de la Serre 1996: 29).

When French interests were not served by the CFSP in the post-Maastricht period, the CFSP was often abandoned for unilateralism or ad-hocery within a *directoire*. Perhaps the best illustration was the so-called Contact Group on Bosnia (see Exhibit 9.4). In particular, Italy complained bitterly about the breaking of EU ranks by the Germans, French and British, its own exclusion from the group and the setting of a precedent for ad hocery when the CFSP was still so young and fragile.[8] Yet Carl Bildt, the former Swedish Prime Minister and the EU's High Representative in Bosnia from 1995 to 1997, spoke for many when he let it be known privately that he favoured some form of *directoire* as the only way to make the CFSP work. Moreover, the Contact Group was only one example of small group diplomacy outside the CFSP: for example, the 'Quint' brought together the UK, France, Germany, Italy and Spain to discuss relations with Turkey. Looking ahead, it seemed clear that 'the

Exhibit 9.3 The Balladur Plan and 'stability pacts'

One of the first joint actions undertaken by the EU in late 1993 was an initiative to convene a series of pan-European conferences to try to settle ethnic and border disputes in Central and Eastern Europe before they arose. First proposed by the French Prime Minister, Edouard Balladur, the ostensible purpose of the 'stability pacts', as they came to be known, was to encourage Central and East European states – such Hungary and Romania – to agree bilateral compacts. The EU oiled the wheels with aid funding and paid for the cost of the conferences, which brought together more than 50 European states, using the Council budget. The 'stability pacts' were viewed as a major success for the CFSP (see Ginsberg 1995).

The EU joint action evolved 'dramatically from scepticism to success' (Ueta 1997: 92). The original proposal was tabled by the French at the 1993 Copenhagen summit. Under the title of *Plan Balladur*, it was detailed to the point of including a schedule with provisions for a final, high profile conference to be held in Paris at the end of the French 1995 Council presidency. To many, the Plan seemed a rather blatant attempt by Balladur to boost his foreign policy profile ahead of his bid for the French presidency in 1995. It received a frosty reception in many Central and East European capitals, where the Plan was viewed as an unnecessary – even illegal – act of interference by the EU in the domestic affairs of sovereign states (see MacManus 1998).

In the event, three factors were crucial to the initiative's success. First, despite initial doubts, Germany decided to back the Plan. In political terms, the French clearly intended the Balladur Plan to ensure that Central and Eastern Europe did not become a sort of German *domaine réservé*. The tabling of the Plan was preceded by virtually no consultation with Bonn, where it was condemned as having the potential to delay EU enlargement. In the event, the French won over the Germans, largely because they allowed the German Council presidency of late 1994 (which directly preceded the 1995 French presidency) to 'run with' the idea of a support programme, designed in Bonn and implemented by the Organisation for Security and Cooperation in Europe (OSCE), to assist local minorities and promote trans-border co-operation. A Franco-German meeting of minds on the stability pacts was symbolised by a newspaper article jointly authored by Balladur and the

→

→

German Chancellor, Helmut Kohl, extolling the virtues of the Plan and published in both France and Germany (Rummel 1996: 56).

Second, the Balladur Plan succeeded because decisions were taken early on to delegate important responsibilities for implementing it to the OSCE. Besides pleasing Germany, traditionally the OSCE's most enthusiastic western supporter, the central role of the OSCE had the politically important effect of moderating resentment of the Balladur Plan in the east (particularly in Russia), where the OSCE enjoyed considerable support. Somewhat cynically, one might conclude that making the OSCE the stability pacts' 'guardian' guaranteed that the EU joint action would be a 'success', since it could step aside after the final conference and avoid any further responsibility for it. More charitably, the stability pacts could be seen as demonstrating that 'interlocking institutions' could work to preserve Europe's post-Cold War security order.

Third, and finally, central and eastern states were persuaded to go along with the EU and sign stability pacts because there were rewards for doing so, even before the big prize of actual EU membership was on offer. At the 1994 Essen European Council, the PHARE aid programme was 're-oriented for the purpose of promoting intra-regional co-operation' (Ueta 1997: 99), thus rewarding states which co-operated with the CFSP joint action in the short term. The stability pacts could be seen as a clear illustration of the maxim that successful CFSP joint actions usually require joint action with pillar I.

The final agreement was signed in Paris in March 1995. It comprised 47 separate agreements between the 'interested countries' (those in Central and Eastern Europe) and the EU or its members, and 76 agreements between the 'interested countries' themselves. The latter included a 'Treaty on Good Neighbourliness' between Hungary and Slovakia, between whom border tensions were previously rife. The diplomatic process that surrounded the Balladur Plan helped to defuse even stronger tensions between Russia and the Baltic states, and Romania and Hungary. Although motivated by the Yugoslavian crisis and inspired by the 1815 Congress of Vienna, Balladur's proposal clearly was based as much on domestic political calculations as on altruism. Ultimately, however, it led to an EU policy initiative that tangibly contributed to the transition to an enlarged EU.

trend towards ad hoc groupings could well be accentuated as the EU enlarges and potentially becomes more unwieldy as a decision-making body' (Cameron 1998: 61).

In particular, considerable ad-hocery is likely to characterise CFSP decision-making related to security and defence. From the mid-1980s onwards, the EU and WEU continued to move closer to one another, despite differences in the two organisations' memberships.[9] The Amsterdam Treaty eschewed an actual merger of the Union and the WEU and made all decisions with military implications subject to strict unanimity. However, the Treaty did refer to the 'progressive', instead of 'eventual', framing of an EU defence policy. It also gave the EU new sanction to perform the so-called 'Petersberg tasks', involving humanitarian and rescue tasks as well as military intervention to try to forestall crises or keep warring factions apart. Here the Amsterdam Treaty drew much inspiration from a paper submitted jointly by Sweden and Finland, which ended up being an important contribution to the 1996–7 intergovernmental conference (IGC). It provided hard evidence that the neutrality of four EU Member States (Austria and Ireland, together with Finland and Sweden) had evolved towards an acceptance of the EU's responsibility for external crises (see Peterson and Bomberg 1998). Moreover, it was possible to argue that the Union stood for a clear set of values in international affairs, as set out clearly in Article 11 of the new treaty: democracy, liberalism, human rights and international co-operation.

Generally, however, the CFSP remained confined to diplomatic gestures or economic actions. The EU continued to lack one of the essential prerequisites of great-power status: a military capability that could be deployed in the pursuit of political goals. More basically, the CFSP suffered from fundamental problems of identity, interests and institutions (Peterson 1998). It was not legitimated by any common 'European identity', shared between average Europeans, thus making it difficult for CFSP decision-makers to compromise national for 'European interests'. In institutional terms, the Monnet method simply did not work. By the late 1990s, foreign policy often still appeared to be 'high politics' and amenable only to intergovernmental decision-making, when amenable to co-operation at all. It remained difficult to refute Hoffmann's (1995: 90) long-standing claim that 'There is no common European outlook. Nor is there a common *projet*, a common conception of Europe's role in world affairs.'

Setting the CFSP: the 'Single' Institutional Framework[15]

At a systemic level of analysis, post-Maastricht CFSP decision-making was overshadowed by bickering about procedure and prerogative: *how* policy would be made, instead of *what* policy would be. At the root of 'the politics of procedure' (Ginsberg 1997) were fierce turf battles, primarily between national foreign ministries and the EU's institutions. Such turf battles raged largely because the CFSP, like the old EPC, 'reflect[ed] the traditional foreign policy activities of Foreign Ministries which [were] gradually being marginalised' (Nuttall 1992: 311). Increasingly, foreign policy in a post-Cold War world was exercised through financial, economic, trade and development aid instruments, which were beyond the remit of pillar II. Logically, perhaps, the turf that remained to foreign ministers and foreign ministries was defended fiercely.

Enormous time and energy was invested in fights about who should decide what (and who should pay for what). These disputes were inevitable because Member States avoided difficult decisions when the CFSP was designed. Precedents were set almost daily by the mere operation of the CFSP after 1993. Formally, at least, the Maastricht Treaty created a single institutional framework, making the Commission, General Affairs Council and COREPER responsible for decisions within *both* pillars I and II, with a view to encouraging more coherence in EU external policy. The treaty institutionalised exchanges between COREPER and the so-called 'Political Directors', or top foreign ministry officials with CFSP responsibilities. Yet the Treaty did not clearly define the roles of either. It certainly did not eliminate rivalries between them, and may even have worsened them by, for example, making COREPER the final prepatory body before the General Council discussed CFSP issues.

Political Directors are based in national capitals and many have direct lines to their foreign ministers. Thus they often have ample opportunity to circumvent COREPER. As Ginsberg (1997: 25) argues, 'Since Directors work for national foreign ministers, they cannot be expected to play the role of ensuring interpillar consistency'. In a majority of EU Member States, the Political Director is officially a superior of its permanent representative. The uneasy relationship between COREPER and Political Directors fuels the impression that the single institutional framework is 'too weak to overcome the practical problems . . . which arise each time the Union wants to use more than one policy component to deal with a particular issue in international relations' (Rummel 1996: 4).

Meanwhile, despite its new (non-exclusive) right of initiative under the terms of Maastricht, the Commission proposed very little. Instead, it preferred to snipe from the sidelines and urge that the CFSP be broadened to embrace 'the possible effects on the Union's stability and security of changing patterns of economic activity, population movements driven both by unrest and by economic attraction, and cultural changes' (Commission 1995b: 141). Several CFSP actions, such as a common position on relations with Ukraine, were successful mainly because European *Community*

Exhibit 9.4   Bosnia: the ultimate humiliation of the CFSP

In late 1993, the German Defence Minister, Volker Rühe, announced a beefing up of the 'Eurocorps', which combined military forces from five EU Member States. 'Hardly five days after the Treaty on European Union came into effect,' claimed Rühe, 'we are preparing the ground for its practical implementation.'[10] Less than six months later, the respected French commentator, Dominique Moïsi, concluded that 'Sarajevo ha[d] emptied Maastricht of its meaning'.[11]

Analysis of the Bosnian tragedy became an academic growth industry in the late 1990s.[12] Most analysts lambasted the EU for engaging in ineffectual diplomacy as it insisted that little could be done by outside forces to stop the worst bloodshed and atrocities seen on the European continent since the 1940s. The perceived failure of the EU in the Balkans frequently became the foundation for more general indictment of the CFSP and even of European integration itself (see Pfaff 1994; Gow 1997; Judt 1997; Rieff 1997).

Defenders of the Union countered that, 'if it failed in its goals [in ex-Yugoslavia], it was not through want of political investment in the cause' (Piening 1997: 11). The CFSP joint action taken to administer and reconstruct the Bosnian city of Mostar helped keep a fragile peace between Muslims and Croats, who the West encouraged to ally against Serb aggression. France and the UK provided the lion's share of troops to guard UN humanitarian convoys, which clearly saved many lives. But the EU also took many ill-judged decisions during nearly four years of civil war in ex-Yugoslavia. In retrospect, three decisions proved particularly damaging to the EU's image and credibility.

The first appeared to have been made in a split second by a single individual. At a very early stage of the conflict in June 1991, Jacques Poos, Luxembourg's Foreign Minister and the Council's President in Office, hailed an EU-brokered cease-fire as proof of the Union's new credentials as a diplomatic power. Speaking off-the-cuff to reporters, Poos claimed, 'This is the hour of Europe, not the hour of the Americans.'[13] The cease-fire quickly fell apart, as did many others after it. The EU had only economic co-operation agreements to offer or withhold from combatants, who showed themselves to be far more concerned with territorial expansion. The Union clearly was not ready or able to bring peace to the Balkans. No other single statement in the history of EPC/CFSP did more than Poos' to widen the 'capabilities–expectations gap' (Hill 1993; 1998).

→

→

A second decision, taken on 16 December 1991 by EU Foreign Ministers, has been analysed more extensively than any other taken under the CFSP. After a long and bitter night of argument, EU Foreign Ministers gave in to Germany and its Foreign Minister, Hans-Dietrich Genscher, and promised to recognise the independence (within a month) of former Yugoslav republics which met certain conditions concerning human rights, commitment to democracy, and so on. In the event, the Germans unilaterally announced (within a week) that they were recognising Croatia and Slovenia regardless of the outcome of an EU investigation into the suitability of breakaway republics for recognition.

Two points are worth making about this decision. First, Germany was far less isolated than it appeared to be, with several other Member States supporting Slovenian and Croatian independence in principle, albeit with less intensity than the Kohl government, which faced heavy domestic pressure to do so (see Zucconi 1996: 241–7). Second, most students of the Yugoslavian civil war concurred with a senior British diplomat, who described the December 1991 Council decision as 'disastrous . . . it made the war in Bosnia inevitable'.[14] The effect of the decision was to encourage the rump, Serb-dominated Yugoslavia, to support the seizure and 'ethnic cleansing' by Bosnian Serbs of Muslim inhabited Bosnia.

Third, and finally, on 26 April 1993, Germany and France agreed to participate in an initiative, backed by the UK together with Russia and the USA, to create the Contact Group, comprising senior officials from these five states, and *only* these five states. The Contact Group's stated mission was to work 'as a matter of urgency towards a full cessation of hostilities for four months' at a time when the fighting was at its worst in Bosnia (Kintis 1997: 160). The slow speed of CFSP deliberations, the disparity in power between large and small EU Member States, and the need to concentrate efforts as national efforts started to diverge may have served to have justified the creation of a *directoire*. However, at this point, the EU essentially ceased to function as a single entity on policy towards Bosnia. The perception that the CFSP had failed in its most crucial test of the post-Maastricht period became almost universal. The European members of the Contact Group eventually shared the diplomatic humiliation of the EU in almost equal measure. Their officials were literally locked out of the rooms at the US airforce base where American diplomats brokered the so-called Dayton Peace Accord for Bosnia in late 1995.

instruments were deployed effectively. In the Ukraine, Community funds were deployed to help pay for the closure of part of the Chernobyl nuclear plant, with the Commission in the lead (Peterson and Ward 1995: 148). However, the EU seemed incapable of doing much of importance that involved speedy co-ordination across pillars.

In particular, the Commission failed to 'punch its weight' in the CFSP during the post-Maastricht period and appeared to have 'little of actual substance to contribute to the development of foreign policy positions and actions' (Allen 1996c: 295). It had very little to do with most joint actions, although common positions were a different matter since most concerned economic sanctions and implicated pillar I. Here the Maastricht Treaty's new provisions (in pillar I) on economic sanctions required a common position (decided by unanimity within pillar II) before the Union could impose them. The CFSP became, in practice, a new hurdle that had to be jumped in order for the Community to take action. The Commission frequently complained that pillar I was being 'contaminated' by the intergovernmentalism of the CFSP.

At the systemic level, the ascendancy of the Council in terms of its power to 'set' the CFSP was unchallenged: the weakness of the Commission and EP in pillar II meant that there was little of the interinstitutional bargaining which was so prominent in pillar I. Yet the CFSP contributed to a general decline in the authority of the General Affairs Council (GAC) in the late 1990s. Foreign ministers had to focus more on foreign policy (that is, 'non-Community') decision-making for a variety of reasons: the more formal decision-making rules of the CFSP required more time than informal policy co-ordination, post-Maastricht turf battles gobbled ministerial time and attention, and the EU was simply more active on matters of foreign policy than it was before 1993. The CFSP contributed to a general overcrowding of the General Council agendas (see Exhibit 9.5), which 'often comprise[d] very big and salient issues, but [were] cluttered up with relatively minor questions, leading to a lack of focus' (Hayes-Renshaw and Wallace 1997: 31). In part because of the CFSP, foreign ministers found that more and more had to be decided in their name by their deputies. Meanwhile they were less and less able to co-ordinate the work of other Councils in any meaningful way.[16] In particular, the increased salience of economic and financial issues in the run-up to EMU elevated the ECOFIN (Council of Economic and Finance Ministers), not least at the GAC's expense.

For their part, foreign ministers often showed themselves fundamentally unable to take clear or sturdy decisions on pillar II questions. In the language of policy analysis, the style of decision-making under the CFSP was 'problem-solving' – taking decisions mostly in isolation from one other – as opposed to 'bargaining', which involves issue linkage, package dealing, side payments, log-rolling, and so on. Crucially, the paramount

Exhibit 9.5 The GAC's impossible agenda

Agenda of the 2078th General Affairs Council meeting, 30–1 March 1998

Items discussed	*Items not discussed*
Enlargement – launch of accession process – opening of accession negotiations	Rwanda
	Enlargement (accession partnerships)
WTO – preparations of second ministerial meeting	Development co-operation – gender issues
Agenda 2000	FYROM – trade in wine
Middle East Peace Process	UN – co-ordination on candidates for Heads of Agencies
Iran	Interinstitutional agreement on CFSP
Influx of Migrants from Iraq and the Neighbouring Region	
South Africa – negotiations on a trade and co-operation agreement	
New Transatlantic Marketplace	
ASEM II	
Relations with the Western Balkans – Kosovo – Croatia	
Policy Planning and Early Warning Unit	
Great Lakes Region (Africa)	

Source: Council of the European Union (1998); reproduced with permission.

'problem' to be solved was usually how to keep up a united front amongst 15 Member States. Generally, it was *not* how to solve the real problems of foreign policy, such as genocide in Rwanda, violations of human rights in Burma or ethnic cleansing in Bosnia. As Nuttall (1994: 25) suggested:

> The deliberations of the Council became those of a diplomatic conference mediating among the domestic interests of the participants, rather than a body working out and implementing a common foreign and security policy reflecting the joint interest of the Community.

In many cases, decisions which 'set' policy did nothing more than agree a common view (or 'common position') on an international matter, with agreement only possible on a lowest common denominator policy: vague, non-committal and, above all, designed to preserve the EU's unity. As a caveat, a number of specific policies, at least four by one count,[17] were 'set' *without* unanimity at the systemic level in the post-Maastricht period. Still, under the CFSP, as under EPC, the Union usually found the most it could do was to decide on forms of words, as opposed to forms of action. In this regard, as much as any other, pillars I and II remained distinctly different from one another.

Policy Networks: the 'Brusselisation' of Foreign Policy?

If the EU often appears to lack single-mindedness or unity of purpose at the 'political' levels of decision-making, there is evidence of increasing harmony at the sub-systemic level. The CFSP has induced policy networks, generally very loose and sometimes only nascent during the EPC era, to become more cohesive. Crucially, however, most remain dominated by mainly national actors, with the EU's supranational institutions mostly marginalised.

From the time that EPC began to function in earnest in the mid-1970s, the great mass of EU foreign policy business has always been done at the working group level (Nuttall 1992: 17–18). The main function of working groups – of which there were around 20 under the CFSP by the late 1990s – is to exchange information in specialised areas such as sub-Saharan Africa, landmines or the OSCE. In principle, no actual decisions are taken at this level. Working groups report to the Political Committee which itself may take decisions on behalf of the Council. In practice, such decisions may be predetermined at the working group level. In any case, if fundamental differences of analysis cannot be reconciled with working groups, decisive action is unlikely at the level of the political directors or Council.

In the post-Maastricht period, most pillar II working groups were gradually consolidated with pillar I Council groups, both to save time and money and to encourage closer inter-pillar co-ordination. Predictably, the process was fraught with conflict between the Political Committee, to whom pillar II groups traditionally reported, and COREPER, to whom most consolidated working groups reported. Generally, consolidation seemed to be favoured by most actual *participants* in working groups, as sectoral experts preferred to be able to discuss the use of a full range of EU policy instruments. Over time, a pragmatic series of *modus vivendi* were reached, with many working groups reporting to the Political Committee on some questions and COREPER on others.

Meanwhile, progressively more authority and expertise on pillar II questions were shifted by Member States from their national foreign ministries to their Permanent Representations (PermReps) in Brussels.

The clearest specific example of the 'Brusselisation' of national foreign policies was the creation of a new group of CFSP counsellors in Brussels (Kiso 1997). The counsellors met weekly, ostensibly to discuss judicial and financial questions, but their remit gradually expanded (especially during crises).

'Brusselisation' was not entirely unwelcome from the Commission's point of view. Sometimes, the Commission found scope to encourage more single-mindedness within Council working groups, particularly after pillar I and II groups were consolidated. As a senior official in the British Foreign Office put it,

> A lot of people in working groups are sent out from national capitals. They know their subject, but often don't know the EU and how it works. That gives the Commission an edge because their guy [sic] usually has been doing his job for 10 years. Plus the Commission often knows where a pot of money, however small, might be found to facilitate some sort of activity, and most specialists naturally want to be 'active' in their area of speciality.[18]

Yet, in contrast to pillar I, the Commission lacked the capacity to set the CFSP agenda. *National* actors, representing either the Council presidency or one of the 'big three', thus tended to assume the role of 'ringleader' in most CFSP policy networks. The lack of any clear 'honest broker' often produced partisanship and stalemate.

The process of 'Brusselisation' also meant that a considerable amount of information on foreign policy was exchanged between national delegations, far more than between sovereign states in any other international organisation. In particular, the COREU network, established under the EPC, provided a secure means of distributing cipher telexes. Still, information exchange did not equate to *common* analysis. The absence of any central authority for policy planning or analysis tended to reinforce disparities in power between large and small Member States. One Commission official complained:

> One of the most intractable problems of the CFSP is that there is little pooled information, apart from that which is circulated on the Coreu network, which facilitates the exchange of (mainly non-sensitive) information amongst EU foreign ministries. The upshot is that ministers and officials come to meetings with briefing papers of widely varying quality, and which are written from a national perspective. Inevitably it is the larger Member States with the necessary resources which make the greatest contribution in terms of information provided. (Cameron 1998: 62)

This pattern persisted in part because the Council Secretariat, which became home to the old EPC Secretariat, was a marginal player in most CFSP policy networks. Its 50 officials, half seconded from national foreign ministries and half permanent, generally lacked the information or resources to challenge national analyses of foreign policy problems as they arose. One negotiator on pillar II questions in the 1996–7 IGC observed that, 'after Maastricht, more resources were put into the Council Secretariat, but it didn't work at all. We ended up with an army of pen pushers in Brussels. Everyone agrees that more common planning and analysis would be a good thing'.[19]

Yet, even post-Amsterdam (see Exhibit 9.1), 'common' planning and analysis will not mean 'Community planning and analysis'. The trend towards Brusselisation, not communitarisation, was clear in decisions taken on the composition of the new CFSP Planning Unit in 1998. It would consist of 20 A-grade (policy level) officials, but only one each from the Commission and WEU, three from the Council Secretariat, and 15 from the Member States (one each).

In short, collective action remains difficult to foster at the CFSP's sub-systemic level because the orientation of the most important decision-makers remains fundamentally national. The Monnet method of 'leaving experts to get on with it' has *not* provoked the communitarisation of foreign policy. The Amsterdam Treaty essentially seems to reinforce the ascendance of the Council over the Commission in decision-making (see Allen 1998). Perhaps above all, when issues preoccupy high-level decision-makers, particularly foreign ministers, the ability of policy networks to shape decisions is strictly limited. The sub-systemic level always matters less when 'high politics' are involved.

Yet, for many practitioners, such as the long-time Belgian Ambassador to the EU, Phillippe de Schoutheete (1986), the process of socialising decision-makers to each other and the CFSP is a crucial prerequisite of EU solidarity in foreign policy. In the language of rational choice theory, the continued interaction of national experts at the working group level means that, to a considerable extent, national preferences are formed more *endogenously*, or within a context of intergovernmental bargaining, than ever before in the history of EPC/CFSP.

The EU joint action to extend the nuclear Non-proliferation Treaty (NPT) in 1995 illustrates these points. As a nuclear power, France's position of general scepticism about the treaty's merits had traditionally precluded a united EU policy. However, in the first multilateral arms control conference of the post-Cold War era, France's position appeared to shift under the influence of an epistemic community of national experts that supported the treaty's extension. In the event, the Union, 'strongly led by France' (Leigh-Phippard 1997: 176), played a crucial role alongside the USA (see Exhibit 9.6) in successfully 'selling' the treaty to reluctant non-nuclear states. Previously belonging to the 'hard core' of national interests, nuclear export policy was 'fully "sucked" into the intergovernmental framework of jointness' which underpins the CFSP (Müller and van Dassen 1997: 69).

The point is that, at the very least, national preferences on many CFSP matters are shaped by interactions between specialists at the sub-systemic level. Their status and work tends to be elevated when they can reach agreement and recommend truly joint positions to the Political Committee and their political masters. The politics of scale, or the notion that the EU is most powerful when it is most united (Ginsberg 1989), start here.

Conclusion

Clearly, foreign policy is unique as an arena for European co-operation. Touching so directly on national sensibilities, foreign policy resists many of the methods that have been successful harbingers of market integration. Foreign policy co-operation requires a distinctive set of decision rules and norms, which in practice may be described as 'Brusselisation', not communitarisation. Given these limitations, the CFSP is a widely inclusive and even sophisticated system of decision-making. Whatever its design faults, the CFSP has had a number of important policy successes in the post-Maastricht period.

Yet this upbeat judgement cannot go unqualified. The frequent obsession of the EU and its Member States with formal decision-making and procedure within pillar II invites charges of navel-gazing. The CFSP has been, and will continue to be, judged largely by its results, and 'The institutional mechanisms of how decisions are reached within the EU are of little interest to the beneficiaries or targets of a given policy' (Piening 1997: 194).

The EU already does a credible job (at least much of the time) of taking *decisions* on matters of foreign policy, and doing it collectively. Cases of national foreign policy decisions taken entirely without reference to the CFSP or the 'other 14' are relatively rare, and probably becoming rarer. However, in foreign policy more than in other EU policy sectors, common 'decisions' do not necessarily produce effective action or policy. The CFSP's central and most serious problem is a lack of policy instruments, which can be deployed to support or enforce policy decisions (see Bildt 1997). The upshot is that the Union makes foreign policy decisions that may be ignored by the outside world. One need not be an unreconstructed realist to believe that the EU will not 'punch its weight' in foreign policy until the CFSP is backed up by the firepower or the unity of purpose which are the hallmarks of a truly great power in international relations. The

Exhibit 9.6 Transatlantic relations: a true partnership?

There is no shortage of scholarship on relations between the EU and the USA (see Featherstone and Ginsberg 1996; Peterson 1996a; Gardner 1997; Ginsberg 1998). The transatlantic relationship is a complex and critical one between two global powers, which often frustrate and annoy each other, but remain each other's best partner. A decision-making approach sheds light on the relationship in particular by highlighting the sharp contrast between frequent tension at the level of 'high politics' and considerable complicity at the sub-systemic level.

A number of transatlantic trade disputes (see Exhibit 4.4), caused considerable bilateral friction in the late 1990s. American policy remained stubbornly unilateralist on Bosnia and Iraq. For instance, neither the EU Council presidency nor any of its Member States were consulted by the Clinton administration when cruise missile attacks were launched against Iraq in 1996 (Piening 1997: 99). The geopolitics of EU enlargement also frayed nerves at the level of 'high politics'. In 1997, the Clinton administration was able to force the pace of NATO enlargement (against the will of many EU Member States) and invite Poland, Hungary and the Czech Republic to join. At the same time, the USA began to try to link the expansion of NATO with EU enlargement. Even as the US Ambassador to NATO acknowledged that such linkage had been 'rejected as Union policy', he argued that 'some parallelism of approach is a factor of life and some parallelism will be valuable for all concerned' (Hunter 1997: 14). An unstated but clear US objective was to push the EU to extend membership to the Baltic republics – Estonia, Latvia and Lithuania – as a way to compensate them for failing to achieve their number one foreign policy goal: early accession to NATO. The Clinton administration found allies on the question of Baltic EU membership in Denmark and Sweden, but southern Member States (led by France) accused the USA of interfering in the EU's own internal affairs.

→

author of the 1975 Tindemans report, designed to identify ways out of the Community's malaise of the period, offered a compelling analysis of the CFSP's malaise 23 years later:

> In order to be able to conduct a foreign policy, one must avail oneself of all possible means, namely political dialogue, economic co-operation, confidence-building measures, political and economic pressure, and the use or threatened use of force. EU diplomacy has all these instruments at its disposal, with the exception of the last of them. (EP 1998: 21)

The central question with which this chapter has grappled is, in many respects, a long-standing and time-honoured one: 'Is there no chance for

→

The decision by the Commission (1997b: 57) to recommend that EU accession negotiations be opened first with Estonia – along with Poland, Hungary, the Czech Republic, Cyprus and Slovenia – was based on 'an objective analysis, in light of the criteria laid down by the [1993] Copenhagen European Council'. But it went some way towards appeasing nearly all concerned, including the Americans (if not the Latvians and Lithuanians or their supporters, the Nordic EU states). One obvious implication of extending the EU's borders closer to Russia, to encompass a region of potential instability, was to highlight the need for a more effective and united CFSP.

On more low-key, even mundane issues, the USA and the EU were working more closely together than was easily imaginable when the clear, common threat from the Soviet Union disappeared in 1989–91. In particular, the New Transatlantic Agenda (NTA), agreed in 1995, moved the USA and the EU from consultation towards actual 'joint action' on a range of policies (see Ginsberg 1998), including many which preoccupied the CFSP, such as human rights, nuclear proliferation, assistance to Palestine and aid to Bosnia.[20] In particular, the Action Plan's most tangible commitments to joint action concerned development co-operation and humanitarian assistance. No precedent existed for truly common transatlantic initiatives on 'pillar II' type issues, which often were the subject of outright ruptures in US–EU relations during the Cold War.

The NTA did not constitute an actual treaty and its long-term significance was uncertain. Still, the USA supported co-operation with the EU on any foreign policy issue that cost money almost instinctually. It became very much a 'superpower on the cheap' as its budget for foreign affairs (leaving aside military spending) was reduced by about half from levels of the early 1980s. The more general point is that tensions at the level of 'high politics' masked increasingly closer co-operation on questions which rarely made headlines, such as banking reform in Ukraine, reinforcing democracy in Haiti or controlling nuclear development in North Korea.

the European [Union]? Is it condemned to be, at best, a success in economics and a fiasco in "high politics?"' (Hoffmann 1995: 96). The answer is not a simple 'yes'. If we conceive of the CFSP as a *process* and consider how far foreign policy co-operation has been advanced in less than 30 years, long-term predictions begin to appear risky. Moreover, it is plausible to argue that, 'in its external relations policy generally, Europe has never been more united than it is today' (Cameron 1998: 76). On the other hand, to give Hoffmann (1995: 84) his due as well as the final word, the CFSP clearly is not what the framers of Maastricht promised it would be, for the simple reason that 'a procedure is not a purpose, a process is not a policy'.

Chapter 10

Conclusion

Explaining the European Union – what it does, how it does it and with what effect – is one of the most daunting challenges facing political science as a discipline. Clearly, there are important differences between being an ordinary nation-state and an EU Member State. The Union is obviously a highly 'differentiated polity' (Rhodes 1997: 7). Eastern enlargement and EMU are likely to transform EU decision-making. Otherwise, the EU resists simple, uncontroversial generalisations.

We have argued that the challenge of understanding the EU is best tackled by examining decision-making at different levels of governance using different 'lenses', or theoretical models. Our framework highlights two kinds of contrasts. First, different actors and factors govern the making of different types of EU decision. Second, enormous differences exist between policy sectors: compare, for example, the Common Agricultural Policy (CAP) with the Common Foreign and Security Policy (CFSP).

Our case studies offer rich detail, but we have made no attempt to be comprehensive. We have touched only fleetingly on transport, energy, the budget or pillar III. At the same time, the application of our framework to the sectors we have covered *does* offer new insights into EU decision-making, three of which we accent here.

First, the EU resists 'meta-theorising'. It is far more amenable to a portfolio of theoretical models, which can describe, explain and (hopefully) predict the outcomes of decision-making at different levels of governance. Policies, especially EU policies, are the products of numerous, sequenced decisions taken at different levels in a multi-level system. We need a range of theories 'pitched' at each of the important levels, and a framework that links them together.

Second, EU decision-making should be approached as 'actor-centred', with explanations derived from 'the interests and strategies of the actors in

252

the EU policy process' (Hix 1998: 48). Winning coalitions are not easy to construct in EU governance, so identifying precisely how they are constructed is crucial. It is too simple to claim that agency matters more than structure in EU decision-making, yet the EU is a surprisingly active system of governance, given its powerful structural barriers to collective action.

Third, a crucial task for any student of the EU is explaining how it *changes*. We have highlighted the sources of unpredictability in EU decision-making, while also noting the Union's recurrent tendency to embrace major, wrenching changes when they are needed to break through political impasse. Consider the frequency of treaty reforms since the mid-1980s: three rounds in just over 10 years. Even if the treaties are mostly left alone in the early 21st century, EMU and enlargement will both force considerable change on EU decision-making.

Our primary purpose here is to identify what we have discovered about EU decision-making that is fresh and original. While highlighting enduring patterns at each level of EU decision-making, however, we also consider how new challenges – above all EMU and enlargement – are likely to force the Union to change. We begin by explaining why our evidence points to the need for an actor-centred approach to EU decision-making, and precisely what this approach implies.

EU Decision-Making: What is New?

We have employed a single framework for analysis of EU decision-making that combines multiple theoretical perspectives. Before considering what new light it sheds, let us first consider what we already 'know'. Broadly, two approaches exist for understanding the EU (see Caporaso 1998). One views the Union as a product of forces *external* to the EU itself: integration results from responses to impulses from beyond Europe, or 'exogenous shocks'. Thus, for example, the 1992 project is explained as the Community's answer to the anti-Europeanism of the US Reagan administration, or declining European competitiveness vis-à-vis Asia (Sandholtz and Zysman 1989).

The second approach highlights the *internal* logic of European integration, usually building on the concept of path dependency. This view assumes that the EU has proved resilient because its policies have blended together both national practices and decision-makers (Pierson 1996). 'Renationalising' EU policies is impossible: it is like trying 'to unmake a stew or cake, starting from finished product and ending with the original ingredients' (Caporaso 1998: 13).

These two approaches are companions masquerading as rivals. The 'exogenous shock' approach is about what drives European integration, as an historical process. The path dependence school is more about EU policy-making, as a political process. The essential point is that European integration and EU policy-making shape, define and determine one another. The process of European integration has produced relatively frequent, dramatic institutional change since the mid-1980s. Meanwhile, in most sectors, EU policy-making has produced relatively consistent outcomes, which usually change incrementally when they change at all.

We explain this apparent paradox by suggesting that decisions that determine the path of European integration are fundamentally different from those that set or shape EU policies. Different levels of governance are implicated. Different decision-makers, motivated by different concerns, dominate each level. What is consistent across all levels of EU decision-making is that the Union institutionalises co-operation, even if it often lacks institutions (in the traditional sense of the term) to facilitate meaningful bargaining. Whether bargaining is formal or informal, the EU socialises decision-makers to one another and offers new supranational solutions to national problems. It thus encourages new types of agency in what is perceived as a positive sum game.

It is easy to underestimate the EU's ability to make policy because it appears to have so many veto points, while also depending fundamentally on consensus. Yet the EU frequently agrees policies of fundamental importance to its Member States and citizens. Given all the reasons to assume that the EU would produce little more than impasse and stalemate, it is a remarkably active and productive system of government.

If the EU offers considerable scope for political agency, how do we explain the behaviour of its agents (or actors)? Interests and strategies are determined in important respects by the identities of actors: how they define themselves in relation to other actors who are potential allies or adversaries in the pursuit of collective action. To an extent unseen in other systems of government, actors in EU decision-making have multiple identities: national and supranational, political and apolitical, sectoral and institutional, and so on. Their actions may be motivated by different rationalities at different times, particularly in a system where the rules differ so much between policy 'episodes' and change so frequently. Thus we are wise to 'hold open the question of the orientations of political [and non-political] actors to the rules that constrain them' (Marks 1996a: 5; see also Marks *et al.* 1996a; Richardson 1996a).

Moreover, in EU decision-making the rules are often vague, contentious or 'shiftable'. The rules, like nearly everything else, may even be negotiable. As such, 'it is the men [sic] who govern the processes, and not the processes that govern the men' (Rosenthal 1975: 14). To be more modern (and politically correct), it is frequently the political agency of actors which determines outcomes as much or more than the rules or structures that constrain them. This view is at the centre of an 'actor-centred' perspective on EU decision-making.

An actor-centred perspective also assumes that the rationality of EU actors – or the values that motivate their behaviour – is not only determined by their institutional or political affiliation. It may also be moulded fundamentally by their acclimation to the process of repeated bargaining at the EU level. One important implication is that a rigid conceptual distinction between 'national governments' and 'supranational institutions' is unsustainable. On the one hand, national leaders may become so acclimated to EU decision-making that they may appear to act on the basis of 'supranational ideology', or the perceived need to strengthen European structures, even as they seek to defend national interests. Consider François Mitterrand's support for dramatic moves to strengthen the EU's structures in response to the French economic crisis of the early 1980s and the perceived threat to France of German unification in the early 1990s. On the other hand, if officials in the EU's institutions truly left their national orientations at the door, presumably there would be no point in the intense bargaining between Member States over placement of officials in the upper echelons of the EU's institutions (see Page 1997).

To illustrate the point another way, it is widely accepted that the system of private interest lobbying in France is underdeveloped (at least in Anglo-Saxon terms). Yet, the managing director of Shandwick Europe, Europe's largest public affairs agency, argues that 'the best lobbyists in Europe are the French'. Why? Because French interest groups 'make their influence felt through the [EU's] institutions themselves via civil servants and political networking'.[1] This judgement is counterintuitive, but entirely compatible with an actor-centred perspective: it allows that national interests may be actively expressed and pursued in all institutions and at all levels of EU decision-making. The EU is constructed in a way that allows plenty of space for 'national agency'. In this context, Moravcsik's (1993), liberal intergovernmentalism (LI) tells us both more and less than it claims to: more because the EU's supranational structures are permeated by national 'interests' and individuals willing to defend them, and less because LI assumes a clear dichotomy between 'national governments' and 'supranational actors'.[2]

At the same time, the EU's supranational institutions operate with considerable autonomy, at least compared to the institutions of other international organisations. Their functions, strategies and behaviour 'may reflect not so much the preferences and intentions of their member state principals but rather the preferences, and the autonomous agency, of the supranational institutions themselves' (Pollack 1997a: 107). What matters is which actors act as agents for their institutions, and what motivates them. The structural terrain of the EU offers considerable scope for creative, independent agency that is relatively unconstrained by formal affiliations, rules or institutions.

An actor-centred view also assumes weak links between agents and principals, or EU decision-makers and the constituents they represent. Some EU scholars have begun to detect *stronger* agent–principal links. They claim that the 'politics of the EU' are becoming 'normalised', or more like national politics, featuring the 'mobilization of citizens, private groups and office-holders to secure outputs close to their interests, values and ideologies' (Hix 1998: 42). Witness, for example, the emergence of stronger trans-European party federations (particularly given the advent of co-decision) and innovations such as meetings of Christian Democratic and Socialist leaders prior to every European Council.

Yet the 'day-to-day role and impact of these federations is . . . marginal' (Wessels 1997b: 33). More generally, 'normalised' politics are precluded by the EU's vast number of procedures for decision-making, reliance on backroom bargaining and blurred lines of accountability. The politics of the EU remain underdeveloped, and its democratic legitimacy weak.

In this context, one group of (especially continental) scholars argues that the Union is being judged by the wrong standards: majoritarian democracy is peculiar to the nation-state, and for good reason (see Dehousse 1995; Majone 1996a, 1996b; Joerges and Neyer 1997). For advocates of the 'new governance', the EU's legitimacy is functional, not representative. Diffusing the Union's regulatory powers to specialised independent agencies, which are required to act in the 'public interest', enhances it. Thus 'democracy needs to be redefined and reconstructed to fit the EU' (Hix 1998: 51). Freed from traditional pluralist pressures, technocrats can design EU policies so that everybody wins. The idea here is to liberate the EU from actor-centred politics by defining more tightly the 'orientations' of actors and making the rules under which they operate much clearer.

This normative set of arguments would be easier to accept if there was a clear division of labour between the EU and national levels. Much of the traditional work of the nation-state – the provision and regulation of money, food and a clean environment – is now primarily the domain of the EU (see Sbragia 1993). Even in 'apolitical' areas (such as anti-dumping policy) the EU often cannot decide without provoking intense ideological divisions between its Member States (see Holmes and Kempton 1996). Whether or not the EU could ever establish itself in the minds of European citizens as a benign technocracy, it is worth asking whether it could sustain such a status for very long. As it is now, EU decision-makers generally operate with both surprisingly wide discretion and predictably low legitimacy.

Punctuating Equilibriums, Making History

We have found the EU to be an unusually differentiated polity, in which broad policy initiatives are difficult to co-ordinate. An equally enduring trend in EU decision-making is that major change in *policy* often seems impossible without a change in *process*. The result is constant tinkering with process, which produces a kind of 'organic accretion' of decision-making procedures. As a senior Swedish official put it:

> Most of our procedures are so complicated because they are revised versions of revised versions of past versions. There's rarely much attempt made to find the optimum, it is more often a case of sticking a new procedure onto the old one, which of course is treated with reverence because so much blood was spilt to agree it.[3]

Even when governments meet in intergovernmental conferences (IGCs) with the express intent to alter the EU's institutions, participants quickly realise that 'There are no simple alternatives to the present arrangements. There are no quick institutional fixes' (McDonagh 1998: 17). Yet fundamental institutional change enters the realm of the possible, as well as the practical, when existing EU policy simply does not work any more. 'Path dependency' often seems more powerful at the systemic than at the super-systemic level, and more of a deterrent to *policy* change than to *institutional* change. Most EU policies are made in sectoral 'villages', in which past bargains are spoken of with sanctimony, as the outcomes of careful compromise and delicate balancing of interests. When a clear majority of Member States cannot agree on policy change, existing EU policy becomes entrenched simply owing to an apparent lack of alternatives. EU policies – the banana regime, subsidies for collaborative R&D, or uniform water quality standards – frequently survive past their 'sell-by' dates.

The 'easier' choice often becomes high-level intervention to push through history-making decisions that change the way the EU operates. Put another way, policy change occurs by changing the way the EU makes decisions about policy. Decisions concerning the EU's budget (see Exhibit 10.1) illustrate the point clearly. Member States that made large net contributions to the budget, particularly Germany and the Netherlands, began to agitate for a 'fairer' distribution of costs and benefits by the late 1990s. They thus gave licence to supporters of CAP reform to propose radical changes in the making and financing of EU agricultural policy. Without a history-making decision to change the system by which states paid for the EU, radical CAP reform was difficult to imagine, regardless of pressures for reform arising from the EU's imminent enlargement.

Exhibit 10.1   Paying for the privilege: the EU's budget

Traditionally, the Byzantine system of financing the EU has resisted radical change. In the early 1980s, Margaret Thatcher successfully exploited a 'policy window' to secure a rebate for the UK, which reduced the imbalance between its payments to the EU's common budget and its receipts. Generally, however, the need for unanimous agreement on changes to the system kept the status quo in place. Germany bore the burden of its massive net contribution without much complaint, with most German political elites considering it an acceptable price to pay for the wealth, prosperity and peace engendered by the EU.

This cosy consensus was shattered in 1998 when Helmut Kohl began to insist, in the heat of an election campaign, that a unified and relatively poorer Germany would start to withhold EU budget payments unless its net contribution was reduced. After Kohl was defeated in the 1998 German election and was replaced by Gerhard Schröder, the Commission elected to do the previously unthinkable: it tabled a report which indicated, for the first time, precisely how much each Member State paid into and received back from the EU's budget. Its decision to do so, in a document with the innocuous title, *Financing the European Union* (Commission 1998c), was motivated by three factors.

First, the Commission sought to expose the UK's rebate as both anachronistic and 'anti-Communautaire'. Much had changed since the Thatcher era. In particular, the reduction in the CAP's share of the budget from 70 per cent in the early 1980s to less than half by 1998 meant that the UK's budgetary imbalance was no longer unique. By this time, Germany, the Netherlands, Sweden and Austria all made relatively larger net contributions. Moreover, the UK's rebate distorted an otherwise reasonably equitable system of contributions. For example, Germany's 26 per cent share of EU gross

→

An important clue to understanding why, paradoxically, it is often easier to reform the EU's institutions than to reform EU policy is the Union's relatively weak mechanisms for policy co-ordination at the systemic level. Over time, the General Affairs Council (of foreign ministers) has lost much of its grip on EU decision-making. Meanwhile, the burgeoning power of ECOFIN (the Council of Economic and Finance ministers) means that some of the most conservative, inward-looking, nationally-focused ministers and ministries – with whom most members of national cabinets have inherently hostile relations – now often sit at the apex of EU decision-making. Overall, the recipe is one for policy stagnation.

At first glance, the European Council seems an unlikely candidate to break through the morass and put the EU out of its policy misery when

→

national product (GNP) was more or less reflected in its 28.2 per cent contribution to the Union's budget. Greece had 1.5 per cent of GNP and a 1.6 per cent contribution to the budget, while the relevant figures for France were 17.2 and 17.5 per cent. But the UK, which had increased its share of wealth since the Thatcher era, had 16.1 per cent of GNP while paying only 11.9 per cent of the Union's budget (after its rebate). The only other country clearly out of step was Italy, with 14.2 per cent of GNP and a payment equal to 11.5 per cent of the EU's budget.

Second, the Commission saw a new 'policy window' opening for CAP reform. It boldly suggested that as much as one-quarter of CAP spending could be renationalised, with national exchequers paying direct income subsidies to farmers. The effect would be to slice a significant chunk off the net contributions of Germany and the Netherlands, both of which insisted that CAP and budgetary reform be linked and decided upon at the same time. The foundations for a package deal, in advance of the 1999 German Council presidency, were laid.

Third, while reform of the budgetary system required unanimous agreement, renationalising a share of the CAP only required a qualified majority decision. The political impossibility of radically changing the budget system suited the Commission because it was clear that the only major changes that were politically realistic were changes on the spending side. Thus new prospects arose for shifting EU spending away from the CAP to other, 'sexier' purposes such as regional policy, research or external relations. The budget deal agreed at the 1999 Berlin summit was a typically diluted Euro-compromise (with the UK keeping its rebate) but the Commission's boldness in proposing to renationalise a large slice of the CAP shows that the EU is not always or entirely path-dependent: when it sets its mind to the task (or is forced to), the EU possesses the political agency to choose a different path.

what it is doing, and usually *has been doing* for years, simply does not work any more. How can impossibly busy political leaders, meeting for the equivalent of less than a working week in any given year, be a source of control and innovation? Asked about the European Council's new pillar II prerogatives under the Amsterdam Treaty, a senior British official was incredulous: 'Come on. The European Council is an incompetent body, and to give them military decision-making power is silly.'[4]

Yet the European Council is, in many respects, the most supple, unconstrained source of *agency* in EU decision-making. Its overwhelmingly political rationality allows it to surmount inevitable technical roadblocks to institutional change – and thus policy reform – when change is needed. This rationality is reflected in the European Council's institutional make-up and authority, which cannot be challenged at any other level of EU governance:[5]

> No national officials are present (other than the country that holds the six-month Presidency). This distinguishes European Councils from meetings at ordinary ministerial level. (I recall [the German Foreign Minister Hans-Dietrich] Genscher once comparing the throng at a Foreign Ministers' meeting in Luxembourg to a plenary session of the Chinese Communist Party.) It is not just a question of numbers. It is a question of atmosphere, of moving from the details to the essentials. It is a question of cutting deals (McDonagh 1998: 18).

Many of these deals 'make history'. They touch the highest political levels even if they are formally 'made' elsewhere.[6] Our framework treats history-making decisions as a distinct analytical category. First, they are taken at levels of governance above and beyond the control of narrowly concerned 'sectoral' decision-makers. Second, most are taken, usually after 'hardball' intergovernmental bargaining, on the basis of distinctly political rationality.

In this context, it is worth considering Bulmer's (1998: 367) argument that 'changing EU governance is *not* just a product of "history-making" decisions'.[7] Of course, some European Court of Justice (ECJ) decisions 'make history' and are taken on the basis of rationality that is, at least in appearance, more 'legal' than political. However, we have highlighted a range of ECJ decisions, from *Cassis de Dijon* to the Franzen case (see Exhibits 2.4 and 3.1), which suggest that the ECJ is not simply an apolitical, legalistic adjudicator. An enduring trend in EU decision-making seems to be that the ECJ will hand down a decision that fundamentally changes the way the EU works *only* if it has some kind of 'cover' in the form of past political choices to take the Union down a certain path (see Dehousse 1998).

Moreover, we have found few cases of truly transformative decisions that were not the results of intergovernmental bargains and conscious political choices at the highest political levels. Sometimes history-making decisions are taken, formally at least, at 'lower' levels of governance. The Merger Control Regulation (see Exhibit 3.3), which revolutionised EU competition policy, appeared to emerge as a combined product of decisions taken by the General Affairs Council, Court and Commission. However, we doubt that the MCR could have been agreed without the 1972 mandate of the European Council (before it was even called the 'European Council') for beefed-up EU powers to police mergers. More-over, the fact that the General Council took the formal decision on the MCR certainly does not mean that the decision did not preoccupy decision-makers at the highest political levels.

Of course, the intergovernmental bargaining which precedes history-making decisions does not proceed unconstrained. Again, we see clear virtues in combining the insights of liberal intergovernmentalism (LI) as a theory of EU bargaining, and neo-functionalism as a theory of contextual change. Put another way, LI is our best theory for explaining the *agency* which produces 'big decisions', while neo-functionalism is a plausible theory of the way EU *structures* evolve to constrain such agency. To illustrate the point, LI does an excellent job of explaining the original decision to make a commitment to EMU in 1990–91 (see Moravcsik 1998), while neo-functionalism highlights the host of functional and political spill-overs that shaped this choice and constrained subsequent ones. For example, the political arguments for creating the Euro were underpinned by simple functional reasoning, which held that the Union could not have a truly 'single' market without a single currency. After EMU, powerful new pressures arose for mechanisms that could produce more unified EU positions in international economic diplomacy. 'And while we are at it,' argued the French and others, 'we might as well create a new "economic government" to ensure political control over EMU' (see Exhibit 10.2). It is impossible to explain the very considerable changes in EU decision-making arising from EMU – with many more ahead in the 21st century – without a theory to explain why, in structural terms, European integration frequently begets more European integration.

However, this process is hardly a 'straight', linear or untroubled one. The EU tends to change according to a pattern of 'punctuated equilibriums'. To understand it, it helps to visualise the way that Arctic ice flows gradually become packed together by sea currents and then periodically burst apart. Pressures build up over time and then suddenly are released, allowing chunks of ice to float freely again.[8] Similarly, pressures often build for EU policy change while enlargement expands the range of national preferences and reinforces political stalemate (see Corbey 1995; Kirman and Widgrén 1995). The status quo is then altered dramatically and quite suddenly, particularly by agreement on package deals. Such decisions unblock political impasse and allow the EU to 'float freely' forward. However, whether the EU can continue to move forward using the same methodology in a Union of far more diverse preferences and, probably, far more entrenched impasse remains a very open question.

Setting Policies: Making Everyone 51 per cent Happy

If decisions are viewed as answers to different kinds of questions (see Peterson 1995a), it is clear that some EU decisions are, effectively, answers to *two* questions: what does the EU do and how does the EU change? The

Exhibit 10.2   'Don't laugh!' The launch of EMU

Rarely are decisions that make EU history greeted by laughter. Yet, the claim by the French President, Jacques Chirac, that the Dutchman, Wim Duisenberg, had 'voluntarily' decided to serve a shortened term as the first President of the new European Central Bank (to make way for a French successor) was greeted by guffaws from assembled journalists. After the gruelling Brussels European summit, during which decisions were also made about which EU Member States would join the 'first wave' of a single currency, Chirac's irritated injunction, 'Don't laugh!' (*On ne rit pas!*),[9] will surely become part of EU lore.

The decision to create the Euro was one of the most audacious in the history of European integration. The Maastricht Treaty, ratified in 1993, set out a timetable for the launch of EMU by 1999 (at the latest). Member States which met a set of economic 'convergence criteria' (on public debt, inflation, interest rates, annual budget deficits and exchange rates) were eligible to join. Only Greece clearly failed to meet the criteria by 1998, while Denmark, Sweden and the UK elected, for various reasons, not to join the 'first wave'. By the time the remaining 11 Member States moved towards the launch of the Euro (with actual notes and coins to be in circulation by 2002), the main features of the future system for decision-making concerning the Euro were clear:

- The European Central Bank (ECB), based in Frankfurt, would issue and manage the Euro. Its six-member executive committee would be headed by a President (for eight years, but possibly less in the case of Duisenberg) and operate with a German-style commitment to independence and price stability. The ECB was set to enjoy one of the strongest legal forms of independence ever created for any central bank.
- The European System of Central Banks (ESCB) would bring the heads of national central banks together with the ECB's executive committee to form a governing council to determine overall policy and (crucially) to set interest rates.

→

launch of the Euro illustrates that the EU sometimes cannot avoid 'making history' almost every time it sets policy in areas where its competence is entirely new. However, most systemic level decisions are relatively undramatic: they determine what the EU *does* as a system of governance, as opposed to how the Union *changes*. They are a product of EU policy-making, as opposed to European integration, even though these two processes are fundamentally interrelated.

EMU offers glimpses of the Union's future, and illustrates both recurrent patterns and evolving trends in EU decision-making.[11] Time-honoured principles informed choices concerning EMU: the perceived need to

$\longrightarrow$

- ECOFIN (Council of Economic and Finance Ministers) was established by the 1990s as one of the EU's most powerful decision-makers, eclipsing the power of Foreign Ministers. By the late 1990s, for example, no European Council took place without ECOFIN's participation. ECOFIN (a French acronym) included Ministers from *all* EU Member States (both EMU 'ins' and 'outs') and retained responsibility for broad macroeconomic policy.

- The 'Euro-11' Council was a new creation, bringing together Finance Ministers *only* from EMU Members. Its role was unclear, but it was likely to extend to international representation of the 'Euro-zone' (such as in the International Monetary Fund). Euro-11 became the focus of French-backed efforts to create an 'economic government' to ensure political control of EMU.

- The Economic and Financial Committee would group together national treasury officials, central bankers and two members of the European Commission to prepare ministerial meetings. It seemed certain to become the scene for informal, backroom bargaining at the centre of a new EMU policy network.

- The European Commission remained at the centre of a system of institutionalised peer review: monitoring national economic performances and even retaining the power to recommend fines for profligate states which violated the economic criteria for membership of EMU.

- The European Parliament (EP) vetted appointees to the ECB and secured the right to have the Bank's President report to it four times a year. Appearing before MEPs soon after the May 1998 EMU summit, Duisenberg reiterated that 'in future the decision to resign [early] will be my decision alone. This must be clearly understood'. He even described the informal understanding to appoint a French successor as 'slightly absurd'.[10] The point, amply illustrated, is that virtually everything is negotiable in EU politics, even history-making decisions.

maintain (at least the appearance of) consensus, the imperative to 'strike a deal' and avoid impasse, the willingness to treat everything, including previously agreed rules about compliance, as negotiable, and the powerful urge to keep the European project moving forward. Decisions concerning the launch of the Euro taken at the 1998 Brussels summit illustrate the power of determined agency at the super-systemic level (see Exhibit 10.2): a range of history-making decisions were taken that defied or ignored the preferences of the EU's monetary policy network.

But the launch of the Euro also reveals a number of new trends in EU decision-making that we have highlighted throughout this study. First,

EMU shows that the Union has, perhaps reluctantly, begun to embrace the notion of 'flexible integration': allowing sub-groups of Member States to move forward on their own. The creation of the Euro raises stark questions about which EU economic policies should be set exclusively by 'ins', and which should feature input from 'outs'.

Second, EMU arguably illustrates the exhaustion of the 'Monnet method' and the rise of an alternative methodology: 'policy transfer' (see Begg and Peterson 1999). Policy transfer is what happens when governments learn from each other (see Dolowitz and Marsh 1996; Peters 1997). 'Benchmarking', or agreeing standards that national policies should aim to achieve, together with institutionalised peer review became the preferred methodology not only for creating the Euro, but also for lowering unemployment, harmonising taxation systems and achieving more uniform application of internal market rules (Commission 1998d). For Member States, institutionalised policy transfer preserves the appearance, at least, of 'non-interference in each other's affairs' while still encouraging convergence. As a senior Commission official suggested, 'We've discovered the power of benchmarking, almost by accident. Governments loathe being at the bottom of the pile in any comparative exercise.'[12] The comparative exercise with the highest stakes, of course, was the effort by Member States to meet the EMU convergence criteria.

Third, EMU gives the Union new global responsibilities. It thus creates new pressures, visible also in foreign and defence policy, to devise stronger mechanisms to facilitate internal EU consensus on external policy matters. France tabled proposals in 1998 to agree Euro-zone positions in advance of International Monetary Fund and World Bank annual meetings, and generally to ensure that the Euro was backed by an active EU approach to international financial issues. Significantly, the UK – not a Euro-zone member – broadly supported the proposals. Moreover, after insisting that the Amsterdam Treaty recognise the primacy of NATO on European security issues,[13] the British government under Tony Blair was out in front of discussions a year later on incorporating the Western European Union (WEU) as the EU's 'pillar IV'. In a global system increasingly marked by new regional alliances – *Mercosur*, NAFTA (the North American Free Trade Association), the Asia–Pacific Economic Cooperation Forum (APEC) and so on – and more constrained by international rules (not least from the World Trade Organisation: WTO), the EU clearly needs to reconsider how it sets external policies.

Fourth, and finally, EMU represents a significant heightening of familiar tensions between efficiency and democratic accountability in EU decision-making. A particularly fiery debate arose in 1998 on rules governing the secrecy of decision-making by the new European Central Bank (ECB). As usual, the treaty itself was vague, indicating that 'the proceedings of the meetings [of the ECB] shall be confidential. The Governing Council may decide to make the outcome of its deliberations public'.[14] The practice of the UK's Monetary Policy Committee (MPC), created by the Blair government, which set British interest rates, was to publish its voting records, a practice criticised by Wim Duisenberg (see Exhibit 10.2) as leading to 'increased uncertainty'.[15] Yet the British Finance Minister Gordon Brown insisted that:

> People will want to know why a decision has been made. They will want to know what is the likely effect on their economy . . . It is important for reasons of transparency and accountability, and therefore shared understanding of what is happening, that the proper and full reasons for decisions are given.[16]

Ensuring transparency and accountability remains difficult at the systemic level, in part because very few decisions that set EU policy are taken by policy generalists. The systemic level is dominated by ministers, Commissioners, MEPs and others who are policy specialists. The fragmentation of EU governance starts here. Yet policy innovation increasingly requires co-ordination across traditional policy sectors. Thus separate, linked, compatible decisions must be cajoled out of different versions of the Council. Responsibility for co-ordinating the Council's work clearly must fall to some authority that is more continuously engaged in EU matters than the European Council, and more politically weighty than COREPER. The problem is that the General Affairs Council has become increasingly unable to co-ordinate the work of the Council. By 1998, Delors spoke for many in complaining, 'We are confronted now with a situation that cannot last. No one is in control.'[17]

Proposals to create some kind of 'super-Council', perhaps consisting of vice-prime ministers or the personal representatives of prime ministers, began to gain ground. The problems of representation in a 'super-Council' were thorny, particularly given the abundance of coalition governments in the EU and prime ministers and vice-prime ministers from different political parties. The best reasons for thinking they would, eventually, be surmounted were EMU, which clearly demanded more cross-policy co-ordination, and enlargement, which threatened political drift in an EU of far more diverse national preferences.

The EU's expanding external policy responsibilities also pushed in this direction. Part of the rationale for a 'super-Council' was that the EU would be more consistent and forceful as an international actor if foreign ministers were free to focus exclusively on external policy. As we have seen (especially in trade policy) internal EU policy agreement is often more difficult to achieve than agreement with third countries. The EU thus not only requires some body that can co-ordinate its internal policies, but one that can reconcile the Union's internal policies with its external commitments.

Even if the EU of the 21st century finds ways to become a more cohesive system of governance, it is likely to find that other patterns of decision-making that we have highlighted will persist and endure. One is the interinstitutional dynamic of setting policy. As we have seen, the Council does not, as intergovernmentalists sometimes assume, set policy by itself in many sectors. In some, such as competition policy, the Commission has explicit and primary powers (as in policing mergers) to set policy. Under co-decision, nothing may be agreed at the 'policy decision point' without the agreement of the European Parliment (EP).

Inevitably, the difficulty of aggregating interests and shaping policies to the point where interinstitutional consensus emerges means that stalemate is frequent. The problem will be, if anything, worse after eastern enlargement. Breaking the logjam often requires high-level intervention to alter institutions or decisions rules, or strike package deals. Yet the EU has another weapon against inertia. The power of the internal market – the largest in the capitalist world – often *forces* the EU to make decisions, thus overcoming its innate tendency to delay decisions. In the case of 'novel foods', imports of Japanese cars, and packaging waste, the EU had no choice but to make a decision, *any* decision, because the status quo was unsustainable. In such cases, the Commission is usually empowered.

We have seen that the role of the Council presidency may also be accentuated under these circumstances. Whether the EU moves towards some system of 'team presidencies' after eastern enlargement or preserves the existing system of rotating the presidency every six months, it is clear that the Council presidency system is an essential lubricant in EU decision-making. In particular, it brings home civil servants into the 'game' of Brussels-based decision-making in a way that is both valuable and difficult to do in any other way.

The many cases we have uncovered of Council presidencies compromising national interests for the sake of a 'deal' is indicative of a wider point: the EU is a highly consensual system, to the extent that most EU policy outcomes 'are second choice for all participants' (Marks *et al*. 1996a: 372). Put another way, there are very few 'home runs' hit in EU decision-making, or cases in which one Member State, interest group or EU institution gets everything it wants without having to compromise. Even what Héritier (1996) calls 'qualified home runs' are 'hit' very rarely, if ever.[18] EU decision-making almost never produces 'winner take all' outcomes, and they become increasingly unlikely each time the EU enlarges.

Still, experienced students of politics in national settings might well ask: how is *any* important EU policy ever 'set', even in a Union of 15 Member States, given its diffusion of power, lack of a 'government', and sectoral fragmentation? Moreover, does not the systemic level feature, in somewhat weaker form, the same barriers to decision which exist at the super-systemic level: multiple veto points and a strong emphasis on consensus?

The answer seems to be, first, that process is important and sometimes even dominant: EU decision-making socialises actors to compromise in order to reach consensus. It is tempting to argue that *process* matters more than *outcome* at the systemic level. In other words, the content of policies may be less important than the process by which they are agreed (see especially Chapter 6). When actors become socialised to one another, to bargaining by a set of rules (formal or informal) and to giving ground in order to strike a 'deal', they begin to view the process as natural, normal and applicable to the next issue which arises. Put simply, co-operation becomes 'institutionalised' when 'individuals repeatedly interact, when they have a great deal of information about each other, and when small numbers characterise the group' (North 1990: 12).

Of course, *the* key resource at the systemic level is skill in constructing coalitions. Interests must somehow be aggregated, particularly by 'finding and maintaining a collective identity' (Fligstein 1997: 398). The nature of the collective identity may vary: it may be national (the 'France–Commission nexus'), institutional (as in COREPER) or political (the socialist party 'cohort'), but the EU's policy structures are constructed in such a way as to make interest aggregation more likely and feasible within policy *sectors*. Thus policy specialists in agriculture, trade or monetary policy in the EU's various institutions bargain with each other on the assumption that deals struck between them will have positive-sum outcomes for their sector. Meanwhile, decisions taken at a higher political level (by the General Council or the college of Commissioners) are less controllable by sectoral specialists. In the language of institutional theory, policy specialists organise their policy 'field' into a 'frame', and as it 'begins to cohere . . . they act to propagate that frame and the social order it implies' (Fligstein 1997: 403).

Thus we end up with a theoretical explanation for both continuity and change at the systemic level. The power of path dependency in EU decision-making reflects the ability of actors to defend the status quo in their sector, particularly by appealing to the sanctity of past bargains or their sector's contribution to European unity. Cynically, we might conclude that the most organised EU policy 'frames' defend 'haves' from threats posed by 'have-nots', and thus prevent policy change. However, the EU offers considerable scope for rewriting the rules. Its institutions remain fundamentally experimental and offer 'a hospitable framework for evolutionary change', facilitating 'new bargains and compromises between the players' (North 1990: 89–90). We have seen that it is sometimes possible for 'challenger groups' to propose 'rules to reorganize the field. Their ability to do so will depend on their being able to convince a larger number of actors that changing the rules is in their interests' (Fligstein 1997: 403). The recent history of the EU offers examples of coalitions that have successfully 'jumped' the systemic level of EU decision-making and mobilised opinion in support of history-making decisions, which in turn made policy change possible. The European Round Table of Industrialists (ERT) clearly did so in the case of the 1992 project, as did the environmental lobby prior to the Maastricht Treaty.

It is difficult to be very precise, in theoretical terms, about what causes 'policy windows' to appear which allow political agents to challenge the EU's status quo. However, we *can* see that the dichotomy between 'exogenous shock' and path dependency explanations of the EU's history is a rather artificial one. Exogenous shocks – competitive advances by Japanese high-tech industries or the Chernobyl nuclear accident – clearly influence decision-making at the super-systemic level. Path dependency helps explain why, at the *systemic* level, EU policy usually does not change very radically or often.

Of course, eastern enlargement is, in many ways, incompatible with the 'policy path' on which the EU has been set in many sectors. However, eastern enlargement is unlikely to alter the present pattern of shifting coalitions between EU policy sectors. As Winkler (1998: 403) argues, 'there is no fixed coalition structure in the EU. Different coalition structures simultaneously exist for different issue areas and, moreover, coalition structures change over time'. Thus there is no Franco-German alliance on food policy, but a traditionally solid one on the CAP. The Netherlands and the UK are allies on most external trade questions, but not bananas.

It is safe to assume that shifting coalitions will continue to be a primary feature of an enlarged EU, with the Central and Eastern Europe countries (CEECs) voting with poorer states on many issues (internal market, cohesion policy) and, say, Germany on others (CFSP, border controls). In short, eastern enlargement is likely to continue to reinforce the EU's sectoral fragmentation. It will also create a structure for decision-making in which effective agents will require even more sophisticated skills to coax policy deals which leave all at least 51 per cent happy.

Policy Networks: Agency Begins at 'Home'

Arguably, the ubiquity of policy networks in EU decision-making reflects a more general shift in international relations 'away from the state – up, down, and sideways – to supra-state, sub-state, and, above all, non-state actors' (Slaughter 1997: 183). The result, according to Keohane (1998: 93) is a new 'transgovernmental society in the form of networks amongst individuals and non-governmental organizations'. The problem is that governance by policy networks is not very democratic: the same type of 'democratic deficit' which plagues the EU is becoming visible in 'many of the world's most important international institutions' (Keohane 1998:91).

If we are right to assume that much EU decision-making effectively occurs informally within policy networks, then such normative concerns inevitably arise. One of the fundamental problems of governance in a 'differentiated polity' is ensuring that policy specialists do not govern in ways that violate the collective interests of the polity. Specialised expertise is a considerable barrier to entry to most EU policy networks. Perhaps the primary lesson of the 'beef crisis' (Exhibit 5.2) is that all the political will in the world often cannot shift many EU decisions made on the basis of technocratic expertise. The indignant response of Friends of the Earth, who were highly successful in mobilising opposition to the 'Novel Foods Regulation', shows that political agency at the sub-systemic level requires considerable technical expertise:

> Roundup (of which the active ingredient is glyphosate) is NOT used in conjunction with the genetically modified maize 'Bt 176', which is, in fact, marketed by Novartis, NOT Monsanto. As most people involved in the GMO debate will know, the Novartis 'Bt 176' maize (in addition to being insect-resistant and carrying an antibiotic marker gene) is resistant to another chemical, gluphosinate.[19]

The highly technical content of EU policy reinforces fragmentation at the sub-systemic level. The problems of trying to construct an EU rural policy in the face of the competing agendas of CAP, cohesion and environmental policy networks is indicative. Even in trade policy, where the EU has clear incentives to speak with a single voice, battles are rife between trade and agriculture policy networks and their 'sherpas'. Note Franz Fischler's bitter 1997 attack on the WTO's lack of 'clear democratic controls', a remark which reportedly left Leon Brittan 'incandescent with rage'.[20]

One technique for overcoming fragmentation and legitimising bargaining which otherwise would take place in backrooms is to assemble broad, 'formal' policy networks and make their memberships and decisions public. The EU has far more such forums now than in the past and, in important ways, is a more 'transparent' polity (see Peterson 1995c). The Bangemann Group, Social Dialogue and European Science and Technology Assembly are all indicative of efforts to achieve more transparent interest mediation as policy is formulated. But they also show that the Commission continues to retain 'virtually a free hand in creating new networks' (Marks *et al.* 1996a: 359).

More formalised, purpose-built policy networks, along with an expanded EU policy remit, means that interest groups must 'fight for tickets'
or admission to such forums. Actors that fail must find innovative ways to
influence their deliberations without achieving actual membership. As one
experienced Brussels lobbyist observed:

> The most important change that has occurred in recent years in Brussels is the
> growth of 'secondary lobbying'. It's a consequence of the increased crowding,
> increased pressure on the 'ear time' of people in the EU's institutions. It also has
> occurred because the nature of the issues has become more extrinsic, rather than
> purely technocratic . . . Secondary lobbying means not only lobbying
> institutions, but lobbying other 'players': other business groups, consumer
> groups, green groups. People who you know have the ears of the institutions.[21]

Yet actors who enjoy such access tend to have entry to specific, policy-
concerned segments of the EU. Rarely does any lobbyist achieve 'membership' of multiple policy networks in different sectors. Secondary lobbying
is essential in a system where influence is wielded quite narrowly.

Of course, the actors with the 'broadest' influence across a range of EU
policy sectors are the Member States themselves (see Grande 1996; Kohler-
Koch 1996). It is plausible to believe that the EU 'strengthens the state' at
the sub-systemic level, and privileges public over private actors. Formally,
at least, only the EU's Member States are powerful at every level of EU
decision-making, and in every policy sector. Consequently it is clear that
policy networks effectively prepare the ground for policy-setting only
when they offer adequate representation to national interests. Recent
evidence suggests that most Council working groups contribute to 'network[s] with a clear focus' (Beyers and Dierickx 1998: 313), while also
introducing an element of intergovernmentalism into bargaining within
them. However, crucially, it is the EU's institutions – the Commission, the
Council presidency and General Secretariat – that occupy 'the hub of the
informal communication network[s]' (Beyers and Dierickx 1998: 313).
Actors from these institutions are at the 'hub' of most policy networks,
primarily because they have privileged access to information. Moreover,
intergovernmentalism within policy networks is tempered by the power of
sectoral interests, which often 'round off' the rough edges of national
identities.

In particular, the EU's growing external policy responsibilities give
specialised policy networks powerful incentives to become more integrated, decisive, and capable of mitigating the Union's internal political
divisions. We have noted, particularly in chapter 9, the fundamental
differences between decision-making in pillars I and II, and the problems
of extending the unity that has given rise to, say, monetary union to

traditional questions of foreign policy. The EU is far from having a truly 'common' foreign policy or a single 'foreign service', yet the creation of the Euro has effects here, too. Witness the convening of a 1998 conference bringing together all 111 heads of the European Commission's external delegations with external affairs Commissioners, the EP and officials in the relevant Directorates General (DGs) to discuss how to promote the single currency abroad. By this time, the EU and its Member States were under new pressures to exploit the Commission's external 'reach', with 128 delegations and offices world-wide, to maximise the Union's diplomatic clout.[22] The creation of the Euro, eastern enlargement and diplomatic initiatives such as the Barcelona process in the Mediterranean region provide new incentives for EU diplomats, regardless of their national or institutional affiliation, to co-operate.

More generally, in 'internal' policy networks as much as external ones, we have found that the EU does not empower only one kind of actor at the sub-systemic level. Increasingly, it gives voices to 'progressive', forward-thinking political forces which might not get a hearing in national systems of government.[23] Especially where co-decision applies and the EP has the most 'pull', the Union offers more effective representation to consumer, environmental and social interests than it ever has before, including representation at the sub-systemic level.

On the other hand, most of the EU's agenda remains fundamentally neo-liberal, thus privileging narrow interests over broad ones, and producers over consumers. The Commission's (1998f) attempts to put flesh on the bones of EU social policy, such as through its multi-annual 'Social Action Programmes', have resulted in empty exhortations more often than concrete new policies. One attempt by the EU's talented Commissioner for consumer affairs, Emma Bonino, to impose a ban on phthalates – potentially dangerous chemicals contained in children's toys – unleashed furious lobbying by the European chemicals policy network. The initial result was a feeble Commission opinion, which merely urged EU governments to carry out their own studies on the matter. Consumer lobbyists insisted that the incident 'show[ed] how powerful the industrial lobby is. No action is going to be taken until there are corpses on the table. The Commission is politically bankrupt in terms of consumer protection'.[24]

Of course, the relatively narrow concern of the EU with promoting trade limits the range of interests that are welcome participants in EU decision-making. Most sectors feature policy networks which are dominated by elites, feeding the claim that the EU suffers from an 'advocacy void' (Aspinwall 1998). However, the nature of EU governance is constantly changing. Most of the most important changes in the 1990s have rendered it, on balance, more accessible to European citizens, not less.

Conclusion

We conclude by posing two final questions. The first is methodological: how well does our framework for analysis work? The second is substantive: how durable is the European Union?

Our framework is synthetic, combining insights from a range of theoretical models and implicitly rejecting the claim that any tells us 'all we need to know'. It has already provoked plenty of criticism. Armstrong and Bulmer (1998: 42) argue that 'All levels of decision-making require an institutional framework . . . therefore new institutionalist analysis should simply be adjusted to take account of the different scope of the decisions concerned.' Rhodes *et al.* 1996: 374) applaud the 'common-sense appeal' of our model but complain that it is 'difficult to apply consistently' because its 'criteria are broad'. In particular, they criticise the distinction between history-making and policy-setting decisions, on the grounds that it resurrects 'the means and ends distinction with all its known ambiguities and problems'. Warleigh (1998: 10) describes our framework as 'something of a watershed in EU theory, being located at the interface of IR [international relations] and comparative politics approaches'. Yet he argues that 'it is subject to its own problems (mixing approaches from different academic traditions, difficulties in combining macro and micro theories)'. For him, the 'problem of competing truths' is endemic to synthetic theory, which becomes 'reducible to the dominant perspective which informs any scholar attempting to make it' (Warleigh 1998: 9).

Our framework also steps into the firing line of critics who claim that 'policy networks are unable to deploy any theoretical power in explaining policy process and policy outcome' (Börzel 1998: 354). Policy network analysis is dismissed as 'much too vague', with some scholars claiming that only in cohesion policy 'does the term "network" seem appropriate' (Lane 1997: 206). Peters (1998b: 26) is not alone in urging that 'theoretical meat must be put on these strong metaphorical bones' (see also Le Galés and Thatcher 1995).

We have tried to meet these criticisms. We have shown that one level of decision-making, particularly the systemic, is far more 'institutionalised' than others. We have offered clear, simple criteria to categorise different types of EU decision, specifying, for example, that history-making decisions are choices which determine, fundamentally, the way the Union works. They implicate the very highest political levels and – because they are transformative – they concern both means and ends. Decisions at the systemic level are nearly always about ends, while most 'policy-shaping' decisions are about means. We see virtues in 'mixing approaches from different academic traditions', particularly given the traditional dominance of European integration studies by IR scholars. We are not sure what our 'dominant perspective' is, but certainly do not feel shackled by 'competing truths'. Following Sbragia (1993), we view liberal intergovernmentalism as a plausible theory of EU bargaining, while neo-functionalism (usually) helps explain change in the structural context of EU decision-making. It seems silly to declare one or the other the 'winner' in some imaginary competition.

Policy network analysis tells us little about *formal* policy process, but it helps us explain why and how formal process is sometimes trumped by informal bargaining. Many policies that we have studied were 'shaped' in important ways by policy networks that were able to load the decision-making process in favour of some options over others. Certainly, quite a lot of work on policy networks has been quite vague, and we have tried to be 'sharper'. We have no doubt that policy networks exist outside the realm of cohesion policy. Thus far, there exists no predictive theory of policy networks, but we have tried to put 'theoretical meat on metaphorical bones'. In particular, we have contrasted policy communities (as in the CAP) with issue networks (in, say, environmental policy) by identifying the factors that produce these different structures (primarily resource dependencies) and exploring the implications for policy outcomes. We would challenge any researcher investigating the European Union to deny that policy networks (or something like them) are an essential form of EU governance. Our work suggests that policy network analysis is 'an indispensable part of any political scientist's toolkit' (Rhodes *et al.* 1996: 385), specifically for understanding the EU's murky and underresearched sub-systemic level. It does not *give* us many answers, but directs our attention to where many answers may be found.

Our second, substantive question arises from the view, expressed inter alia by the British Foreign Secretary, Robin Cook, that the 'high tide of European integration has passed'.[25] Put another way, by the Danish Prime Minister Pol Nyrup Rasmussen, there exist no 'big decisive new issues in the EU requiring new treaties ... There will always be elderly gentlemen who dream of great projects, but do not necessarily have the support of the people'.[26] Particularly given the EU's lack of democratic legitimacy, perhaps EMU will be the last 'great project' of European integration. Eastern enlargement certainly renders new ones difficult.

It is impossible not to be struck by the EU's fragility as it enters the 21st century. EMU and enlargement have much in common: both pose profound new challenges and risks to the European Union. The basic question arises: is the EU *safe*?[27] In other words, is this fundamentally experimental, unevenly institutionalised and frequently crisis-ridden polity durable enough to withstand new and profound challenges and responsibilities?

History is littered with instances when international co-operation broke down under pressure. In particular, a traditional international relations paradigm lends credibility to claims such as Helmut Kohl's that sustaining European integration is a 'matter of war and peace', or Martin Feldstein's (1997) assertion that armed conflict could result from the collapse of EMU (see Moravcsik and Nicolaïdis 1998: 36). Yet the EU has institutionalised co-operation on a historically unprecedented scale for more than 40 years. The Union is unlikely to fall apart, but far more likely to stagnate and become immobilised without institutional and policy reforms, and far more radical ones than the EU is used to agreeing. The argument of one of the first political scientists ever to investigate European integration remains valid:

> While it does not seem likely that anyone will break up the Community . . . the danger of stagnation through inability to take key decisions is a real one. The ponderous Community decision-making process could overheat: package deals and brinkmanship tactics by governments and the Commission could lead to an accumulation of frustrations and ultimately to the collapse of the system. But nobody desires such an outcome for nobody would gain from it, not even those who are most unhappy with the present orientation of the Community. (Lindberg 1965: 80)

Those who are 'most unhappy' with the present orientation of the EU inevitably highlight its lack of democratic credibility. The 'new governance' school, which argues that majoritarian democracy is impossible at the EU level anyway (so why bother?), sometimes seems content in its assumptions simply because there are few violent, anti-EU citizen protests. Yet it probably remains true, as Helen Wallace suggests (1997: 4), that the Union's 'durability is a function of whether the results it produces are worthwhile to the participants; the process is more results-dependent than habit-dependent'. The new governance school performs the valuable service of seeking ways to improve the quality of the EU's 'results', or its policies. But in judging the *quality* of policy, surely one important criterion must always be how many actors have a voice in shaping it. We have been struck by how few actors sometimes shape, even make, important EU policy decisions. The EU's 'backbone' is firmly intergovernmental and, in key respects, elite-dominated.

Elite actors who dominate EU decision-making have become socialised to a permanent system of bargaining to which they are 'locked in'. At times, the system moderates the naked pursuit of national interests only marginally, but there are costs for Member States who blatantly trample the 'Community interest' in seeking national advantage. The point was illustrated in the small hours of the morning at a press conference, when a weary Jacques Chirac tried to justify his decision to insist on a French candidate as the first President of the ECB (see Exhibit 10.2): 'One has to defend one's own interests . . . we are in a system of Europe of nations where each nation defends its interests.' Sitting at his shoulder, a worried Dominique Strauss-Kahn, the French Finance Minister, scrawled a note and passed it to Chirac, prompting the French President to amend his comment: 'a Frenchman isn't there to defend French interests but to run the money'.[28]

Our *tour d'horizon* of EU decision-making may leave many readers thinking that the Union is not only democratically deficient, but also not very efficient. Many of its procedures seem undemocratic, indefensible or unsustainable (or all three). The reader who draws this conclusion might wish, however, to stop and consider how 'young' the EU is as a polity, and how recently it has been transformed from 'a system essentially concerned with the *administration of things* to one concerned with the *governance of people*' (Shackleton 1997: 70).

It also is worth recalling how decisions about relations between European states were made before the EU existed. We are satisfied to give McDonagh (1998: 17), a practitioner long at the centre of EU decision-making, the final word (almost): 'The decision-making mechanisms of the European Union are, of course, quite hilarious, but not quite as funny as the centuries of war which preceded them.' Warts and all, the EU remains the most successful experiment in international co-operation in modern history, and it is likely to remain so.

Notes

Introduction

1. We are grateful to David Allen for his thoughtful comments on this point. The EU's governing Treaties also change frequently. When we refer to 'the Treaty' in this book, we generally mean the consolidated version of the EU and EC Treaties incorporating the changes made by the Amsterdam Treaty. Even the name of the international organization to which 'the Treaty' gives life has changed repeatedly. We follow the convention of consistently calling the EU by its most recent name. Finally, of course, the EU has recently changed its basic unit of account. We provide all monetary figures in Euros, even in (the majority of) cases where we refer to amounts which pre-date EMU and previously existed in ECUs (which became Euros at a rate of 1:1 on 31 December 1998).
2. In choosing this method of presentation, we have been inspired by Norman Davies' (1996) magisterial, single-volume history of Europe.
3. We have benefited from discussion of this point with William Wallace and Gary Marks.
4. We welcome comments, suggestions and criticism:
   jcms@gla.ac.uk *or* eeb1@stir.ac.uk.

Chapter 1   Making Sense of EU Decision-Making

1. Majone (1996b: 265) cites French *Conseil d'Etat* statistics, from the early 1990s when the EU's legislative output was at its peak, and concludes that Delors' prediction does 'not lack empirical support'. Hooghe and Marks (1997: 25) concur that Delors' prediction 'has a solid basis in reality', while cautioning that 'such data should be evaluated carefully'. What is entirely unambiguous is that far less than 80 per cent of social legislation was decided at the EU level by the late 1990s.
2. Emphasis added. For our purposes, 'supranational' means transcending national boundaries, authority or interests.
3. We dismiss the notion that the EU is a 'state', or that it is in the process of eclipsing the nation-state (Joerges 1991; Peterson 1997). The EU is, put simply, one level for decision-making among several for governing Europe.
4. However, a variety of works have appeared with 'decision-making' in their titles or sub-titles. See Bulmer and Wessels (1987), Keohane and Hoffmann (1991), Kirchner (1992).
5. The simple lesson of IR scholarship on 'levels of analysis' is that explaining change in international relations tends to require explanations which focus on at least three levels of analysis: individual leaders, individual states and the international system as a whole. See also Waltz (1954).

6. We are grateful to Simon Bulmer for helping us to sharpen our thinking on this issue.
7. We are grateful to Nick Ziegler for helping us to sharpen this point.
8. Interview, Brussels, 26 October 1995.
9. Dick Leonard in *Financial Times*, 17 September 1998.
10. Quoted in *European Voice*, 5–11 December 1996.
11. The strength of Pierson's account – its ambition to be a general explanation of EU decision-making – is also its major weakness. It criticises LI for focusing overmuch on 'history-making' decisions, but then posits theoretical arguments (if not a general theory) which, apparently, apply to *any* EU decision. For example, the insight that 'long term effects are often heavily discounted' (Pierson 1996: 135) seems, logically, to apply to decisions which set policy more than decisions which 'make history' (by, for example, changing the EU's institutions), since the short-term political benefits of the former are likely to outweigh those of the latter.
12. There are perhaps more analyses of the Amsterdam Treaty than it really deserves (see Devuyst 1999; Ludlow 1997; Moravcsik and Nicolaïdis 1998, 1999; Peterson and Jones 1999).
13. A treaty is not a constitution: the former is an agreement between governments, while the latter is usually taken to mean an agreement between a government and its citizens.
14. Interview, Brussels, 7 October 1997.
15. Interview, Brussels, 8 October 1997.
16. This distinction is a useful one but it cannot be applied strictly to the EU given conventional usage of the term 'EU institutions' to refer to the Commission, Council, EP and so on. See Pollack (1997a: 99).
17. QWERTY is the 'word' formed by reading laterally across a computer keyboard starting with the letter 'Q' in the upper left-hand corner. This peculiar organisation of letters became standardised when typewriters began to be mass-produced in the early 20th century and has persisted to this day, even though it is not the most efficient means to fast or accurate typing (see David 1985). Keyboards designed specifically for people who suffer from repetitive strain injury often offer a 'non-QWERTY' layout option, which causes less strain on the user.
18. For this analogy we are grateful to Simon Gage (to whom we apologise for using it!).
19. It seems unfortunate that much of the policy literature treats policy network analysis and new institutionalism as branches of the same approach (Rhodes 1995; Lowndes 1996).
20. Article 155 prior to the Amsterdam Treaty. Emphasis added.
21. Implementation is a crucial part of the EU policy process, and 'post-decisional' politics clearly matter (see Jordan 1997), but we consider implementation mostly to be beyond the scope of our study. We do note that there is good evidence to suggest that there is more variety in the implementation of EU policy between sectors than between states, which may be taken as supportive of a policy networks approach.

22. This exhibit draws heavily on Peterson (1997) and has benefited considerably from comments from Michael Shackleton.
23. Article 189b prior to the Amsterdam Treaty.
24. Andrew Moravcsik suggested this form of words in his contribution to a panel on policy networks at the European Community Studies Association conference in Seattle, Washington in May 1997.
25. By 1998, negotiations were under way with 12 applicant states, although six (Cyprus, the Czech Republic, Estonia, Hungary, Poland and Slovenia) received 'fast-track' treatment and others (Bulgaria, Latvia, Lithuania, Malta, Romania and Slovakia) began negotiations on 'preparations for accession'.
26. Quoted in *Financial Times*, 19 October 1998.
27. Quoted in *European Voice*, 30 July–5 August 1998.

Chapter 2   Institutions, Rules, Norms

1. This introductory section draws heavily on Peterson and Jones (1999).
2. For definitional purposes, *agents* are actors that exert power or produce effects in EU decision-making. *Agency* is the act of exerting such power and tangibly affecting outcomes. *Structure* is the pattern of organisation in EU governance, particularly the institutions and formal decision rules set out in the EU's treaties or other written agreements (such as interinstitutional agreements, institutional rules of procedure, and so forth) or accepted by convention.
3. For reasons of space, we leave it to George (1996: ch. 2) and especially Nugent (1994: pt 2) to explain the roles of the Court of First Instance, Economic and Social Committee, Committee of the Regions, Court of Auditors and European Investment Bank.
4. Sometimes, as Bonvicini and Regelsberger (1987: 162) observe, presidency conclusions are so detailed that they may be transformed directly into Community law.
5. The European Council has the prerogative to 'reconstitute' itself as the Council of Ministers to take a legally binding decision. The phrase 'the Council' generally refers to the Council of Ministers, and not the European Council.
6. Notably, one of the first acts of the new Social Democrat-led German government elected in 1998 was to shift most responsibility for EU policy coordination away from the Economics Ministry to the Finance Ministry, thus creating the potential for more national interest-oriented German diplomacy in the EU.
7. Interview, Copenhagen, 5 January 1996.
8. Delors, quoted in *Financial Times*, 20 May 1998.
9. Article 138b prior to the Amsterdam Treaty. Of course, the Council has long enjoyed the same prerogative under Article 208 (152 prior to Amsterdam).
10. Interview, Brussels, 16 November 1995.
11. Interview, Brussels, 17 July 1997.
12. Interview, Brussels, 9 February 1994. Interestingly, this official later himself became a member of *cabinet*. Asked to reaffirm the veracity of his previous

statement on the role of *cabinets*, he responded, 'Yes, it is still true. Maybe they are more like mini-COREPERS, but nothing has changed.' Interview, Brussels, 11 October 1995.

13. As a caveat, representatives of interest groups are most prevalent in advisory committees, which are relatively 'upstream' in the EU's policy process, whereas the most powerful 'downstream' committees – those closest to the 'policy decision point' – consist almost exclusively of national officials.

14. For example, the EP's Energy and Research Committee met on 26 January 1994 at a crucial stage in the negotiations on the Framework IV research programme. In an exchange with MEPs, the President-in-Office of the Research Council, the Greek Industry Minister (and future Prime Minister) Konstantinos Simitis, was asked by one (German) MEP whether there was anything the Council could do about the 'recent increase in the number of millionaires in Europe'.

15. Precise totals are disputed. See Nugent (1994: 309), Westlake (1994a: 39), Wallace and Young (1996), Earnshaw and Judge (1997).

16. Article 30 prior to the Amsterdam Treaty.

17. Article 100 prior to the Amsterdam Treaty.

18. Here we seem to have a case of a decision that made history, but did *not* preoccupy the highest political levels. However 1979 was back in the 'days when integrationist advances were given a favourable welcome by well-disposed elites and were ignored by the vast majority of the population' (Dehousse 1998: 184). These days seem long gone.

19. In particular, the linkage between the two was enshrined in the Amsterdam Treaty. At Spain's insistence, an annex on institutional reform was included which stated that a change in the composition of the Commission would happen *only* if there was agreement on the reweighting of votes in the Council.

20. The only exception, for very complicated reasons, is Luxembourg, which may stand to gain power.

21. Interview, German Permanent Representation to the EU, Brussels, 26 October 1995. Germany lost an appeal to the ECJ to have the regime declared null in 1993, with the Court finding that the new banana arrangements did not cause 'serious and irreparable damage' to Germany (see Stevens 1996: 346).

22. *The Economist*, 11 October 1997.

23. We are grateful to Lionel Barber for suggesting this point to us.

Chapter 3   The Internal Market

1. Until 1992, the internal market was primarily the responsibility of DG III (Industry).

2. The 'common market' is a concept which, in modern, practical terms, derives from measures which are not mandated in the EU's treaties but which affect the establishment or functioning of unrestricted trade and free movement. The 'internal market' is legally defined in Article 3 as 'characterised by the

abolition, between Member States, of obstacles to the free movement of goods, persons, services and capital'.

3. In practice, the single market is really more about *intra*-industry trade – of the sort that leads to a computer being assembled from parts manufactured by many different suppliers – than about the sort of inter-industry trade which underpins comparative advantage. It is also more about dynamic change, or measures taken by firms to make themselves more competitive, to which intense rivalry is central, than about 'static' comparative advantages. We are grateful to Iain Begg for setting us straight on these points.

4. Interview, Brussels, 26 October 1995.

5. David Petrie, chair of the committee for the defence of foreign lecturers, quoted in *European Voice*, 16–22 July 1998. By this point, the Italian practice had been condemned repeatedly by the EP and in three separate ECJ decisions.

6. By 1996, all continental EU Member States plus Norway and Iceland, as members of the Nordic Passport Union, were members or on the road to becoming members of Schengen. The only exceptions amongst EU members were Ireland and the UK, whose island geographies and concerns about terrorism in Northern Ireland made membership problematic.

7. Article 100 prior to the Amsterdam Treaty.

8. The relevant Treaty article was Article 36 (30 after the Amsterdam Treaty), which allowed restrictions on imports or exports on grounds of 'public morality, public policy or public security', amongst others.

9. See the Commission's 1998 survey of national car prices at http:// europa.eu.int/en/comm/dg04/aid/en/car.html.

10. Cited in *European Voice*, 23–9 April 1998.

11. Quoted in *European Voice*, 20–26 February 1997.

12. We are grateful to Helen Wallace for making this point to us.

13. See *European Voice*, 16–22 April 1998.

14. Articles 85 and 86, respectively, prior to the Amsterdam Treaty.

15. Article 93 prior to the Amsterdam Treaty.

16. Quoted in *European Report*, 15 January 1994.

17. Quoted in *Agence Europe*, 10 March 1994.

18. Quoted in *Agence Europe*, 14/15 March 1994

19. Quoted in *Financial Times*, 13 October 1994.

20. An eclectic array of actors lent their support to the 1992 project. The EP played a crucial role, particularly Altiero Spinelli, one of the Community's original Founding Fathers and the prime mover behind the EP's Draft Treaty on European Union in 1984, which many analysts have viewed as critical to the EU's general relaunch in the period (see Corbett 1987).

21. *Europemballage Corporation and Continental Can Co. Inc.* v. *Commission*, Case 6/72.

22. *British American Tobacco Co. Ltd.* v. *Commission* (142/84) and *R.J. Reynolds Industries Inc.* v. *Commission* (156/84) became 'joined cases' (see Armstrong and Bulmer 1998: 115).

23. Quoted in *Financial Times*, 16–17 December 1995.

24. Quoted in *European Voice*, 29 February 1996.

25. The report is now updated each year. The original survey – COM (96) 520 final – is available at the same web-site as Commission (1998d).
26. Interview, Brussels, 8 October 1997.
27. Emphasis in original. Notably, by late 1998, a new 'Single Market Scoreboard' showed that over 85 per cent of all internal market legislation had been transposed into national law in all 15 Member States. See http:// europa.eu.int/comm/dg15/en/update/score/score1.htm.
28. Prior to Amsterdam, Article 90.
29. European Parliament delegations to the Conciliation Committee, 'Progress report for the second half of 1994', PE 211.522/rev. 2/ann., 1 March 1995.
30. Interview, Brussels, 19 October 1995.
31. A second 'multi-directive' regulating standards for noise, anti-tampering measures, tyres and so on was passed in February 1997 after co-decision. The EP won a variety of concessions, although not enough to satisfy bikers' groups which complained they had been 'betrayed in conciliation' (Milward 1997: 14).
32. Interview, London, 6 June 1996.
33. Quoted in *European Report*, 15 January 1994.
34. Quotes from Barton and Bangemann taken from untranslated transcripts of Parliamentary debate, Strasbourg plenary session, 7 February 1994.
35. *Agence Europe*, 23 March 1994 and interview, EP Secretariat, Brussels, 24 March 1994.
36. Interview, Brussels, 18 September 1996.
37. Letter from Milward published in *European Voice*, 12–18 September 1996. See also Milward (1997).
38. Bernd Thomas of BMW, quoted in *Agence Europe*, 15 January 1994.
39. Interview, Brussels, 31 October 1995.
40. Interview, UK Permanent Representation, Brussels, 5 October 1995.
41. Interview, Brussels, 29 September 1998.
42. Interview, Brussels, 18 October 1995.
43. See report on the Internal Market Council of 27 November 1997 in *Monthly Report on Europe* (EIS), December 1997, p.III.11–14.
44. Unanimous Council votes (leaving aside the UK) remained a prerequisite for policies relating to social security, protection of workers after their dismissal, co-determination, conditions of employment for non-EU nationals, and financial contributions for promotion of employment (except for the European Social Fund).
45. Ironically, Renault was one of the first European multinationals (in 1995) to conclude a voluntary consultative agreement with its workers after the Works Council directive was passed.
46. *Financial Times*, 17 March 1997. The only taxi driver (in Paris) who asked to be interviewed by us for the present study insisted that, in the wake of Vilvoorde, 'Europe, for us, means unemployment.'
47. Quoted in *Financial Times*, 6 June 1997.
48. See *European Voice*, 21–8 March 1996.
49. The Ivory Coast's Minister for Raw Materials, Alain Gauze, quoted in *Financial Times*, 23 October 1997.

50. Quoted in *European Voice*, 30 October–5 November 1997.
51. See EIS, *Monthly Report on Europe*, March 1998.
52. *Financial Times*, 13 September 1994.
53. Quoted in *This Week in Europe*, 7 March 1996, WE/8/96, European Commission Office, London.
54. Stéphane Garelli quoted in *Agence Europe*, 7 September 1995.
55. Table available from http://www.imd.ch/wcy.

Chapter 4   External Trade Policy

1. Strictly speaking, of course, the 'EU' is the 'European Community' on all matters of trade policy, since the relevant treaty articles are all EC articles and the EU is not, strictly speaking, a member of the World Trade Organisation.
2. 'Colbertiste' is a label which, in our experience, French diplomats are often happy to use to refer to themselves. Jean-Baptiste Colbert was a 17th century French minister to Louis XIV who pioneered a 'specially *dirigiste* form of mercantilism' (Davies 1996: 618).
3. Considerable liberalisation did take place in the 1990s, with one study concluding that increased consumer willingness to buy cars made in other EU countries was one of the biggest changes prompted by the 1992 project (see Ernst and Young 1997).
4. John Lawson of Salomon Smith Barney, quoted in *Financial Times*, 8 May 1998.
5. *New York Times*, 12 August 1991.
6. Quoted in *Financial Times*, 9 September 1993.
7. One of the most conspicuous changes caused by the Amsterdam Treaty's renumbering of most EU Treaty articles was that Article 113 (on the CCP) became Article 133. Thus the long-familiar label for one of the EU's most powerful committees, 'the Article 113 Committee', was made moot and the 'Article 133 Committee' was born. For the sake of simplicity (and modernity!), we use Article 133 throughout this chapter, even when the relevant Treaty article was actually 1., 1 the pre-Amsterdam Treaty EU. The same goes for Articles 300 (formerly 228) and 310 (formerly 238).
8. Of course, both the 'common market' and a 'common commercial policy' were prominently featured in the original Treaty of Rome.
9. Quoted in *Financial Times*, 9 September 1993.
10. Quoted in *Le Monde*, 20 September 1993 (our translation).
11. Quoted in *Financial Times*, 12 July 1993.
12. Quoted in Nugent (1994: 390).
13. Nevertheless, Leon Brittan later claimed that 'The unanimous conclusions of the joint Council of September 20 have exorcised the spectre of the internal Community quarrels which had long blocked the negotiations.' Quoted in *Financial Times*, 6–7 November 1993.
14. Article 133 (113 before Amsterdam) specifically states that the Council 'shall act by a qualified majority', although the inclusion of services and intellectual

property in the Round lent credibility to the French argument that they could use their veto. Webber (1998: 579) argues that the Uruguay Road 'should be seen as a victory for France and therefore as evidence that the threat of a national veto has not yet become a "dull weapon" in the EU'.

15. The 'TRIPs' ('trade-related intellectual property') agreement extended global trade rules to the protection of patents, trademarks or copyright. It was a crucial building block of the Uruguay Round, especially as the number of goods embodying intellectual property rights – particularly in high-tech industries and pharmaceuticals – grew enormously in the years prior to the Round, as did incidences of counterfeiting or infringement (see Footer 1998: 327–8).

16. Quoted in Devuyst (1995: 462).

17. The legal uncertainty about representation following the Court's 1994 opinion had still not been formally settled by 1999, with no Code of Conduct yet agreed between the Commission and Council.

18. The bill had extraordinary and perverse effects. One was that one three-year-old boy, a friend of the present authors' son, could have been arrested upon entering the USA under the terms of Helms-Burton because his grandparents had bought him shares in a firm with investments in Cuba. A planned trip to Disneyworld in Florida by the three-year-old had to be postponed pending a political solution to the dispute.

19. Quoted in *Financial Times*, 2 October 1996.

20. Article 235 prior to the Amsterdam Treaty.

21. Article 164 prior to the Amsterdam Treaty.

22. Quoted in *Financial Times*, 21 February 1997.

23. The 10 Asian members of ASEM are Brunei, China, Japan, Indonesia, Malaysia, Singapore, South Korea, the Philippines, Thailand and Vietnam.

24. Here we draw on comments made by Robert Madelin of the European Commission during a presentation he gave to a conference on 'New Dimensions of European Union Commercial Policy' on 17 October 1997.

25. See Eizenstadt's comments as reported in the *Financial Times*, 16 February 1996.

26. While it might seem counterintuitive that private firms might engage in pricing strategies which lead to losses, dumping often occurs when firms want to offload stocks or cut their losses on uncompetitive products. Or they might offer products as 'loss leaders' as a way to increase their market share, perhaps even putting their competitors out of business. Frequently, firms that are caught dumping are state-owned or subsidised, and thus can absorb losses because of government hand-outs.

27. Patrick Messerlin of the *Institut d'Etudes Politiques de Paris*, quoted in *Financial Times*, 20 September 1994.

28. Ultimately, only the UK voted against the proposals when they were approved by the General Affairs Council meeting on 8 February 1994. See *Agence Europe*, 9 February 1994.

29. Interview, Brussels, 11 March 1994.

30. Quoted in *Financial Times*, 27 September 1996.

31. Portugal also voted 'no' in protest over an unrelated matter. Belgium, as the main port through which Germany's bananas travelled, backed liberalisation

but voted for the BTR, as did the Netherlands. The governments of both later protested that they were misled about the proposal.
32. Statement of the Caribbean Banana Exporters Association, quoted in *Financial Times*, 29 July 1998.
33. Quoted in *European Voice*, 16–22 October 1997.
34. Both quoted in *Financial Times*, 2 July 1997. BEUC is the *Bureau Européen des Unions de Consommateurs*.
35. Quoted in *Financial Times*, 17–18 January 1998.
36. The only exception, of course, is the European Economic Area agreement, which gives Norway, Iceland and Liechtenstein (but not Switzerland) full access to the EU's internal market.
37. Interview, Brussels, 11 March 1994.
38. Interview, Brussels, 16 July 1997.
39. Quoted in *Financial Times*, 17–18 September 1994.
40. Quoted in *Financial Times*, 13 July 1998.
41. Interview, Brussels, 16 July 1997.
42. Quoted in *The Guardian Weekly*, 17 November 1996.
43. Quoted in *Financial Times*, 12 May 1996.
44. Quoted in *Financial Times*, 10 December 1996.
45. Commission official quoted in *European Voice*, 2–8 July 1998.
46. Quoted in *Financial Times*, 10 June 1997.
47. Quoted in *Financial Times*, 20 June 1997.
48. Quoted in *Financial Times*, 9 January 1998.
49. Quoted in *Financial Times*, 15 April 1998.

Chapter 5   The Common Agricultural Policy

1. Linked supply and processing industries substantially enhance both the economic and political importance of the agricultural sector (see Grant, 1997b: 21–4).
2. Article 39 prior to the Amsterdam Treaty.
3. We owe this characterisation primarily to Wyn Grant.
4. Interviews with officials in British and German Permanent Representations, Brussels, December 1995.
5. Quoted in *Financial Times*, 8 July 1998.
6. Traditionally, Creutzfeldt-Jakob disease was confined to elderly people, whereas younger people, including children, contracted the new variant.
7. A high rate of BSE in Portugal led to an export ban on Portuguese beef in late 1998.
8. Quoted in *Financial Times*, 17 May 1996.
9. In the event, the ban (except for Northern Irish beef) remained in place until late 1998.
10. Quoting from a 1990 internal memorandum.
11. Prior to the Amsterdam Treaty, Article 37 was 43, Article 95 was 100a.
12. Prior to the Amsterdam Treaty, Article 130r.

13. The 'Mansholt riots' help explain why the Belgian police have always responded since with huge numbers of police and large amounts of riot control equipment to any political demonstration in Brussels.
14. The Cairns group is an alliance of 14 agricultural exporters – including Argentina, Australia, Chile, New Zealand and Canada – which is named after the Australian resort where its delegates first met.
15. Interview with official in UK Permanent Representation, Brussels, 19 October 1994.
16. Quoted in *European Voice*, 30 July–5 August 1998.
17. See 'Survey: agriculture', *European Voice*, 27 February–5 March 1997.
18. In some cases, such as milk quotas, a qualified majority is needed to renew or extend the provisions. We thank Alan Swinbank for making this point to us.
19. This exhibit draws heavily on Peterson and Bomberg (1998).
20. Interview at UK Permanent Representation, Brussels, 7 December 1995.
21. The Commission in 1998 tabled controversial reforms to the EU's wine regime, which included increased subsidies of almost 20 per cent.
22. We are grateful to Wyn Grant for drawing this point to our attention.
23. Quoted in *Financial Times*, 9 July 1998.
24. Quoted in *Financial Times*, 13 October 1998. By this time, the EU provided around 80 per cent of the nearly €7.5 billion paid annually in subsidies to French farmers.
25. Article 100 prior to the Amsterdam Treaty.
26. This exhibit draws heavily on Peterson (1997).
27. Quoted in *European Voice*, 26 March–1 April 1998.

Chapter 6   Cohesion Policy

1. Article 2 of the Maastricht (and Amsterdam) Treaty.
2. Quoted in the *Financial Times*, 18 December 1997.
3. Article 130d prior to the Amsterdam Treaty.
4. After Danish voters refused to ratify the Maastricht Treaty in their June 1992 referendum, the European Council at the Edinburgh summit agreed to offer the Danes certain 'opt-outs' related to EMU, common defence arrangements, citizenship and co-operation on justice and home affairs. Following a 'yes' vote in a second Danish referendum held in May 1993, the Treaty finally came into force in November 1993.
5. Interview, German Permanent Representation, Brussels, 7 December 1995.
6. Interview with senior official in the Commission's Secretariat-General, Brussels, 7 November 1995.
7. Quoted in the *Financial Times*, 21 July 1993.
8. The 1.27 per cent of total gross national product ceiling agreed at the 1992 Edinburgh summit remained.
9. Spanish State Secretary for Europe, Ramon de Miguel, quoted in the *Financial Times*, 18 November 1997.
10. The *Economist*, 10 July 1993.

11. Interview with senior official in the Commission's Secretariat-General, Brussels, 7 November 1995.
12. Interview, German Permanent Representation, Brussels, 7 December 1995.
13. *Financial Times*, 21 July 1993.
14. *Financial Times*, 21 October 1993.
15. Quoted in the *Scotsman*, 30 December 1994.
16. Quoted in the *Financial Times*, 18 December 1997.
17. Interview, 6 November 1995, Brussels.
18. Interview with official in the Permanent Representation of a large Member State, Brussels, 7 December 1995.
19. Interview, Brussels, 14 July 1997.
20. Interview, Brussels, 6 November 1995.
21. EU central governments have charged that CI funding is spread too thinly to have much of an impact, and that CIs either interfere with the internal affairs of Member States or duplicate efforts under way in other EU-funded programmes. These complaints do not emanate only from Britain: German officials (particularly in the Ministry of Finance) often voice similar reservations.
22. Quoted in the *Financial Times*, 28 April 1997.
23. The EP must assent to the general regulations (formerly the framework and co-ordinating regulations) governing the reform of the structural funds included in Agenda 2000.
24. For instance, by providing comfortable 'phasing out' periods for regions set to lose their objective status.
25. The Economic and Social Committee, or 'EcoSoc', is a consultative body which comprises over 200 representatives of socioeconomic interests, such as employers, trades unions, and non-governmental organisations. See George (1996: 26–8).
26. Interview with official in the Commission's Secretariat-General, Brussels, 19 September 1995.
27. Interview with official in the Commission's Secretariat-General, 19 September 1995, Brussels.
28. Previously Article 146.
29. Quoted in Bomberg and Peterson (1998: 232).
30. This central control is near absolute in the case of the Cohesion Fund, which requires neither partnership nor additionality (see Allen 1996a).
31. This exhibit draws heavily on Bomberg and Peterson (1998).
32. Interview, Brussels, 14 July 1997.
33. Interview, UK Permanent Representation to the EU, Brussels, 30 October 1995.
34. Quoted in Bomberg and Peterson (1998: 233).
35. Ansell *et al.* (1997) capture this cross-cutting dynamic with their application of 'dual networks' in which the relationship between any two actors (say, SNA and Commission) is always conditioned by the existence of a second network (say, a domestic network made of up SNAs and central government actors).
36. See *Financial Times*, 28 April 1997.

37. Other explanations for non-spending include the bureaucratic complexity compliance may require or Member States' weak commitment to spending in declining regions. In the Agenda 2000 debate, the underspending of funding was cited by the Netherlands and Germany in support of their argument that planned expenditures of structural funds were too high. See the *Financial Times*, 1 December 1997.
38. See *European Voice*, 5 November 1998.
39. The potentially insatiable appetite of the CEECs for cohesion funding led to a proposal – contained in *Agenda 2000* – to limit any state's receipts from the structural funds to 4 per cent of its total GDP. The limit was defended as justified by the limited capacity of the CEECs to absorb cohesion funding.
40. Quoted in the *Financial Times*, 20 October 1998.

Chapter 7 Environmental Policy

1. The precise number of legislative acts is open to debate and depends on how liberally one defines the term 'environmental legislation'. For contending figures (and definitions) see Haigh (1992), Johnson and Corcelle (1995a), Golub (1996a), McCormick (1998). This confusion underlines the extent to which environmental policy merges with other policy sectors, especially consumer and internal market.
2. The term had already been in vogue for several years, popularised by the World Commission on Environment and Development's Brundtland Report in 1987. The report concluded that economic growth was based overwhelmingly on exploiting finite resources and argued that policy-makers and citizens needed to consider the longer-term consequences of development.
3. Article 235 previous to the Amsterdam Treaty.
4. Interview, Brussels, 3 October 1995.
5. Interview, Brussels, 8 November 1995.
6. The European Environmental Bureau is a pan-European federation representing over 150 national environmental organisations.
7. Quoted in *European Voice*, 30 May 1996.
8. Quoted in *European Voice*, 30 May 1996.
9. Interview, Brussels, 17 November 1995.
10. Interview, Brussels, 17 November 1995.
11. See *European Voice*, 4 June 1998.
12. In many respects, the UK's record at the 'post-decision' or implementation stage is not as poor as that of other Member States, including 'greener states' such as the Netherlands. See Richardson (1996d: 165).
13. For instance, the UK has taken a lead role in pushing for eco-audits, while Germany has resisted such measures (Weale 1996: 603).
14. Geography helps explain this preference. Much of the pollution produced in the UK is either blown to other countries (say, in the form of acid rain which drifts to Scandinavia) or washed away onto other shores.
15. Interview, UK Permanent Representation to the EU, Brussels, 18 October 1995.

16. Quoted in Golub (1996a: 690).
17. Interview, Brussels, 7 December 1995.
18. Interview, Brussels, 27 October 1995.
19. See the remarks of Michael Grubb, member of the Intergovernmental Panel on Climate Change, commenting on the EU's resistance to allowing trade in emission quotas, in the *Financial Times*, 12 June 1997.
20. Andrew Kerr, European Co-ordinator of World Wide Fund for Nature's Climate Change Campaign, 'WWF's Climate News' 23, March 1998, www.panda.org/climate/news.
21. UK Environment minister Michael Meacher, quoted in *ENDS Environment Daily*, 17 June 1998.
22. See *European Voice*, 12-18 June 1997.
23. Integrated pollution control attempts to regulate pollutants released into *all* environmental media (air, water, land) within a single framework (see Skea and Smith 1998).
24. Interview, Brussels, 17 November 1995.
25. Interview, Brussels, 6 December 1995.
26. Articles 100 and 235 prior to the Amsterdam Treaty.
27. The ban on imports was replaced by the introduction of standards of 'humaneness' (such as a shorter 'killing time') and eventual phase-out of such traps.
28. Interview, Brussels, 17 November 1995.
29. Article 100a prior to the Amsterdam Treaty.
30. Quoted in the *Independent*, 8 May 1990.
31. Quoted in Bomberg (1998b:43).
32. In relative terms DGXI's staff (around 490) and budget (around €137 million in 1996) appear to be those of a middle ranking DG. However, over half its staff are temporary, and its budget is small considering the scope of its responsibilities (McCormick 1998).
33. Interview with official in the Permanent Representation of a large Member State, Brussels, 18 October 1995.
34. Interview, member of the Environment Commissioner Carlo Ripa di Meana's *cabinet*, 28 January 1993, Brussels.
35. Interview, UK Permanent Representation to the EU, Brussels, 27 October 1995.
36. Interview, Brussels, 17 November 1995.
37. Interview, Brussels, 29 September 1995.
38. Interview, Brussels, 8 November 1995.
39. This case draws on Bomberg (1998b).
40. Quoted in the *Financial Times*, 29 December 1993.
41. The Industry Council for Packaging and the Environment (INCPEN), European Recovery and Recycling Association (ERRA), Association of Plastics Manufactures in Europe (APME) and the European Organisation for Packaging and the Environment (EUROPEN) were among the most active. In addition to individual lobbying, several packaging and producer groups joined forces under the Packaging Chain Forum (PCF).
42. Interview, Brussels, 14 March 1994.

Chapter 8   Research and Technology Policy

1. This term is used here in its most expansive sense to refer to all activities of the EU which involve the promotion of innovation, including demonstration projects and the deregulation of markets for new technologies.
2. This section draws heavily on Peterson (1996b).
3. Directive 89/552/EEC of 3 October 1989.
4. Quoted in *Agence Europe*, 21–2 February 1994; *European Report*, 26 February 1995.
5. See *European Report*, 26 February 1994.
6. See report on green paper in *Agence Europe*, 26 March 1994.
7. Quoted in *Financial Times*, 3 February 1995.
8. See Philippe Douste-Blazy, the French Culture Minister, quoted in *European Report*, 18 October 1995.
9. Article 130 prior to the Amsterdam Treaty.
10. Article 85 prior to the Amsterdam Treaty.
11. Article 130a, which became 158 after the Amsterdam Treaty.
12. These figures reflect *all* EU spending on research, including financing from the Structural Funds. See Commission (1994a: 243). The relatively small number of EUREKA projects which featured participation by Greece (25), Ireland (14) and Portugal (48) may be grasped by considering equivalent figures for France (256), Germany (234), Switzerland (124) or even Hungary (35). See EUREKA secretariat (1996: 9).
13. By 1998, EUREKA included founding members Norway, Switzerland and Iceland, but also Slovenia, Hungary, Poland, the Czech Republic, Romania, and even Russia.
14. Quoted in Peterson (1993a: 189).
15. Interview, Brussels, 26 February 1995.
16. Dutch EUREKA official, quoted in Peterson (1993a: 188).
17. Interview, Brussels, 20 October 1994.
18. Quoted in EIS, *Monthly Report on Europe*, February 1998, p.III.33.
19. Jack Metthey, quoted in EIS, *Monthly Report on Europe*, November 1997, p.III.31
20. This exhibit is derived mainly from Peterson (1995b).
21. Quoted in *Agence Europe*, 11 March 1994.
22. Interview with member of Leon Brittan's *cabinet*, cited in Peterson (1995b: 401).
23. At the time, the author cited here was a British MEP and vice-chairman of the EP's Energy, Research and Technology committee.
24. Article 90 prior to the Amsterdam Treaty.
25. Iain Vallance, chairman of British Telecommunications, quoted in *Financial Times*, 10 July 1996.
26. The result was a new Treaty Article 16, which recognised the 'place occupied by services of general economic interest in the shared values of the Union as well as their role in promoting social and territorial cohesion'. The new article was significant in view of enlargement, as only about half of all households in the CEECs had a telephone by 1998.

27. Interview, UK Permanent Representation to the EU, Brussels, 18 September 1995.
28. Interview, DG XII, Brussels, 24 February 1994.
29. Interview, DG XII, Brussels, 24 February 1994.
30. Quoted in *European Voice*, 27 June–3 July 1996.
31. Interview, Brussels, 26 September 1995.
32. Interview, Brussels, 15 November 1995.
33. Quoted in EIS, *Monthly Report on Europe*, December 1997, p.III.29.
34. Quoted in *Financial Times*, 27 June 1996.

Chapter 9   The Common Foreign and Security Policy

1. *The Economist*, 14 December 1991.
2. This section draws heavily on Peterson and Sjursen (1998b).
3. *The Economist*, 14 December 1991.
4. A British Foreign Office plan, which clearly bore the fingerprints of the former British Ambassador to the EU, Sir John Kerr, proposed that the WEU essentially be abolished, with its political functions taken over by the EU and its military role shifting to NATO. It also called for the creation of an EU Council of Defence Ministers, which would be able to call on NATO's European forces in European missions.
5. The relatively small Italian-led military force sent to Albania in 1997 was heavily dependent for its effectiveness on a considerable contribution from France (1000 of a total of 6000 troops), particularly given the UK's decision not to take part in the operation.
6. In other words, a positive vote would require a minimum number of votes under QMV by a group of states representing a minimum percentage of the EU's total population.
7. Interview, French Ministry of Foreign Affairs, Paris, 30 June 1997.
8. Later, Italy became a member of the Contact Group, with its admission propitiated by its lead role in the Albanian crisis of 1997.
9. By 1997, the WEU included all EU Member States except Austria, Denmark, Finland, Ireland and Sweden, which themselves were 'associate members' of the defence alliance.
10. Quoted in *Agence Europe*, 6 November 1993. In practice, the Eurocorps – with forces from Germany, France, Luxembourg, Spain and Belgium – remained operationally dependent on American hardware and transport well into the late 1990s. It was never deployed in Bosnia.
11. Quoted in *Agence Europe*, 7–8 March 1994.
12. Two of the best treatments are Woodward (1995) and Zucconi (1996).
13. Quoted in *Financial Times*, 1 July 1991.
14. Interview, UK Permanent Representation to the EU, Brussels, 8 October 1997.
15. This section draws heavily on Peterson (1998).
16. An informal 'Gymnich' meeting of Foreign Ministers (named after the German castle where the first such meeting was held in the 1980s) held under

the 1998 Austrian presidency considered a report which presented a litany of recent GAC violations of official guidelines for EU decision-making. It also criticised Foreign Ministers for tolerating a proliferation of specialised Councils, a concentration of meetings in June and December, their poor preparation, and overcrowding with too many delegates. The potential of the exercise to be a serious review of EU decision-making was, however, limited by the GAC's typical lack of time: time for debate on the report was limited to one morning and one afternoon. See *European Voice*, 3–9 September 1998.

17. Michael E. Smith (1997) found that unanimity 'was not strictly observed' on a directive concerning the clearing of anti-personnel mines, financial sanctions against Bosnia, some disbursement decisions concerning the Bosnian city of Mostar, and a decision prohibiting payments made under contracts subject to the EU embargo against Haiti.

18. Interview, London, 19 August 1997.

19. Interview, British Foreign Office, London, 8 July 1997.

20. The text of the documents is available on the Internet at http://www.cec.lu/en/agenda/tr01.html.

Chapter 10 Conclusion

1. See interview with Volker Stoltz in *European Voice*, 20–26 February 1997. This assertion probably would come as no surprise to Page (1997: 16), who notes Ezra Suleiman's description of the role of the *Grands Corps* in France's domestic administration as 'part of a network within and beyond the administration, which enables them to arbitrate conflicts and co-ordinate policies'. Page (1997: 55) also suggests that France appears to defend its 'national flags' in the Commission's upper administration more effectively than any other Member State.

2. Take, for example, Moravcsik's claim (1995: 622) that 'Where the preferences of supranational authorities are more stable than those of governments . . . the former may be able to act incrementally to increase their power.'

3. Interview, Brussels, 1 May 1996.

4. Interview, London, 19 August 1997.

5. Of course, the ECJ can strike down any decision taken in the name of the Union by any EU institution. However, as we have argued, the ECJ often operates at the same level as the European Council, that is the 'super-systemic' level that transcends the day-to-day operation of the EU as a political system.

6. To illustrate the point, consider the famous case of a Transport Council that nodded through a massive raft of legislation – nearly all as 'A' points – to make the former East Germany part of the EU in 1990 (see Spence 1991).

7. Consider the specific examples Bulmer (1998: 367) uses to illustrate this argument: 'rolling medium-term policy programmes, such as the Framework programmes . . . environmental action programmes and others in areas such as social affairs or equal opportunities, or the Lomé convention'. Arguably, all either do touch the highest political levels of decision-making, or are

essentially declaratory, and thus do not fundamentally change the way the EU works, even if some (such as EAPs) may produce a kind of 'soft law'.

8. An alternative analogy – in some ways, a seductive one — comes from the realm of solid state physics: 'explosive crystallisation'. Sometimes crystals take a very long time to form, but crystallise very quickly (in microseconds) when they do. The result is stunning crystal patterns, bringing order out of 'chaos'. Here is the rub: high-level political deals which unblock impasse and allow EU decision-making to move forward often do *not* result in a new kind of 'order', or one which is more patterned than in the past. A look at the Maastricht or Amsterdam Treaties, with their long lists of protocols, exemptions and annexes, suggests that the ice flow analogy – with chaos emerging out of a kind of order (resulting from political impasse) – is the more apposite one. Thanks to Simon Gage for his advice on this point.

9. Quoted in *Financial Times*, 4 May 1998.

10. Duisenberg's statement to the May 1998 EMU summit as reproduced in *Financial Times*, 4 May 1998, and Duisenberg, quoted in *European Voice*, 14–19 May 1998. On the eve of the Euro's launch, Duisenberg caused uproar by telling *Le Monde* (30 December 1998), when asked whether he would resign after four years, '*La réponse est non*'.

11. We are grateful to Helen Wallace for suggesting this distinction.

12. Interview, *cabinet* of Commission President Santer, Brussels, 29 September 1998.

13. A new Treaty article (17) post-Amsterdam mentioned NATO for the first time ever in the history of EU treaty-making, stating that any EU decisions on defence 'shall respect the obligations of certain Member States, which see their common defence realised in NATO'.

14. This language was contained in a protocol to the Maastricht Treaty.

15. Excerpt from Duisenberg's evidence to the EP in early 1998, quoted in the *Financial Times*, 24 September 1998.

16. Quoted in *European Voice*, 2–8 July 1998.

17. Quoted in *European Voice*, 16–22 July 1998.

18. The metaphor itself seems disposable, given that there is no such thing as a 'qualified home run' in baseball: a batter either touches all bases to score a 'run' or they do not, and there exists no in-between.

19. Gill Lacroix of Friends of the Earth Europe, Biotechnology Programme, in a letter printed in *European Voice* (9–15 June 1998) after the newspaper ran a lengthy feature on the GMO debate.

20. Quoted in *Financial Times*, 5 September 1997.

21. Interview, EU Committee of the American Chamber of Commerce of Belgium, Brussels, 15 September 1994 (quoted in Peterson 1997: 18).

22. By some estimates, the Commission had Europe's fourth-largest network of foreign missions after the UK, France and Germany by the late 1990s, at a time when national spending on foreign affairs generally was falling (see Allen 1998; *European Voice*, 3–9 September 1998).

23. To give a tangible example, the British Minister for Consumer Affairs, Nigel Griffiths, publicly disowned the advice of a government-convened task force of British businesspeople in 1998 on the EU's 'burden of proof' directive,

which proposed that the burden of proof regarding faulty goods should rest with suppliers, not buyers. Griffiths welcomed the EU as a legitimator of his 'robust views on behalf of consumers', particularly as a member of a New Labour government preaching the virtues of deregulation and free enterprise. Quoted in the *Financial Times*, 14 May 1998.

24. Axel Singhofen of Greenpeace, quoted in the *Financial Times*, 2 July 1998.
25. Quoted in *The Economist*, 3 January 1998.
26. Quoted in the *Financial Times*, 29 May 1998.
27. David Allen has posed this precise question in a number of conferences or settings that we have been privileged to attend.
28. Quoted in the *Financial Times*, 4 May 1998.

Guide to Further Reading

Chapter 1

Three recent, stimulating contributions to the theoretical literature – Armstrong and Bulmer (1998), Moravcsik (1998) and Sandholtz and Stone Sweet (1998) – are usefully reviewed by Puchala (1999). Marks *et al.* (1996a), Pierson (1996), Hooghe and Marks (1997) and Wessels (1997a) are also essential. The framework for analysis used throughout the book was first developed in Peterson (1995a). Allison (1971) remains a classic application of decision-making as an approach to studying politics.

Chapter 2

The best general overview of the EU's institutions remains Nugent (1994). The classic work on the European Council, soon to be updated, is Bulmer and Wessels (forthcoming). Hayes-Renshaw and Wallace (1997), read alongside Westlake (1995), gives a comprehensive picture of the Council and all of its offshoots. The long-standing dearth of works on the Commission has recently been filled, perhaps to capacity: see Christiansen (1996), Cini (1996), Cram (1997), Laffan (1997b), Nugent (1997, 1999), Page (1997), and Peterson (1999). There is far less work on the European Parliament, but see Westlake (1994b) and Corbett *et al.* (1995) for overviews. On the ECJ, Dehousse (1998) and Weiler (1993, 1997) are essential. On rules of EU decision-making, see Wallace (1996a). Kirman and Widgrén (1995) and Raunio and Wiberg (1998) offer analysis based on 'power indexes'. Armstrong and Bulmer (1998) provide extensive coverage of norms in EU decision-making.

Chapter 3

When political scientists write on the internal market, they tend to focus on one of three sets of issues. One is the internal market's implications for European institution-building (see Allen 1992; Cameron 1992; Pinder 1993). A second is its effects in specific economic sectors, such as financial securities or pharmaceuticals (Coleman and Underhill 1995; Greenwood 1995b). A third is broad principles or goals of the 1992 project, such as deregulation or 'mutual recognition' of national standards (Majone 1990; Woolcock 1994; Sun and Pelkmans 1995). Some recent work transcends these relatively narrow categories: see Mazey and Richardson (1992), Wallace and Young (1996) and (especially) Armstrong and Bulmer (1998). An enormous amount of information on the internal market, especially progress towards its completion, is available on the European Commission's web-site: http:europa.eu.int/comm/dg15/en.htm

Chapter 4

General treatments of the politics of EU trade policy are thin on the ground. On the Uruguay Round, see Devuyst (1995), Paemen and Bensch (1995) and Woolcock and Hodges (1996). Eeckhout (1994) is strong on the legal implications of EU trade policy, while Moore (1994) offers an interesting (if dated) study of trade policy developments in the early 1990s. Hanson (1998) offers a fresh and provocative analysis.

Chapter 5

Professor Wyn Grant of the University of Warwick maintains a 'CAP web-site' which is almost miraculous in its clarity of analysis. This chapter contains a considerable amount of information obtained from: http://members.tripod.com/ ˜WynGrant/WynGrantCAPpage.html. Non-net surfers should see Grant (1997c), along with Rieger (1996) and Swinbank (1996a, 1996b).

Chapter 6

George (1996, ch. 12) gives a broad overview of the historical development of cohesion policy. Allen (1996a) and Pollack (1995) offer the best intergovernmentalist accounts of cohesion policy formulation, whilst Hooghe (1996b) and Marks *et al* (1996a) examine cohesion policy decision-making in the context of multi-level governance. A focus on sub-national actors is offered by Ansell *et al*. (1997), Bache *et al*. (1996), Bomberg and Peterson (1998) and McAleavey and De Rynck (1997). For thoughtful speculation on the future of cohesion policy, see Hooghe (1998).

Chapter 7

Judge's edited collection (1993a) and Sbragia's overview (1996) cover the primary players and dynamics shaping the development of the EU's environmental policy. Conceptual treatments of environmental policy decision-making include Baker *et al*. (1997), Golub (1996a), Weale (1996) and Zito (1995). Bomberg (1998a) offers an analysis of green parties and NGOs in the decision-making process, whereas the role of particular Member States is emphasised by Andersen and Liefferink (1997) and Lowe and Ward (1998).

Chapter 8

For a general overview of RTD policy, see Peterson and Sharp (1998), which contains an extensive *Guide to Further Reading* of its own. Sandholtz (1992) remains an important piece of work in this area of decision-making.

Chapter 9

Peterson and Sjursen (1998a) contains a variety of different perspectives on the CFSP, with Hill (1998) worth reading carefully. The contribution of each Member State to the CFSP is covered with considerable insight in Hill (1996a). Piening (1997) does a good job of putting the CFSP in the context of EU external policy more generally. Holland (1997) provides detailed assessments of individual EU foreign policy actions.

Chapter 10

Caporaso (1998) and Hix (1998) are both good overviews of the state of play in academic scholarship on the EU. On agency and structure in EU decision-making, see Pollack (1997a). Marks (1996a) and Richardson (1996a) both make cases for an 'actor-centred' perspective on EU decision-making. McDonagh (1998) and Moravcsik and Nicolaïdis (1998, 1999) offer insights into the negotiations on the Amsterdam Treaty.

Bibliography

Adam, G. (1994) 'Euro-conflict over research cash', *Times Higher Education Supplement*, 25 March: 13.

Allen, D. (1992) 'European union, the Single European Act and the 1992 programme', in D. Swann (ed.) *The Single Market and Beyond*, London: Routledge.

—— (1996a) 'Cohesion and structural adjustment', in H. Wallace, and W. Wallace, (eds) *Policy-Making in the European Union*, Oxford: Oxford University Press.

—— (1996b) 'Conclusions: the European rescue of national foreign policy?' in C. Hill (ed.) *The Actors in Europe's Foreign Policy*, London: Routledge.

—— (1996c) 'Competition policy: policing the single market', in H. Wallace and W. Wallace (eds) *Policy-Making in the European Union*, Oxford: Oxford University Press.

—— (1998) '"Who speaks for Europe?": the search for an effective and coherent external policy', in J. Peterson and H. Sjursen (eds) *A Common Foreign Policy for Europe? Competing Visions of the CFSP*, London: Routledge.

Allison, G.T. (1971) *Essence of Decision: Explaining the Cuban Missile Crisis*, Boston: Little, Brown and Company.

Alter, K.J. (1998) 'Who are the "Masters of the Treaty"?: European governments and the European Court of Justice', *International Organization* 52, 1: 121–47.

Alter, K.J. and Meunier-Aitsahalia, S. (1994) 'Judicial politics in the European Community: European integration and the pathbreaking *Cassis de Dijon* case', *Comparative Political Studies* 26, 4: 535–61.

Andersen, M.S. and Liefferink, D. (eds) (1997) *European Environmental Policy: The Pioneers*, Manchester: Manchester University Press.

Andersen, S.S. and Eliassen, K.A. (1996) 'EU-lobbying: between representativity and effectiveness', in S.S. Andersen and K.A. Eliassen (eds) *The European Union: How Democratic Is It?* London and Thousand Oaks: Sage.

Anderson, C. (1995) 'Economic uncertainty and European solidarity revisiting: trends in public support for European integration', in C. Rhodes and S. Mazey (eds) *The State of the European Union Volume 3: Building a European Polity?*, Boulder CO, and Essex: Lynne Rienner and Longman.

Anderson, J. (1990) 'Skeptical reflections on a "Europe of the Regions": Britain, Germany and the ERDF', *Journal of Public Policy* 10: 41–7.

—— (1996) 'Germany and the structural Funds: unification leads to bifurcation', in L. Hooghe (ed.) *Cohesion Policy and European Integration*, Oxford: Oxford University Press.

Ansell, C., Parsons, C. and Darden, K. (1997) 'Dual networks in European regional development Policy', *Journal of Common Market Studies* 35, 3: 347–76.

Armstrong, H. and Taylor, J. (1993) *Regional Economics and Policy*, London: Harvester.

Armstrong, K. and Bulmer, S. (1996) 'United Kingdom', in D. Rometsch and W. Wessels (eds) *The European Union and Member States: Towards Institutional Fusion?*, Manchester: Manchester University Press.

—— (1998) *The Governance of the Single European Market*, Manchester: Manchester University Press.

Armstrong, K. and Shaw, J. (eds) (1998) 'Integrating Law', special issue of the *Journal of Common Market Studies* 36: 2: 147–272.

Arp, H. (1995) *Multiple Actors and Arenas: European Community regulation in a polycentric system – a case study of car emission policy*, PhD thesis, Florence: European University Institute.

Artis, M.J. and Lee, N. (1994) (eds) *The Economics of the European Union*, Oxford and New York: Oxford University Press.

Ashford, D.E. (1982) *Policy and Politics in France: Living With Uncertainty*, Philadelphia: Temple University Press.

Aspinwall, M. (1998) 'Collective Attraction - the New Political Game in Brussels', in J. Greenwood and M. Aspinwall (eds) *Collective Action in the European Union*, London: Routledge.

Aspinwall, M. and Greenwood, J. (1998) 'Conceptualising Collective Action in the European Union: an Introduction' in J. Greenwood and M. Aspinwall (eds) *Collective Action in the European Union*, London: Routledge.

Atkinson, A.B. (1997) 'The Economics of the Welfare State: an Incomplete Debate', *European Economy*, 4, Reports and Studies, Brussels: DG II, European Commission.

Avery, G. (1984) 'The Common Agricultural Policy: A Turning Point', *Common Market Law Review* 21: 481–504.

Babarinde, O. (1995) 'The Lomé Convention: An Ageing Dinosaur in the European Union's Foreign Policy Enterprise' in C. Rhodes and S. Mazey (eds) *The State of the European Union Volume 3: Building a European Polity?*, Boulder, CO and Essex: Lynne Rienner and Longman.

Bache, I., George, S. and Rhodes, R.A.W. (1996) 'The EU, Cohesion Policy and Subnational Authorities in the UK', in L. Hooghe (ed.) *Cohesion Policy and European Integration*, Oxford: Oxford University Press.

Bachrach, P. and Baratz, M.S. (1963) 'Decisions and Nondecisions: an Analytical Framework', *American Political Science Review* 57, 4: 639–57.

—— (1970) *Power and Poverty*, London and New York: Oxford University Press.

Baker, S., Milton, K. and Yearley, S. (eds) (1994) *Protecting the Periphery: Environmental Policy in Peripheral Regions of the European Union*, London: Frank Cass.

Baker, S. Kousis, M. Richardson, D. and Young, S. (eds) (1997) *The Politics of Sustainable Development. Theory, Policy and Practice Within the European Union*, London: Routledge.

Bangemann, M. (1992) *Meeting the Global Challenge: Establishing a Successful European Industrial Policy*, London: Kogan Page.

Barber, L. (1998) 'Life After Boris', *Financial Times*, 15 April: 22.

Baumgartner, F.R. and Jones, B.D. (1993) *Agendas and Instability in American Politics*, Chicago: University of Chicago Press.

Begg, I. (1996) 'Introduction: Regulation in the European Union', *Journal of European Public Policy* 3, 4: 525–35.

—— (1997) 'Reform of the Structural Funds after 1999' *European Policy Paper*, No. 5, July, Center for West European Studies, University of Pittsburgh.

Begg, I. and Peterson, J. (1999) 'Editorial Statement', *Journal of Common Market Studies* 37, 2: 1–12.

Bellier, I. (1995) 'Une Culture de la Commission Européenne?', in Y. Mény, P. Muller and J.-L. Quermonne (eds) *Politiques Publiques en Europe*, Paris: l'Harmattan.

—— (1997) 'The Commission as an Actor: an Anthropologist's View', in H. Wallace and A. Young (eds) *Participation and Policy-Making in the European Union*, Oxford: Clarendon Press.

Benedick, R. (1991) *Ozone Diplomacy. New directions in Safeguarding the Planet*, Cambridge, MA: Harvard University Press.

Benz, A. (1988) 'German regions in the European Union: from joint policy-making to multi-level governance', in P. Le Galès and C. Lequesne (eds) *Regions in Europe*, London: Routledge.

Beyers, J. and Dierickx, G. (1998) 'The working groups of the Council of the European Union: supranational or intergovernmental negotiations', *Journal of Common Market Studies* 36, 3: 289–317.

Bildt, C. (1997) 'The Global Lessons of Bosnia', in PMI (ed.) *What Global Role for the EU?* Brussels: Philip Morris Institute for Public Policy.

Bomberg, E. (1994) 'Policy Networks on the Periphery: EU Environmental Policy and Scotland', *Regional Politics and Policy* 4: 45–61.

—— (1998a) *Green Parties and Politics in the European Union*, London: Routledge

—— (1998b) 'Policy Networks in the EU: Explaining EU Environmental Policy', in D. Marsh (ed.) *Policy Networks in Comparative Perspective*, Milton Keynes: Open University Press.

Bomberg, E. and Peterson, J. (1993) 'Prevention from Above? Preventive Policies and the European Community' in M. Mills (ed.) *The Politics of Prevention and Health Care* Aldershot: Avebury Press.

—— (1998) 'European Union Decision Making: the Role of Sub-National Authorities', *Political Studies* 46, 2: 219–35.

Bonvicini, G. and Regelsberger, E. (1987) 'The Decision-making Process in the EC's European Council', *The International Spectator* 22, 3: 152–75.

Borrell, B. (1995) *EU Bananarama 111*, Policy Research Working Paper 1386, Washington DC: World Bank.

Börzel, T.A. (1998) 'Rediscovering Policy Networks as a Modern Form of Government', *Journal of European Public Policy* 5, 2: 354–9.

Bradley, K.S.C. (1992) 'Comitology and the Law: Through a Glass, Darkly', *Common Market Law Review* 29: 631–721.

Brenton, P., Scott, H. and Sinclair, P. (1997) *International Trade: A European Text*, Oxford: Oxford University Press.

Brittan, L. (1994) 'The world economy after the Uruguay Round', speech delivered at the Centre for European Policy Studies, Brussels, 17 January.

—— (1996) 'New tactics for EU trade', *Financial Times*, 11 November: 20.

Buiges, P., Ilzkovitz, F. and Lebrun, J.-F. (1990) 'The impact of the internal market by industrial sector', *European Economy: Social Europe*, special edition, 3–7.

Buiges, P., Jacquemin, A. and Sheehy, J. (1995) 'European integration and the internal market programme', Brussels: mimeo.

Buitendijk, G.J. and van Schendelen, M.P.C.M. (1995) 'Brussels Advisory Committees: a Channel for Influence', *European Law Review* 20: 37–56.

Bulmer, S. (1994) 'Institutions and Policy Change in the European Communities', *Public Administration* 72: 3: 423–44.

—— (1996) 'The European Council and the Council of the European Union: Shapers of a European Confederation', *Publius* 26, 4: 17–42.

—— (1997) 'Shaping the Rules? The Constitutive Politics of the EU and German Power', in P. Katzenstein (ed.) *Tamed Power: Germany in Europe*, Ithaca: Cornell University Press.

—— (1998) 'New Institutionalism and the Governance of the Single European Market', *Journal of European Public Policy* 5, 3: 365–86.

Bulmer, S. and Paterson, W. (1987) *The Federal Republic of Germany and the European Community* (London: Allen and Unwin).

Bulmer, S. and Wessels, W. (1987) *The European Council: Decision-Making in the European Community*, London: Macmillan.

—— (forthcoming) *The European Council*, 2nd edn, London: Macmillan.

Burley, A.-M. and Mattli, W. (1993) 'Europe before the court: a political theory of legal integration', *International Organization* 47, Winter: 41–76.

Butler, M. (1986) *Europe: More Than a Continent*, London: Heinemann.

Cameron, D.R. (1992) 'The 1992 Initiative: causes and consequences', in A. Sbragia (ed.) *Euro-Politics: Institutions and Policymaking in the 'new' European Community*, Washington, DC: Brookings Institution.

Cameron, F. (1998) 'Building a Common Foreign Policy: Do Institutions Matter?', in J. Peterson and H. Sjursen (eds) *A Common Foreign Policy for Europe? Competing Visions of the CFSP*, London: Routledge.

Campbell, J.L., Hollingsworth, J.R. and Lindberg, L.N. (eds) (1991) *Governance of the American Economy*, Cambridge: Cambridge University Press.

Caporaso, J. (1998) 'Regional Integration Theory: Understanding Our Past and Anticipating Our Future', *Journal of European Public Policy* 5, 1: 12–16.

Caporaso, J. and Keeler, J.T.S. (1995) 'The European Union and Regional Integration Theory' in C. Rhodes and S. Mazey (eds) *The State of the European Union: Building a European Polity*, Boulder, CO and Essex: Lynne Rienner and Longman.

Carnegie Endowment (for International Peace) (1996) *Reflections on Regionalism*, Washington DC: Brookings Institution.

Cawson, A. (1995) 'High definition television in Europe', *Political Quarterly* 66, 2, April–June: 35–54.

Cawson, A. and Holmes, P. (1995) 'Technology policy and competition issues in the transition to advanced television services in Europe', *Journal of European Public Policy* 2, 4: 650–71.

Cecchini, P. with Catinat, M. and Jacquemin, A. (1988) *The European Challenge 1992: the Benefits of a Single Market*, Aldershot: Wildwood House.

Christiansen, T. (1996) 'A maturing bureaucracy? The role of the Commission in the policy process', in J. Richardson (ed.) *European Union: Power and Policy-Making*, London: Routledge.

Cini, M. (1996) *The European Commission: Leadership, Organisation and Culture in the EU Administration*, Manchester: Manchester University Press.

Cockfield, A. (1994) *The European Union: Creating the Internal Market*, Chichester: John Wiley & Sons.

Colebatch, H.K. (1998) *Policy*, Buckingham: Open University Press.

Coleman, W.D. (1998) 'From Protected Development to Market Liberalism: Paradigm Change in Agriculture', *Journal of European Public Policy* 5, 4: 632–51.

Coleman, W.D. and Underhill G.R.D. (eds) (1995) 'The Single Market and global economic integration', special issue of *Journal of European Public Policy* 2/3.

Collins, K. and Earnshaw, D. (1993) 'The Implementation and Enforcement of European Community Environmental Legislation' in Judge, D. (ed.) *A Green Dimension for the European Community? Political Issues and Processes*, London: Frank Cass.

Collins, R. (1994) 'Unity in Diversity? The European Single Market in Broadcasting and the Audiovisual, 1982–92', *Journal of Common Market Studies* 32, 1: 89–102.

Commission of the European Communities (1985a) 'Completing the Internal Market: Community Legislation on Foodstuffs', COM (85) 603 final.

—— (1985b) 'Completing the Internal Market: White Paper from the Commission to the European Council', COM (85) 310 final.

—— (1991) 'European Industrial Policy for the 1990s', *Bulletin of the European Communities* 3/91, document based on COM (90) 556, SEC (91) 565 and SEC (91) 629, Luxembourg: Office for Official Publications of the European Communities.

—— (1992a) Eurobarometer, No. 37, June, Luxembourg: Office for Official Publications of the European Communities.

—— (1992b) *Research After Maastricht: An Assessment, A Strategy*, Communication for the Commission to the Council and European Parliament, SEC (92) 682 final, Bull. supplement 2/92, Brussels.

—— (1992c) *Towards Sustainability: A European Community Programme of Policy and Action in Relation to the Environment and Sustainable Development*, European Documentation Series, Luxembourg: Office for Official Publications of the European Communities.

—— (1993) *Growth, Competitiveness and Employment: the Challenges and Ways Forward Into the 21st Century*, COM (93) 700, final.

—— (1994a) *The European Report on Science and Technology Indicators 1994*, Report EUR 15897 EN, Luxembourg: DG XII.

—— (1994b) *Europe's Way to the Information Society: An Action Plan*, IP/94/683, Brussels, 20 July.

—— (1994c) 'An industrial competitiveness policy for the European Union', Communication from the Commission to the Council and Parliament and to the

Economic and Social Committee and the Committee of the Regions, drawn up on the basis of COM (94) 319 final, *Bulletin of the European Union*, supplement 3/94, Brussels.

—— (1995a) 'Completion of the internal market: Community legislation on foodstuffs', COM (85) 603, Brussels.

—— (1995b) *Report on the Operation of the Treaty on European Union*, Brussels, SEC (95) 731.

—— (1995c) *Third Survey on State Aid in the European Union in the Manufacturing and Certain Other Sectors*, Luxembourg: Office for the Official Publications of the EU.

—— (1996a) *First Report on Economic and Social Cohesion, 1996*, Luxembourg: Office for Official Publications of the European Communities.

—— (1996b) *I&T Magazine News Review*, Brussels: DGs III and XIII, 19, April.

—— (1996c) *Reinforcing Political Union and Preparing for Enlargement. Commission Opinion for the Intergovernmental Conference 1996*, Luxembourg: Office for the Official Publications of the European Communities, 28 February.

—— (1996d) *Structural Funds and Cohesion Fund, 1994–99. Regulations and Commentary*, January.

—— (1997a) *Action Plan for the Single Market*, Communication of the Commission to the European Council, CSE (97) 1 final, Brussels, 4 June.

—— (1997b) *Agenda 2000 – For a Stronger and Wider Union*, COM(97) 2000 final, Brussels, 15 July.

—— (1997c) *The Commission's Work Programme for 1998*, COM (97) 517 final, 15 October.

—— (1998a) 'Agenda 2000: the legislative proposals', Spokesman's Service, 18 March.

—— (1998b) *Fifth Survey on State Aid in the European Union in the Manufacturing and Certain Other Sectors*, COM 97/170.

—— (1998c) *Financing the European Union*, DG XIX, 7 October.

—— (1998d) *The Impact and Effectiveness of the Single Market*, communication from the Commission to the European Parliament and Council, available from http://europa.eu.int/comm/dg 15/en/update/impact/smtocen.htm

—— (1998e) *Proposed Regulations Governing the Reform of the Structural Funds 2000–2006*, 18 March.

—— (1998f) *Social Action Programme 1998–2000* (Brussels), IP/98/383.

Conzelmann, T. (1995) 'Networking and the politics of EU regional policy: lessons from North Rhine–Westphalia, Nord–Pas de Calais and North West England', *Regional and Federal Studies* 52: 134–172.

Corbett, R. (1987) 'The 1985 intergovernmental conference and the Single European Act', in R. Pryce (ed.) *The Dynamics of European Union*, London: Croom Helm.

—— (1994) 'Representing the people', in A. Duff, J. Pinder and R. Pryce (eds) *Maastricht and Beyond: Building the European Union*, London: Routledge.

—— (1998) *The European Parliament's Role in Closer European Integration*, Basingstoke: Macmillan.

Corbett, R., Jacobs, F. and Shackleton, M. (1995) *The European Parliament*, 3rd edn, London: Cartermill.

Corbey, D. (1995) 'Dialectical Functionalism: Stagnation as a Booster of European Integration', *International Organization* 49, 2: 254–84.

Council of the European Union (1997) 'Luxembourg European Council, 12 and 13 December 1997 – Presidency Conclusions', Brussels: General Secretariat, R109VDAT.doc.

—— (1998) 'Press release: 2087th Council meeting', Brussels: General Secretariat, 7095/98 (Presse 86 - G).

Court of Auditors (1992) 'Special Report No 3292 Concerning the Environment Together with the Commission's replies', *Official Journal* 92/C245/01, September.

Cowles, M.G. (1995) 'Setting the agenda for a new Europe: the ERT and EC 1992', *Journal of Common Market Studies* 33, 4: 501–26.

Cox, A. (1994) 'Derogation, Subsidiarity and the Single Market', *Journal of Common Market Studies* 32, 3: 127–47.

Cram, L. (1994) 'The European Commission as a multi-organization: social policy and IT policy in the EU', *Journal of European Public Policy* 1, 2: 195–217.

—— (1997) *Policy-Making in the EU: Conceptual Lenses and the Integration Process*, London: Routledge.

Dai, X., Cawson, A. and Holmes, P. (1996) 'The rise and fall of High Definition Television: the impact of European technology policy', *Journal of Common Market Studies* 34, 4: 149–66.

Dashwood, A. (1983) 'Hastening Slowly: the Community's path towards harmonisation', in H. Wallace, W. Wallace, and C. Webb (eds) *Policy-making in the European Community*, Chichester: John Wiley.

Daugbjerg, C. (1998) 'Similar Problems, Different Policies: Policy Networks and Environmental Policy in Danish and Swedish Agriculture', in D. Marsh (ed.) *Comparing Policy Networks*, Buckingham: Open University Press.

David, P. (1985) 'Clio and the economics of QWERTY', *American Economic Review* 75: 332–7.

Davies, N. (1996) *Europe: a History*, Oxford and New York: Oxford University Press.

Dehousse, R. (1995) 'Institutional Reform in the European Community: Are There Alternatives to the Majoritarian Avenue?', in J. Hayward (ed.) *The Crisis of Representation in Europe*, London: Frank Cass.

—— (1998) *The European Court of Justice*, Basingstoke: Macmillan.

Dekker, D. (1984) *Europe 1990: An Agenda for Action*, Eindhoven: N.V. Philips.

de Schoutheete P. (1986) *La Coopération politique européenne*, Brussels: Editions Labor.

Devuyst, Y. (1992) 'The EC's Common Commercial Policy and the Treaty on European Union: An Overview of the Negotiations', *World Competition: Law and Economics Review* 16, December: 67–80.

—— (1995) 'The European Community and the conclusion of the Uruguay Round', in C. Rhodes and S. Mazey (eds) *The State of the European Union Volume 3: Building a European Polity?*, Boulder, CO and Essex: Lynne Rienner and Longman.

—— (1999) 'The Community Method After Amsterdam', *Journal of Common Market Studies* 37, 1: 109–20.

Dinan, D. (1994) *Ever Closer Union? An Introduction to the European Community*, Basingstoke and Boulder, CO: Macmillan and Lynne Rienner.

—— (1998) 'Reflections on the IGCs' in P.H. Laurent and M.Maresceau (eds) *The State of the European Union, Vol. 4: Deepening and Widening*, Boulder, CO: Lynne Rienner.

Dolowitz, D. and Marsh, D. (1996) 'Who Learns What from Whom: a Review of the Policy Transfer Literature', *Political Studies* 44, 2: 343–57.

Donnelly, M. and Ritchie, E. (1994) 'The college of Commissioners and their *cabinets*', in G. Edwards and D. Spence (eds) *The European Commission*, Essex: Longman.

Earnshaw, D. and Judge, D. (1993) 'The European Parliament and the Sweeteners Directive: From Footnote to Inter-Institutional Conflict', *Journal of Common Market Studies* 31, 1: 103–116.

—— (1997) 'The Life and Times of the European Union's Cooperation Procedure', *Journal of Common Market Studies* 35, 4: 543–64.

Edwards, G. (1996) 'National Sovereignty vs. Integration? The Council of Ministers', in J. Richardson (ed.) *European Union: Power and Policy-Making*, London: Routledge.

Edwards, G. and Phillipart, E. (1999) 'The Provisions on Closer Cooperation in the Treaty of Amsterdam – the Politics of Flexibility in the European Union', *Journal of Common Market Studies* 37, 1: 87–108.

Edwards. G. and Pijpers, A. (eds) (1997) *The Politics of European Treaty Reform: the 1996 Intergovernmental Conference and Beyond*, London: Pinter.

Edwards, G. and Spence, D. (1994) *The European Commission*, Essex: Longman.

Eeckhout, P. (1994) *The European Internal Market and International Trade: a Legal Analysis*, Oxford: Clarendon Press.

Ehlermann, C.-D. (1984) 'How Flexible is Community Law? An unusual approach to the concept of two speeds', *Michigan Law Review* 82: 1274–93.

Ehrlich, E. (1996) 'Success judged on expectations more than performance', *European Voice* Survey on Environment, 30 May: 18.

Elizalde, J. (1992) 'Legal Aspects of Community Policy on Research and Technological Development (RTD)', *Common Market Law Review* 29: 309–46.

Elkington, J. and Hailes, J. (1988) *The Green Consumer Guide*, London: Gollancz.

Emerson, M., Aujean, M., Catinat, M., Goybet, P., and Jacquemin, A. (1988) *The Economics of 1992: the Commission's Assessment of the Economic Side Effects of Completing the Internal Market*, Oxford: Oxford University Press.

EP (1998) *Report on the Gradual Establishment of a Common Defence Policy for the European Union* (Brussels), PE 224.862/final, DOC_EN/RR/352/352586, 30 April (Rapporteur: Mr Leo Tindemans).

—— (1999) Committee of Independent Experts – First Report on Allegations regarding Fraud, Mismanagement and Nepotism in the European Commission (Brussels), 15 March, http://www.europar/.eu.int/experts/en/default.htm.

Epstein, P.J. (1997) 'Beyond Policy Community: French Agriculture and the GATT', *Journal of European Public Policy* 4, 3: 355–72.

Ernst and Young (1997) *The Single Market Review*, London: Kogan Page.

EUREKA secretariat (1996) *EUREKA Project Report 1995*, Brussels.

Evans, P., Jacobson, H. and Putnam, R. (eds) (1993) *Double-Edged Diplomacy: International Bargaining and Domestic Politics*, Berkeley: University of California Press.

Falkner, G. (1996) 'European Works Councils and the Maastricht Social Agreement: Towards a New Policy Style?', *Journal of European Public Policy* 3, 2: 192–208.

Featherstone, K. (1994) 'Jean Monnet and the "Democratic Deficit" in the European Union', *Journal of Common Market Studies* 32, 2: 149–70.

Featherstone, K. and Ginsberg, R. (1996) *The United States and the European Community in the 1990s*, 2nd edn, London and New York: St Martin's Press.

Federation of Swedish Industries (1996) *The Price of Protection*, Stockholm, April.

Feldstein, M. (1997) 'EMU and International Conflict', *Foreign Affairs* 76, 6: 60–73.

Fennell, R. (1987) *The Common Agricultural Policy of the European Community*, 2nd edn, London: Granada.

Fenno, R. (1996) *Senators on the Campaign Trail: the Politics of Representation*, Norman, OK: University of Oklahoma Press.

Fligstein, N. (1997) 'Social skill and institutional theory', *American Behavioral Scientist* 40, 4 (February): 397–405.

Fligstein, N. and Brantley, P. (1995) 'The 1992 single market program and the interests of business', in B. Eichengreen and J. Frieden (eds) *Politics and Institutions in an Integrated Europe*, New York: Springer Verlag.

Footer, M.E. (1998) 'The EU and the WTO Global Trading System', in P.-H. Laurent and M. Maresceau (eds) *The State of the European Union, Vol. 4: Deepening and Widening*, Boulder, CO and Essex: Lynne Rienner and Longman.

Fraser, M.W. (1996) 'Television', in H. Kassim and A. Menon (eds) *The European Union and National Industrial Policy*, London: Routledge.

Friedman, J.W. (1990) *Game Theory with Applications to Economics*, Oxford: Oxford University Press.

Friedrich, A., Tappe, M and Wurze, R. (1998) 'The Auto/Oil Programme: Missed Opportunity or Leap Forward?', Centre for European Union Studies Working Paper. No 2/98, University of Hull: Centre for European Union Studies.

Gardner, A. (1997) *A New Era in US-EU Relations? The Clinton Administration and the New Transatlantic Agenda*, Aldershot: Avebury Press.

Garrett, G. (1992) 'International cooperation and institutional choice: the European Community's Internal Market', *International Organization*, 46 (Spring): 533–60.

—— (1995) 'The politics of legal integration in the European Union', *International Organization* 49, Winter: 171–81.

Garrett, G. and Tsebelis, G. (1996) 'An institutionalist critique of intergovern-mentalism', *International Organization* 50, 2 (Spring): 269–99.

Garrett, G. and Weingast, B. (1993) 'Ideas, interests and institutions: constructing the European Community's internal market', in J. Goldstein and R.O. Keohane (eds) *Ideas and Foreign Policy*, Ithaca: Cornell University Press.

Garrett, G., Kelemen, R. D. and Schutz, H. (1998) 'The European Court of Justice, national governments, and legal integration in the European Union,' *International Organisation* 52, 1: 149–76.

GATT Secretariat (1993) *Trade Policy Review Mechanism: European Communities*, Geneva, 19 April, C/RM/S/36A.

George, S. (1996) *Politics and Policy in the European Union*, 3rd edn, Oxford: Oxford University Press.

Geyer, R. and Springer, B. (1998) 'EU Social Policy After Maastricht: the Works Council Directive and the British Opt-Out', in P-H. Laurent and M. Maresceau (eds) *The State of the European Union Volume 4*, Boulder CO and Essex: Lynne Rienner and Longman.

Ginsberg, R.H. (1989) *Foreign Policy Actions of the European Community*, London: Adamantine/Lynne Rienner.

—— (1995) 'The European Union's Common Foreign and Security Policy: Retrospective on the First Eighteen Months', in F. Cameron, R. Ginsberg and J. Janning (eds) *The European Union's Common Foreign and Security Policy: Central Issues . . . Key Players*, Washington, D.C.:US Army War College.

—— (1997) 'The EU's CFSP: the Politics of Procedure', in M. Holland (ed.) *Common Foreign and Security Policy: the Record and Reforms*, London: Cassell.

—— (1998) 'U.S.–E.U. Relations: the Commercial, Political, and Security Dimensions', in P-H. Laurent and M. Maresceau (eds) *The State of the European Union Volume 4*, Boulder CO and Essex: Lynne Rienner and Longman.

Golub, J. (1996a) 'Sovereignty and Subsidiarity in EU Environmental Policy', *Political Studies* 44, 4: 686–703

—— (1996b) 'State Power and Institutional Influence in European Integration: Lessons from the Packaging Waste Directive', *Journal of Common Market Studies* 34, 3: 313–41.

—— (1996c) 'Why did they sign? Explaining EC Environmental policy bargaining', paper presented to the 37th Annual Convention of the International Studies Association, 16–20 April 1996, San Diego.

Gomez, R. (1998) 'The EU's Mediterranean policy: common foreign policy by the back door?', in J. Peterson and H. Sjursen (eds) *A Common Foreign Policy for Europe? Competing Visions of the CFSP*, London: Routledge.

Gow, J. (1997) *Triumph of the Lack of Will: International Diplomacy and the Yugoslav War*, New York: Columbia University Press.

Grande, E. (1996) 'The State and Interest Groups in a Framework of Multi-Level Decision-Making: the Case of the European Union', *Journal of European Public Policy* 3,3: 318–8.

Grant, C. (1994) *Delors: Inside the House that Jacques Built*, London: Nicholas Brealey.

Grant, W. (1993) 'Pressure groups and the European Community: an overview', in S. Mazey and Richardson (eds) *Lobbying in the European Community*, Oxford and New York: Oxford University Press.

—— (1994) *Pressure Groups, Politics and Democracy in Britain*, 2nd edn, Hemel Hempstead: Philip Allan.

—— (1995) 'Is agricultural policy still exceptional?', *Political Quarterly* 66, 3: 156–69.

—— (1997a) 'BSE and the politics of food', in P. Dunleavy, A. Gamble, I. Holliday and G. Peele (eds) *Developments in British Politics V*, Basingstoke: Macmillan.

—— (1997b) 'The CAP in the global agricultural economy', paper presented to the International Political Studies Association conference, Seoul, South Korea, August.

—— (1997c) *The Common Agricultural Policy*, London: Macmillan.

Gray, P.S. (1992) 'Subsidiarity and EC food law', unpublished paper, DG XII, mimeo.

—— (1993) 'International view of the new labels', presented to ILSO conference on food, nutrition and labelling, Bahamas, 25 January.

Greenwood, J. (1995a) (ed.) *European Casebook on Business Alliances*, Hemel Hempstead and Englewood Cliffs, NJ: Prentice-Hall.

—— (1995b) 'The pharmaceutical industry: a European business alliance that works' in J. Greenwood (ed.) *European Casebook on Business Alliances*, London and New York: Prentice Hall.

—— (1997) *Representing Interests in the European Union*, Basingstoke: Macmillan.

—— (1998) 'The Professions' in Greenwood, J. and Aspinwall, M. (eds) (1998) *Collective Action in the European Union*, London: Routledge.

Greenwood, J. and Aspinwall, M. (eds) (1998) *Collective Action in the European Union*, London: Routledge.

Greenwood, J. and Ronit, K. (1991) 'Medicine regulation in Denmark and the UK: reformulating interest representation to the transnational level', *European Journal of Political Research* 19: 327–59.

—— (1995) 'European bioindustry', in J. Greenwood (ed.) *European Casebook on Business Alliances*, Hemel Hempstead and Englewood Cliffs, NJ: Prentice-Hall.

Greenwood, J., Grote, J.R. and Ronit, K. (eds) (1992) *Organized Interests and the European Community*, London: Sage.

Grieco, J.M. (1995) 'The Maastricht Treaty, Economic and Monetary Union and the Neo-realist Research Programme', *Review of International Studies* 21, 1: 21–40.

Griffiths, R. T. (1995) '1958–73', in K. Middlemas, (ed.) *Orchestrating Europe: the Informal Politics of the European Union*, London: Fontana.

Grilli, E. (1993) *The European Community and the Developing Countries*, Cambridge: Cambridge University Press.

Guzzetti, L. (1995) *A Brief History of European Union Research Policy*, Brussels: European Commission, DG XII Studies 5, October.

Haas, E. (1964) *Beyond the Nation-State: Functionalism and International Organization*, Stanford: Stanford University Press.

Haas, E. (1968) *The Uniting of Europe: Political, Social, and Economic Forces, 1950–7*, Stanford: Stanford University Press.

Haas, E. (1975) *The Obsolescence of Regional Integration Theory*, Berkeley, CA: Institute of International Studies.

Haas, P. (1992) 'Epistemic Communities and International Policy Coordination', *International Organization* 46, 1: 1–35.

Haas, P. (1993) 'Protecting the Baltic and North Seas', in P. Haas, R.O. Keohane, and M. Levy, (eds) *Institutions for the Earth: Sources of Effective International Environmental Protection*, Cambridge, MA: MIT Press.

—— (1998) 'Compliance with EU Directives: Insights from International Relations and Comparative Politics', *Journal of European Public Policy* 5, 1: 17–37.

Haigh, N. (1992) *Manual of Environmental Policy: The EC and the UK*, London: Longman.

Haigh, N. and Baldcock, D. (1989) *Environmental Policy and 1992*, London: Department of the Environment.

Handoll, J. (1995) *Free Movement of Persons in the European Union*, Chichester: John Wiley & Sons.

Hanson, B.Y. (1998) 'What Happened to Fortress Europe?: External Trade Policy Liberalization in the European Union', *International Organization* 52, 1: 55–85.

Harvie, C. (1994) *Rise of Regional Europe*, London: Routledge

Hay, C. (1995) 'Structure and Agency', in D. Marsh and G. Stoker (eds) *Theory and Methods in Political Science*, Basingstoke: Macmillan.

Hayes-Renshaw, F. and Wallace, H. (1997) *The Council of Ministers*, Basingstoke: Macmillan.

Hayward, J. (ed.) (1995) *Industrial Enterprise and European Integration: From National to International Champions in Western Europe*, Oxford: Oxford University Press.

Hayward, K. (1994) 'European Union policy and the European aerospace industry', *Journal of European Public Policy* 1, 3: 347–65.

Heclo, H. (1978) 'Issue Networks and the Executive Establishment', in A. King (ed.) *The New American Political System*, Washington DC: American Enterprise Institute.

Heinelt, H. (1996) 'Multilevel Governance in the European Union and the Structural Funds', in H. Heinelt, and R. Smith, (eds) *Policy Networks and European Structural Funds*, Aldershot: Avebury.

Heinelt, H. and Smith, R. (eds)(1996) *Policy Networks and European Structural Funds*, Aldershot: Avebury.

Héritier, A. (1996) 'The accommodation of diversity in European policy-making and its outcomes: regulatory policy as a patchwork', *Journal of European Public Policy* 3, 2: 149–67.

Hildebrandt, P. (1992) 'The European Community's environmental policy, 1957–1992: from incidental measures to an international regime?', *Environmental Politics* 1: 13–44.

Hill, C. (1993) 'The capability-expectations gap, or conceptualising Europe's international role', *Journal of Common Market Studies* 31, 3: 305–28; reprinted in S. Bulmer and A. Scott (eds) (1994) *Economic and Political Integration in Europe: Internal Dynamics and Global Context*, Oxford: Blackwell.

—— (ed.) (1996a) *The Actors in Europe's Foreign Policy*, London: Routledge.

—— (1996b) 'United Kingdom: Sharpening Contradictions', in C. Hill (ed.) *The Actors in Europe's Foreign Policy*, London: Routledge.

—— (1997) 'The Actors Involved: national perspectives', in E. Regelsberger, P. de Schoutheete de Tervarent and W. Wessels (eds) *Foreign Policy of the European Union: From EPC to CFSP and Beyond*, London: Lynne Rienner.

—— (1998) 'Closing the Capabilities–Expectations Gap' in J. Peterson and H. Sjursen (eds) *A Common Foreign Policy for Europe? Competing Visions of the CFSP*, London: Routledge.

Hindley, B. and Lal, D. (1994) *Trade Policy Review 1994*, London: Centre for Policy Studies.

Hix, S. (1998) 'The Study of the European Union II: the "New Governance" Agenda and Its Rival', *Journal of European Public Policy* 5, 1: 38–65.

Hoffmann, S. (1995) *The European Sisyphus: Essays on Europe 1964–1994*, London and Boulder, CO: Westview.

Holland, M. (ed.) (1997) *Common Foreign and Security Policy: the Record and Reforms*, London: Cassell.

Holmes, P. and Kempton, J. (1996) 'EU Anti-Dumping Policy: a Regulatory Perspective', *Journal of European Public Policy* 3, 4: 647–64.

Holmes, P. and McGowan, F. (1997) 'The Changing Dynamic of EU-Industry Relations: Lessons from the Liberalization of European Car and Airline Markets', in H. Wallace and A. Young (eds) *Participation and Policy-Making in the European Union*, Oxford: Clarendon Press.

Holmes, P. and Smith, A. (1995) 'Automobile industry', in P. Buiges, A. Jacquemin and A. Sapir (eds) *European Policies on Competition, Trade and Industry*, Aldershot: Edward Elgar.

Hooghe, L. (1995) 'Subnational mobilisation in the European Union', *West European Politics* 18, 1: 175–98.

—— (1996a) 'Building a Europe with the Regions: The Changing Role of the European Commission', in L. Hooghe (ed.) *Cohesion Policy and European Integration*, Oxford: Oxford University Press.

—— (ed.) (1996b) *Cohesion Policy and European Integration*, Oxford: Oxford University Press.

—— (1996c) 'Introduction: Reconciling EU-Wide Policy and National Diversity', in L. Hooghe (ed.) *Cohesion Policy and European Integration*, Oxford: Oxford University Press.

—— (1998) 'EU cohesion policy and competing models of European capitalism', *Journal of Common Market Studies* 36, 4: 457–78.

Hooghe, L. and Keating, M. (1994) 'The politics of European Union regional policy', *Journal of European Public Policy* 11, 3: 367–93.

Hooghe, L. and Marks, G. (1997) 'Contending Models of Governance in the European Union', in A.W. Cafruny and C. Lankowski (eds) *Europe's Ambiguous Unity*, Boulder and London: Lynne Rienner.

—— (1999) 'Making of a Polity: the Struggle Over European Integration', in H. Kitschelt, P.Lange, G. Marks and J. Stephens (eds) *Continuity and Change in Contemporary Capitalism*, Ithaca, NY: Cornell University Press.

Hosli, M. (1993) 'Admission of the European Free Trade Association States to the European Community: Effects on Voting power in the European Community Council of Ministers', *International Organization* 47, 4: 629–643.

Hull, R. (1993) 'Lobbying Brussels: a View from Within', in S. Mazey and J. Richardson (eds) *Lobbying in the European Community*, Oxford and New York: Oxford University Press.

Hunter, R. (1997) 'Equal Partners Need a Common Destiny', *European Voice*, 20–6 February: 14.

Hussain, I. (1992) 'Domestic priorities and European imperatives: a comparative study of farm policy in France and Germany', paper presented to the annual meeting of the Western Political Science Association, San Francisco, 19–22 March.

Jacquemin, A. and Sapir, A. (eds) (1991) *The European Internal Market: Trade and Competition*, Oxford: Oxford University Press.

Jacquemin, A. and Wright, D. (1993) 'Corporate strategy and European challenges post-1992', *Journal of Common Market Studies* 31, 4: 525–37.

Janis, I. (1982) *Groupthink: Psychological Studies of Policy Decisions and Fiascoes*, 2nd edn, Boston: Houghton Mifflin.

Jeffrey, C. (1995) 'Regional information offices and the politics of "third level" lobbying in Brussels', paper presented to the University Association for Contemporary European Studies conference on 'The Europe of the Regions', Leicester University, 6 October.

—— (1996) 'Towards a "third level" in Europe? The German Länder in the European Union', *Political Studies* 44: 253–266.

Jervis, R. (1976) *Perception and Misperception in World Politics*, Princeton: Princeton University Press.

Joerges, C. (1991) 'Markt ohne Staat? Die Wirschaftsverfassung der Gemeinschaft und die regulative Politik', in R. Wildenmann (ed.) *Staatswerdung Europas? Optionen für eine Europäische Union*, Baden-Baden: Nomos.

Joerges, C. and Neyer, J. (1997) 'Transforming Strategic Interaction into Deliberative Problem-Solving: European Comitology in the Foodstuffs Sector', *Journal of European Public Policy* 4, 4: 609–25.

Johnson, C. (1984) 'Introduction: the idea of industrial policy', in C. Johnson (ed.) *The Industrial Policy Debate*, San Francisco: Institute for Contemporary Studies.

Johnson, S. and Corcelle, G. (1995) *The Environmental Policy of the European Communities*, 2nd edn, London: Kluwer Law International.

Johnston, M. T. (1994) *The European Council: Gatekeeper of the European Community*, Boulder, CO: Westview.

Jones, B. and Keating, M. (eds) (1995) *The European Union and the Regions*, Oxford: Clarendon Press.

Jordan, A. (1997) 'Overcoming the Divide Between Comparative Politics and International Relations Approaches to the EC: What Role for "Post-Decisional Politics"?', *West European Politics* 20, 4: 43–70.

—— (1999) 'European Community Water Policy Standards: Locked in or Watered Down?', *Journal of Common Market Studies* 37, 1: 13–37.

Judge, D. (ed.)(1993a) *A Green Dimension for the European Community? Political Issues and Processes*, London: Frank Cass

—— (1993b) ' "Predestined to save the earth": the environment committee of the European Parliament', in D. Judge (ed.) *A Green Dimension for the European Community. Political Issues and Processes*, London: Frank Cass.

Judge, D. and Earnshaw, D. (1994) 'Weak European Parliament influence? A study of the environment committee of the European Parliament', *Government and Oppositions* 29: 262–76.

Judt, T. (1997) *A Grand Illusion? An Essay on Europe*, London: Penguin.

Kassim, H. (1995) 'Air transport champions: still carrying the flag', in J. Hayward (ed.) *Industrial Enterprise and European Integration: From National to International Champions in Western Europe*, Oxford: Oxford University Press.

—— (1996) 'The impact of European Union action on national policy and policy-making in the air transport sector', in H. Kassim and A. Menon (eds) *The European Union and National Industrial Policies*, London: Routledge.

Katzenstein, P. J. (1977) 'Conclusion: domestic structures and strategies of foreign economic policy', *International Organization* 31, 4: 879–920.

Keating, M. and Jones, B. (1995) 'Nations, regions and Europe: The UK experience', in B. Jones and M. Keating (eds) *The European Union and the Regions*, Oxford: Clarendon Press.

Kenis, P. and Schneider, V. (1987) 'The EC as an international corporate actor: two case studies in economic diplomacy', *European Journal of Political Research* 15, 4: 437–57.

Keohane, R. and Hoffmann, S. (1991) 'Institutional Change in Europe in the 1980s', in R.O. Keohane, and S. Hoffman (eds) *The New European Community: Decisionmaking and Institutional Change*, Boulder, Colorado: Westview Press.

Keohane, R. (1998) 'International Institutions: Can Interdependence Work?', *Foreign Policy* II0, Spring: 82–96.

Kingdon, J. (1984) *Agendas, Alternatives and Public Policies* , New York: Harper Collins.

Kintis, A. (1997) 'The EU's Foreign Policy and the War in Former Yugoslavia', in M. Holland (ed.) *Common Foreign and Security Policy: the Record and Reforms*, London: Pinter.

Kirchner, E. (1992) *Decision-Making in the European Community: the Council Presidency and European Integration*, Manchester: Manchester University Press.

Kirman, A. and Widgrén, M. (1995) 'European economic decision-making policy: progress or paralysis?', *Economic Policy* 21, October: 423–60.

Kiso, J.O. (1997) 'CFSP Heads Into Uncharted Waters', *European Voice*, 4–10 September: 15.

Kohler-Koch, B. (1994) 'Changing Patterns of Interest Intermediation in the European Union', *Government and Opposition* 29, 2: 166–80.

—— (1996) 'Catching Up with Change: the Transformation of Governance in the European Union', *Journal of European Public Policy* 3, 3: 359–80.

—— (1997) 'Organised Interests in European Integration', in H. Wallace and A. Young (eds) *Participation and Policy-Making in the European Union*, Oxford: Clarendon Press.

Krasner, S. (1984) 'Approaches to the State', *Comparative Politics* 16, 2: 223–246.

Krugman, P.R. (1991) 'Is Bilateralism Bad?', in E. Helpman and A. Razin (eds) International Trade and Trade Policy, Cambridge, MA: MIT Press.

—— (1994) 'Competitiveness: a dangerous obsession', *Foreign Affairs* 73, 2: 28–44.

Labouz, M-F (1998) 'A propos des lois américaines Helms-Burton et d'Amato-Kennedy', in European Commission (ed.) *The European Union in a Changing World*, a selection of conference papers presented at the Third ECSA–World European Community Studies Association Conference, Brussels, 19–20 September 1996, Luxembourg.

Laffan, B. (1996) 'The IGC and Institutional Reform of the Union', in G. Edwards and A. Pijpers (eds) *The Politics of European Treaty Reform: the 1996 Intergovernmental Conference and Beyond*, London: Pinter.

—— (1997a) *The Finances of the European Union*, London: Macmillan.

—— (1997b) 'From Policy Entrepreneur to Policy Manager: the Challenge Facing the European Commission', *Journal of European Public Policy* 4, 3: 422–38.

—— (1998) 'The European Union: a distinctive model of internationalization', *Journal of European Public Policy* 5, 2: 235–53.

Laffan, B. and Shackleton, M. (1996) 'The Budget', in Wallace H. and Wallace W.(eds) *Policy-Making in the European Union*, Oxford, Oxford University Press.

Lamassoure, A. (1995) 'Transcript of press conference given by M. Alain Lamassoure, Minister Delegate for European Affairs', *Statements*, SAC/95/48, London: French Embassy.

Lane, J.-E. (1997) 'Governance in the European Union', *West European Politics* 20, 4: 200–208.

Lane, J.-E., Maeland, R. and Berg, S. (1996) 'Voting power under the EU constitution', in S.S. Andersen and K.A. Eliassen (eds) *The European Union: How Democratic Is It?* London: Sage.

de La Serre, F. (1996) 'France: the Impact of François Mitterrand', in C. Hill (ed.) *The Actors in Europe's Foreign Policy*, London: Routledge.

de La Serre, F. and Wallace, H. (1997) 'Les coopérations renforcées: une fausse bonne idée?', *Etudes et Recherches* (Paris: Notre Europe), 2, juin.

Le Galés, P. and Lequesne, C. (eds) (1998) *Regions in Europe*, London: Routledge.

Le Galés, P. and Thatcher, M. (eds) (1995) *Les Réseaux de Politique Publique: Débat autour des 'Policy Networks'*, Paris: L'Harmattan.

Leigh-Phippard, H. (1997) 'Multilateral Diplomacy at the 1995 NPT Review and Extension Conference', *Diplomacy and Statecraft* 8, 2: 167–90.

Lequesne, C. (1993) *Paris-Bruxelles: Comment Se Fait la Politique Européenne de la France*, Paris: Presses de la Fondation Nationale des Sciences Politiques.

Lewis, J. (1998) 'Is the "Hard Bargaining" Image of the Council Misleading? The Committee of Permanent Representatives and the Local Elections Directive', *Journal of Common Market Studies* 36, 4: 479–504.

Liberatore, A. (1997) 'Integrating Sustainable Development', in S. Baker, M. Kousis, D. Richardson, and S. Young, (eds) *The Politics of Sustainable Development. Theory, Policy and Practice Within the European Union*, London: Routledge.

Lindberg, L. (1965) 'Decision Making and Integration in the European Community', *International Organization* 19, 1: 56–80.

—— (1970) 'Political Integration as a Multidimensional Phenomenon Requiring Multivariate Measurement', *International Organization* 24, 4: 649–731.

Lindberg, L. and Scheingold, S.A. (1970) *Europe's Would-Be Polity: Patterns of Change in the European Community*, Englewood Cliffs, NJ: Prentice-Hall.

—— (eds) (1971) *Regional Integration: Theory and Research*, Cambridge, MA: Harvard University Press.

Lodge, J. (1989) 'Environment: Towards a clean green–blue EC?', in J. Lodge (ed.) *The European Community and the Challenge of the Future*, London: Pinter.

Long, T. 'Shaping Public Policy in the European Union: A Case Study of the Structural Funds', *Journal of European Public Policy* 2: 672–9.

Lowe, D. (1996) 'The Development Policy of the European Union and the Mid-Term Review of the Lomé Partnership', *The European Union 1995: Annual Review of Activities* (published by *Journal of Common Market Studies*) 34: 15–28.

Lowe, P. and Ward, S. (eds.) (1998) *British Environmental Policy and Europe. Politics and Policy in Transition*, London: Routledge.

Lowi, T. (1972) 'Four Systems of Policy, Politics and Choice', *Public Administration Review* 32, 4: 298–310.

Lowndes, V. (1996) 'Varieties of New Institutionalism: A Critical Appraisal', *Public Administration* 74, 2: 181–97.

Ludlow, P. (1991) 'The European Commission', in R.O. Keohane, and S. Hoffmann (eds) *The New European Community: Decisionmaking and Institutional Change*, Boulder, CO: Westview Press.

—— (1992) 'Europe's Institutions: Europe's Politics', in G.F. Treverton (ed.) *The Shape of the New Europe*, New York: Council on Foreign Relations Press.

—— (1997) *Preparing Europe for the 21st Century: The Amsterdam Council and Beyond*, Brussels: Centre for European Policy Studies.

McAleavey, P. (1993) 'The politics of European Regional Development Policy: Additionality in the Scottish coalfields', *Regional Politics and Policy* 3: 88–107.

—— (1994) 'The Political Logic of the European Community Structural Funds Budget: Lobbying Efforts by Declining Industrial Regions', *EUI Working Paper*, RSC No. 942, Florence: European University Institute.

McAleavey, P. and De Rynck, S. (1997) 'Regional or Local? The EU's Future Partners in Cohesion Policy', *EUI Working Paper*, RSC No. 97/55. Florence: European University Institute

McCormick, J. (1998) 'Environmental Policy Deepening or Widening?', in P-H. Laurent and M. Maresceau (eds) *The State of the European Union*, Volume 4, Boulder CO and Essex: Lynne Rienner and Longman.

McDonagh, B. (1998) *Original Sin in a Brave New World: an Account of the Negotiation of the Treaty of Amsterdam*, Dublin: Institute of European Affairs.

McDonald, M. (1997) 'Identities in the European Commission' in N. Nugent (ed.) *At the Heart of the Union: Studies of the European Commission*, London: Macmillan.

McFarland, A. (1987) 'Interest Groups and Theories of Power in America', *British Journal of Political Science* 17: 129–47.

McGowan, F. and Wallace, H. (1996) 'Towards a European Regulatory State', *Journal of European Public Policy* 3, 4: 560–76.

McHugh, Fiona (1996) 'Blunders delay banking proposal', *European Voice*, 18–24 April: 3.

McLaughlin, A. (1994) 'The EU-Japan Understanding on Cars: Engineering Elements of a Consensus', in R. Pedlar and R. van Schendelen (eds.) *Lobbying in the European Union*, Aldershot: Dartmouth.

McLaughlin, A. and Jordan, G. (1993a) 'Corporate lobbying in the European Community', *Journal of Common Market Studies* 31, 2: 192–211.

—— (1993b) 'The rationality of lobbying in Europe: why are Euro-groups so numerous and so weak?', in S. Mazey and J. Richardson (eds) *Lobbying in the European Community*, Oxford and New York: Oxford University Press.

MacManus, C. (1998) 'Poland and the Europe Agreements: the EU as a Regional Actor', in J. Peterson and H. Sjursen (eds) *A Common Foreign Policy for Europe? Competing Visions of the CFSP*, London: Routledge.

MacMullen, A. (1997) 'European Commissioners 1952–1995: National Routes to a European Elite', in N. Nugent (ed.) *At the Heart of the Union: Studies of the European Commission*, London: Macmillan.

McNamara, K. (1998) *The Currency of Ideas: Monetary Politics in the European Union*, Ithaca, NY: Cornell University Press.

Majone, G. (ed.) (1990) *Deregulation or Re-regulation?*, London: Pinter.

—— (1993) 'The European Community Between Social Policy and Social Regulation', *Journal of Common Market Studies* 31, 2: 153–70.

—— (1994) 'Independence vs Accountability: Non-Majoritarian Institutions and Democratic Government in Europe', in J. Hesse, (ed.) *European Yearbook of Public Administration and Comparative Government*, Oxford: Oxford University Press

—— (1996a) *Regulating Europe*, London: Routledge.

—— (1996b) 'A European regulatory state?', in J. Richardson (ed.) *European Union: Power and Policy-Making*, London: Routledge.

—— (1997) 'From the Positive to the Regulatory State: Causes and Consequences of Changes in the Mode of Governance', *Journal of Public Policy* 17, 2: 139–67.

March, J. and Olsen, J. (1989) *Rediscovering Institutions*, New York: The Free Press.

Marginson, P. and Sisson, K. (1998) 'European collective bargaining: a virtual prospect?', *Journal of Common Market Studies* 36, 4: 529–48.

Marks, G. (1992) 'Structural policy in the European Community', in A. Sbragia (ed.) *Euro-Politics: Institutions and Policy-Making in the 'New' European Community*, Washington, DC: Brookings Institution.

—— (1993) 'Structural policy and multi-level governance in the EC', in A. Cafruny and G.G. Rosenthal (eds) *The State of the European Community II*, Boulder, CO and Essex: Lynne Rienner and Longman.

—— (1996a) 'An actor-centered approach to multilevel governance', paper presented to the APSA meeting, San Francisco, 29 August–1 September.

—— (1996b) 'Exploring and Explaining Variation in EU Cohesion Policy', in L. Hooghe (ed.) *Cohesion Policy and European Integration*, Oxford: Oxford University Press

Marks, G., Hooghe, L. and Blank, K. (1996a) 'European Integration from the 1980s: State-Centric v. Multi-Level Governance', *Journal of Common Market Studies* 34, 3: 341–78

Marks, G., Nielsen, F., Ray, L. and Salk, J. (1996b) 'Competencies, cracks and conflicts: regional mobilization in the European Union', in G. Marks, F.W. Scharpf, P.C. Schmitter and W. Streeck (eds) *Governance in the European Union*, London and Thousand Oaks, CA: Sage.

Mason, M. (1994) 'Elements of consensus: Europe's response to the Japanese automotive challenge', *Journal of Common Market Studies* 32, 4: 433–53.

Matláry, J.H. (1997) *Energy Policy in the European Union* London: Macmillan.

Mattli, W. and Slaughter, A.-M. (1995) 'Law and politics in the European Union: a reply to Garrett', *International Organization* 49, 1: 183–90.

—— (1998) 'Revisiting the European Court of Justice', *International Organization* 52, 1: 177–209.

Mazey, S. (1998) 'The European Union and Women's Rights: From the Europeanisation of National Agendas to the Nationalization of a European Agenda?', *Journal of European Public Policy* 5, 1: 131–52.

Mazey, S. and Mitchell, J. (1993) 'Europe of the Regions: territorial interests and European integration: the Scottish experience', in S. Mazey and J. Richardson (eds) *Lobbying in the European Community*, Oxford: Oxford University Press.

Mazey, S. and Richardson (1992) 'British Pressure Groups in the European Community: The Challenge of Brussels', *Parliamentary Affairs* 45, 1: 92–107.

—— (1993a) Effective business lobbying in Brussels', *European Business Journal* 5, 4: 14–24.

——(eds) (1993b) *Lobbying in the European Community*, Oxford and New York: Oxford University Press.

—— (1995) 'Promiscuous Policy-Making: the European Policy Style?', in C. Rhodes and S. Mazey (eds) *The State of the European Union Volume 3:* Boulder, CO and Essex: Lynne Rienner and Longman.

Mény, Y., Muller, P. and Quermonne J-L. (eds) (1995) *Politiques Publiques en Europe*, Paris: L'Harmattan.

Messerlin, P. (1996) 'France and trade policy', *International Affairs* 72, 2: 293–309.

Metcalfe, L. (1992) 'After 1992: can the Commission manage Europe?', *Australian Journal of Political Science* 51, 1: 117–30.

Middlemas, K. (1995) *Orchestrating Europe: the Informal Politics of the European Union 1973–95*, London: Fontana Press.

Milner, H. (1993) 'Maintaining international commitments in trade policy', in B. Rockman and K. Weaver (eds) *Do Institutions Matter? Government Capabilities in the United States and Abroad*, Washington, DC: Brookings Institution.

Milward, A. (1992) *The European Rescue of the Nation-State*, London: Routledge.

Milward, S. (1997) 'Sound Approach to Power Play', *European Voice*, 6–12 March: 14.

Monar, J. (1994) 'Interinstitutional agreements: the phenomenon and its new dynamics after Maastricht', *Common Market Law Review* 31: 693–719.

—— (1997) 'The Financial Dimension of the CFSP', in M. Holland (ed.) *Common Foreign and Security Policy: the Record and Reforms*, London: Cassell.

Monnet, J. (1978) *Memoirs*, London: Collins.

Moon, B.E. (1996) *Dilemmas of International Trade*, Boulder CO and Oxford: Westview.

Moore, L. (1994) 'Developments in Trade and Trade Policy', in M.J. Artis and N. Lee (eds) *The Economics of the European Union: Policy and Analysis*, Oxford: Oxford University Press.

Moravcsik, A. (1991) 'Negotiating the Single European Act', in R.O. Keohane and S. Hoffmann (eds) *The New European Community*, Boulder, CO: Westview.

—— (1993) 'Preferences and power in the European Community: a liberal intergovernmentalist approach', *Journal of Common Market Studies* 31, 4: 473–524.

—— (1994) 'Why the European Community strengthens the state: international cooperation and domestic politics', *Center for European Studies Working Paper*, 52, Cambridge, MA: Harvard University Press.

—— (1995) 'Liberal intergovernmentalism and integration: a rejoinder', *Journal of Common Market Studies* 33, 4: 611–28.

—— (1998) *The Choice for Europe*, Ithaca, NY: Cornell University Press.

Moravcsik, A. and Nicolaïdis, K. (1998) 'Federal Ideals and Constitutional Realities in the Amsterdam Treaty', in G. Edwards and G. Wiessala (eds) *The European Union 1997: Annual Review of Activities*, Oxford and Malden, MA: Blackwell for the *Journal of Common Market Studies* 36: 13–38.

—— (1999) 'Negotiating the Treaty of Amsterdam: Interests, Influence, Institutions', *Journal of Common Market Studies* 37, 1: 59–85.

Müller, H. and van Dassen, L. (1997) 'From Cacophony to Joint Action: Successes and Shortcomings of the European Nuclear Non-Proliferation Policy', in M. Holland (ed.) *Common Foreign and Security Policy: the Record and Reforms*, London: Cassell.

Neville-Rolfe, E. (1984) *The Politics of Agriculture in the European Community*, London: European Centre for Political Studies.

Niskanen, W.A. (1973) *Bureaucracy: Servant or Master?*, London: Institute of Economic Affairs.

North, D.C. (1990) *Institutions, Institutional Change and Economic Performance*, Cambridge and New York: Cambridge University Press.

Nugent, N. (1994) *The Government and Politics of the European Union*, 3rd edn, Basingstoke: Macmillan.

—— (1995) 'The leadership capacity of the European Commission', *Journal of European Public Policy* 2, 4: 602–23.

—— (ed.) (1997) *At the Heart of the Union: Studies of the European Commission*, London: Macmillan.

—— (1999) *The European Commission*, London: Macmillan.

Nuttall, S. (1992) *European Political Cooperation*, Oxford: Clarendon.

—— (1994) 'Keynote article: the EC and Yugoslavia – Deux ex Machina or Machina sine Deo?', in N. Nugent (ed.) *The European Union 1993: Annual Review of Activities*, Oxford: Blackwell, for the *Journal of Common Market Studies* 32: 11–25.

Oliver, P. (1996) *Free Movement of Goods in the European Community*, London: Sweet and Maxwell.

Olson, M. (1965) *The Logic of Collective Action*, Cambridge, MA: Harvard University Press.

Paarlberg, R. (1997) 'Agricultural Policy Reform and the Uruguay Round: Synergistic Linkage in a Two-Level Game?', *International Organization* 51, 3: 413–44.

Paemen, H. and Bensch, A. (1995) *From the GATT to the WTO: the European Community in the Uruguay Round*, Louvain: Leuven University Press.

Page, E. (1997) *People Who Run Europe*, Oxford: Clarendon Press.

Pedlar, R.H. (1994) 'Fruit Companies and the Banana Trade Regime (BTR)', in R.H. Pedlar and M.P.C.M. Schendelen (eds) *Lobbying in the European Union*, Aldershot: Dartmouth.

Pelkmans, J. (1995) 'Comments', in A. Sykes (ed.) *Product Standards for Integrated Goods Markets*, Washington, DC: Brookings.

Peters, B.G. (1997) 'Policy Transfers Between Governments: Administrative Reforms', *West European Politics* 20, 4: 71–88.

—— (1998a) *Comparative Politics: Theory and Method*, London: Macmillan.

—— (1998b) 'Policy Networks: Myth, Metaphor and Reality' in D. Marsh (ed.) *Comparing Policy Networks*, Buckingham: Open University Press.

Peterson, J. (1989) 'Hormones, Heifers and High Politics: Biotechnology and the Common Agricultural Policy', *Public Administration* 67, 4: 455–71.

—— (1991) 'Technology policy in Europe: explaining the Framework programme and EUREKA in theory and practice', *Journal of Common Market Studies* 29, 1: 269–90.

—— (1993a) *High Technology and the Competition State: an Analysis of the Eureka Initiative*, London: Routledge.

—— (1993b) 'Towards a common European industrial policy? The case of High Definition Television', *Government and Opposition* 28, 4: 496–511.

—— (1994) 'Subsidarity: a Definition to Suit Any Vision?', *Parliamentary Affairs* 47, 1: 116–32.

—— (1995a) 'Decision-making in the European Union: towards a framework for analysis', *Journal of European Public Policy* 2, 1: 69–93.

—— (1995b) 'EU research policy: the politics of expertise', in C. Rhodes and S. Mazey (eds) *The State of the European Union Volume 3:* Boulder, CO and Essex: Lynne Rienner and Longman.

—— (1995c) 'Playing the transparency game: policy-making and consultation in the European Commission', *Public Administration* 73, 3: 473–92.

—— (1996a) *Europe and America: the Prospects for Partnership*, 2nd edn, London: Routledge.

—— (1996b) 'European Union industrial policy', in P. Barbour (ed.) *The European Union Handbook*, Chicago and London: Fitzroy Dearborn.

—— (1996c) 'Research and development policy', in H. Kassim and A. Menon (eds) *The European Union and National Industrial Policy*, London: Routledge.

—— (1997) 'States, societies and the European Union', *West European Politics* 20, 4: 1–24.

—— (1998) 'Introduction: the European Union as a Global Actor', in J. Peterson and H. Sjursen (eds) *A Common Foreign Policy for Europe? Competing Visions of the CFSP*, London: Routledge.

—— (1999) 'The Santer era: the European Commission in normative, historical and theoretical perspective', *Journal of European Public Policy* 6, 1: 46–65.

—— (2000) *Power, Decision and Policy in the European Union*, Oxford: Oxford University Press.

Peterson, J. and Bomberg, E. (1998) 'Northern enlargement and EU decision-making', in P-H. Laurent and M. Maresceau (eds) *The State of the European Union Volume 4*, Boulder CO and Essex: Lynne Rienner and Longman.

Peterson, J. and Cowles, M. G. (1998) 'Clinton, Europe and Economic Diplomacy: What makes the EU different?', *Governance* 11, 3: 251–71.

Peterson, J. and Jones, E. (1999) 'Decision-Making in an Enlarging European Union', in J. Sperling (ed.) *Two Tiers or Two Speeds? The Double Expansion of NATO and the EU*, Manchester: Manchester University Press.

Peterson, J. and Sharp, M. (1998) *Technology Policy in the European Union*, London: Macmillan.

Peterson, J. and Sjursen, H. (eds) (1998a) *A Common Foreign Policy for Europe? Competing Visions of the CFSP*, London: Routledge.

Peterson, J. and Sjursen, H. (1998b) 'Conclusion: the Myth of the CFSP?', in J. Peterson and H. Sjursen (eds) *A Common Foreign Policy for Europe? Competing Visions of the CFSP*, London: Routledge.

Peterson, J. and Ward, H. (1995) 'Coalitional instability and the multidimensional politics of security: a rational choice argument for US-EU cooperation', *European Journal of International Relations* 1, 2: 131–56.

Pfaff, W. (1994) 'Nations Can Resolve to Act, But Europe Isn't a Nation', *International Herald Tribune*, 1 February: 17.

Piening, C. (1997) *Global Europe: the European Union in World Affairs*, Boulder, CO: Lynne Rienner.

Pierson, P. (1995) 'Fragmented welfare states: federal institutions and the development of social policy', *Governance* 8, 4: 449–78

—— (1996) 'The Path to European Integration: A Historical Institutionalist Analysis', *Comparative Political Studies* 29, 2: 123–63.

Pijpers, A. (1991) 'European Political Cooperation and the Realist Paradigm', in M. Holland (ed.) *The Future of European Political Cooperation*, London: Macmillan.

—— (1997) 'Order and Flexibility in the EU: the Case of the Second Pillar', paper presented to the conference on Order and Flexibility in the European Union, Cambridge, 20 June.

Pinder, J. (1993) 'The Single Market: a step towards union', in J. Lodge (ed.) *The European Community and the Challenge of the Future*, London: Pinter.

Pollack, M. (1995) 'Regional actors in an intergovernmental play: the making and implementation of EC structural policy', in C. Rhodes and S. Mazey (eds) *The State of the European Union Volume 3:* Boulder, CO. and Essex: Lynne Rienner and Longman.

—— (1997a) 'Delegation, Agency and Agenda-Setting in the European Union', *International Organization* 51, 1: 99–134.

—— (1997b) 'Representing Diffuse Interests in EC Policy-Making', *Journal of European Public Policy* 4, 4: 572–90.

Polsby, N. (1980) *Community Power and Political Theory*, 2nd enlarged edn, New Haven, CT and London: Yale University Press.

Poncet, J.-F. and Barbier, B. (1989) *1992: Les Conséquences pour l'Economie Française du Marché Intérieur Européen*, Paris: Economica.

Porter, M. and Butt Philip, A. (1993) 'The Role of Interest Groups in EU Environmental Policy Formulation: A Case Study of the Draft Packaging Directive', *European Environment* 3,1: 16–20

Pou Serradell, V. (1996) 'The Asia-Europe Meeting (ASEM): a historical turning point in relations between two regions', *European Foreign Affairs Review* 1, 2: 185–210.

Preston, C. (1995) 'Obstacles to EU enlargement: the classical Community method and the prospects for a wider Europe', *Journal of Common Market Studies* 33, 3: 451–63.

—— (1997) *Enlargement and Integration in the European Union*, London: Routledge.

Puchala, D. (1999) 'Institutionalism, Intergovernmentalism and European Integration', *Journal of Common Market Studies* 37, 2: 317–31.

Putnam, R. (1988) 'Diplomacy and the logic of two-level games', *International Organization* 42, Summer: 427–60.

Raunio, T. and Wiberg, M. (1998) 'Winners and losers in the Council: voting power consequences of EU enlargements', *Journal of Common Market Studies* 36, 4: 549–62.

Read, R. (1994) 'The EC International Banana Market: the Issues and the Dilemma', *The World Economy* 17, 2: 219–36.

Rehbinder, E. and Steward, R. (eds) (1985) *Environmental Protection Policy, Volume 2*, Florence: European University Institute.

Reich, R. (1991) *The Work of Nations: Preparing Ourselves for 21st Century Capitalism*, New York: Albert Knopf.

Rhodes, C. and Mazey, S. (1995) 'Introduction: Integration in Theoretical Perspective' in C. Rhodes and S. Mazey (eds) *The State of the European Union Volume 3: Building a European Polity?* Essex and Boulder CO, Longman and Lynne Rienner.

Rhodes, R.A.W. (1988) *Beyond Westminster and Whitehall*, London: Unwin Hyman.

—— (1990) 'Policy Networks: A British Perspective', *Journal of Theoretical Politics* 2: 293–317.

—— (1995) 'The Institutional Approach', in D. Marsh and G. Stoker (eds) *Theory and Methods in Political Science*, Basingstoke: Macmillan.

—— (1997) *Understanding Governance: Policy Networks, Governance, Reflexivity and Accountability*, Buckingham: Open University Press.

Rhodes, R.A.W, Bache, I. and George, S. (1996) 'Policy Networks and Policy Making in the EU: A Critical Appraisal', in L. Hooghe (ed.) *Cohesion Policy and European Integration*, Oxford: Oxford University Press.

Ricardo. D. (1911) *The Principles of Political Economy and Taxation*, London: J.M. Dent and Son; first published 1817.

Richardson, J. (1996a) 'Actor based models of national and EU policy-making', in H. Kassim and A. Menon (eds) *The European Union and National Industrial Policy*, London: Routledge.

—— (1996b) 'Eroding EU Policies: Implementation Gaps, Cheating and Re-Steering', in J. Richardson (ed.) *European Union: Power and Policy-Making*, London: Routledge.

—— (1996c) 'Policy-Making in the EU: Interests, Ideas and Garbage Cans of Primaeval Soup', in J. Richardson (ed.) *European Union: Power and Policy-Making*, London: Routledge.

—— (1996d) 'Water', in H. Kassim and A. Menon (eds) *The European Union and National Industrial Policy*, London: Routledge

Rieff, D. (1997) *Slaughterhouse: Bosnia and the Failure of the West*, New York: Touchstone Books.

Rieger, E. (1996) 'The Common Agricultural Policy: external and internal dimensions', in H. Wallace and W. Wallace (eds) *Policy-Making in the European Union*, 3rd edn, Oxford: Oxford University Press.

Risse-Kappen, T. (1996) 'Exploring the Nature of the Beast: International Relations Theory Meets the European Union', *Journal of Common Market Studies* 34, 1: 53–80.

Rometsch, D. (1996) 'Germany', in D. Rometsch and W. Wessels (eds) *The European Union and Member States: Towards Institutional Fusion?*, Manchester: Manchester University Press.

Rometsch, D. and Wessels, W. (1994) 'The Commission and the Council of Ministers' in G. Edwards and D. Spence (eds) *The European Commission*, Essex: Longman.

—— (eds) (1996) *The European Union and Member States: Towards Institutional Fusion?*, Manchester: Manchester University Press.

Roper, J. (1997) 'Flexibility and Legitimacy in the Area of the Common Foreign and Security Policy', paper presented to the European Institute for Public Administration Colloquium on 'Flexibility and the Amsterdam Treaty', Maastricht, 27–8 November.

Rosenthal, G.G. (1975) *The Men Behind the Decisions*, Farnborough: D.C. Heath.

Ross, G. (1995) *Jacques Delors and European Integration*, New York and London: Polity Press.

Rummel, R. (1996) 'Germany's role in the CFSP: "Normalität" or "Sonderweg"?' in C. Hill (ed.) *The Actors in Europe's Foreign policy*, London: Routledge.

Sabatier, P. (1998) 'The Advocacy Coalition Framework: Revisions and Relevance for Europe', *Journal of European Public Policy* 5, 1: 98–130.

Sabatier, P.A. and Jenkins-Smith, H.C. (eds) (1993) *Policy Change and Learning: An Advocacy Coalition Approach*, Boulder, CO and Oxford: Westview.

Sandholtz, W. (1992) *High-Tech Europe: the Politics of International Cooperation*, Berkeley: University of California Press.

—— (1993) 'Choosing Union: Monetary Politics and Maastricht', *International Organization* 47, 1: 1–39.

—— (1996) 'Membership Matters: Limits of the Functional Approach to European Institutions', *Journal of Common Market Studies* 34, 3: 403–29.

—— (1998) 'The Emergence of a Supranational Telecommunications Regime' in W. Sandholtz and A. Stone Sweet (eds) *European Integration and Supranational Governance*, Oxford: Oxford University Press.

Sandholtz, W. and Stone Sweet, A. (eds) (1998) *European Integration and Supranational Governance*, Oxford: Oxford University Press.

Sandholtz, W. and Zysman, J. (1989) '1992: recasting the European bargain', *World Politics* 42, 1: 95–128.

Saryusz-Wolski, J. (1994) 'The reintegration of the "old continent"', in S. Bulmer and A. Scott (eds) *Economic and Political Integration in Europe*, Oxford and Cambridge, MA: Blackwell.

Sbragia, A. (1993) 'The European Community: a Balancing Act', *Publius* 23: 23–38.

—— (1996) 'Environmental Policy' in H. Wallace and W. Wallace (eds) *Policy-Making in the European Union*, Oxford: Oxford University Press.

—— (1998) 'Institution-Building from below and above: The European Community in Global Environmental Politics' in W. Sandholtz, and A. Stone Sweet, (eds) *European Integration and Supranational Governance*, Oxford: Oxford University Press.

Scharpf, F. (1988) 'The Joint-decision Trap: Lessons from German Federalism and European Integration', *Public Administration* 66, 3: 239–78.

—— (1994a) 'Community and Autonomy: Multi-Level Policy-Making in the European Union', *Journal of European Public Policy* 1, 2: 219–42.

——. (1994b) 'Politiknetzwerke als Steuerungssubjekte', in H.-U. Derlien, U. Gerhardt and F. Scharpf (eds) *Systemrationalität und Partialinteresse*, Baden-Baden: Nomos.

Schattschneider, E.E. (1960) *The Semi-Sovereign People*, New York: Holt, Rinehart and Winston.

Schneider, V., Dang-Nguyen, G. and Werle, R. (1994) 'Corporate Actor Networks in European Policy-Making: Harmonizing Telecommunications Policy', *Journal of Common Market Studies* 32, 4: 473–98.

Schreiber, K. (1991) 'The new approach to technical harmonization and standards', in L. Hurwitz and C. Lequesne (eds) *The State of the European Community: Politics, Institutions and Debates in the Transition Years*, Boulder, CO and Essex: Lynne Rienner and Longman.

Scott, A., Peterson, J. and Millar, David (1994) 'Subsidiarity: A "Europe of the Regions" Vs. the British Constitution?', *Journal of Common Market Studies* 32, 1: 47–67.

Scott, F. (1977) *Sweden: the Nation's History*, Minneapolis: University of Minnesota Press.

Shackleton, M. (1991) 'Budgetary policy in transition', in L. Hurwitz and C. Lequesne (eds) *The State of the European Community: Policies, Institutions and Debates in the Transition Years*, Boulder, CO and Essex: Lynne Rienner and Longman.

—— (1997) 'The Internal Legitimacy Crisis of the European Union', in A.W. Cafruny and C. Lankowski (eds) *Europe's Ambiguous Unity*, Boulder, CO and London: Lynne Rienner.

Sharp, M. and Shearman, C. (1987) *European Technological Collaboration*, London: Routledge and Kegan Paul.

Singer, J. D. (1961) 'The Levels of Analysis Problem in International Relations', *World Politics* 14, 2: 77–92.

Skea, J. and Smith, A. (1998) 'Integrating Pollution Control', in P. Lowe and S. Ward (eds) *British Environmental Policy and Europe*, London: Routledge.

Skjaerseth, J. (1994) 'The Climate Policy of the EC: Too Hot to Handle?', *Journal of Common Market Studies* 32, 1: 25–45.

Skogstad, G. (1994) 'Agricultural Trade and the International Political Economy', in R. Stubbs and G. Underhill (eds) *Political Economy and the Changing Global Order*, London: Macmillan.

—— (1998), 'Ideas, Paradigms and Institutions: Agricultural Exceptionalism in the European Union', *Governance* 11, 4: 463–90.

Slaughter, A. M. (1997) 'The Real New World Order', *Foreign Affairs* 76, 5: 183–97.

Smith, D.L. and Wanke, J. (1993) 'Completing the single European market: an analysis of the impact on the Member States', *American Journal of Political Science* 37, 2: 529–54.

Smith, M. (1998) 'Does the Flag Follow Trade? "Politicisation" and the Emergence of a European Foreign Policy', in J. Peterson and H. Sjursen (eds) *A Common Foreign Policy for Europe? Competing Visions of the CFSP*, London: Routledge.

Smith, M.E. (1997) 'What's Wrong with the CFSP? The Politics of Institutional Reform', in P-H. Laurent and M. Maresceau (eds) *The State of the European Union, Volume 4*, Boulder, CO and Essex: Lynne Rienner and Longman.

Smith, M.J. (1990) *The Politics of Agricultural Support in Britain*, Aldershot: Dartmouth.

Socialist Group of the European Parliament (1989) 'Comitology: Why it Is, Why it Matters, Parliament's Position', information document, PE/GS/230/90, 23 October.

Spence, D. (1991) *Enlargement without Accession: the EC's Response to German Unification*, London: Royal Institute of International Affairs.

—— (1993) 'The role of the national civil service in European lobbying: the British case', in S. Mazey and J. Richardson (eds) *Lobbying in the European Community*, Oxford: Oxford University Press.

Staniland, M. (1995) 'The United States and the external aviation policy of the EU', *Journal of European Public Policy* 2, 1: 19–40.

Stevens, C. (1996) 'EU Policy for the Banana Market: the External Impact of Internal Policies', in H. Wallace and W. Wallace (eds) *Policy-Making in the European Union*, 3rd edn, Oxford: Oxford University Press.

Stone Sweet, A. and Sandholtz, W. (1997) 'European Integration and Supranational Governance', *Journal of European Public Policy* 4, 3: 297–317.

Streeck, W. (1997) 'Industrial Citizenship Under Regime Competition: the Case of the European Works Councils', *Journal of European Public Policy* 4, 4: 643–64.

Streeck, W. and Schmitter, P. (1991) 'From National Corporatism to Transnational Pluralism: Organised Interests in the Single European Market', *Politics and Society* 19, 2: 133–64.

Sun, J.-M. and Pelkmans, J. (1995) 'Regulatory competition in the Single Market', *Journal of Common Market Studies* 33, 1: 67–89.

Sutherland, P. (1988) 'The Parliament and the Commission: partners or protagonists?', in J.V. Louis (ed.) *Le Parlement Européen dans l'évolution Institutionnelle*, Brussels: Editions de l'université de Bruxelles.

—— (1995) 'Introduction', in H. Paemen and A. Bensch (eds) *From the GATT to the WTO: the European Community in the Uruguay Round*, Louvain: Leuven University Press.

Swann, D. (1993) *Competition and Competition Policy*, London: Methuen.

Swinbank, A. (1989) 'The Common Agricultural Policy and the politics of European decision making', *Journal of Common Market Studies* 27, 4: 303–22.

—— (1996a) 'The CAP Decision-Making Process', in C. Ritson and D. Harvey (eds) *The Common Agricultural Policy*, London: CAB International.

—— (1996b) 'The European Union Common Agricultural Policy', in P. Barbour (ed.) *The European Union Handbook*, Chicago and London: Fitzroy Dearborn.

Swinbank, A. and Tanner, C. (1995) *Farm Policy and Trade Conflict: the Uruguay Round and CAP Reform*, Ann Arbor: University of Michigan Press for the Trade Policy Research Centre.

Taylor, P. (1989) 'The New Dynamics of EC Integration in the 1980s', in J. Lodge (ed.) *The European Community and the Challenge of the Future*, London: Pinter.

Teasdale, A. (1995) 'The Luxembourg Compromise', in M. Westlake, *The Council of the European Union*, London: Cartermill.

Thagesen, R. and Matthews, A. (1997) 'The EU's Common Banana Regime: An Initial Evaluation', *Journal of Common Market Studies* 35, 4: 615–27.

Towers Perrin (1998) *The Human Resources Implications of EMU*, London: Towers Perrin with Deutsche Bank, June.

Tranholm-Mikkelsen, J. (1991) 'Neofunctionalism: Obstinate or Obsolete?', *Millienium* 20: 1–22.

Tsebelis, G. (1994) 'The power of the European Parliament as a conditional agenda-setter', *American Political Science Review* 88, 1: 128–42.

—— (1995) 'Decision Making in Political Systems: Veto Players in Presidentialism, Parliamentarianism, Multicameralism and Multipartyism', *British Journal of Political Science* 25, 3: 289–325.

Tsoukalis, L. (1993) *The New European Economy: The Politics and Economics of Integration*, 2nd edn, Oxford: Oxford University Press.

Ueta, T. (1997) 'The Stability Pact: from the Balladur Initiative to the EU Joint Action', in M. Holland (ed.) *Common Foreign and Security Policy: the Record and Reforms*, London: Cassell.

Urry, M. (1997) 'Will the New CAP Fit?', *Financial Times*, 22–3 November: 1.

van Schendelen, M.C.P.M. (1993) *National Public Policy and Private EC Lobbying*, Aldershot: Dartmouth.

—— (1996) '"The Council decides": does the Council decide?', *Journal of Common Market Studies* 34, 4: 531–48.

Vasey, M. (1985) 'The 1985 farm price negotiations and the reform of the Common Agricultural Policy', *Common Market Law Review* 22: 649–72.

Vogel, D. (1996) *Trading Up: Consumer and Environmental Regulation in a Global Economy*, Cambridge, MA: Harvard University Press.

Vosgerau, H-J (1994) 'Replacing trade policies by international competition policy', paper presented to the ESRC conference on the Single European Market, Exeter, 8–11 September, mimeo, Univeristy of Konstanz.

Wallace, H. (1977) 'The establishment of the Regional Development Fund: common policy or pork barrel?', in H. Wallace, W. Wallace and C. Webb (eds) *Policy-Making in the European Community*, Chichester: John Wiley and Sons.

—— (1993) 'European governance in troubled times', in S. Bulmer and A. Scott (eds) *Economic and Political Integration in Europe*, Oxford: Blackwell.

—— (1996a) 'The institutions of the EU: experience and experimentation', in H. Wallace and W. Wallace (eds) *Policy-Making in the European Union*, 3rd edn, Oxford: Oxford University Press.

—— (1996b) 'Politics and policy in the EU: The challenge of governance', in H. Wallace and W. Wallace (eds) *Policy-Making in the European Union*, 3rd edn, Oxford: Oxford University Press.

Wallace, H. (1997) 'Introduction', in H. Wallace and A. Young (eds) (1997) *Participation and Policy-Making in the European Union*, Oxford: Clarendon Press.

Wallace, H. and Young, A. (1996) 'The single market: a new approach to policy', in H. Wallace and W. Wallace (eds) *Policy-Making in the European Union*, Oxford: Oxford University Press.

—— (eds) (1997) *Participation and Policy-Making in the European Union*, Oxford: Clarendon Press.

Waltz, K. (1954) *Man, the State and War*, New York: Columbia University Press.

—— (1993) 'The Emerging Structure of International Politics', *International Security* 18, (Fall): 44–79.

Ward, N. (1998) 'Water Quality', in P. Lowe, and S. Ward, (eds) *British Environmental Policy and Europe. Politics and Policy in Transition*, London: Routledge.

Warleigh, A. (1998) 'Synthetic and Confederal Understandings of the European Union', *West European Politics* 21, 3: 1–18.

Weale, A. (1996) 'Environmental Rules and Rule-Making in the European Union', *Journal of European Public Policy* 3, 4: 594–611.

Weale, A. and Williams, A. (1992) 'Between economy and ecology: the single market and the integration of environmental policy', *Environmental Politics* 1, 4: 45–64.

Webber, D. (1998) 'High midnight in Brussels: an Analysis of the September 1993 Council Meeting on the GATT Uruguay Round', *Journal of European Public Policy* 5, 4: 578–94.

Weaver, R.K. and Rockman, B.A. (eds) (1993) *Do Institutions Matter? Government Capabilities in the United States and Abroad*, Washington, DC: Brookings Institution.

Weiler, J.H.H. (1993) 'Journey to an Unknown Destination: a Retrospective and Prospective of the European Court of Justice in the Arena of Political Integration', *Journal of Common Market Studies* 31, 4: 417–46.

—— (1997) 'The Reformation of European Constitutionalism', *Journal of Common Market Studies* 35, 1: 97–131.

Wendt, A. (1987) 'The Agent–Structure Problem in International Relations Theory', *International Organization* 41, 3: 335–70.

Werts, J. (1992) *The European Council*, Amsterdam: Elsevier Publishers.

Wessels, W. (1997a) 'An Ever Closer Fusion? A Dynamic Macropolitical View on Integration Processes', *Journal of Common Market Studies* 35 (2): 267–99.

—— (1997b) 'The Growth and Differentiation of Multi-Level Networks: A Corporatist Mega-Bureaucracy or an Open City?', in H. Wallace and A. Young (eds) *Participation and Policy-Making in the European Union*, Oxford: Clarendon Press.

Wessels, W. and Rometsch, D. (1996) 'European Union and National Institutions', in D. Rometsch and W. Wessels (eds) *The European Union and Member States: Towards Institutional Fusion?*, Manchester: Manchester University Press.

Westlake, M. (1994a) *The Commission and the Parliament*, London: Butterworths.

—— (1994b) *A Modern Guide to the European Parliament*, London: Pinter.

—— (1995) *The Council of the European Union*, London: Cartermill.

Westwood Digital (1998) *The Single European Aviation Market: the First Five Years*, Cheltenham.

Wiberg, H. (1996) 'Third Party Intervention in Yugoslavia: Problems and Lessons', in J. de Wilde and H. Wiberg (eds) *Organized Anarchy in Europe: The Role of Intergovernmental Organizations*, London and New York: Tauris Academic Studies.

Williams, R. (1973) *European Technology: the Politics of Collaboration*, London: Croom Helm.

Wincott, D. (1995) 'Institutional interaction and European integration: towards an everyday critique of liberal intergovernmentalism', *Journal of Common Market Studies* 33, 4: 597–609.

Winkler, G.M. (1998) 'Coalition-sensitive voting power in the Council of Ministers: the case of eastern enlargement', *Journal of Common Market Studies* 36, 3: 391–404.

Winters, L.A. (1994) 'The EC and World Protectionism: Dimensions of the Political Economy', Discussion paper no. 897, February, London: CEPR.

Wishlade, F. (1996) 'EU Cohesion Policy: Facts, Figures, and Issues', in L. Hooghe (ed.) *Cohesion Policy and European Integration*, Oxford: Oxford University Press.

Woods, N. (1995) 'Economic Ideas and International Relations: Beyond Rational Neglect', *International Studies Quarterly* 39, June: 161–80.

Woodward, S.L. (1995) *Balkan Tragedy: Chaos and Dissolution After the Cold War*, Washington, DC: Brookings Institution.

Woolcock, S. (1994) *The Single European Market: Centralization of Competition Among National Rules?*, London: Royal Institute of International Affairs.

Woolcock, S. and Hodges, M. (1996) 'EU policy in the Uruguay Round', in H. Wallace and W. Wallace (eds) *Policy-Making in the European Union*, 3rd edn, Oxford: Oxford University Press.

Wright, V. (1996) 'The national coordination of European policy-making: negotiating the quagmire' in J. Richardson (ed.) *European Union: Power and Policy-making*, London: Routledge.

—— (1998) 'Intergovernmental relations and regional government in Europe: a sceptical view', in P. Le Galès and C. Lequesne (eds) *Regions in Europe*, London: Routledge.

Zito, A. (1995) 'Integrating the Environment into the European Union: the history of the controversial carbon tax', in S. Mazey and C. Rhodes (eds) *The State of the European Union*, Vol. 3, Boulder CO and Essex: Lynne Rienner and Longman.

Zucconi, M. (1996) 'The European Union in the Former Yugoslavia', in A. Chayes and A. Chayes (eds) *Preventing Conflict in the Post-Communist World: Mobilizing International and Regional Organizations*, Washington, DC: Brookings Institution.

Index